Penguin Books

The Read-Aloud Handbook

Jim Trelease works full-time addressing parents, teachers, and professional groups on the subjects of children, literature, and television. A graduate of the University of Massachusetts, he was for twenty years an award-winning artist and writer for *The Springfield* (MA) *Daily News.*

Initially self-published in 1979, *The Read-Aloud Handbook* has had five American editions along with British, Australian, and Japanese editions. Mr. Trelease is also the editor of two popular read-aloud anthologies for Penguin: *Hey! Listen to This,* for grades K–4; and *Read All About It!,* for preteens and teens.

Since 1983, Mr. Trelease has devoted his full time to lecture work and seminars with parents and teachers throughout North America. He has been profiled in *Smithsonian* and *Reader's Digest*. The father of two grown children, he lives in Springfield, Massachusetts, with his wife, Susan.

Jim Trelease's lectures are available on both video and audiocassette. For information, write Reading Tree Productions, 51 Arvesta Street, Springfield, MA 01118. On the World Wide Web, his site is www.trelease-on-reading.com.

The
Read-Aloud
Handbook

—

FIFTH EDITION

Jim Trelease

Penguin Books

PENGUIN BOOKS
Published by the Penguin Group
Penguin Putnam Inc., 375 Hudson Street,
New York, New York 10014, U.S.A.
Penguin Books Ltd, 27 Wrights Lane,
London W8 5TZ, England
Penguin Books Australia Ltd, Ringwood,
Victoria, Australia
Penguin Books Canada Ltd, 10 Alcorn Avenue,
Toronto, Ontario, Canada M4V 3B2
Penguin Books (N. Z.) Ltd, 182–190 Wairau Road,
Auckland 10, New Zealand

Penguin Books Ltd, Registered Offices:
Harmondsworth, Middlesex, England

The Read-Aloud Handbook first published in the United States of America
in Penguin Books 1982
First revised edition published 1985
Second revised edition (under title *The New Read-Aloud Handbook*)
published 1989
Third revised edition published 1995
This fourth revised edition published 2001

5 7 9 10 8 6 4

Portions of this work were originally published in pamphlet form.

Page 403 constitutes an extension of this copyright page.

Library of Congress Cataloging-in-Publication Data

Trelease, Jim.
The read-aloud handbook / Jim Trelease.—5th ed.
p. cm.
Includes bibliographical references (p.) and indexes.
ISBN 0-14-100294-8
1. Oral reading.   I. Title.

LB1573.5 .T68 2001
372.45'2—dc21

2001021012
Printed in the United States of America
Set in Bembo
Designed by Susan Hood

To my grandsons, Connor and Tyler—
the best audiences an old reader-aloud could hope to find.

And to Alvin R. Schmidt, a ninth-grade English teacher
in New Jersey who found the time forty-seven years ago
to write to the parents of one of his students to tell them
they had a talented child. That vote of confidence
has never been forgotten.

Acknowledgments

This book could not have been written without the support and cooperation of many friends, associates, neighbors, children, teachers, and editors. I especially wish to acknowledge my everlasting gratitude to the memory of Mary A. Dryden, of Springfield, Massachusetts, for beginning it all by convincing me to visit her class thirty-four years ago in the school that is now named in her honor.

I am also deeply indebted to Dick Garvey and Carroll Robbins, my former editors at *The Springfield* (MA) *Daily News,* for their long-standing support of staff involvement with the community's schoolchildren. It was this policy that provided the early impetus for my experiences in the classroom. At the same time, I am particularly grateful to my dear friend Jane Maroney, whose guiding hand helped shape the initial concept of this book.

It is impossible to express adequately the gratitude I feel toward the hundreds of individuals who, over the last twenty years, have taken the time to share with me their personal experiences with reading and children, only a fraction of which can I use in each edition. For this edition, I am especially grateful to Robert Allen, Melissa Olans Antinoff, Ellen Beck, Dr. G. Kylene Beers, Pat Brown, Helen Cox, Chris Erskine, Mike and Sally Hard, Kristin Hallahan, the Hassett family, Lee Sullivan Hill, Linda and Frank Van Hoegarden, Jade Hogan, Derek and Kelly Kline, the Kunishima family, Margie McPartland, Charli O'Dell, Mike Oliver, Tom O'Niell, Jr., Elizabeth and Connor Reynolds, Amber Soucy, Meghan Sullivan, Bob Tebo, Marcia Thomas and her family, Jamie and Tyler Trelease, and Karleen Waldman.

For the many clerical and manuscript needs that accompany a revision, I thank my long-suffering assistant, Linda Long, as well as Kathi Botta and Helen Soucy for their daily support.

In addition, I would like to thank my neighbor Shirley Uman, whose enthusiasm for my self-published edition back in 1979 spilled over at a family reunion within hearing distance of a then-fledgling literary agent, Raphael Sagalyn, who carried it home to Penguin Books; Dr. Bee Cullinan for her early encouragement; Dr. Stephen Krashen for his assiduous enthusiasm; my Penguin editors, Kathryn Court and Caroline White, for their faith and support; Stan Reeves, lifetime reader extraordinaire; and a lovely woman named "Florence of Arlington," who wrote the fateful letter to "Dear Abby" in 1983 that changed the Treleases' lives forever.

And, finally, I thank my family—near and far—for their patience during the long absences required for each revised edition.

Contents

Introduction   xi

1. Why Read Aloud?   1

2. When to Begin Read-Aloud   28

3. The Stages of Read-Aloud   60

4. The Do's and Don'ts of Read-Aloud   99

5. Sustained Silent Reading: Reading-Aloud's Natural Partner   106

6. Libraries: Home, School, and Public   143

7. Lessons from Oprah, Harry, and the Internet   169

8. Television   194

9. How to Use the Treasury   214

Treasury of Read-Alouds   218
   Wordless Books   219
   Predictable Books   220
   Reference Books   222
   Picture Books   223
   Short Novels   270

Full-Length Novels	284
Poetry	323
Anthologies	327
Fairy and Folk Tales	330
Appendix A: A Note for Doomsayers Who Think Things Have Never Been Worse	333
Appendix B: Internet Sites for Children's Literature and Education	340
Notes	349
Bibliography	373
Subject Index for the Text	379
Author–Illustrator Index for the Treasury	395

Introduction

> You may have tangible wealth untold:
> Caskets of jewels and coffers of gold.
> Richer than I you can never be—
> I had a mother who read to me.
> —Strickland Gillilan,
> "The Reading Mother,"
> *Best Loved Poems*
> *of the American People*

Taped inside my copy of *Charlotte's Web* are a note and a photograph of a little boy beside a cake. They were sent to me by a stranger named Kelly Kline, a parent in Cleona, Pennsylvania: "Dear Mr. Trelease—I heard you speak at Lebanon Valley College, Pennsylvania, last month. I was the mother who had just finished reading *Charlotte's Web* to my three-year-old son, Derek. We thought you would get a kick out of our 'Wilbur' cake. I forgot to mention, when I finished reading the book, his next four words were, 'Mom—read it again!' Guess what we're doing? You got it—we're on Chapter 17."

Upon investigation, I learned that Derek's mother did not start reading to him when he was three. Beginning with the day he was born, she did not let a day go by without a story—often more than one. She began with Jack Prelutsky's *Read-Aloud Rhymes for the Very Young,* along with nursery rhymes. What started as a handful of books from the library grew into bagsful of books, so by age three he was ready for his very first novel.

By the age of four, he had taught himself to read. Not with a commercial phonics program, however. One thing can be said in favor of such products; they're right when they claim, "There are only forty-four sounds in the English language." And all of those forty-four sounds—every ending, blending, and diphthong—can be found in *Good Night Moon, Make Way for*

Derek

Ducklings and *Charlotte's Web.* Which is just the way Mrs. Kline gave them to Derek. Although she was trained as a teacher, she did no formal teaching with Derek other than to answer his questions and read to him.

Now I want you to jump ahead to the day Derek sat down at the kindergarten learning table for the first time. Think about the dozen novels he'd heard by that day; the thousand picture books he'd heard, as well as the ones he'd read himself; and the tens of thousands of words he knew from all those readings. And then I want you to think about the child on his left and the one on his right—who, if they were typical American kindergarten children, had heard no novels and only a handful of tired picture books over the last five years.

Which child had the larger vocabulary with which to understand the teacher? Which one had the longer attention span with which to work in class? Mrs. Kline brought a child to the classroom door ready and willing to learn. Did she have to invest $230 in a seventeen-pound box of flashcards and phonics tapes? Did she have to enroll Derek in an elite and expensive preschool? Did she have to bring him down to the computer store and plug him into expensive software? All Kelly Kline needed—all anyone needs—is a free public library card and the determination to invest her mind and time in her child's future. The investment can be as small as fifteen minutes a day. Nothing on Wall Street will ever pay dividends as rich as that.

When I talked with Kelly Kline for the fourth edition of this book, Derek was six years old and reading picture books to his mother, and she had just finished reading *Maniac Magee* by Jerry Spinelli and Roald Dahl's *Matilda* to Derek. For this fifth edition, I checked in with the Klines to find Derek in the middle of reading *Harry Potter and the Goblet of Fire,* having "aced" all his final exams in sixth grade, and getting ready for four honors classes in seventh grade.

Every child cannot be a Derek, but every child should have the chance

Derek was given. Extensive research has proven that reading aloud to a child is the single most important factor in raising a reader. These inexpensive fifteen minutes a day are the best-kept secret in American education.

If reading to children were common instead of a rarity, we'd be facing fewer academic and social problems in this nation. Students' achievements have not kept pace with the increasing complexity of the world around them. Consider these findings that even the optimists can't deny:

- In spite of numerous reform efforts, higher standards, twelve years under Democrats and eighteen under Republicans, there has been no significant change in students' reading scores between 1971 and 2000.[1]
- Only 37 percent of high school students score high enough on reading achievement tests to handle adequately college-level material—yet almost 70 percent attempt college.[2]
- 80 percent of college faculty members report that entering freshmen cannot read well enough to do college work.[3]
- An examination of college remedial classes showed a marked increase in the enrollment numbers for reading classes, with the greatest deficiency being reading speed and comprehension.[4]

This book is about changing those patterns. It's a book for new parents, veteran parents, grandparents, teachers, principals, day-care providers, and librarians—anyone who feeds the minds and affects the lives of children, and thus the future.

This is not a book about teaching a child *how* to read; it's about teaching a child to *want* to read. "What we teach children to love and desire," goes an education adage, "will always outweigh what we teach them to do." The fact is that some children learn to read sooner than others, and some better than others. There is a difference. For the parent who thinks sooner is better, who has an eighteen-month-old child barking at flashcards, my response is: *Sooner is not better.* Are the dinner guests who arrive an hour early better guests than those who arrive on time? Of course not.

However, I am concerned about the child who needlessly arrives late, who then struggles through years of pain with a book. Not only will he miss out on large portions of what he needs to know in school, he experiences a pain connection with print that will stay with him for a lifetime.

It also might be helpful to know this is really two books in one. The first half is the evidence in support of reading aloud, and the second half is the Treasury of Read-Alouds, a beginner's guide to recommended titles, from picture books to novels. The listing is intended to take the guesswork out of reading aloud for busy parents and teachers (many of whom were never read to in their own childhoods), who want to begin reading aloud but don't have the time to take a course in children's literature. Since the Treasury is annotated with grade levels, it doesn't have to be read all at once; if you have a toddler, you needn't concern yourself with the novels for a few years. Before using the Treasury, however, you might want to read chapter 9 (How to Use the Treasury).

For those returning readers who wonder how this edition differs from the previous four, I assure you none of the fundamentals has changed. Statistics have been updated and exciting new research and anecdotes added. Since the last edition, major national and international studies have been done on children's reading, but the one I found to be the most sobering and informative involved 42 families whose daily conversations with their children were taped and entered in a database. After nearly three years of entries, the researchers counted the number and kinds of words the children heard. The differences ranged from one socioeconomic group hearing 13 million words to another one with 45 million words. Since kindergarten vocabulary is the biggest predictor of school success, this difference in words would be terribly important. Those differences are explored throughout this edition.

In the last two editions I've told the story of an inner-city junior high principal who brought his school's scores from last to first place using a simple reading formula. When that formula was seen in the Japanese edition of my book, the SSR (sustained silent reading) part of it caught the eye of Japanese school officials and has now been adopted by 3,500 elementary and middle schools there (see chapter 1).

Almost 20,000 new children's books have been published since the last edition, and I've collected what I hope are some of the best read-alouds from that total and added them to the Treasury, which still includes the best titles from previous editions.

Three subjects are brand-new to this edition, subjects that for all intents and purposes didn't exist twenty years ago when the first edition was published: Oprah Winfrey, the Harry Potter books, and the Internet. In chapter 7, I look at the lessons those influences offer those who wish to create lifetime readers.

There is also a chapter on television. It's a reasoned and, I hope, enlightening one, to be used in controlling the use of the medium, not eliminating it. As you'll see in the research, there is a clear connection between over-viewing of TV and underachievement in the classroom. In chapter 8, I answer the parent's question, "What can you do about it?"

In writing each edition, my foremost perspective has been that of a parent—because that is how I came to write this book in the first place. But in the intervening years, half of my time has been spent working with classroom teachers—the people who must pick up the pieces when parents don't do their jobs. More than fifty colleges and universities now use this book in their education classes. Therefore I've included annotations for those who require such data for their research or classes, but have placed most of it in the endnotes so it will not intrude on the normal reading process. And because there are certain questions that are always asked by parents and teachers, I've arranged each chapter under the headings of those questions—like the following:

How Did a Parent Come to Write This Book?

Back in the 1960s, I was a young father of two children and working as an artist and writer for a daily newspaper in Massachusetts. Each night I read to my daughter and son, unaware of any cognitive or emotional benefits that would come of it. I had no idea what it would do for their vocabulary, attention span, or interest in books. I read for one reason: because *my* father had read to *me*. And because he'd read to me, when my time came I knew intuitively there is a torch that is supposed to be passed from one generation to the next.

As a school volunteer in Springfield, Massachusetts (I'd been visiting classrooms on a weekly basis for several years, discussing my careers as artist and writer), I was invited one day to speak to a sixth-grade class.

After spending an hour with the class, I gathered my materials and prepared to leave, when I noticed a little novel on the shelf near the door. It was *The Bears' House* by Marilyn Sachs, and it caught my eye because I'd just finished reading it to my daughter.

"Who's reading *The Bears' House*?" I asked the class. Several girls' hands went up.

"I just finished reading it," I said. Their eyes lit up. They couldn't believe it. This man, who had just told them stories about how he got started in newspapers, this man, whose drawings and stories they had been clipping out of the paper for the last month—this man was reading one of *their* books?

So I explained about my children, Elizabeth and Jamie, and how I read to each of them every night. I told them how, when my children were little, they were mostly interested in the pictures. That was fine with me because I was an artist and I was interested in the pictures, too. I told them my story about Robert McCloskey and *Make Way for Ducklings*. "Did you know," I said, "that Mr. McCloskey had a dreadful time drawing those ducks? He finally brought six ducklings up to his apartment in order to get a closer look. In the end, because they kept moving around so much, do you know what he did? You may find this hard to believe, but I promise you it's true: in order to get them to hold still, he slowed them down by getting them drunk on wine!"

The class clapped their approval of McCloskey's unorthodox approach.

Then we talked about *The Bears' House*: what it was about (for those in the room who had not read it); what the students liked about it; and what else they had read by the author. I asked the rest of the class what they had read lately. There was an avalanche of hands and a chorus of books. It was forty-five minutes before I could say good-bye.

In the days following the visit I pondered what had happened in that classroom. The teacher subsequently wrote to say that the children had begged and begged to go to the library in order to get the books I'd talked about. I wondered what it was that I had said that was so unusual. I had just talked about my family's favorite books.

All I was doing was giving book reports. As soon as I called it that I realized what was so special about it. It probably was the first time any of them had ever heard an adult give a book report—an unsolicited one, at that. I thought of how few of them had ever heard a teacher say, "You'll have to bear with me today, class, I'm a little fuzzy-headed this morning. I stayed up until three o'clock this morning reading the most wonderful book. I just couldn't put it down. Would you like to hear what the book was about?"

I'd piqued the children's interest by giving them a book report. But an even better description of it would be "a commercial." So I made a resolution: from then on, whenever I visited a classroom, I would save some time at the end to talk about reading. I'd begin by asking the class, "What have you read lately? Anybody read any good books lately?"

In the ensuing years, to my dismay, I discovered they didn't read much. They weren't reading much in the remedial classes or in the classes for the gifted and talented. Nor was there any difference between the public schools and the parochial schools. But ever so slowly I began to notice one difference. There were isolated classrooms where the kids *were* reading— reading a ton! How is it, I puzzled, these kids are so turned on to reading while the class across the hall (where I was the previous month) wasn't reading anything? Same principal, same neighborhood, same textbooks. What's up?

When I pursued it further I discovered the difference was standing in the front of the room: the teacher. In nearly every one of the turned-on classes, the teacher read to the class on a regular basis. Maybe there is something to this—more than just the feel-good stuff I got from reading to Elizabeth and Jamie. So off to the libraries of the local teacher colleges I went, looking for answers. And there I discovered the research showing that reading aloud to children improves their reading, writing, speaking, listening—and, best of all, their *attitudes* about reading. There was one big problem with the research: the people who should have been reading it weren't reading it. The teachers, supervisors, and principals didn't know it even existed. Indeed, as I was soon to discover, there were many schools where teachers were forbidden to read aloud to students, a rule created out of the misconception that such behavior was a waste of instructional time and would make the children lazy. I also found that most parents and teachers were unaware of good children's books. When I pressed some of my newspaper colleagues (most of whom were college graduates) about reading to their children, I'd get answers like, "Oh, I tried that but the books are so boring neither of us could stay awake."

In the late 1970s, when I realized there was nothing generally available for parents on reading aloud, not even book lists (except those included in children's literature textbooks), I decided to compile my own. Initially, it was a modest self-publishing venture (costing me $650 for the first printing—the family vacation money for one summer), with local bookstores taking copies on consignment. Within three years the booklet sold 20,000 copies in thirty states and Canada. By 1982, Penguin Books had seen a copy and asked me to expand it into the first Penguin edition of the book you are reading now. There have also been British, Australian, and Japanese editions.

Even in this—the growth of this book—we can see the metaphor of "passing torches." A few months after the first Penguin edition of *The Read-Aloud Handbook* was published, someone gave a young graduate student a copy of the book on the occasion of his becoming a new parent. He was also doing part-time carpentry work, and he was hired by an Arlington, Virginia, couple to do some work in anticipation of their new baby. He gave them a copy of the book. This Arlington mother, though, did more than just read it. She wrote an unsolicited "book report" about it to a national syndicated newspaper columnist—a woman named Abigail Van Buren. And when her letter appeared with "Abby's" response on February 23, 1983, almost overnight Penguin had orders for 120,000 copies of the book. As you can imagine, she's now known in our house as "*Dear, Dear* Abby."

I share that background with you not in a self-congratulatory way but rather as evidence in support of a major thesis of this book: The cultural problems of our nation are not insurmountable; we know how to cure many of them, and you can help. I propose that you—one parent, one grandparent, one teacher, or one librarian—can make a lasting difference. So sprinkled throughout the first half of this book are examples of people who made the world a better place for one child, a dozen, hundreds, and thousands. Few of them are famous. Most are folks you probably never heard of—like Kelly and Derek Kline—but I think you'll remember them after you've met them here.

Isn't It the Teacher's Job to Do All This?

At the end of kindergarten, a child has been in school a total of 700 hours. The politicians are quick to point out, "An awful lot of teaching and learning better take place in those 700 hours, and if it doesn't, we've got to hold those teachers and teachers' unions accountable!" I don't have a problem with that—as long as we're fair and hold the right teacher accountable for the right number of hours. For while the child has been in school for 700 hours by age six, the same child at the same age has been *outside* school for 52,000 hours.[5]

Which teacher has a better chance of affecting that child: the classroom teacher who had him for 700 hours or the *home* teachers—the parents, grandparents, the aunts and uncles, or the nanny—who had the child for 52,000 hours? No contest.

There are, of course, those parents who cannot or will not do the job. I recall the kindergarten teacher in Lodi, California, who described for me her daily challenges: thirty-one children speaking ten different primary languages. For a variety of reasons but none provable, she suspects several of the children are being abused at home. Her students' homes include a level of poverty unimaginable to America's middle and upper class. "One child wanted to show me all the words he could write but had no paper at home to write on. In desperation, he finally found a lightbulb wrapper. Then, ever so carefully, so as not to rip the corrugated paper, he printed and printed until he had filled the entire surface with his words."

Such a child represents both the challenges in our classroom society *and* the possibilities. For that child, the classroom teacher is the last hope, the "last stop for gas before the beltway of adulthood," as Phyllis Theroux once put it. If the teacher finds a way to turn the child on to the joy of reading and to create a lifetime reader, that student has a much greater chance of growing up and doing the right things with his or her child, thus making a future teacher's burden less heavy.

Unfortunately, at-risk students usually reside in the most dangerous neighborhoods, attend schools in the worst physical condition (including the worst classrooms and school libraries—chapter 6), and are taught by high-turnover faculties that have the largest number of uncertified and underpaid teachers in America. So when a politician suggests that we punish the low-scoring schools by cutting their funding, someone needs to tell them publicly, "We already have!"

What Can We Tell Parents of At-Risk Families?

Poverty parents love their children as much as affluent parents do. A telling difference lies in what one knows or doesn't know about what's good for a child. For example, the poverty parent may think if a child is happy and quiet in front of a television set, that's good. The educated parent is more apt to know that too much TV is harmful and further knows that children should be read to daily.

The Early Childhood Longitudinal Study, Kindergarten Class 1998–99, which has been following 22,000 children from kindergarten through fifth grade,[6] showed these marked differences. Welfare children were less likely to have been read to by a parent each day. While poor families can afford to buy fewer books, it should be noted that everyone is welcome to help themselves to the public library's shelves. The poverty child's lack of book time was evidenced in the child's attention span in kindergarten, where teachers reported the higher the education level of the parent, the longer the child's attention span.[7]

In spite of the daunting statistics listed above, there are children who emerge from poverty zones and rise to great heights. And they're doing it as early as kindergarten. The aforementioned U.S. kindergarten study showed that among children coming from a single-parent home in which the mother was a high school dropout, 52 percent achieved on the lowest reading levels, *but*—6 percent (two children in twenty) performed at the *highest* level.

Moreover, 40 percent of college students from the wealthiest quartile graduate with a four-year degree while only 6 percent of those in the lowest quartile graduate.[8] You can focus on those who didn't make it *or* you can say, "Wait a minute! In a given year, six percent of the most at-risk children graduate from college!"

In a 1996 study of 2,420 immigrant children in California, many from families in which neither parent had a high school diploma, there were significant numbers who were outscoring and out-graduating their native-born peers. Further examination of those children showed a strong correlation between the amount of homework, television viewing, and school absences and the child's grade-point average.[9]

All of this proves that poverty children are not doomed to low achievement *if the right things happen*. The enabling factor is almost always a parent or relative—someone close to the child in the early years—who avoids the wrong things and does the right things at the right time.

Can You Give an Example of an At-Risk School Achiever?

Several examples of at-risk achievers come to mind immediately, but the first is Dr. James Comer, who holds two doctorates (medicine and psychiatry), is a Yale professor, is the recipient of thirty-six honorary degrees, and is founder of the Comer Project used in 700 schools in twenty-six states. If that doesn't make him unique enough, Comer is also the son of a woman who had a total of nine months' education in her childhood. A sharecropper's daughter, Maggie Comer worked as a domestic and raised five children who hold thirteen college diplomas among them.

How did she do it? To start, while she cleaned people's homes she kept her eyes and ears open. Simply put, she spied! She saw how the rich people did things, the networking they did to give their children the best chances, the museum trips they scheduled, the music lessons they saved for, the phone calls they made to insure their children had the right teachers or that school problems were addressed, the emphasis they placed on homework, and the books and newspapers they had in their homes.

And then she and her steelworker husband sacrificed, demanded, inspired, scolded, and cheered their children. And remember, she had only nine months of schooling in her entire life.

In chapter 8 (TV), there is yet another example of a parent who did the difficult things—a semi-literate single parent, suffering from depression,

Dr. James Comer

with only a third-grade education, who raised the world's premier pediatric brain surgeon.

As much as anything else, this is a "spy" book. It contains the strategies that have been spied in homes and classrooms that produce happy, achieving children. If we don't find a way to spread those strategies beyond the select group that hold them now, America will face a seizure of monstrous proportions. Two small news items reinforce that prediction: (1) The distribution of wealth between rich and poor in the U.S. is the equivalent of Guatemala's,[10] and (2) at our present rate of incarceration, we'll soon have more people in prison than in college.[11]

As Brown University's Ruth J. Simmons puts it, we must find a way to mainstream the children who have been marginalized. While America's white population grows smaller and its minorities grow larger, it can't continue to draw from a pool of college-educated future leaders that boasts fewer and fewer minorities. Historian John Hope Franklin warned, "You can't have an elite society that ignores all these other people. That is how a society collapses."[12]

How Do I Convince My Husband He Should Be Doing This with Our Children?

As it happens, fathers are my special project. But there is always a shortage of fathers at my seminars, no matter where I travel. The one place where there is never a shortage of males is in our remedial reading classes, where boys make up more than 70 percent of the enrollment.[13] In *American* remedial classes, that is. Boys don't constitute 70 percent of the remedial students in many other countries. In Israeli remedial classes, there are *no* gender differences.[14] In Finland, England, Nigeria, India, and Germany, the girls outnumber the boys.[15] So it can't be genetics.

The findings of sociologists like Professor Cornelius Riordan show an alarming pattern that superintendents, principals, and teachers need to confront parents with every school year: According to Riordan's and others' research,[16] boys are more likely than girls to repeat a grade or drop out of school, suffer from more learning disabilities, are three times more likely to be enrolled in special-education classes, are more likely to be involved in criminal and delinquent behavior, are less likely to be enrolled in college-prep classes, have lower educational expectations, lower reading and writing scores, read less for pleasure, and do less homework. Even those males who eventually reach college are less likely to graduate than females, largely due to their macho-male behavior while they are there; as Riordan notes, "while in college they spend more time than women exercising, partying, watching TV, or playing video games."[17]

Not too many years ago it was a commonly accepted fact that girls surpassed boys in the early grades, but that boys bounced back in later grades and surpassed the girls. That's a thing of the past. Thanks to concerted social and academic efforts, girls' high school and college scores have risen for the last two decades. But during the same period, the boys' scores have taken a nosedive.

An immediate measure of the downshift among young males in the last decade can be seen in the number of students taking the Advanced Placement exams (see chart below). AP courses allow achieving high school students to gain college credit while still in high school. As the chart shows, the girls' rate of AP courses has shown a steady climb, while the boys' rate has taken two dips and allowed a wide margin to grow between the sexes since 1984. If the adage "We raise our daughters, but love our sons" applies here, then it's a bitter indictment of parent behavior, particularly fathers.

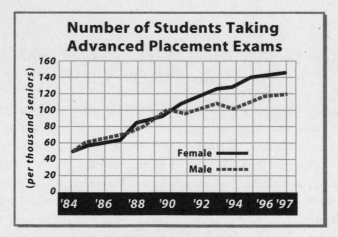

From *Trends in Educational Equity of Girls & Women*[18]

In 1970, males outnumbered females in college enrollment by a ratio of 59 to 41. By 2000, that ratio had been reversed to 57 to 43 in favor of women. Granted, the women's movement raised the bar for female achievement in the classroom, but what's going on with the guys?

I propose there's been one significant change in the value system of the male culture. What entered the system between 1970 and 2000? Try ESPN and round-the-clock sports. By 2000, moms were "taking their daughters to work," but dads were taking their sons to the stadium.

Three decades ago, sports existed on TV only two days and one night a week. By the mid-1990s, sports had its own channels, and additional stations carried everything from rodeo and wrestling to stock-car racing and golf—twenty-four hours a day. And the audiences were nearly all male.

The boy who only sees his father focusing on athletics, who lives in a home or culture where it's all sports all the time, will allot far less value and time to school than to athletics. The end result has been higher sports scores, lower school scores. It may be resulting in other antisocial behavior, but that's for someone else's book to decide.[19]

The strange thing is this "dumbing of daddy" seems to affect families at all education levels. In a study comparing poverty-level families and university-educated families, fathers read to the children only 15 percent of the time, mothers 76 percent, and others 9 percent. This finding was the same for both family groups.[20]

The right call for fathers is to be involved intellectually as well as athletically with a child. If a child must wait until junior high or middle school before encountering a male in the act of reading, the idea that reading is for girls will already have taken deep root in his mind. We have to short-circuit that dangerous thinking and convince American males that it is not only possible but *preferable* for fathers to be athletically *and* intellectually involved in their children's lives. A father can play catch in the backyard after dinner and, on the same night, read to the child for fifteen minutes. He can take him to the basketball game on Friday night and to the library on Saturday morning.

The odds are against a child whose role model at home is seldom if ever seen or heard reading, but that wasn't the case with Thomas Belmore. Much to his father's surprise and pleasure, eleven-year-old Thomas finished the 732-page *Harry Potter and the Goblet of Fire* in one week. "I never remember reading a 700-page book when I was a kid. It's amazing!" his father exclaimed to me. Actually, there was nothing amazing about it at all. It was entirely predictable.

What made it predictable was the photograph seen on this page of Kent Belmore, a father (who also happens to be an Episcopal priest) in Atlanta,

*Father and son
at curbside, Atlanta*

Georgia, sitting at curbside reading to seven-year-old Thomas while the two waited for the school bus each morning. I first saw the photo in the *Atlanta Journal*[21] back in September 1996 and immediately put Reverend Belmore on my list of people to interview for this fifth edition of *The Read-Aloud Handbook*.

Their curbside routine continued rain or shine all the way up to fifth grade, bringing father and son closer together and laying a foundation for literacy. "Along the way, I met books I'd never known as a child. I never had a Roald Dahl!" Reverend Belmore explained. "Every day it was the best fifteen minutes of my day!" Clearly he enjoyed the books, but he is actually referring to the emotional bond that is built between parent and child (and teacher and class) through sharing books. Few things bring people together as closely as regular visits to the barnyard with Fern and Charlotte (*Charlotte's Web*).

A study of boys in Modesto, California, found that: (1) boys who were read to by their fathers scored significantly higher in reading achievement; and (2) where fathers read recreationally, their sons read more and scored higher than did boys whose fathers did little or no recreational reading. When the dads were surveyed, only 10 percent reported having fathers who read to them when they were children.[22] Somewhere along the line, we must find a way to break that pattern of ignorance.

Is Reading Still Important in the Video Age?

Reading is the *heart* of education. The knowledge of almost every subject in school flows from reading. One must be able to read the word problem in math in order to understand it. If you cannot read the science or social studies chapter, you cannot answer the questions at the end of the chapter. The complicated computer manual is essential to its operation, but it must be read.

One can arguably state: reading is the single most important social factor in American life today. Here's a formula to support that. It sounds simplistic, but all its parts can be documented, and while not 100 percent universal, it holds true far more often than not.

1. The more you read, the more you know.[23]
2. The more you know, the smarter you grow.[24]
3. The smarter you are, the longer you stay in school.[25]
4. The longer you stay in school, the more diplomas you earn and the longer you are employed—thus the more money you earn in a lifetime.[26]

5. The more diplomas you earn, the higher your children's grades will be in school.[27]
6. The more diplomas you earn, the longer you live.[28]

The opposite would also be true:

1. The less you read, the less you know.
2. The less you know, the sooner you drop out of school.
3. The sooner you drop out, the sooner and longer you are poor.
4. The sooner you drop out, the greater your chances of going to jail.[29]

The basis for that formula is firmly established: poverty and illiteracy are related—they are the parents of desperation and imprisonment.

♦ 82 percent of prison inmates are school dropouts.[30]
♦ Inmates are twice as likely to be ranked in the bottom levels of literacy as is the general population.[31]
♦ 60 percent of inmates are illiterate.[32]
♦ 63 percent of inmates are repeat offenders.[33]

Why are such students failing and dropping out of school? Because they cannot read—which affects the entire report card. Change the graduation rate and you change the prison population—which changes the entire climate of America. The higher a state's high school graduation rate, the smaller its prison population.[34]

So common sense should tell us that reading is the ultimate weapon—destroying ignorance, poverty, and despair before they can destroy us. A nation that doesn't read much doesn't know much. And a nation that doesn't know much is more likely to make poor choices in the home, the marketplace, the jury box, and the voting both. And those decisions ultimately affect an entire nation—the literate and the illiterate.

The challenge therefore is to convince future generations of children that carrying books is more rewarding than carrying guns.

One note of caution to the reader: Because it doesn't do much good if we only know what *helps* in education and remain ignorant of what *hurts,* I have included both aspects in this book. The truly dreadful, if not dumb, things we parents, teachers, librarians, and administrators do with reading and children will not be eliminated by ignoring them. Some would prefer that such things as the lack of reading done by teachers or the gap in reading scores between white and minority students not be addressed publicly.[35] I strongly disagree. The light of public scrutiny will do much to eliminate such stains.

The statistics you find in the early chapters of this book can be interpreted to mean that today's student scores pale when compared with those of students fifty years ago. Such conclusions are erroneous. Today's average student is as smart—if not smarter—than his predecessors. If you wish to read the evidence, see Appendix A on page 333. The critical difference is not in the scores but in the world—it's a lot more complicated today. Yesterday's scores—if they *were* all that good—are not good enough today. The approaches endorsed in this book would change school scores significantly for the majority and enable today's student to better cope in a very complicated world.

The Read-Aloud Handbook

Chapter 1

Why Read Aloud?

Perhaps it is only in childhood that books have any deep influence on our lives . . . in childhood all books are books of divination, telling us about the future, and like the fortune-teller who sees a long journey in the cards or death by water, they influence the future. I suppose that is why books excited us so much. What do we ever get nowadays from reading to equal the excitement and the revelation of those first fourteen years?

—Graham Greene,
The Lost Childhood and Other Essays

IN this chapter, we will examine both sides of *Why*: why it is so important for us to read to children *at this particular point in history*; and why reading aloud is so effective.

A decade ago on a lovely autumn morning, I visited the same kindergarten room I had attended as a child at Connecticut Farms Elementary School in Union, New Jersey. Gazing up at me were the upturned faces of about fifteen children, each of them seated expectantly on their story rugs. "How many of you want to learn to read this year?" I asked.

Without a second's hesitation, every hand shot into the air, many accompanied by boasts like "I already know how!" Their excitement matches what every kindergarten teacher has told me: Every child begins school wanting to learn to read. In other words, we've got 100 percent enthusiasm and desire when they start school.

Several months later, the National Reading Report Card[1] told the rest of the story:

♦ Among fourth-graders, 45.7 percent read something for pleasure every day.

- Among eighth-graders, only 27 percent read for pleasure daily.
- By twelfth grade, only 24.4 percent read anything for pleasure daily.
- Fourth-grade weekly library use was 40 percent but dropped to 10 percent by senior year.

As I noted in the introduction, the nation's reading scores haven't changed in thirty years, despite school reforms. We have 100 percent interest in kindergarten but lose 75 percent of our potential lifetime readers by senior year. Any business that kept losing 75 percent of its customer base would be in Chapter 11 overnight. And *that's* why the scores haven't improved in three decades.

A school's objective should be to create lifetime readers—graduates who continue to read and educate themselves throughout their adult lives. But the reality is we create schooltime readers—graduates who know how to read well enough to graduate. And at that point the majority take a silent vow: If I never read another book, it'll be too soon.

In the dawning hours of our awareness, 1983, a national committee was created to discover the causes of this crisis and its solution. It was called the Commission on Reading, organized by the National Academy of Education and the National Institute of Education and funded under the U.S. Department of Education. It consisted of nationally recognized experts in how children develop, how they learn language, and how they learn to read. Since nearly everything in the curriculum of school rested upon reading, the consensus was that reading was at the heart of either the problem or the solution.

As the most important discipline in education, reading generates more than 1,200 research projects annually. It took the commission two years of poring through more than 10,000 research projects done in the last quarter century to determine what works, what might work, and what doesn't work.

In 1985, the commission issued its report, *Becoming a Nation of Readers.* It is, in my subjective opinion, the most important and "commonsense" education document in twenty-five years. Among its primary findings, two simple declarations rang loud and clear:

- "The single most important activity for building the knowledge required for eventual success in reading is *reading aloud* to children."[2]
- The commission found conclusive evidence to support reading aloud not only in the home but also in the classroom: "It is a practice that should continue throughout the grades."[3]

In its wording—"the single most important activity"—the experts were saying reading aloud was more important than worksheets, homework, assessments, book reports, and flashcards. One of the cheapest, simplest, and oldest tools of teaching was being promoted as a better teaching tool than anything else in the home or classroom. What exactly is so powerful about something so simple you don't even need a high school diploma in order to do it?

How Do You Get *Better* at Reading?

It boils down to a simple, two-part formula:

♦ The more you read, the better you get at it; the better you get at it, the more you like it; and the more you like it, the more you do it.
♦ The more you read, the more you know; and the more you know, the smarter you grow.

Contrary to what alarmists would have us believe, we are not a nation of illiterates. The average American student *can* read. And 95 percent of twenty-one- to twenty-five-year-olds, our alumni, can perform routine tasks using printed information (one paragraph of simple sentences).[4] Sixty-three percent go on to advanced education, compared to only 20 percent in 1940. As I explain in Appendix A (page 333), today's students not only don't think any less or any slower than their grandparents did, they're actually smarter. But the needs of today's world are far more complex than those of 1940, growing more complex by the hour, and outstripping the small progress being made by most American students, particularly minorities. Seventy percent of the reading material in a cross section of jobs nationally is written on *at least* ninth-grade level.[5]

How Is Today's World More Complex?

The contrast between yesterday and today in America can be seen in Baltimore, Maryland, in the life of a forty-two-year-old resident that *The New York Times* described as Joe, and that of his son, Joe, Jr.[6] Back in 1965, Joe, Sr., had no trouble landing a full-time job with the biggest employer in Baltimore, Bethlehem Steel, despite literacy skills that allowed him to read only the simplest of sentences. Twenty years later, his son was job hunting with the same reading skills his father had and the difference was staggering. First, Bethlehem Steel was gone. Second, the largest employer in Baltimore was Johns Hopkins University Medical Center. And third, even a college diploma wouldn't guarantee a job at Johns Hopkins.

There are 150,000 Joes living in Baltimore, a situation duplicated in every urban center across America, to say nothing of rural America.

But the changing world versus the unchanging reading patterns of young Americans is only *part* of the problem. Equally important is the out-of-sight problem: If American children are not getting any smarter, those in other countries *are.* Impoverished nations we left in our academic dust in the past are now on equal footing, thanks to their educational improvements.

What effect would a rise in, let's say, India's scores have upon the U.S.? In the 1960s, America had a healthy lead in engineering and math skills. Then India's scores began to rise. As soon as they neared us, companies like Motorola, I.B.M., and Texas Instruments shipped them business. By 1993, most of the state-of-the-art components for Motorola's handheld satellite telephone system (invented in the U.S.) were being made in India by engineers now as skilled as ours but willing to work for much less money. Thus 10,000 computer jobs went out of the country.[7]

Five years ago only Israel and India were competing with U.S. workers in the computer industry, but with the arrival of the Internet came a third party: the Philippines. Two factors give the Philippines a leg up on other Asian nations when it comes to the Internet: (1) English is taught throughout the grades; and (2) there is a 95 percent literacy rate. Since English dominates the Internet and more than 80 percent of information stored in computers worldwide is in English, employees who are English-literate hold the advantage.

What Are Today's Student Reading Scores?

Couple the above international examples with these classroom challenges:

- ◆ At our highest-rated colleges and universities, 99 percent of seniors could identify "Beavis and Butthead," but 78 percent couldn't identify the last line of the Gettysburg Address—even with multiple choice.[8]
- ◆ Of the nearly 63 percent of high school students who attempt college, only 37 percent score high enough on reading achievement tests to handle college-level material.[9]
- ◆ Even in the most elite high schools, only one-third of students have the grades, course work, and test scores that indicate they can do college work.[10]

- Almost 50 percent of those who try four-year colleges fail to achieve a degree.[11]
- Only 5 percent of twelfth-graders are able to write on the level of a college freshman.[12]
- Less than 5 percent of high school seniors can read on the level of *The New York Times,* and 63 percent are not reading on the level of a tabloid newspaper. More than 75 percent, however, can read on at least a primary, fourth-grade, level.[13]
- In comparing 1999 reading scores with those of 1971, there is little or no improvement in student scores, despite standard raising and curriculum changes. The only appreciable changes were improvements in minority scores from 1971 to 1984; since then, improvement has stalled, leaving minorities approximately 35 points behind whites on the NAEP assessments.[14]

The reading stagnation is evident not only at the bottom or middle of the class, it is there at the top as well. Scholar and author Jacques Barzun writes of a committee interviewing 150 young people—three top students from each state—to award ten full scholarships worth $60,000 each. "One member of the committee asked every candidate this question: 'Did you, during the past year, read a book that was not assigned? If so, please tell us a little something about that book.' Only one student out of the 150 was able to comply."[15]

The scores tell us that many of our students know how to read, but their behavior as children and adults tells us they don't like it enough to do it very often. We've taught children *how* to read but forgotten to teach them to *want* to read.

If a nation doesn't read much, it doesn't know much. Thomas Jefferson explained the danger in that when he wrote: "If a nation expects to be ignorant and free, in a state of civilization, it expects what never was and never will be."[16]

So where do we go from here? We follow the advice of the man who founded compulsory education back in the 1830s, Horace Mann: "Men," he wrote, "are cast iron; but children are wax."

We begin with the "wax"—children—and we use the findings of the Commission on Reading to shape them: We read aloud to them throughout the grades. Simple. And unlike most reforms, it will not increase the tax rate 1 percent!

How Can Something as Simple as Reading to a Child Be So Effective?

We read to children for all the same reasons we talk with children: to reassure, to entertain, to bond; to inform or explain, to arouse curiosity, to inspire. But in reading aloud, we also:

+ Condition the child's brain to associate reading with pleasure
+ Create background knowledge
+ Build vocabulary
+ Provide a reading role model

Let's look at how we create lifetime readers. There are two basic reading "facts of life" that are ignored in many education circles, yet without these two principles working in tandem, little else will work in education reform.

Reading Fact No. 1: *Human beings are pleasure-centered.*
Reading Fact No. 2: *Reading is an accrued skill.*

Let's examine Fact No. 1: *Human beings are pleasure-centered.* Human beings will voluntarily do over and over that which brings them *pleasure.* That is, we go to the restaurants we *like,* order the foods we *like,* listen to the radio stations that play the music we *like,* and visit the in-laws we *like.* Conversely, we avoid the foods, and music, and in-laws we *dislike.* Far from being a theory, this is a physiological fact. When our senses send electrical and chemical messages to the "pleasure" or "unpleasure centers" of the brain, we respond positively or negatively.

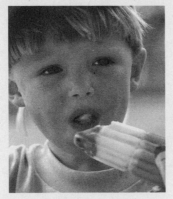

Pleasure dictates our choice of flavors, music, friends, and how we use our time.

An eminent animal psychologist at the American Museum of Natural History built a case for reducing all behavior to two simple responses: approach and withdrawal. We approach what causes pleasure, and we withdraw from what causes unpleasure or pain.[17]

Pleasure could be called the *glue* that holds our attention—but it only holds us to what we like. As long as we're enjoying a movie, we're connected. When we cease to enjoy it, we disconnect. It applies to nearly everything we do willingly. Every time we read to a child, we're sending a "pleasure" message (glue) to the child's brain. You could even call it a commercial, conditioning the child to associate books and print with pleasure. There are, however, "unpleasures" associated with reading and school. The learning experience can be tedious or boring, threatening, and without meaning—endless hours of worksheets, hours of intensive phonics instruction, and hours of unconnected-test questions. If a child seldom experiences the "pleasures" of reading and meets only the "unpleasures," then the natural reaction will be withdrawal.

And that brings us to Reading Fact No. 2: *Reading is an accrued skill.* That means reading is like riding a bicycle, driving a car, or sewing: in order to get better at it you must do it. And the more you read, the better you get at it.

The last twenty-five years of reading research[18] confirms this simple formula—regardless of sex, race, nationality, or socioeconomic background. Students who read the most, read the best, achieve the most, and stay in school the longest. Conversely, those who don't read much, *cannot* get better at it. And most Americans (children and adults) don't read much, and therefore aren't very good at it.[19]

Why don't they read much? Because of Reading Fact No. 1: the large number of "unpleasure" messages they received throughout their school years, coupled with the lack of "pleasure" messages in the home, nullify any attraction from the book. They avoid books and print the same way a cat avoids a hot stove burner. There is ample proof for all these hypotheses in my answer to the next question.

Which Country Has the Best Readers and Why?

One of the most comprehensive international reading studies was conducted in 1990 and 1991 involving thirty-two countries, and assessed 210,000 nine- and fourteen-year-olds.[20] Of all those children, which ones read best?

For nine-year-olds, the four top nations were: Finland (569); U.S. (547); Sweden (539); and France (531).

But the U.S.'s position dropped to a tie for eighth when fourteen-year-olds were evaluated. This demonstrates that American children *begin* reading on a level that is among the best in the world, but since reading is an accrued skill and U.S. children appear to do less of it as they grow older, their scores decline when compared with countries where children read more as they mature.

Can Finland's High Score Be Attributed to Any Advanced Reading Start?

Just the opposite. Finland's high scores should give pause to those who think an earlier reading start ("hothousing") will produce better results. There was only three months' difference in age between the first-place Finnish children and second-place American students, yet the Finnish children are introduced to formal reading instruction only at age seven, *two years later than American children,* and still managed to surpass them by age nine. Chapter 8 includes information on the television viewing habits of Finnish children, which has an impact on their scores, along with exceedingly large amounts of print in the home.

What Factors Were Common to the Best Student Readers Around the World?

Two of the factors that produced higher achievements (two others will be found later in chapter 6: Libraries) are:

* The frequency of teachers reading aloud to students
* The frequency of SSR (sustained silent reading/pleasure reading in school). Children who had daily SSR scored much higher than those who had it only once a week.

Those two factors also represent the two Reading Facts we've just examined. Wherever in the world it is done, in the home or in the classroom, reading aloud serves as a commercial for the pleasures of reading. This is the catalyst for the child wanting to read on his own. But it also provides a reading foundation by nurturing the child's listening. *Listening comprehension comes before reading comprehension.*

Consider, for example, the word "enormous." If a child has never *heard* the word "enormous," he's unlikely ever to *say* the word. And if he's neither *heard* it nor *said* it, imagine the difficulty when it's time to *read* it and *write* it. The listening vocabulary is the reservoir of words that feeds the speaking vocabulary, the reading vocabulary and the writing vocabulary— *all at the same time.*

Little wonder Tom Parker, former admissions director at Williams College and now at Amherst College, tells parents who ask about improving their child's SAT scores, "The best SAT-preparation course in the world is to read to your children in bed when they're little. Eventually, if that's a wonderful experience for them, they'll start to read themselves." Parker, who has interviewed some of America's finest applicants, claims he's never met a student with high verbal SAT scores who wasn't a passionate reader.[21] And the SAT-prep course can't package that passion, but *parents* can.

Where Does Phonics Come into All This?

There's more than enough research to validate the importance of phonics in children's reading. Children who understand the mechanics of reading—who know that words are made up of sounds and can break the sound code—have a great advantage. But teaching a boy *how* to scrub his neck is no guarantee he'll have a clean neck, even if he knows how to use the washcloth and soap. The missing ingredient is motivation; he knows *how* but doesn't *want* to wash the neck. But when that boy meets the right girl, he'll have a clean neck—thus you need the combination of know-how *and* motivation.

Phonics drills don't motivate—they can't. What motivates people to come back to ball games are favorite teams and favorite players. What motivates folks to come back to bookstores and libraries are favorite authors and favorite books. And that's the story behind the front-page headline in *The New York Times,* March 19, 1998:

Experts Call for Mix of 2 Methods
To Teach Reading: Phonics and Meaning[22]

The article described the 390-page report from the National Research Council, commissioned by the U.S. Department of Education, that found the most effective teaching of reading took place when *both* phonics and whole-language methods were used in tandem, urging an end to the reading wars that had wrenched school districts for twenty-five years. These findings were the result of a two-year study analyzing decades of reading research.

For some people phonics almost becomes an article of religious faith.

Giving them the benefit of the doubt, I combed both the Old and New Testaments, but the closest I came was "Phoenicians."

This is not to say phonics isn't important. It is, and good "whole language" classes include phonics. A knowledge of phonics gives the reader a key by which he or she can unlock a word they don't recognize by sight. It makes the word "elephant" comprehensible—but only if you've ever *heard* the word "elephant." But if you've never heard it, how will you know if you're sounding it out correctly? Then, if you've never seen an elephant or at least a picture of one, you'll be in a pickle to *understand* the word you sounded out. Phonics is very dependent upon the person's background knowledge of words and things.

That's why when the Ohio legislature awarded grants of up to $15,000 to thirty-seven schools that agreed to incorporate systematic phonics instruction in their reading instruction, including daily letter and sound drills, seventeen improved and seventeen declined—including six that dropped to less than a 22 percent proficiency rating.[23] High poverty was named as a culprit for the phonics failure, and poverty is nearly always associated with poor background knowledge.

What Is "Background Knowledge"?

The easiest way to understand it is to read the following two paragraphs and see if there is a difference in your understanding of each. (I'm assuming you're a good enough reader to be able to decode or "sound out" all the words.)

1. Mike Piazza and Robin Ventura singled to start the eighth inning. After a Braves pitching change to bring in Mike Remlinger, Melvin Mora—the first of a series of pinch-hitters—came to the plate for Benny Agbayani. Mora bunted, moving Piazza and Ventura over.

2. Kallis and Rhodes put on 84 but, with the ball turning, Mark Waugh could not hit with impunity and his eight overs cost only 37. The runs still had to be scored at more than seven an over, with McGrath still to return and Warne having two overs left, when Rhodes pulled Reiffel to Beven at deep square leg.

Was there a difference in your comprehension? You probably had an easier time with the first paragraph, an account of a baseball game in 1999. The second paragraph came from an account of the World Cricket Championship in the same year. Any confusion was because the less one knows about a subject or the vocabulary associated with that subject, the slower one must read, the more difficult reading comprehension becomes, and the less one understands.[24] "Sounding out" the cricket paragraph wouldn't have helped much, would it?

Background knowledge is one reason why children who read the most (or those who travel the most) bring the largest amount of information to the table and thus understand more of what the teacher or the textbook is teaching. Thus children whose families bring them to museums and zoos, who visit historic sites, who travel abroad or camp in remote areas, accumulate huge chunks of background knowledge without even studying.

When students at the University of Virginia, ranked among the best in the U.S., had to read sections of Hegel's "Metaphysics," their speed and comprehension slowed considerably. But they had no difficulty in reading an account of Lee's surrender at Appomattox, Virginia—because they had background knowledge of the persons, places, and events involved in the latter reading.

On the other hand, students at a community college in Richmond, Virginia, experienced comprehension problems with even the Appomattox account. Researchers found most of the students were not only ignorant of Generals Grant and Lee, but of the name "Appomattox" as well. And these were students living in the state of Virginia![25] The less you know about a subject, the more difficult the reading becomes.

Unfortunately, the lack of background knowledge surfaces very early in a child's school life. In the ongoing study of 22,000 kindergartners, government researchers found that more than 50 percent of children coming from the lowest education and income levels finished in the bottom quartile in background knowledge.[26] Three-year-olds living in the shadow of St. Louis's airport didn't know there were *people* in the planes flying over their homes until their Head Start program took a class trip to the airport. Imagine the difference that made in their understanding of the word "plane." Sometimes background knowledge is just a case of traveling a mile from your own home.

How Is My Child Going to Get Better at Reading If *I'm* Doing the Reading?

Each time you read aloud to a child or class, you offer yourself as a role model. One of the early and primary abilities of children is imitation.[27] They imitate much of what they see and hear, and it is this ability that allows a fifteen-month-old child to say his first words. By age two, the average child expands his vocabulary to include nearly three hundred words, and it triples again in the next year. By age four, the child already understands two-thirds to three-quarters of the words he will use in future daily life.[28] Once he learns to talk, he'll average as many as ten new words a day—not one of which is on a flashcard.[29] Much of that pace is determined, however, by the amount and richness of the language he hears from you and others around him.

Most young parents think children are somehow programmed to speak the language automatically. Most, however, express surprise at how quickly the child imitates what he sees on television—especially the commercials. No matter how often children see a particular commercial, the same fascination is reflected in their eyes each time.

With that in mind, we would do well to learn from Madison Avenue and adapt their advertising formula to sell a product called Reading:

1. Read to children while they are still young enough to want to imitate what they are seeing and hearing.
2. Make sure the readings are interesting and exciting enough to hold their interest while you're building up their imaginations.
3. Keep the initial readings short enough to fit their attention spans and gradually lengthen both.

Neither books nor people have Velcro sides—we don't naturally attach to each other. In the beginning there must be a bonding agent—parent, relative, neighbor, teacher, or librarian—someone who attaches child to book.

None of this is complicated. Anyone who can read can do it with a child, and even illiterates can do it with the right technology (like books on tape from the library—see the "audio books" listing in the subject index on page 379). When you look at all the arguments in its favor, how could we *not* read aloud to children? Nonetheless, the Carnegie Foundation found that "Only half of infants and toddlers are routinely read to by their parents, and many parents do not engage in other activities to stimulate their child's intellectual development. It is not surprising, then, when teachers report that 35 percent of American kindergarten children arrive at school unprepared to learn."[30] Nor does the pattern improve much with age. Looking at children in general and not just toddlers, a 1990 survey showed only 20 percent of parents had a daily involvement with reading and their child; if you include the ones who involved themselves two to three times a week, the figure improves to only 42 percent.[31]

Saddest of all, the most at-risk children are the least likely to be read to. The U.S. government's research with 22,000 kindergartners and their families showed that the lower the parents' income and education, the less chance the child would be read to, and more than 50 percent were not read to daily.

What Are the Skills a Child Needs for Kindergarten?

There is one skill that matters above all others, because it is the prime predictor of school success or failure: the child's vocabulary upon entering school. Yes, the child goes to school to learn new words, but the words he or she *already knows* determine how much of what the teacher says will be understood. And since most instruction for the first four years of school is oral, the child who already has the largest vocabulary will understand the most, while the child with the smallest vocabulary grasps the least.

Once they begin reading, that personal vocabulary will feed comprehension, but a small vocabulary will frustrate it. And, of course, school tests grow increasingly complicated with each grade. That's why school-entry tests on vocabulary predict so accurately.

If No Child Is Born with Words Already in His Head, How Do Some Kids Get a Head Start on Vocabulary?

Conversation is the prime garden in which vocabulary grows, but conversations vary greatly from home to home. Consider the important, eye-opening findings of Drs. Betty Hart and Todd Risley at the University of Kansas from their research on children's early lives.

Published as *Meaningful Differences in the Everyday Experience of Young American Children,*[32] the research began in response to the four-year-olds in the university lab school. With many children, the lines were already drawn. Some were far advanced and some far behind. When these same children were tested at age three and then again at nine, the differences held. What caused the differences so early?

The researchers began by identifying 42 normal families—no drug, alcohol, or spouse abusers, and non-transient—representing three socioeconomic groups: welfare, working class, and professional. Beginning when the children were seven months old, researchers visited the homes for one hour a month, and continued their visits for two and one-half years. During each visit, the researcher tape-recorded and transcribed by hand any conversations and actions taking place in front of the child.

Through 1,300 hours of visits, they accumulated 23 million bytes of information for the project database, categorizing every word (noun, verb, adjective, etc.) said in front of the child. They also defined the kind of sentences used with the child, breaking them down to three distinct types:

♦ Question ("Can you find the ball?")
♦ Affirmation ("You're so smart!")
♦ Prohibition ("Stop that! Bad boy!")

The project held some surprises: Regardless of socioeconomic level, all 42 families said and did the same things with their children. In other words, the basic *instincts* of good parenting are there for most people, rich or poor.

And then the researchers received the data printout and saw the "meaningful differences" among the 42 families.

When the daily number of words for each group of children was projected across four years, the four-year-old child from the professional family will have heard 45 million words, the working-class child 26 million, and the welfare child only 13 million. All three children will show up for kindergarten on the same day, but one will have heard 32 million fewer words—which is a *gigantic* difference.

None of this has anything to do with how much a parent loves a child. They all love their children and want the best for them, but some parents have a better idea of what needs to be said and done to reach that best. They know the child needs to hear words *repeatedly* in meaningful sentences and questions, and they know that plunking a two-year-old down in front of a television set for three hours at a time is more harmful than

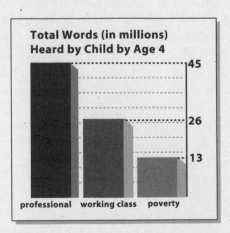

Total Words (in millions) Heard by Child by Age 4

professional   working class   poverty

meaningful. In a few short years, when it is time to read, those numbers will play a big role, for the frequency with which a child has met a word will affect how quickly he can decode it[33] and understand it.[34]

Were There Differences in the Kinds of *Sentences* the Children Heard?

The professional child heard 32 compliments an hour, working class averaged 12 affirmations, and the poverty child heard just 5 encouragements in an hour. Imagine the impact on a child's self-esteem and confidence from 32 positive statements an hour—one every other minute!

Conversely, the professional child heard the fewest negatives in the space of an hour—5, compared to 7 for the working-class child and 11 for welfare. For America's most at-risk children, that comes to a total of 104,000 encouragements and 228,000 discouragements by age four. The professional child arrives at the kindergarten door thinking he's a world-beater, while the at-risk child arrives with a mindset of "can't do" because people at home have been telling him so for years.

The message of *Meaningful Differences* is unambiguous: It's not the toys in the house that make the difference in children's lives; it's the words in their ears. The least expensive thing we can give a child outside of a hug turns out to be the most valuable: *words.* You don't need a job, a checking account, or even a high school diploma to talk with a child. Sadly, I've not heard even one of the nation's so-called "education candidates" address the issues in the *Meaningful Differences* report.

The immediate effect of this vocabulary gap presents itself when the child starts school. Two significant studies of student vocabularies in first through third grades showed children from high-income families with 30 to 50 percent larger vocabularies than peers in low-income families, a factor that allows them to understand and decode words faster, read more, and thus widen the gap further.[35] In order for the poverty child to make up the lost ground before fifth grade, he would need to learn an extra 170 vocabulary words for each week of the school year, along with the 116 he's already supposed to be learning—a daunting task, to say the least.

Then What Hope Is There for Children Coming from At-Risk Homes?

The most encouraging of all the long-term studies on children in poverty is the Carolina Abecedarian Project.[36] Begun in the early 1970s, the study followed 111 low-income children in Chapel Hill, North Carolina; 57 were assigned to a high-quality, year-round day-care program and 54 to a control group that didn't receive the same treatment. The day-care children received nutritional food supplements in the early years and social services until age eight. A central focus of the day care was a language-enrichment program. To encourage that, the staff-to-child ratio for infants was 1 to 3, and 1 to 7 for preschoolers. Children stayed in the program for five years, costing a total of $11,000 per child by today's standards, and were evaluated through age twenty-one.

At age twenty-one, when compared to their control-group peers, the Abecedarian students had higher IQs, were retained in grade far less, had higher reading achievement, had slightly higher math scores, were twice as likely to be in post-secondary schools by age twenty-one, and delayed having a child by two full years.

There are those who will balk at spending that kind of money ($2,200 annually per child for five years) in order to break the cycle of school failure in a family. But if you put that figure into perspective, it's a simple choice: Society can spend the $11,000 total while he is a child, or they can risk paying $27,500 *a year* when he's an adult and must be incarcerated. A RAND study[37] showed that for *each person* who is moved from the status of high school dropout to graduate, the following *annual* savings occur by age thirty:

- Social program savings (jail, Medicaid, food stamps, AFDC): $4,121
- Increase in graduate's tax payment: $1617
- Increase in graduate's disposable income: $2,449

By these calculations, the $11,000 cost of enriched child care could be repaid in less than two years, and after that the savings are all profit for the community and country. If the person goes beyond high school, the savings are even greater.

Where Is the Richer Vocabulary: Conversation or Reading?

Most conversation is plain and simple, whether it's between two adults or with children. It consists of the five thousand words we use all the time, called the Basic Lexicon. (Indeed, 83 percent of the words in normal conversation with a child come from the most commonly used thousand words, and it doesn't change much as the child ages.[38]) Then there are another five thousand words we use in conversation less often. Beyond that ten thousand mark are the "rare words," and these play a critical role in reading. The eventual strength of our vocabulary is determined not by the common ten thousand words but by how many "rare words" we understand.

If we don't use these rare words very often in conversation, where do we find them? The chart below shows that *printed text* contains the most rare words.

Whereas an adult only uses nine rare words (per thousand) when talking with a three-year-old, you'll find three times as many in a children's book, and more than seven times as many in a newspaper. As you can see, oral communication (including a TV script) is decidedly inferior to print when building vocabulary. As soon as the chart moves to printed material (children's book), the number of rare words increases significantly. This poses serious problems for at-risk children who watch large amounts of TV, hear fewer words, and encounter print less often at home. Such children face a gigantic word-gap that impedes reading progress throughout school. And that gap can't possibly be breached in 120 hours of summer school, as some propose.[40]

Regular family conversations will take care of the basic vocabulary, but

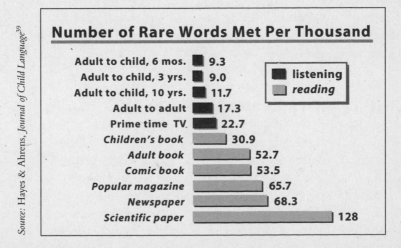

Source: Hayes & Ahrens, *Journal of Child Language*[39]

Number of Rare Words Met Per Thousand

listening
reading

Adult to child, 6 mos.	9.3
Adult to child, 3 yrs.	9.0
Adult to child, 10 yrs.	11.7
Adult to adult	17.3
Prime time TV	22.7
Children's book	30.9
Adult book	52.7
Comic book	53.5
Popular magazine	65.7
Newspaper	68.3
Scientific paper	128

when you read to the child you leap into the rare words that help most when it's time for school and formal learning. Simultaneously, you're familiarizing the child with books and print in a manner that brings him or her pleasure.

But What If the Parent Doesn't Have a Good Vocabulary? How Can You Give What You Don't Have?

It's a question I've heard from parents who are school dropouts or for whom English is a second language. And while there are few easy answers in parenting, this one is easier than most. There is a public agency that comes to the rescue in such instances; in fact, it's been doing this job for more than a century. What the agency does is take all the nouns, verbs, and adjectives a person would ever need, and bundles them into little packages for anyone to borrow—free. They only ask that you bring the "packages" back in a few weeks. I'm referring to books in the American free public library—the "people's university."

If you think it's simplistic that libraries can fix people's language and knowledge problems, then you must be unaware of the many success stories involving libraries and immigrants throughout the twentieth century.

How Can Illiterate Parents Read to Their Child?

That would have been a harder question to answer forty years ago, but today's library has thousands of children's and adult books on audiocassette (audio books) that can be borrowed, with the book, so the parent and child can follow along with the tape. I go into this in more detail in chapter 6 and show how schools are using such tapes to reach reluctant or learning-disabled students. It's a very viable option. (See also "audio book" in subject index.)

What About Those Worksheets My Kid Brings Home—Do They Really Help?

The original intention of a worksheet was intelligent: to discover which students didn't understand the lesson, so the teacher could work with them individually. Unfortunately, she also had to keep the rest of the class busy while she was doing that, so she passed out more worksheets. Thus the assessment tool became a crowd control device. To make matters worse, they multiplied faster than the loaves and fishes, often reaching 1,000 per child per school year. As you can see in chapter 6, a fully stocked classroom library would have kept them just as busy—and with better results.

The most frustrating aspect of this practice is that research shows no correlation between the number of worksheets a student does and how good a reader the child eventually becomes.[41] Nonetheless, many schools continue to ignore the research. School districts like Dallas advise principals that a school of 500 students should plan for 60,000 sheets of paper for duplication of worksheets each month.[42]

Since 1972, the National Assessment of Educational Progress (NAEP) has tracked the reading scores of fourth-, eighth-, and twelfth-graders. They found the highest scorers were those taught with trade books (as opposed to basal textbooks) and those who did the most pleasure reading. With these findings in mind, how are we supposed to react to NAEP's report that found 38 percent of the fourth-graders were below even the *minimal* level of reading achievement,[43] one-third of all students were using workbooks and worksheets on a daily basis,[44] and 44 percent of the fourth-graders had no regularly scheduled SSR time?[45]

The ultimate damage from the avalanche of worksheets can be seen in a 1983 World Series incident when a stadium elevator, jammed with reporters rushing to the locker room level for their post-game interviews, stopped at the executive level. Waiting to get on was a distinguished-looking, silver-haired gentleman. Before he could enter, the young elevator operator barred his way and barked, "Full! Press!" The man, lacking a press tag, graciously stepped back and stared blankly over the heads of the reporters while the door closed.

When someone asked the operator if she knew who that was, she shrugged and said, "Sure. Mr. Coffee." The young woman had closed the door on one of the greatest players ever to wear a professional uniform—Joe DiMaggio. But her generation had never been fed Joe DiMaggio as a Hall of Fame center fielder or "Joltin' Joe." Her generation had only known him in retirement, as the television spokesperson for Mr. Coffee.[46] As they say, what you are fed is what you consume and eventually believe.

If you are fed reading as six worksheets a day, 1,000 sheets a year, under the pronouncement, "Boys and girls, it's time for reading," by the time you reach fourth grade you think worksheets are reading and you mistakenly think you hate reading.

Why Don't They Cash In the Worksheets for Library Books?

In 1989, three researchers at the State University of New York at Albany tabulated the cost of one year's worth of worksheets for a second-grade child. Not including the cost of the school building's utilities (heat, etc.) and the salary of the teacher, it came to an average of $59.98 per child. The researchers' conclusion was that most schools find it easier to make twenty-five copies of a piece of paper than to purchase books. The approximately $60 spent on worksheets could purchase twenty children's trade paperbacks for the child, or five hundred for the entire class.[47]

How Important Is It That the Parent Be a Reader?

My favorite example is the study of 30 men who were identified as growing up in working-class, blue-collar families. (This is potent proof of the aforementioned RAND study of what happens to income and human potential when we move people up the education ladder.) Fifteen of the 30 men eventually became college professors and 15 remained in blue-collar careers. In handpicking the 30, the researchers made sure all came from similar socioeconomic childhoods with similar family traumas (family alcoholism, parent death, divorce, etc.).

If the 30 men began life in similar circumstances, how to explain the 15 who rose so far above their beginning stations? In extensive interviews with the 30, significant differences appeared regarding books and reading as children.

- 12 of the 15 professors were read to or told stories by their parents, compared to only 4 of the blue-collar workers.
- 14 out of 15 professors came from homes where books and print were plentiful; among blue-collar workers, only 4 had books.
- 13 of the professors' mothers and 12 of the fathers were identified as frequent readers of newspapers, magazines, or books; blue-collar workers identified 6 mothers and 4 fathers.
- All of the 15 professors were encouraged to read as children, compared with only 3 of the blue-collar workers.

A significant part of the study was what the 15 professors found motivating or interesting in their childhood reading. They found answers or information relating to problems in their lives. The book, in a manner of speaking, became food for the starving child. Typical in this respect was Professor Respondent #2, "a sociologist whose mother died when he was seven years old, with the result that the respondent was put into an orphanage, where he stayed until he was 'on his own' at about age seventeen. This respondent experienced great anxiety at being put into an orphanage and he identified the chief problem as being the 'uncertainty of what happens to orphans.'"

He explained: "'All of a sudden my mother was dead and I was in this place. I felt I didn't know what would happen to me. I was scared and had continually in my mind the question of what would happen to me and to others in that place. What happened to kids in orphanages?'

"In the orphanage library, at about age eight, this respondent discovered the Horatio Alger books. The discovery had a profound impact on him because all of a sudden he 'realized that he could create his own life' even if he was in an orphanage. He had been looking for an answer to the question of what would become of him and now he *realized that what would become of him was up to him.* Horatio Alger books provided him with the *model of a boy whose life was his own* and who could create it as he chose."[48]

Why Is Fiction Important?

With all the focus on reading achievement and scores, it's very easy to overlook the *purpose* of literature. Jack London didn't write *The Call of the Wild* to boost SAT scores. *Les Miserables* wasn't created to improve vocabulary. Ultimately, the purpose of literature is to provide meaning in our lives—which is really the purpose of all education. Child psychologist Bruno Bettelheim says that finding this meaning is the greatest need and most difficult achievement for any human being at any age. Who am I? Why am I here? What can I be?[49] In *The Uses of Enchantment,* Bettelheim writes that the two factors most responsible for giving the child this belief that he can make a significant contribution to life are parents or teachers and literature; that is, life experience and stories *about* life experience.

Literature is considered such an important medium—more than television, more than films, more than art or overhead projectors—because literature brings us closest to the human heart. And of the two forms of literature (fiction and nonfiction), the one that brings us closest and presents the meaning of life most clearly to the child is fiction. That is one reason most of the recommendations for read-alouds at the back of this book are fiction.

Three-time Pulitzer Prize–winning novelist and poet Robert Penn Warren wrote that we read fiction because:

- We like it.
- There is conflict in it—and conflict is at the center of life.
- Its conflict wakes us up from the tedium of everyday life.
- It allows us to vent our emotions with tears, laughter, love, and hate.
- We hope its story will give us a clue to our own life story.
- It releases us from life's pressures by allowing us to escape into other people's lives.[50]

Has Anyone Ever Applied These Ideas to an At-Risk School?

Just as parents in low-income situations need to be reminded their task is not insurmountable, so too do educators who work with children coming from those homes. Reading achievement and "pleasure" do not have to be mutually exclusive. During his ten years as principal of Boston's Solomon Lewenberg Middle School, Thomas P. O'Neill, Jr., and his faculty proved it. The pride of Boston's junior high schools during the 1950s and early 1960s, Lewenberg subsequently suffered the ravages of urban decay, and by 1984, with the lowest academic record and Boston teachers calling it the "loony bin" instead of the Lewenberg, the school was earmarked for closing. But first, Boston officials would give it one last chance.

The reins were handed to O'Neill (no relation to the former Speaker of the House), an upbeat, first-year principal and former high school English teacher whose experience there had taught him to "sell" the pleasures and importance of reading.

The first thing he did was abolish the school's intercom system ("As a teacher I'd always sworn someday I'd rip the thing off the wall. Now I could do it legally") and then set about establishing structure, routine, and discipline. "That's the easy part. What happens *after* is the important part— *Reading.* It's the key element in curriculum. IBM can teach our graduates to work the machine, but *we* have to teach them to read the manual." In O'Neill's first year, sustained silent reading (see chapter 5) was instituted for the nearly 400 pupils and faculty for the last ten minutes of the day—during which everyone in the school read for pleasure. Each teacher was assigned a room—much to the consternation of some who felt those last ten minutes could be better used to clean up the shop or gym. "Prove to me on paper," O'Neill challenged them, "that you are busier than I am, and I'll give you the ten minutes to clean." He had no takers.

Within a year, critics became supporters and the school was relishing the quiet time that ended the day. The books that had been started during SSR were often still being read by students filing out to buses—in stark contrast to former dismissal scenes that bordered on chaos.

The next challenge was to insure that each sixth-, seventh-, and eighth-grade student not only *saw* an adult reading each day, but also *heard* one. Faculty members were assigned a classroom and the school day began with ten minutes of reading aloud—to complement the silent ending. Soon reading aloud began to inspire awareness, and new titles sprouted during SSR. In effect, the faculty was doing what the great art schools have always done: providing "life" models from which to draw.

In the first year, Lewenberg's scores were up; the second year, not only did the scores climb but so too did student enrollment in response to the school's new reputation.

Three years later, in 1988, Lewenberg's 570 students had the highest reading scores in the city of Boston, there was a fifteen-page waiting list of children who wanted to attend, and O'Neill was pictured by *Time* as a viable alternative to physical force in its cover story on Joe Clark, the bull-horn and bat-toting principal from Paterson, New Jersey.[51]

Today, Tom O'Neill is retired, but the ripple effect of his work has reached shores that not even his great optimism would have anticipated. In the early 1990s, a junior high school civics teacher in Japan, Hiroshi Hayashi, read the Japanese edition of *The Read-Aloud Handbook*. Intrigued by the concept of SSR and Tom O'Neill's example, he immediately decided to apply it in his own school. Contrary to what most Americans believe, few Japanese public school students are singleminded overachievers, and many are rebellious or reluctant readers—if they are readers at all.[52]

Although SSR was a foreign concept to Japanese secondary education, Hayashi saw quick results in his junior high school with just ten minutes at the start of the morning. Unwilling to keep his enthusiasm to himself, he

Thomas P. O'Neill, Jr.

spent the next two years sending forty thousand handwritten postcards to administrators in Japanese public schools, urging them to visit his school and adopt the concept. His personal crusade has won accolades from even the faculty skeptics: to date, more than thirty-five hundred Japanese schools use SSR to begin their school day, and their ranks are increasing each year.

The response to Hayashi's initial campaign caught the eye of a Japanese book wholesaler who soon published "A Guide to SSR in the Morning." At one junior high using SSR, students were reading 2.9 books a month. By contrast, a 1997 survey by the Japan School Library Association found 55.3 percent of the country's junior high students read nothing at all.[53]

My Husband and I Are Short on Time, So Where Do We Find the Time for This?

The last time I checked, everyone still gets twenty-four hours a day—no more, no less. There is no shortage of time. For three decades, two professors have been doing a study of people's daily schedules, using thousands of personal time diaries.[54] This decade shows Americans have *five more free hours a week than they did ten years ago.* The reason they feel so stressed is because they are continually multitasking. Instead of simply driving the child to a soccer game, we're driving *and* making an appointment on the cell phone. At the game, we're networking with a neighbor about the refreshments at the preschool picnic, watching the game, and taking calls on the ubiquitous cell phone. We're not out of time—we're out of *breath.*

To easily disprove the time myth, count the number of video stores you pass in one day, then count the number of channels on your TV, and finally count the number of cars in your local mall at 7:30 in the evening. If Americans were out of time, the video stores would be in bankruptcy court, you'd have only ten TV channels (one set to a house), and the mall parking lot would be three-quarters empty.

We have time for what we value. The people who found the time to read to a child and to themselves yesterday had the same twenty-four hours as the person who had no time to read, but did watch their favorite team on TV or the afternoon soap they taped, did find the time to talk on the phone for thirty-five minutes, and did find the time to run over to the mall for an errand.

Time is the great filtering agent in success. The athletes, accountants, writers, readers—anyone in pursuit of success—must put in the time to be successful. It's a bit easier for the reader because in the early years, someone else can put in the time; that is, the parent or caregiver can read to the child. On the other hand, if that time is not put in then, the child alone will need to do it when he or she reaches school age. Schools for at-risk students that have high achievement levels also require 70 percent more time spent in school and on assignments than do other non-achieving schools.[55] But the common denominator is time.

In closing this chapter, let's consider what impact some downtime might have on a child's reading attitudes, as well as his relationship with a parent. Chris Erskine, columnist for the *Los Angeles Times,* shares a father–son reading relationship that evolved from a case of mononucleosis.

BOOK HABIT PUTS DAD, SON ON THE SAME PAGE[56]
by Chris Erskine

The boy reads the paragraph, then stops. He likes this paragraph. To him, it is rich with truth, almost profound. He reads it again.

> *People have been trying to understand dogs ever since the beginning of time. One never knows what they'll do. You can read every day where a dog saved the life of a drowning child, or lay down his life for his master. Some people call this loyalty. I don't. I may be wrong, but I call it love—the deepest kind of love.*

"That's true, isn't it, Dad?" the boy says after reading it the second time. "This stuff about dogs."

I nod, and we read aloud some more, first him, then me, sharing this book page by page, chapter by chapter, front to back.

"You really like books, don't you, Dad?" he asks as we pause between chapters.

"They're all right," I say.

Truth is, I like books the way I like cold, foamy drinks in the summer and baseball in the fall. Basically, I live for them.

And now the boy is discovering books too. Almost by accident, the twelve-year-old is finding enjoyment in the simple act of reading, a kind of intimacy there is no real expression for.

"Know what 'camaraderie' is?" I ask him at one point.

"Like being friends?" he says.

"Like being pals," I say. "You've become pals with your books."

"Sorry, Dad. I don't get you."

"That's all right," I say. "Just keep reading."

Six months ago, he was indifferent to books. He read only when he had to. And even then, not always.

Six months ago, if someone had offered a magic potion to make him love to read, I would've paid a fortune for it. Even though I don't have a fortune, I would've paid one, borrowing the fortune at 15 percent interest and paying it back in huge installments over sixty years.

Back then, he thought books were for dorks, prematurely mature boys who couldn't hit a fast ball or snag a line drive. Books were for indoor people, people who shunned sunlight and all the other good things in life.

Then, one day, the boy flopped down on the couch and didn't flop back up again.

"Mono?" I asked the doctor.

"Mono," the doctor said.

It was just the bad break he needed. Mono. And for two weeks, he became what he'd always despised—an indoor person.

The mono made him so sleepy, he couldn't watch TV. It left him so weak, he couldn't lift a book.

So I began to read to him. Like when he was four, I would read to him, hamming it up and trying to bring the words to life.

As he got stronger, we would alternate reading pages aloud, first him, then me. Then, with time, we would alternate chapters. And when he finally recovered, we still alternated chapters.

Now every night before bed, he grabs some book and calls to me. And together we read, elbow to elbow, page by page.

"Dad, you listening?" he'll say.

"Huh?"

"Your turn to read."

"OK," I say, shaking myself awake. And we read some more.

He likes adventure stories mostly. *Old Yeller. Where the Red Fern Grows. Hatchet.* Stories about boys lost in the woods with only their dogs and their hunting rifles. Stories he gobbles up like movie-house popcorn.

And now this love for reading has gotten so out of hand, he'll even read a daily newspaper, starting with the sports section and working his way forward, the way his dad does.

He reads the sports section the way people read the wills of rich relatives, scouring the fine print, then rereading the parts he doesn't fully understand.

Mostly, he likes the obscure facts, the stuff he thinks only he will discover.

"Mondesi is only hitting .194," the boy says in disbelief. ".194!"

Each morning, he leans down close to the page, getting his elbows in the newsprint, crinkling the page as he shoves closer to the breakfast table.

The smaller the print, the closer he gets. The smaller the print, the more he cherishes the information.

"Catfish Hunter threw five no-hitters in high school," he says, reading some factoid deep inside sports. "Five no-hitters!"

He stores up these facts for later use, balling them up in his brain like pieces of string, ready to call on them at just the right time, during playground discussions or dugout debates.

"The All-Star game is July 7," he says, pointing to a piece of type no thicker than an eyelash. "July 7 at Coors Field."

There's a pause as he hunts for more factoids, more of the trivia that makes a boy a boy, or a man a man. Or, maybe best of all, a little of both.

"Dad, you listening?" he finally says, both our noses buried in the morning paper.

"Huh?"

"You listening, Dad?"

"Always," I say.

Chapter 2

When to Begin Read-Aloud

In every task the most important thing is the beginning . . . especially when you deal with anything young and tender.

—Plato, *The Republic*

"How old must a child be before you start reading to him?" That is the question I am most often asked by parents. The next is: "When is the child too old to be read to?"

In answer to the first question, I ask one of my own. "When did you start *talking* to the child? Did you wait until he was six months old?"

"We started talking to him the day he was born," parents respond.

"And what language did your child speak the day he was born? English? Japanese? Italian?" They're about to say English when it dawns on them the child didn't speak *any* language yet.

"Wonderful!" I say. "There you were holding that newborn infant in your arms, whispering, 'We love you, Cindy. Daddy and I think you are the most beautiful baby in the world.' You were speaking multisyllable words and complex sentences in a foreign language to a child who didn't understand one word you were saying! And you never thought twice about doing it. But most people can't imagine *reading* to that same child. And that's sad. If a child is old enough to talk to, he's old enough to read to. It's the same language."

Obviously, from birth to six months of age we are concerned less with "understanding" than with "conditioning" the child to your voice and the sight of books. Dr. T. Berry Brazelton, when he was chief of the child development unit of Boston Children's Hospital Medical Center, observed that new parents' most critical task during these early stages is learning how to calm the child, how to bring it under control, so he or she can begin to look around and listen when you pass on information.[1] Much the same task confronts the classroom teacher as she faces a new class each September.

Is *In Utero* Learning" a Myth?

We've long known the human voice is one of the most powerful tools a parent has for calming a child. And what many previously suspected is now firmly established in research indicating that the voice's influence starts *even earlier than birth*. University of North Carolina psychologist Anthony De-Casper and colleagues explored the effects of reading to children *in utero,* thinking that infants might be able to recognize something they had heard prenatally.

DeCasper asked thirty-three pregnant women to recite a specific paragraph of a children's story three times a day for the last six weeks of pregnancy. Three different paragraphs were used among the thirty-three women, but each woman used just one passage for the entire recitation period. Fifty-two hours after birth, the newborns were given a special nipple and earphones through which they could hear a woman (not the mother) reciting all three paragraphs. By measuring each child's sucking rate, researchers concluded the infants preferred the passages their mothers had recited during the third trimester.[2]

"The babies' reactions to the stories had been influenced by earlier exposure," DeCasper concluded. "That constitutes learning in a very general way." In a similar experiment with reading to fetuses during the two and one-half months before birth, DeCasper found the child's heartbeat increased with the new story, and decreased with the familiar one.[3] Both of these experiments clearly establish that a child becomes familiar with certain sounds while *in utero* and begins associating those tones with comfort and security. The baby is being conditioned—his first class in learning. Imagine how much can be accomplished when a child can see and touch the book, understand the words, and feel the reader.

What About Reading Aloud to "Special Needs" Children?

In *Cushla and Her Books,* author Dorothy Butler described how Cushla Yeoman's parents began reading aloud to her when she was four months of age.[4] By nine months the child was able to respond to the sight of certain books and convey to her parents that these were her favorites. By age five she had taught herself to read.

What makes Cushla's story so dramatic is that she was born with chromosome damage that caused deformities of the spleen, kidney, and mouth cavity. It also produced muscle spasms—which prevented her from sleeping for more than two hours a night or holding anything in her hand until she was three years old—and hazy vision beyond her fingertips.

Until she was three, the doctors diagnosed Cushla as "mentally and physically retarded" and recommended that she be institutionalized. Her parents, after seeing her early responses to books, refused; instead, they put her on a dose of fourteen read-aloud books a day. By age five, Cushla was found by psychologists to be well above average in intelligence and a socially well-adjusted child.

The story of Cushla and her family has appeared in each edition of *The Read-Aloud Handbook* and each time it was my hope it would inspire an unknown reader someplace. One day I received a letter from Marcia Thomas, then of Memphis, Tennessee:

> Our daughter Jennifer was born in September 1984. One of the first gifts we received was a copy of *The Read-Aloud Handbook*. We read the introductory chapters and were very impressed by the story of Cushla and her family. We decided to put our daughter on a "diet" of at least ten books a day. She had to stay in the hospital for seven weeks as a result of a heart defect and corrective surgery. However, we began reading to her while she was still in intensive care; and when we couldn't be there, we left story tapes and asked the nurses to play them for her.
>
> For the past seven years we have read to Jennifer at every opportunity. She is now in the first grade and is one of the best readers in her class. She consistently makes 100 on reading tests and has a very impressive vocabulary. She can usually be found in the reading loft at school during free time, and at home she loves to sit with my husband or me and read a book.
>
> What makes our story so remarkable is that Jennifer was born with Down Syndrome. At two months of age, we were told Jennifer most likely was blind, deaf, and severely retarded. When she was tested at age four, her IQ was 111.

For the fourth edition of this book, I needed Mrs. Thomas's permission to use her letter. Since the family had moved in the intervening years, it took me a while to find them, but finally I did. And on the summer after-noon I called, Jennifer—who was about to enter fourth grade and was reading on grade level—was entertaining her former third-grade teacher for lunch, sharing some of her favorite books. For the fifth edition of the book, I called shortly after Jennifer had finished her freshman year of reg-ular high school classes in Concord, Massachusetts, where she'd received the English department's "high achievement" citation for straight A's.

Of all the parents I've ever had in my audience, the one who *least* needed my message was Geri Kunishima in Honolulu, Hawaii. Nonethe-less, there she was in 1992 and again in 1993, and also in 1998. A classroom teacher as well as a parent, Geri and her husband, Lindy, have three chil-dren—two girls and a boy. Six months after Steven was born, Geri began to suspect something was wrong with him; the doctors told her to relax.

At eighteen months, still unable to walk or talk, the child was found to be suffering from hypoplasia of the vermis. Simply put, the transmitter for the brain's messages had not developed—and never would. The doctor's verdict left no room for hope. "He will never walk or talk, or do much of anything that requires muscle control. He will be profoundly retarded, un-educable in all but the simplest tasks," the doctor explained, and then sug-gested eventual institutionalization.

When Geri Kunishima recovered from the initial shock and depression, she recalled how she and Lindy had read aloud to the girls when they were Steven's age. The older daughter, Trudi, claimed to see a spark in the boy's eyes—something waiting to be reached. Maybe a daily read-aloud would help.

So began a nightly program of someone sitting and reading with Steven each evening while dinner was being prepared. Cushioned by floor pillows and supporting his head so he could see the pages, he was read to. Book af-ter book, night after night. Nothing seemed to register. There was no re-action from Steven, just a blank stare.

And then one day, three months later, when Trudi announced it was time for a story, she was amazed to see him begin to pull himself across the floor to the bookcase. Pawing at the books, he smacked one until it opened. Then he stared at the animals on the page. The scene was repeated the following night—same book, same page. "He's got a memory!" the family exulted.

The Kunishimas then increased their efforts. There were more books, and more muscle exercise. The brain often compensates for damage in one area by opening alternate routes, Geri reasoned, and this may be happen-ing with Steven. His progress was slow and painful but the work bore fruits. Though unable to speak words at age four and a half, he was speaking a few within a year. And more the next. Walking and schoolwork amounted to climbing mountains, but the Kunishimas never quit. By age thirteen, Steven was walking and talking, and played a little basketball—though not very well. More important, he was reading and writing—on grade level.[5]

I last saw Steven when he was an honor-role freshman in high school. Today his family runs a special school in Hawaii for children with learning disabilities, with instruction based on what they learned from Steven.

If the Yeomans, the Thomases, and the Kunishimas can accomplish all they did with their children, imagine how much can be realized by the average family if they begin reading to a child early and in earnest.

What Could You Expect If You Started Reading to a Child on *Day One*?

Erin had no idea what a lucky girl she was when Linda Kelly-Hassett and her husband, Jim, brought her home from the hospital that Thanksgiving Day in 1988—but she soon found out. A few years later, I found out, too, when Erin's mom shared with me her journal of reading experiences. Since I didn't keep such a document with my own children, and since Linda began even earlier than I did (ignorant parent that I was back in those days), I think her words speak louder than anything I might write in this space.

Linda had been an elementary-grade teacher for twenty-two years when Erin was born, and a devoted reader-aloud to her students. Everything she did in class, and recommended to the parents of her students, she applied to Erin. Not every parent has the time to do all that Linda did, but if they did even half as much, all children's futures would be brighter. You should

Erin Hasset

note the unforced and gradual manner in which books were introduced to Erin, and the way in which they were tied to everyday events.

Erin's first book, on her first day of life, was *Love You Forever* by Robert Munsch. My husband videotaped me reading it. He was unfamiliar with the story and was moved to tears as we rocked "back and forth, back and forth." That video went to relatives and friends, helping to bring Erin into their lives in a special way, and it also went to my former class of third-graders—planting a seed for the next generation.

Erin's first four months saw mostly soft chunky books, board books, and firmer-paged, lift-the-flap books. These were not only read but tasted and enjoyed. When she was four months old she began to enjoy time in her johnny-jump-up, often spending forty-five minutes at a time, two or three times a day, jumping happily to poems, songs, and pop-up books. Over and over we read poems from *Read-Aloud Rhymes for the Very Young* by Jack Prelutsky, sang along with the Wee Sing tapes, and popped up and out with books like *Who's Peeking at Me?* by Kees Moerbeek.

The enjoyment of johnny-jump-up diminished around eight months when crawling and seeking her own entertainment took over. She loved tearing paper at this time, so we put out lots of magazines, but only very durable books. At reading time we stayed with the same kind of book until she was around ten months. At this stage, I became so eager to read story books to her that I decided to read these to her while she was in her highchair (so she couldn't tear the pages). It worked beautifully and provided some surprises.

For starters, we never had any food battles because I was too busy reading to let myself become overly concerned with her food intake. As I read, she ate her finger foods while I spooned in some baby fruit and veggies. Mealtime was fun, positive, and usually ended with her pointing to the bookshelf and requesting another "Boo(k)." This practice set a precedent that followed through the years. I continued to read to her at breakfast and lunchtime. When she had friends over, we always had a story or two at snack time. Using big books from my teaching days is a special treat.

Several memorable events happened during this period of early reading. My husband was transferred to the east coast and got home every other weekend. Between Erin's tenth and fifteenth months, we were pretty much by ourselves when eating, so mealtime reading grew in length. It was nothing for her to actively listen to stories from twenty to forty minutes after a meal. A note in my journal for February 4, 1990, reads: "9 books after breakfast; 10 books and 4 poems after lunch; 7 books after dinner." This was not an unusual day's reading.

Ten days later, February 14, 1990, I wrote this entry: "After breakfast, Erin asked for a book. Since we were moving at the end of the month, I read her *Good-Bye House* by Frank Asch. She kept asking for another book as soon as I finished one. I ended up reading seventy-five minutes, covering twenty-five books. At fourteen months of age she had sustained interest in the stories—actively listening, pointing, saying words, and making sounds."

I want to note that all these books were familiar to Erin. She did not immediately take to a new book. I would introduce it to her over a period of days. The first day we would look at the cover and "talk" about it. On the second day, I would then proceed to read the first page or so. I would read a few more pages each additional day until about the fifth or sixth day, when the book would be familiar enough for me to read it in its entirety.

Shortly after our move to Pennsylvania, I was reading her *The Very Hungry Caterpillar* by Eric Carle—as I had been doing for the last six months. This time, during the reading of the second sentence ("One Sunday morning the warm sun came up and—pop!— out of the egg came a tiny and very hungry caterpillar"), while I was still forming my mouth to say "pop," Erin said the word "pop!" and with perfect inflection. She was seventeen months that day and it was the start of her inserting words into familiar stories. What an addition to an already pleasant experience.

Beyond the love of reading nurtured by these parent-child experiences, Erin's verbal skills were growing. She spoke in complete sentences at twenty-one months and had a vocabulary of 1,000 words by twenty-four months—all achieved without flashcards or "drill and skill." Erin's father wasn't excluded from the readings, and the two had a collection of books she labeled "Daddy Books" that became a personal cache.

With all of this reading, Erin's attention span and interests grew by leaps and bounds. By four years of age, she was listening to hundred-page novels along with her picture books. When it came time to attend school, Erin's mom decided to use her own years of professional teaching experience and home-school Erin. Home schooling wasn't a political or religious issue with the Hassetts; they felt that their only child should receive the best they could possibly give her—a veteran twenty-two-year teacher called Mom. Furthermore, with the head start she received at home, much of her first years in formal school would have been redundant and probably bored her to tears. In the ensuing years, Linda and Erin would be involved in weekly cooperative ventures with other community homeschoolers, and by age twelve, Erin was also taking band and physical education at the local middle school for 310 minutes a week.

Aware of the bonding that occurs during read-aloud, as well as the difference between a child's listening level and reading level (more on that later), the Hassetts continued to read to Erin. For a list of all the novels heard by Erin from ages four to twelve, see my web site (www.trelease-on-reading.com/erinlist.html). They also brought their readings alive every chance they could. When a family vacation took them to the Midwest, the Hassetts made sure Erin had a chance to visit the Ingalls's homesteads, including the chance to place flowers on their graves while wearing her specially made *Little House on the Prairie* dress.

Erin's progress in learning to read is a story in itself. After expressing a desire at age five to know her letters and sounds, she quickly mastered them but balked at formal reading. Listening to Mom and Dad reading novels was still a daily experience, but when her mother began to press her about reading herself in first grade, Erin declared, "I don't want to read those dumb books, those baby books (primers and easy-readers). I'm not going to read until I can do chapter books."

Her mother backed off—to a degree. There was a local Head Start program of four- and five-year-olds whom Linda and Erin had begun visiting as volunteers once a week, and one of the activities was reading to the children. Since the children quickly began to look up to Erin, she hedged on her determination and agreed to read some "big books" like Eric Carle's *The Very Hungry Caterpillar* to these classes. Obviously, Erin had learned *how* to read.

Finally, in the summer between first and second grade, the Hassetts were visiting friends who had a daughter three years older than Erin. Though the two girls went to bed at the same time, Erin was a night owl and not at all tired. When she was told she could read in bed, the older girl gave her some chapter books she had outgrown. The next morning, Erin came down to breakfast, handed her mother a novel and said, "I read that last night." Thinking she meant she had glanced through it, Linda said that was nice and didn't think more about it. When it happened with a second novel the following morning, Linda asked her to read aloud a chapter. Erin did, with perfect inflection, and didn't miss a word.

By the end of third grade, Erin was scoring in the ninety-ninth percentile in reading and listening comprehension, as well as vocabulary—and she had never done a workbook page in her life. Nearing age twelve, she read the 732-page *Harry Potter and the Goblet of Fire* in a weekend. Far from being a bookworm, she loves swimming, softball, and singing as a member of the Longmont (Colorado) children's chorale.

Through the years, thanks to that initial letter from her mom, I've lunched and dined with Erin, even interviewed her in front of seminar audiences in Pennsylvania and Colorado. She is poised, enthusiastic, articulate, still girlish, and one of the most extraordinary children I've ever known. Despite her abilities and accomplishments, Jim and Linda continue to read to her. Does she still enjoy it? That can be answered by her special wish for her twelfth birthday, which the family planned to celebrate in Hawaii: She wanted to finish hearing the last page of their five hundredth shared novel on the beach at the exact hour and minute she was born twelve years ago. (She got her wish.)

Erin's advantages are what the Albany (New York) Area Reading Council had in mind in their little brochure for new parents: "All babies are born equal. Not one can . . . speak, count, read, or write at birth. . . . But by the time they go to kindergarten they are *not equal!*"[6] The difference, of course, is between the parents who "raise" their children, as opposed to parents who "watch" them grow up.

Can You Recommend Something That Will Teach My Child to Read Before Kindergarten?

We can have instant pudding, instant photos, instant coffee—but there are no instant adults. Yet some parents are in a hurry to make their children old before their time. Finland has higher reading scores than the U.S., despite that its laws forbid the formal teaching of reading until the child is seven years of age.[7] In fact, in Elley's thirty-two-country study of more than two hundred thousand readers, four of the top ten countries don't begin formal reading instruction until age seven.[8]

No less an authority than Dr. T. Berry Brazelton is on record as noting that an interest in your child's intellectual growth is important, but you can expect negative consequences if this interest takes the form of an obsession with teaching your child to read.

"I've had children in my practice," Brazelton explained to National Public Radio's John Merrow, "who were reading from a dictionary at the age of three and one-half or four, and had learned to read and type successfully by age four. But those kids went through a very tough time later on. They went through first grade successfully, but second grade they really bombed out on. And I have a feeling that they've been pushed so hard from outside to learn to read early, that the cost of it didn't show up until later."

Testimony to the importance of an *unforced* learning schedule in these formative years comes from all corners of the fields of psychology and education—including one that dates back nearly three thousand years: "Avoid compulsion and let early education be a matter of amusement. Young children learn by games; compulsory education cannot remain in the soul," was the advice offered by Plato to parents. Many of the parents who are rushing to buy commercial phonics programs often are ignorant of the fact that most three- and four-year-olds are incapable of making the subtle sound distinctions needed for intensive phonics instruction. More often than not, the child ends up "barking" at type to please the parent, but feeling like a trained seal. That's hardly a pleasant introduction to the world of print.

None of these experts is saying that "early reading" is intrinsically bad; rather, they feel the early reader should arrive at the skill naturally, on his own, without a structured time each day when the mother or father sits down with him and teaches him letters, sounds, and syllables. The "natural way" is the way Scout learned in Harper Lee's *To Kill a Mockingbird*—by sitting on the lap of a parent and listening, listening as the parent's finger moves over the pages, until gradually, in the child's own good time, a connection is made between the sound of a certain word and the appearance of certain letters on the page.

For a child who is developmentally ready (physically, cognitively, and emotionally), consider this book as a reference guide: *Teaching a Child to Read with Children's Books* by Mark B. Thogmartin.[9] Experienced classroom teacher, headmaster, Reading Recovery practitioner, and parent are the perspectives the author brings to this excellent book. His strategies are supported with strong research and hands-on experience. His philosophy is simple: You get better results from a child if you combine phonics with *good children's literature*. Forget the expensive quick-fix commercial products! This is cheaper and more reliable. Although the book is aimed largely at the home-schooling audience, any parent wishing to support the work of the classroom will benefit from it.

When Do You Start the Teaching?

Are you kidding? The day you pick up a book and start reading is the first lesson. That's why those Finnish students are such good readers; they're surrounded by reading role models in the home and community. The best "copycats" on the face of the earth are children. Nothing demonstrates it better than the following research project and two anecdotes:

In the first instance, researchers found that deaf babies of deaf parents, having watched their parents using sign language, begin imitating this communication behavior by using significant hand gestures at ten months of age. These hand gestures are used in the same way that hearing children string together certain sounds or noises like "babababa" or "dadadada." For deaf children, these as yet meaningless gestures would be the equivalent of hearing children's "babbling."[10]

Even our subtlest behavior with print can be absorbed by children. Linda and Frank Van Hoegarden approached me after a lecture one evening at Maerker School in Westmont, Illinois, and told me about their page-ripping daughter, Ann. From the day Ann was born, there had always been a wealth of reading material in her home, and from the very beginning, her parents read to her. However, at fifteen months of age, she began to exhibit a disturbing habit. She'd pick up books, carefully turn two or three pages, then rip out the next page, throw it aside, turn a few more pages, rip out another page and throw it aside. She did this with books, she did it with magazines, and in each case she did it methodically.

Her parents patiently explained to her that this was "naughty." They went out of their way to demonstrate the gentle way to handle a book. It didn't work. As soon as she was alone with a book, she would rip into it with enthusiasm and determination. Her parents had heard of children eating books, even ripping pages while trying to turn them, but they couldn't understand a fifteen-month-old ripper who approached the destruction with such *confidence*.

Then late one evening, the parents were relaxing, watching TV, when Linda looked over at Frank and saw it all fall into focus. There was Frank casually paging through a magazine that had come in the mail that day. He turned a few pages, ripped out one of the stiff advertisement inserts, threw it aside, turned some more pages, and ripped out another. Linda finally discovered their daughter's "ripping role model."

How Is My Child's Reading Going to Get Better If *I'm* Doing the Reading?

Listening comprehension feeds reading comprehension. Sounds complicated, right? So let's make it simple. We'll use the most frequently used word in the English language: *the*. I always ask my lecture audiences if there is anyone present who thinks this little three-letter word is a difficult word to understand, and out of three hundred people I'll get about five who raise their hands—amid snickers from the rest.

I then ask those who *didn't* raise their hands "to pretend I am a Russian exchange student living in your home. It's also important to know there is no equivalent word in Russian for 'the,' as we use it. Indeed, many languages don't have such articles—Chinese, Japanese, Korean, Persian, Polish, Punjabi, Croatian, and Vietnamese.

"Now, as the Russian exchange student, I've been living in your home and listening to you and your family for three weeks when one day I come to you and say, 'Don't understand word you use over and over. What means word "the"?'"

How would you begin to explain the meaning of the word to this person? No one ever volunteers to explain it, and everyone laughs in embarrassment. Explaining this simple word turns out to be pretty difficult. Nevertheless, we do know how to *use* it. And we knew it when we showed up for kindergarten.

How did you learn it? One morning when you were three years old, did your mother take you into the kitchen, sit you down at the table with a little workbook, and say, " 'The' is a definite article. It comes before nouns. Now take your green crayon and underline all the definite articles on the page"? Of course not.

We learned the meaning of this tiny but complex word by *hearing* it. In fact, we heard it three ways:

1. We heard it over and over and over (immersion).
2. We heard it being used by superheroes—Mom, Dad, brother and sister (role models).
3. We heard it in a meaningful context—the cookie, the nap, the crayons, and the potty.

Whenever an adult reads to a child, three important things are happening simultaneously and painlessly: (1) a pleasure-connection is being made between child and book; (2) both parent and child are learning something from the book they're sharing (double learning); and (3) the adult is pouring sounds and syllables called words into the child's ear.

Inside the ear these words collect in a reservoir called the listening vocabulary. Eventually, if you pour enough words into it, the reservoir starts to overflow—pouring words into the speaking vocabulary, reading vocabulary, and writing vocabulary. And all have their origin in the listening vocabulary.

One-on-one time is a key factor in how soon a child learns the purpose of books.

How Can I Expand My Child's Attention Span?

The best tool for expanding attention span is one-on-one time with the child; it is by far the most effective teaching/bonding arrangement ever invented. In studying methods to reverse language problems among disadvantaged children, Harvard psychologist Jerome Kagan found intensified one-on-one attention to be especially effective.[11] His studies indicated the advantages of reading to children and of listening attentively to their responses to the reading, but they also point to the desirability of reading to your children separately, if possible.

I recognize this approach poses an extra problem for working mothers and fathers with more than one child. But somewhere in that seven-day week there must be time for your child to discover the specialness of you, one-on-one, even if it's only once or twice a week.

One-on-one time between adult and child—be it reading or talking or playing, is essential to teaching the *concept* of books or puppies or flowers or water. Once the concept of something has been learned, then the foundation has been laid for the next accomplishment: attention span. Without a concept of what is happening and why, a child cannot and will not attend to something for any appreciable amount of time.

Here, for example, are two concepts entirely within the grasp of a three-year-old:

+ The telephone can be used to make and receive calls.
+ Books contain stories that give me pleasure if I listen and watch.

Nearly twenty years ago, my friend and neighbor Ellie Fernands, now an elementary school principal, returned to teaching after a hiatus of ten years. Since her former experience was in junior high, this new job—*pre-*

school—was almost extraterrestrial. I vividly recall Ellie telling me of her experiences one day with those two concepts: telephone and books. She said, "All morning the three-year-olds used the toy telephone in class to make pretend calls to their mothers for reassurances that they'd be picked up and brought home. They dialed make-believe numbers, talked for long periods of time, and even used telephone etiquette." Understanding the *concept* of the telephone, these children were able to use and enjoy it for a considerable length of time. Their telephone attention span was excellent.

Let's compare that with story time in the same class. "Thirty seconds after the story began, two of the children stood up and moved away from the circle, obviously bored. More children quickly joined them. Within two minutes, half the children had abandoned the story." (Ellie later learned that one of the two children who listened through the entire story was a child who had been read to from day one.)

The difference between the attention spans for each of these two activities is based on the *concept* that each child brought to the activity. Where a child had little or no experience with books, it was impossible for him to have a concept of them and the pleasure they afford. No experience means no attention span.[12]

Short attention spans among three-year-olds is not unusual, but when they continue into the early primary grades, there is cause for alarm. With parents averaging about eleven minutes a day of one-on-one time with a child, it's little wonder I receive letters like this from a speech and language clinician in a Massachusetts school system:

> My language development program is focused on reading aloud to my students. The impetus for this began when, much to my dismay, my caseload of language-delayed kids was rising by leaps and bounds. Before coming to this city, I had worked extensively with culturally deprived and abused children; their language delays were understandable. But why, in this middle-class to upper-middle-class community, was there a rising number of primary children who lacked vocabulary development, memory skills, processing abilities? They often seemed to lack motivation, had limited imaginations and attention spans, and found it difficult to follow directions. In addition, only a handful were diagnosed as learning disabled.
>
> As I became more familiar with the children and their family situations, several possible causes appeared. Many of them have been in child care from infancy and/or early childhood. Many presently go to a child-care situation after school. Many parents admitted they had little time or energy to read to them. Nor did they

have the patience to answer (or find out together) the unending questions of a curious three- or four-year-old. Television served as a babysitter and pacifier.

Some parents were quick to point out the children were read to in child care and had good experiential learning activities in their centers. But somehow, without the cozy, one-on-one giving of a parent or primary caregiver, the "group" input had lost meaningfulness for many of the children.

What About Children Who Can Read Before They Ever Reach School?

Most of us are intrigued by the success secrets of famous people—like a teenage Michael Jordan daily practicing in the dark on a neighborhood playground after being cut from his high school team. Achievers are not born successful, and readers are not born readers. So let's look at the childhood patterns of the "super" readers—the kids who show up for kindergarten *already knowing how to read,* what educators call "early readers."

During the last forty years, intensive studies have been done on such children.[13] The majority of them, I might add, were never formally taught to read at home, nor did they use any commercial reading programs.

The research, as well as studies done on pupils who respond to initial classroom instruction without difficulty, indicates four factors were present in the home environment of nearly every early reader:

1. The child is read to on a regular basis. This is the factor most often cited among early readers. In Dolores Durkin's 1966 study, *all* of the early readers had been read to regularly. Additionally, the parents were avid readers and led by example. The reading included not only books but package labels, street and truck signs, billboards, et cetera.
2. A wide variety of printed material—books, magazines, newspapers, comics—is available in the home. Nearly thirty years later, NAEP studies reported the more printed materials found in a child's home, the higher the student's writing, reading, and math skills.[14]
3. Paper and pencil are readily available for the child. Durkin explained, "Almost without exception, the starting point of curiosity about written language was an interest in scribbling and drawing. From this developed an interest in copying objects and letters of the alphabet."
4. The people in the child's home stimulate the child's interest in reading and writing by answering endless questions, praising the child's efforts

at reading and writing, taking the child to the library frequently, buying books, writing stories that the child dictates, and displaying his paperwork in a prominent place in the home.

I want to emphasize that these four factors were present in the home of nearly *every* child who was an early reader. None of these involved much more than interest on the part of the parent.

Is There Something I Could *Buy* That Would Help My Child to Read Better?

Since parents often think there are quick fixes they can buy, some kind of kit or phonics game to help a child do better at school, years ago I began asking my associates, "What did you have in your home as a child that helped you become a reader? Things your folks had to *buy*." Besides the library card they all named, which is free, their responses form what I call the "Three B's," an inexpensive "reading kit" that nearly all parents can afford.

The first B is Books: Ownership of a book, with the child's name inscribed inside, a book that doesn't have to be returned to the library or even shared with siblings. I still have the first book I ever bought, the first I ever won, and one of the first I ever received as a gift. In a study of Israeli kindergarten children, high achieving readers owned ten times as many books as did the low achievers.[15]

The second B is Book Basket (or magazine rack)—placed where it can be used most often. There is probably more reading done in the bathrooms of America than all the libraries and classrooms combined. Put a book basket in there, stocked with books, magazines, and newspapers.

Put another *book basket* on or near the kitchen table. All those newspaper

A book basket offers easy, immediate access to print during "captive moments."

coin boxes aren't standing in front of fast-food restaurants as decorations. If you sit in your car in the parking lot and watch who uses those coin boxes, invariably it's the person who's eating alone. I'm convinced most human beings want or need to read when they're eating alone. And with more and more children eating at least one daily meal alone, the kitchen is a prime spot for recreational reading. If there's a book on the table, they'll read it—unless, of course, you're foolish enough to have a television in your kitchen, as do 58 percent of parents in America.[16]

And the third B is Bed Lamp: Does your child have a bed lamp or reading light? If not, and you wish to raise a reader, the first order of business is to go out and buy one. Buy the lamp, install it, and say to your child: "Elizabeth, we think you're old enough now to stay up later at night and read in bed like Mom and Dad. So we bought this little lamp and we're going to leave it on an extra fifteen minutes (or longer, depending on the age of the child) *if* you want to read in bed. On the other hand, if you don't want to read—that's okay, too. We'll just turn off the light at *the same old time.*" Most children will do anything in order to stay up later—even read.

At What Age Should I *Stop* Reading to My Child?

Almost as big a mistake as not reading to children at all is stopping too soon. The national Commission on Reading stated reading aloud is "a practice that should continue throughout the grades."[17] In this recommendation the commission was really asking us to model on one of the most successful businesses of all time—McDonald's. This fast-food chain has been in business for almost a half century, and never once has it cut its advertising budget. Every year McDonald's spends more money on advertising than it did the previous year, which comes to more than one million dollars *per day*. Its marketing people never think, "Everyone has heard our message. They should be coming to us on their own, instead of our spending all this money advertising."

Every time we read aloud to a child or class, we're giving a commercial for the pleasures of reading. But unlike McDonald's, we cut our advertising each year, instead of increasing it. The older the child, the less he is read to—in the home and in the classroom. Typical is a Connecticut school's 1990 survey of its fourth- through sixth-grade students in a middle-class community: only 8 percent of the students had been read to the previous evening.[18] Most teachers confirm similar findings in their assessments of students in middle and upper grades. A thirty-year survey of graduate students confirms how seldom they were read to in middle and upper grades.[19]

Parents (and sometimes teachers) say, "He's in the top fourth-grade reading group—why should I read to him? Isn't that why we're sending him to school, so he'll learn how to read by himself?" There are many mistaken assumptions in that question.

Let's say the student is reading on a fourth-grade level. Wonderful. But what level is the child *listening* on? Most people have no idea that one is higher than the other—until they stop and think about it. Here's an easy way to visualize it: For seven years, the most popular show on American television was *The Cosby Show,* enjoyed by tens of millions each week—including first-graders. Even in reruns it's still one of the most-watched shows all over the world. What reading level would you estimate the script to have been written on? When a "Cosby" script was submitted to the Harris-Jacobson Wide Range Readability Formula, it came out to approximately fourth-grade level (3.7).[20]

Would those first-graders watching the show be able to read the script of the show? Ninety-nine percent could not. But they could understand it if it was *read to them*—that is, recited by the actors. According to experts who have studied children's listening skills, it is a reasonable assertion that reading and listening skills begin to converge at about eighth grade.[21] Until then, they usually listen on a higher level than they read on. Therefore, children can *hear* and *understand* stories that are more complicated and more interesting than anything they could read on their own—which has to be one of God's greatest blessings for first-graders. The last thing you want first-graders thinking is what they're reading in first grade is as good as books are going to get! First-graders can enjoy books written on a fourth-grade level, and fifth-graders can enjoy books written on a seventh-grade reading level. (This is, of course, contingent upon the social level of the books' subject matter; some seventh-grade material is above the fifth-grader's social experience and might be off-putting.)

Now that I've established the idea in your mind that there is a significant difference between listening level and reading level, you can better understand why one should continue to read aloud to children as they grow older. Beyond the emotional bond that is established between parent and child (or teacher and class), you're feeding those higher vocabulary words through the ear; eventually they'll reach the brain and register in the child-reader's eyes.

That's the argument for continuing the reading to a higher level. Now let's divert to a lower level. If you've got a beginning reader in your home or classroom—five-, six-, and seven-year-olds—and you're still reading to the child, wonderful! Keep it up. But, if you're still reading those Dr. Seuss controlled-vocabulary books to the child—like *The Cat in the Hat* or *Hop on Pop*—you're insulting the six-year-old's brain cells nightly!

Let's look at what you have: One book of 225 words and one six-year-old with a 6,000-word vocabulary. The child has understood and been using all 225 of those words since he was four years old, and this is what you're reading to the child every night. There's something wrong with the child if he's not lying in bed at night thinking, "One of us here is brain dead!"

At age six, you're a beginning reader. As such, you've got a limited number of words you can decode by sight or sound. But you're not a beginning *listener.* You've been listening for six years; you're a veteran listener! Dr. Seuss deliberately wrote the controlled-vocabulary books to be read *by* children to themselves. And just to make sure people understood this was a book to be read *by* the child and not *to* the child, *The Cat in the Hat*'s original dust-jacket copy included the words "many children . . . will discover for the first time that they don't need to be read to any more."[22]

The listening-level-versus-reading-level problem surfaced recently in the annual "Read Across America" event, in which thousands of adults read to nearly ten million children on March 2, Dr. Seuss's birthday. Begun in 1997, it's been a joyous celebration of reading for the nation. The National Education Association (NEA) surveyed a thousand teachers on their favorite choices for the day, and two of the top five were controlled-vocabulary books by Dr. Seuss, like *Green Eggs and Ham* and *The Cat in the Hat*. Since the event occurs in the spring, even a preschool class should be well beyond such low-level listening at that point. If the teachers made those particular choices to honor Seuss's birthday, perhaps someone should explain that he wrote forty-five other books, most of them with more words and imagery than the 225 words in *The Cat in the Hat*.

In chapter 3, I explore what you could be reading instead of controlled-vocabulary books, including some chapter books that kindergarten and preschool teachers have used successfully with classes.

Aren't We Wasting Time Reading to Preteens and Teens?

Here are two arguments in favor of reading to older children. First, do you know anyone who thinks today's teenagers read too much or even enough? Do you think adults in America read enough? If you answer "No" on both counts, then I suggest the old formula—that is, not reading to children as they grow older, instead increasing the amount of work associated with books, such as portfolios, essays, reports, and exams—hasn't worked all that well. It has resulted in huge numbers of schooltime readers who developed a sweat mentality about books and choose to avoid them in adulthood.

While I'm not suggesting school become a vacation, we should accept the fact that when we try to interest children in reading, we're in the sales business. From that perspective, consider the words of David Ogilvy, whose writings were the bible of the advertising industry during the last half of the twentieth century. Ogilvy gave this advice to employees who were writing ads for the likes of Rolls-Royce, Hathaway, Procter & Gamble, Guinness, and Sears: "You cannot *bore* people into buying your product. You can only *interest* them in buying it."[23] Reading is the product being sold here. Every read-aloud is an advertisement for pleasure, every worksheet is an ad for pain. If the pain outweighs the pleasure, the customers go elsewhere.

Awareness must come before desire—as proven in the eight-week study of a kindergarten class that had a good classroom library and a teacher who read aloud daily.[24] The library's books consisted of three kinds: *very* familiar (read repeatedly by the teacher); familiar (read once); unfamiliar (unread).

In monitoring which books the kindergartners selected during their free time, the researchers found they chose the *very* familiar books three times as often and familiar books twice as often as the unfamiliar. In addition, these nonreaders more often imitated the teacher and tried to "read" the *very* familiar and familiar books instead of just browsing through them, as they did with the unfamiliar. The power of advertising!

Taking that concept up to the middle-school level, when the reading habits of thirty eleven- and twelve-year-olds were evaluated, researchers found the children read two kinds of books: series books and recommended books (higher quality literature). The biggest factor in their choosing the higher-level books was the advertising they saw or heard in class. Sixty-eight percent reported the choice came from hearing peers or teachers talking about it or seeing it read as a "hot book" in class. Any teacher who reads to students—older or younger—can attest to the large number of students who independently seek out the book being read in class.

Is There One Book I Can Read to Both My Four-Year-Old and My Nine-Year-Old?

Do they both wear the same size clothes, ride the same size bike, or have the same size friends? Here's a little rule of thumb for parents: If you can't squeeze your kids into the same size underwear, don't try to squeeze them into the same size book! In doing that, you end up watering down the reading material to accommodate the lowest common denominator—the four-year-old—and boring the nine-year-old. The solution is to read to them individually, especially if there is more than three years' difference in their ages.

When my children (now thirty-six and thirty-two) were young, we read the picture books together. But once Elizabeth was ready for novels, I read nearly all of our novels individually—one-on-one. When they're thirty-six and thirty-two, there is no social or emotional gap between them, but when the same two children were eleven and seven, the gap was sizable. The book that Elizabeth could handle at eleven, Jamie either wasn't ready for or interested in at seven.

A father in New Jersey, after hearing me suggest reading to children separately, interjected, "Excuse me, but doesn't that take longer?" Yes it does, sir. But then, parenting is not *supposed* to be a time-saving experience. Parenting is time-*consuming,* time-*investing*—but not time-*saving.*

Is Reading Aloud Only About Vocabulary and Learning?

Beyond the building of attention span and vocabulary, something else is built during these one-on-one hours with a child. When you get to the "heavy stuff" in books, it usually brings to the surface of the child some of his or her own "heavy stuff"—their deepest hopes and fears. And when that happens, if there is not an obnoxious older sister or younger brother present—when it's one-on-one—children will tell you their secrets. And when they share their secrets, the chemistry that occurs is called "bonding"—and that's what *really* holds families together.

Relatively little of what most people do collectively or communally nurtures bonding. Don't tell me the family trip to Disney World is a bonding time. I've been in the lobby of Disney hotels at 9:30 at night and watched the families come back from a day of "bonding." It's not a pretty sight.

When do we bond best with the young? Whenever it's one-on-one: one-on-one walk, one-on-one talk, or one-on-one read. And finally, you will discover you have far fewer arguments or problems with a child when you're in a one-on-one situation.

It is far easier to convince a parent to begin reading to an infant than it is to convince people to begin (or continue) reading to older children. The older the child, the more complicated the books become, and the more enjoyable or meaningful they are for the adult reader as well. Some of the novels I read to Jamie and Elizabeth in their middle-grade years were as good as anything I was reading on my own: *A Day No Pigs Would Die* by Robert Newton Peck; *Slake's Limbo* by Felice Holman; *Roll of Thunder, Hear My Cry* by Mildred Taylor; *North to Freedom* by Ann Holm; *The Foxman* by Gary Paulsen; and Willie Morris's *Good Old Boy*.

Would Reading Aloud to Them Help Children with Grammar?

Grammar is more caught than taught, and the way you catch it is the same way you catch the flu: you're exposed to it. By hearing the language spoken correctly in meaningful sentences, you begin to imitate the pattern—both in what you say and in what you write.

This predicament about grammar is not restricted to ESL (English as a second language) students. If you've listened in on certain conversations, you know that some of our native-born children bring new meaning to the term "English as a second language."

Consider a common speech pattern among native-born adolescents who have not heard a great deal of organized speech and therefore find it difficult to speak coherently. When National Public Radio interviewed high school seniors about their future plans,[25] one teenage girl suggested she might someday want to become a veterinarian, but her immediate plans were less certain. Perhaps that uncertainty had something to do with her ability to express herself clearly. Here is an exact transcription of her remarks to NPR:

> I'm . . . ah . . . actually just kinda like thinking of makin', ya know, more money, gettin' a better job, hopefully, like, movin' out and, like, not depending on my parents as much 'cause I know a lotta my friends, like, they smug up like their parents and stuff, ya know. I don't wanna do that, like, I can be independent, like—do things for my own, ya know, like driving on my own, not having to, like, well—"Am I gonna buy, like, two books or, like, go buy this and that?" I'm just hoping that my life will, ya know, turn out to be a good one, ya know? Hopefully nothin' bad'll happen, like, ya know, 'cause, ya know, I don't take life for granted. I could die like tonight, ya know? It's like I just live life to the fullest. And, ya know, I'm not sayin', ya know, hurry—live like a fool! It's like go skydiving and, ya

know, stuff like that, ya know, like livin' it, like . . . ah . . . I just live like I think I'm supposed to. Like I want to live. Whatever happens, happens!

Using a form of oral shorthand, she punctuated her one-minute response with eleven "ya knows" and eleven "likes." (Approximately one "ya know" or "like" every 2.7 seconds.) Each use represents the speaker's acknowledgment that he or she cannot think of the appropriate word but the listener must surely know it ("ya know"). Such a serious communication defect is often caused by:

1. Spending large amounts of time with peers whose vocabulary is as meager as your own.
2. Spending large amounts of time listening to music lyrics that are indistinct, blurred, or largely vernacular.
3. Spending little or no time reading or hearing complete sentences in meaningful, complicated contexts.

In a nation that becomes more and more a service-oriented economy, oral communication is an essential skill in the workplace. The richer the words you hear, the richer will be the words you give back—in speech or writing. Reading aloud to all students—ESL or native-born—beginning as early in their lives as possible and continuing through the grades, will expose them to a rich, organized, and interesting language model they will at least have as an alternative to the tongue-tied language of their peers.

Discounting sign language and body language, there are two forms of language—spoken and written. While they are intimately related to each other, they are not twins. As I showed in the chart on page 17, written words are far more structured and complicated than spoken words. Conversation is imprecise, rambling, often ungrammatical, and less organized than print. That's why public speakers have scripts and politicians have speechwriters. Therefore, children who enjoy conversations with adults *and* hear stories are exposed to richer language than is the child who experiences only conversation.

In listening to stories being read aloud, you're learning a second language—the *standard* English of books, the classroom, and most of the workplace. Most of us process at *least* two spoken languages—*home* language and *standard* language. The language Mario Cuomo used with his immigrant parents in the Bronx was distinctly different from that which he would use at a political convention. Bill Cosby, talking with relatives in Philadelphia, would speak a language distinctly different from that which he used with his doctoral dissertation committee at the University of Massachusetts. Unfortunately, many children never meet this *standard* language until they arrive at the schoolhouse door. Knowing this language *before* arriving at school jump-starts a child's learning and does it without stress.

This gift of *standard* English cannot be overemphasized. I say that not because I am a native-speaker of English, but for purely practical reasons. Standard English is the primary tongue of the classroom and the business world, yet children who spend 30 percent of their free time watching television learn little of it (see pages 17, 203). In *The Story of English*,[26] we find what amounts to a "state of the language" report on English:

> Of all the world's languages (which now number some 2,700), [English] is arguably the richest in vocabulary. The compendious Oxford English Dictionary lists some 500,000 words; and a further half million technical and scientific terms remain uncatalogued. According to traditional estimates, neighboring German has a vocabulary of about 185,000 words and French fewer than 100,000. . . . Three-quarters of the world's mail, and its telexes and cables, are in English. So are more than half the world's technical and scientific periodicals. It is the language of technology from Silicon Valley to Singapore. English is the medium for 80 percent of the information stored in the world's computers. Nearly half of all business deals in Europe are conducted in English . . . American technology and finance has introduced 20,000 English words into regular use in Japan.

And since 1944, it is the official language governing conversations between pilots and control towers across the world.[27]

Since few of the above actions are conducted using slang or the vernacular, it is imperative that children learn standard English as a future survival tool. Deprived of the language they need to prosper in the world, children are more apt to commit what Nobel Prize–winner Toni Morrison calls "tongue suicide," referring figuratively to frustrated "children who have bitten their tongues off and use bullets instead to iterate the voice of speechlessness."[28]

Today's student needs home English for the neighborhood and standard English in the marketplace, and hearing it aloud is an easy and contagious manner in which to meet it in large doses.

How Do We Improve the Basics Like Writing and Spelling?

By reading, reading, reading. Vocabulary and spelling are not learned best by looking words up in the dictionary. You learn the meanings and spellings in the same way teachers learn the names of students and parents learn the names of neighbors: by seeing them again and again, and making the connection between the face and the name.

Nearly everyone spells by visual memory, not by rules. (There is ample research to indicate that people who have the best recall of graphic or geometric symbols are also the best spellers. This, say the scientists, may have more to do with your memory genetics than with anything else.)[29] Most people, when they doubt the correctness of what they have just spelled, write the word out several different ways and choose the one that looks correct. The more a child reads words in sentences and paragraphs, the greater the chances he will spell words correctly. Conversely, the less you read, the fewer words you meet and the less certain you are of both meaning and spelling.[30] In Dr. Stephen Krashen's book *The Power of Reading,* he cites a research project that shows one exception to this rule that, in fact, proves the rule. One group of professionals—with literacy rates as high as that of physicians—responds negatively to reading and spelling: the more *they* read, the worse they spell. If you guessed "teachers," you're correct. The longer they teach, the worse they spell. Why? Because they're reading more and more students' papers, including their misspellings!

As for writing, there is the traditional approach, what you might call the "Vince Lombardi school of writing." That is, you write, write, write until you bleed it across the paper and the curriculum. You get better at writing the way you get better at tackling! Do it over and over. The trouble with this approach is that it is not supported by research. Students who write the most are not the best writers.[31] Indeed, for all the testing and portfolio collections, and the raising of writing standards over the last fifteen years, the NAEP assessments show no significant change in national writing scores.

Now before someone suffers apoplexy, I'm *not* suggesting we do away with writing in school. I'm just suggesting—strongly—that we back off a bit, that we might be doing *too much* writing in some places. Good writers are like baseball players. Baseball players have to play regularly, but they spend *most* of their time, either in the field or in the dugout, watching *others* run, hit, catch, and throw. Good writers do the same—they write, but they *read* even more—they watch how *other* people throw words around to catch meaning. The more you read, the better you write—and the NAEP Report Card proves it.[32] The highest scoring student writers were not those who wrote the most each day, but rather the students who *read* the most recreationally, had the most printed materials in their homes, and had regular essay-writing in class.

What is flawed in our current writing curriculum is our failure to grasp the simple observation that Jacques Barzun made a few years ago—that writing and speaking are "copycat" experiences—"words get in through the ear or eye and come out at the tongue or the end of a pencil."[33]

We say what we hear and we write what we see. When I ask people in Georgia, "What do you call these things on either side of my nose?" they often respond with something that sounds like, "Those are yer ahzz's (eyes)."

On the other hand, ask folks in New York City the same question, and the answer often sounds like, "Those're yer oiys." Depending on where you live, you can say the word "eyes" one way or another. But in the end, we usually say what we hear most often. That's why my niece and nephew in Georgia don't sound like my cousins in New Jersey, but speak the same language. What goes in the ear comes out the mouth.

To a degree, it's even true with drawing. Ask children in Alaska and Wisconsin to draw pictures of cows and you end up with very different looking cows. All those Alaskan cows look like husky dogs with udders, but those Wisconsin kids draw cows so lifelike you can almost smell them. Why the difference? Cows are tough to draw if you haven't seen them.

The same principle holds for writing. It's tough to write compound, complex, or good old simple sentences if you haven't seen them that often. And when do you see them most often? When you read—over and over and over. Reading only your own written sentences is about as helpful as speaking Spanish to yourself.

Yes, practice is important, but when I encounter school after school in which children spend more time writing than reading, where they complain there's no time for SSR, I'm convinced they've got the cart in front of the horse. Why do some students improve in writing and some do not? To reiterate once again the words of the admissions director of Amherst College: "I've never met a student with high verbal SAT scores who was not an avid reader."[34] The SAT's are not oral exams—they're *written*.

Reading feeds not only writing skill but also writing *style*—without the student even realizing it. One example of this subliminal copycatting can be found in the popular adult mystery writer Tony Hillerman. Hillerman grew up in Oklahoma, a third-generation German-American, and attended an American Indian boarding school for farm children. After earning a journalism degree from the University of Oklahoma, he worked for years as a wire service reporter and then as an editor with the *Santa Fe New Mexican*. With that background, whom did he imitate when he became a novelist? "When my first book (*The Blessing Way*) was published, a reviewer said it was reminiscent of the *Australian* writer Arthur Upfield. I looked at that and said, 'Aw, yeah! I betcha.' So I went to the library and found some Upfield, and sure enough."

The Upfield connection, it turns out, had been established when Hillerman was a young boy, peddling the *Saturday Evening Post*—which often serialized the Australian's novels. In retrospect, Hillerman says, "I went through all my life with these incredible memories from that serial, of the Australian outback and the aboriginal culture. I just loved it."[35]

How Can Read-Aloud Be Incorporated into a Science or Math Class?

Since everything in the curriculum rests upon reading, reading is the foundation of learning—all kinds of reading, from books and magazines to newspapers and journals. If reading is supposed to be important to students, it must first be important to parents and teachers.

Of all the qualities a teacher or parent might possess, the most contagious is enthusiasm. Are you enthusiastic about books? Do your students ever see you with something other than a textbook in your hand? Have you shared with your child or class a book you stayed awake reading until two o'clock in the morning? Have you read aloud a magazine article or newspaper column about something that really interested you? In other words, it's tough to give someone a cold if you don't have one. And it's just as tough to pass on the love of reading if you yourself don't have it.

If you want your science or history class to be alive, wrap the facts and figures, the dates and battles, in flesh-and-blood novels. Read *My Side of the Mountain* by Jean Craighead George, or *Woodsong* by Gary Paulsen, to your science class. Open a history class with five minutes from *My Brother Sam Is Dead* by James and Christopher Collier.

If you feel duty-bound to tie your readings to your subject matter, look into the excellent sixteen-volume series of biographies called *Great Lives* (Atheneum), each volume containing more than two dozen fifteen-page profiles on famous persons in the following fields: American government; exploration; sports; human rights; nature and the environment; American literature; world religions; American frontier; invention and technology;

world government; medicine; human culture; painting; theater; and American journalism.

Is It Ever Too Late to Start Reading to a Child?

They're never too old—but it's not going to be as easy with older children as it is when they're two or six years old.

Because she has a captive audience, the classroom teacher holds a distinct advantage over the parent who suddenly wants to begin reading to a thirteen-year-old. Regardless of how well-intentioned the parent may be, reading aloud to an adolescent at home can be difficult. During this period of social and emotional development, teenagers' out-of-school time is largely spent coping with body changes, sex drives, vocational anxieties, and the need to form an identity apart from that of their families. These kinds of concerns and their attendant schedules don't leave much time for Mom's and Dad's reading aloud.

But the situation is not hopeless *if you pick your spots.* Don't suggest that your daughter listen to a story when she's sitting down to watch her favorite television show or fuming after a fight with her boyfriend. Along with timing, consider the length of what you read. Keep it short—unless you see an interest for more.

When the child is in early adolescence, from twelve to fourteen, try sharing a small part of a book, a page or two, when you see he is at loose ends—and downplay any motivational or educational aspects connected with the reading. When Jamie and Elizabeth were teens, I was always reading excerpts to them from whatever I was reading myself—be it fiction or nonfiction. Late one evening I was reading Ferrol Sam's *Run with the Horseman,* a wonderful Southern novel by a Georgia physician. When I came to an early scene in which a boy has two outrageously funny incidents with a mule in a field and a rooster in an outhouse, I thought, "Oh, Jamie will love these!"

So in the morning, I caught up with him. "Hey, Jamie—listen to this!"

Edging to the door, he said, "Sorry, Dad, but I gotta run. I'm supposed to meet the guys."

"I know, but it'll just take a minute—I promise." Rolling his eyes, he reluctantly sat and I began to read it aloud. And, as I suspected, he loved it. And several hours later he was back with his buddies in tow, asking me to read it to them too.

Because so many parents and teachers seem at loose ends over what to read to this age group, I created an anthology of fifty read-aloud selections for preteens and teens, *Read All About It!* It contains a broad cross section of fiction and nonfiction, short stories and chapters from novels (that will whet the child's appetite for the rest of the book), newspaper columns from people like Bob Greene and Mike Royko, and biographical sketches of each author.

Choosing something to read to teens is never a problem for an avid reader, someone who reads with pleasure and reads widely. For them, the quandary is limiting all the possible readings. If I were to choose at random from my own bookshelves, here are some titles and authors I would read aloud to teens—though they were written with an adult audience in mind:

- Any of Torey Hayden's powerful books about the psychologically damaged children she has worked with through the years: *One Child*; *Just Another Kid*; *Murphy's Boy*; *Somebody Else's Kid*; and *Ghost Girl*. How good are they? Anything that stays in print as long as they must have some great inner strength.
- Jan Brunvand's collections of urban legends, the modern folk tales that keep springing up in America, "Absolutely true, I swear," and always told by a friend of a friend of a friend: *Too Good to Be True: The Colossal Book of Urban Legends*; *The Big Book of Urban Legends*; *The Vanishing Hitchhiker*; *The Choking Doberman*; *The Mexican Pet*; and *Curses! Broiled Again*. (See the synopsis of *Don't Go Near that Rabbit, Frank!* in the Treasury on page 231 for a classic urban legend that teenagers will *devour*.)
- The Pulitzer Prize–winning historian and journalist David McCullough has a brilliant collection of twenty profiles of exceptional men and women from American history entitled *Brave Companions*.
- Alex Kotlowitz, a former award-winning *Wall Street Journal* reporter, has produced two of the most insightful and widely praised books on race in modern America: *There Are No Children Here*, in which he follows two contemporary children's daily lives in one of Chicago's most dangerous public housing projects; and *The Other Side of the River: A Story of Two Towns, a Death, and America's Dilemma*, which follows the trail of a black teenager's body when it mysteriously surfaces in the St. Joseph River in Michigan between Benton Harbor and St. Joseph, two towns divided by water and race.

With Curriculum to Cover, Who's Got Time for Stories?

Far from suggesting the curriculum be abandoned, I say it is enriched and made meaningful by story. Story does not exist to teach reading skills. Story is the vehicle we use to make sense out of the world—even when we sleep. Dreams are our attempt to make sense out of whatever defies logic. Do you know anyone who dreams nonfiction? We dream *story*!

When Roger C. Schank, former head of the Artificial Intelligence Laboratory at Yale University and now a professor of Electrical Engineering and Computer Science, Psychology, and Education at Northwestern University, was building artificial intelligence in computers, he found that human behavior and thinking often boiled down to the stories each of us make, store, and share. Story, he found, is the basic fabric for intelligence because it determines how we think and behave.[36]

Our brains receive thousands of information pieces daily, sometimes hourly. Most of it we can't retrieve even minutes later, while other pieces easily can be found years after they entered our memories. The easy pieces had "labels" on them that allowed us to grasp them—that is, stories about the information, the incident, or the person. Abstract concepts are all too quickly lost in the dust of yesterday. In his book *Tell Me a Story: A New Look at Real and Artificial Memory,* Schank notes, "Stories give life to past experiences. Stories make the events in memory memorable to others and to ourselves."

It is story that focuses our attention, helps us make sense out of the world around us. The politician or preacher who stands before an audience and says, "That reminds me of a story . . ." has its attention immediately. Television's *60 Minutes* is the longest-running and most profitable prime-time show in the history of television, and the person behind its success is producer Don Hewitt, the man who makes the final decisions and cuts. He says, "The secret of *60 Minutes* is so simple I can't believe the formula hasn't been followed by others. It's four words that every kid knows: 'Tell me a story.' I look at things in screening rooms and I say, 'That's an interesting guy and those are some great scenes you've got, but what's the story?' " Without the "story," Hewitt knows the audience is leaving. So teachers who ignore the importance of story do so at their own peril.[37]

How Does This Fit with the Calls for Higher National Standards?

As a nation, we want to be sure to raise *all* the standards. From everything I read and hear, the CEOs and politicians have only emphasized one standard: IQ. And as the demands for higher scores are pressed on superintendent, principal, and teacher, the curriculum narrows to only what will be on the standardized test. Since the tests include only IQ subjects, there remains little or no time for HQ subjects—the heart quotient. Who has time for the teachable moment when the class hamster dies? Who has time to discuss the ethical thing to do when there are no ethics questions on the state standards exam?

As the late Clifton Fadiman once said, "There is no shortage of smart people. We've got lots of those. The real shortage is in *better* people." And you make better people by educating children's brains *and* hearts. Daniel Goleman's bestseller, *Emotional Intelligence,* is perhaps the most eloquent argument in support of that.

Consider the following headlines, all of them involving people of high IQ, graduates of our finest colleges and universities, many with advanced degrees—but one must wonder at their HQ scores:

♦ Nation's Largest Health Care Company Agrees to Pay $745 Million in Fraud Case
♦ Big Law and Auditing Firms to Pay Millions in S & L Suit
♦ Manufacturer Admits to Selling Untested Devices for Heart
♦ Texaco Settles Race Suit for $176.1 Million
♦ Drug Maker Admits It Concealed Test Results That Showed Flaws
♦ Judge Assesses Insurer $730 Million in Fraud Case
♦ Los Alamos Staff Waited 3 Weeks to Tell of Nuclear Data Loss
♦ Jury: Disney Stole Sports Complex Ideas, Must Pay $240 Million
♦ After 9 Years, 46 Deaths, Tiremaker Recalls 6.5 Million Tires

Those headlines weren't caused by a lack of algebraic skills nor were they a result of former remedial students being in charge. The people behind those scandals were the gifted and talented guys, the ones from the head of the class. To ignore students' emotional and social education (as the standards exams do) is to invite a plethora of such headlines and behaviors.

Because literature reaches beyond the dispassionate intellectual, it can also educate the heart. Educators who find "stories" to be a waste of valuable instructional time would do well to pay attention to the likes of the Harvard Business School.[38] When Harvard invited the eminent child psychiatrist Robert Coles to teach a course in ethics, his course syllabus consisted of nothing but literature—stories and novels that grabbed the young business student where it hurts: the heart. Vicariously through literature, Coles's students explored the gradual slope that leads to compromising one's principles, values, and morality. Quoting William Carlos Williams, Coles states his purpose: ". . . to bring the reader up close, so close that his empathy puts him in the shoes of the characters. You hope when he closes the book his own character is influenced."

If all we're doing in school is teaching students how to answer the calls they'll someday get on their pagers or cell phones, then the curriculum is worthless. The most important calls won't come on pagers; instead they'll be the daily calls for love, justice, courage, and compassion. Yes, student exam scores are important, but *both* scores must be addressed—the IQ and the HQ. When we focus exclusively on paper scores, we must remember that the most educated nation in 2000 years led the world in math and science in 1930. It also became the Third Reich. The Holocaust could never have happened if the German *heart* had been as well educated as the German *mind*.

Chapter 3

The Stages of Read-Aloud

Few children learn to love books by themselves. Someone has to lure them into the wonderful world of the written word; someone has to show them the way.

—Orville Prescott,
A Father Reads to His Children

STARING at the thousands of books in the children's section of the local library, a parent is filled with the same panic that faces the beginning artist with an empty canvas: Where to begin?

I suggest that you first consider the child's age and maturity, then make your decisions accordingly. Let's start with the infant level and work our way upward.

Until a child is four months old, it might not matter a great deal *what* you read, as long as you are reading. Doing so lets the child become accustomed to the rhythmic sound of your reading voice and to associate it with a peaceful, secure time of day. Mother Goose, of course, is always appropriate, but my neighbor read aloud Kipling when she was nursing her daughter, who eventually went on to both Princeton and Harvard. Did Kipling have anything to do with that? Not much, compared to her mother's reading to her day in and day out.

Over the last decade, known in some circles as the Decade of the Brain, a heated debate raged over the importance of the infant years in a person's brain development. Although psychologists and neuroscientists have argued in public conferences, news magazines, and professional journals, the jury remains out on exactly how critical *the first three years* of life really are.

Do the doors of opportunity really slam shut after age three, or are there second, third, or fourth chances later on?

I personally tend to compromise between the two extremes: that learning (and life) is easier if the first three years are enriched, but later opportunities can be rewarding if there is an ideal learning environment. Still, later learning will be more arduous. Anyone wishing to pursue the debate will find it fully explored in *The Scientist in the Crib: Minds, Brains, and How Children Learn* by Gopnick, Melzoff, and Kuhl (Morrow); and *The Myth of the First Three Years* by John T. Bruer (Free Press).

As the various sides have attempted to prove their points, good research has emerged to help the parent who wonders: How much of all this does the child *really* understand? For example, researchers at Johns Hopkins University designed a project to determine how much infants really absorb from hearing a story. Teaming with AT&T Labs, they visited fifteen eight-month-old infants in their homes, where the children heard three stories prerecorded on tape.[1] While a child listened, a research assistant paged through cartoon illustrations related to the stories. This was done ten times over a two-week period. Each day's stories were read by one of three different readers and the stories were never in the same order. Additionally, thirty-six frequently used words from the three stories were arranged into three separate twelve-word lists and recorded by the readers, along with three lists that contained none of the words from the stories.

Two weeks after the tenth visit, the children were brought to a laboratory and tested for attention span on the word lists. Having heard the story words thirteen times each day for ten days, the children had listening spans that were significantly longer for those words than they did for the foil words (not in the stories). Infants who had not heard any of the recorded stories showed no attentional differences between the word lists. This clearly shows that measurable long-term storage of sound and word patterns begins as early as eight months of age. Children hearing the most language will have the best chance of having the best language skills.

Coupling research like this with the fetal research reported in chapter 2 should ease any awkwardness you might have about reading to infants. But let me reiterate an earlier statement: None of this is intended to create a super-baby. The focus should be on nurturing whatever abilities are already there, building an intimate bond between parent and child, and constructing a natural bridge between child and books that can be crossed whenever the child is developmentally ready to cross it as a reader.

Which Books Are Best for Infants?

As demonstrated in chapter 1 with the *Meaningful Differences* and "Abecedarian" projects, the more you talk to children during the early years, the greater the natural language growth. In fact, a child's brain growth increases with such intensity to meet the challenge of these new words and experiences that between ages four and ten his brain metabolism (the brain's heartbeat) is twice that of an adult's. That's the reason children are able to learn foreign languages and musical instruments so easily during these years—and need naps so often.[2]

With this in mind, your book selections for the next year should be ones that stimulate your child's sight and hearing—colorful pictures and exciting sounds upon which the child can focus easily. One of the reasons for Mother Goose's success is that she echoes the first sound a child falls in love with—the rhythmic, rhyming "beat-beat-beat" of a mother's heart.

Mother Goose and Dr. Seuss not only rhyme in name and text, they also must have sensed what researchers would later prove. According to learning specialists like Dr. Reid Lyon at the National Institute of Child Health and Human Development in Bethesda, Maryland, the ability to find words that rhyme appears to be an important ability in children. Indeed, kindergartners who struggle to find words that rhyme with "cat" are prime candidates for later reading problems. Moreover, considering the many rhyming chants found in children's games (such as jump-rope rhymes), and popular children's books like Seuss's *The Cat in the Hat,* it's obvious that children find pleasure in words that rhyme. The question is: Why? Researchers say the pleasure is identical to the reasons humans subconsciously enjoy looking at stripes and plaids, or listening to musical harmony—they help to arrange a chaotic world.

With that in mind, Dr. Sally Shaywitz, a Yale School of Medicine brain researcher, recommends that parents frequently read aloud to young children, especially books and stories that rhyme. Rhyming word games are also recommended.

The impact of rhyme can be traced as early as the womb. For one study, women in the last trimester of pregnancy repeatedly read aloud Dr. Seuss's *The Cat in the Hat*; then, fifty-two hours after birth, monitored infants were able to distinguish Seuss's rhyming verse from another book without rhymes.[3]

We don't turn to Mother Goose for the plot. We turn to her because she takes all those sounds, syllables, endings, and blendings, and mixes them in with the rhythm and rhyme of language, for us to feed to a child who already takes delight in rocking back and forth in his crib repeating a single syllable over and over. "Ba, ba, ba, ba, ba . . ."

There are many collections of Mother Goose, but my present favorite is *The Lucy Cousins Book of Nursery Rhymes* (Dutton). Because it is illustrated in primary colors with boldly outlined images (of multi-ethnic characters), this collection of sixty-four Mother Goose rhymes is easy for infants and toddlers to view. (See the listing for this book in the Treasury for related titles.)

Many parents find that singing or reciting these rhymes during the appropriate activity further reinforces the relationship between rhyme and activity in the child's mind. Compact disks, long-playing records and tapes of these rhymes are available at your library and local bookstore.

Also keep in mind the physical bonding that occurs during the time you are holding the child and reading. To make sure you never convey the message that the book is more important than the child, maintain skin-to-skin contact as often as possible, patting, touching, and hugging the child while you read.[4] Linked with the normal parent-infant dialogue, this reinforces a feeling of being well-loved.

What Is Normal Behavior by the Child During Readings?

Recent interest in early learning has spurred investigations on how infants and their parents react in read-aloud situations, though any reading parent can tell you a child's interest in and response to books varies a great deal. But if you are a *new* parent, any seeming lack of interest can be discouraging. Here is a forecast so you'll not be discouraged or think your child is hopeless.

- At four months of age, since he has limited mobility, a child has little or no choice but to listen and observe, thus making a passive and non-combative audience for the parent, who is probably thinking, "This is easy!"
- Your arms should encircle the child in such a way as to suggest support and bonding, but not imprisonment.
- By six months, however, the child is more interested in grabbing the book to suck on it than listening (which he's also doing). Bypass the problem by giving him a teething toy or other distraction.
- At eight months, he may prefer turning pages to steady listening. Allow him ample opportunity to explore this activity, but don't give up the book entirely.

+ At twelve months, the child's involvement grows to turning pages for you, pointing to objects you name on the page, even making noises for animals on cue.
+ By fifteen months and the onset of walking, his restlessness blossoms fully, and your reading times must be chosen so as not to frustrate his immediate interests.

In nearly all these studies,[5] attention spans during infant reading time averaged only *three minutes* in length, though several daily readings often brought the total as high as thirty minutes a day. There are some one-year-olds who will listen to stories for that long in one sitting, but they are more the exception than the rule.

As babies mature, good parent-readers profit from earlier experiences. They don't force the reading times, they direct attention by pointing to something on the page, and they learn to vary their voices between whispers and excited tones. And they learn that attention spans are not built overnight—they are built minute by minute, page by page, day by day.

Once the child begins to respond to the sight of books and your voice, begin a book dialogue, *talking* the book instead of just *reading* it, with questions like, "Isn't this a wonderful book, Jennifer?" Or "Would you like a puppy like that someday?" Even though the baby cannot initially respond, your pausing in the appropriate places for answers creates a kind of oral road map the child will soon follow on her own when she starts to talk.[6]

Talking the book requires your reading the pages to yourself ahead of time, or, in the case below, which has a minimum of print, observing the pictures, then having what amounts to a conversation with the child. Here, beside the words from Eric Hill's *Spot's First Walk,* is a transcript of the dialogue between a mother and her twenty-three-month-old.[7]

Notice how the mother gently works in the actual words of the book (italics), something she conveys by a different voice inflection. The give-and-take on the part of reader and child not only builds language skills; it also holds the child's attention to the book. Moreover, it tallies with the Chinese adage: *Tell* me and I forget. *Show* me and I remember. *Involve* me and I understand. The more the child is involved in the reading process, the more he will understand.

BOOK/TEXT	MOTHER/CHILD
What have you found?	CHILD: What's the dog doing?
	MOM: He's digging in the dirt looking for his bone. Look what he found there.
	C: Oh.

BOOK/TEXT	MOTHER/CHILD
	M: *What have you found,* Spot?
	C: A doggy bone.
	M: Yes, he's found a doggy bone. He's having fun outside.
	C: Yeah.
	M: What is he doing with his feet?
	C: What's he doing with his feet, Mom?
	M: He's digging.
Now for a drink.	C: He's digging.
	M: Look what he's doing next. He's getting a
Don't fall in.	drink. *Now for a drink* of water.
	C: There's a fish.
	M: There's a fish saying, *"Don't fall in, don't fall in."*

Children younger than eighteen months often find it difficult to understand complicated illustrations that adults recognize easily. Book illustrations consisting of many little figures running here and there may be charming to adults but they are incomprehensible to young children. An adult can recognize instantly a three-dimensional rabbit when it is reduced to one dimension on a page, but a fourteen-month-old child is just beginning this complicated process.

To help the child in this task, the picture books you choose now should be uncomplicated—a single image to a page and preferably in color. Plot, if there is any, is secondary to the image.

What Comes After Mother Goose?

During the toddler stage, an important parental role is to serve as a welcoming committee—welcoming the child to your world. Think of yourself as the host of a huge party, with your child as the guest of honor. Naturally, you want to introduce him to all the invited guests to make him feel at home. As the child grows older a huge number of "things" become objects of fascination: holes, cars, snow, birds, bugs, stars, trucks, dogs, rain, planes, cats, storms, babies, mommies and daddies. This stage is called "labeling the environment."

Picture books are perfect teaching vehicles at this stage. Point to the various items illustrated in the book, call them by name, ask the child to say the name with you, and praise any responses. Two books are excellent for this purpose: *The Everything Book* by Denise Fleming (Holt), and *My First*

Word Book by Angela Wilkes (DK). The latter is a collection of photographs of 1000 common items and is aimed at children eighteen to thirty-six months, while *The Everything Book* focuses on infants to eighteen months and contains a smaller number of images, including animals, shapes, colors, rhymes, finger games, food, faces, letters, traffic, and toys.

The very best picture book at this stage may be the one you make, using photographs taken in your home and of your family. Be sure the images are not smaller than four inches, label each with easy-to-read letters, place the picture on cardboard, and cover it entirely with a piece of self-sealing clear plastic. Metal rings through punch holes will hold it all together as a most durable and personalized "book." The materials can be purchased cheaply wherever office supplies are sold.

How Do You Keep the Child from Ripping Pages?

Families accustomed to treasuring every book are sometimes afraid to leave a book in the hands of a baby. Dorothy White, in *Books Before Five,* described a child's early book as the one "fated to suffer every indignity that a child's physically expressed affection could devise—a book not only looked at, but licked, sat on, slept on, and at last torn to shreds." White and her husband wisely decided "that the enjoyment of personal ownership was a fact of life more worth knowing than how to look after this or that. How can one learn to hold, before one has learnt to have?" she asked.[8] The gentle and affectionate way the *parent* treats the book is far more important. But following the parent's example is accomplished only over time.

As the child's concept of books begins to evolve, start an important but subtle reading lesson: labeling the book. Point to the title of the story each time you read it, and begin to use words like *author, pages, pictures, cover, front,* and *back of the book.* Disregard that old third-grade rule about not using your finger when you read. Let your finger occasionally do some

A child should see books at least as often as toys and television.

"walking and talking" by lightly running under the text as you read. By doing so, you gradually teach the child that those black squiggly lines on the page have meaning, that reading begins in the front, at the top, and moves left to right. You show her the essential steps in the act of reading. They are steps we adults take for granted because they're second nature to us now, but they are not second nature to a child.

Fifty years ago, Dorothy Kunyhardt's *Pat the Bunny* began a genre called "interactive" or "touch and feel" books. Today, that book's stereotyped artwork make it outdated for many families, but the genre is very much alive in bookstores. (Libraries don't usually have this kind of book because the moveable parts give it a short shelf-life.) Interactive books allow a child to manipulate a part of the book by lifting a flap or feeling a texture on the page. *I'm a Little Mouse* by Noelle and David Carter, about a mouse meeting neighbor creatures, is printed on heavily textured pages; and Eric Hill's popular series that begins with *Where's Spot?,* which includes sturdy movable flaps that hide surprise images, also includes one with textures called *Spot's Touch and Feel Book.* Busy babies are most interested in busy books like these.

Many publishers are now marketing baby board books, durable volumes printed in nontoxic inks on heavy, laminated pages that are easy for little fingers to turn and can be quickly wiped clean. Place the board books in the high chair, the playpen, and the crib. Let your child see books at least as often as he sees toys and television.

Why Do They Want the Same Book Read Over and Over?

Just as you didn't learn the names of everyone in your neighborhood or parish overnight, children also need repeated readings in order to learn. Thus, although reading a different book every day may keep the adult from being bored, it prevents the child from getting the reinforcement he needs for learning. Prior to age two, repeated readings of fewer books in the family is better than a huge collection read infrequently.

Like their parents, children are most comfortable with the familiar, and when they are relaxed, they're better able to absorb. Those of us who have seen a movie more than once fully realize how many subtleties escaped us the first time. This is even more the case with children and books. Because they're learning a complex language at the adult's speaking pace, there often are misunderstandings that can only be sorted out through repeated readings. Allerton Kilborne, a history teacher in New York City, once told me how, as a child, he used to ask his grandmother "to read the book about the man who got sick," and then hand her Clement Moore's "The Night

Before Christmas." The family couldn't figure out why he called it that until one day his grandmother came to this stanza:

> When out on the lawn there arose such a clatter,
>   I sprang from my bed to see what was the matter.
> Away to the window I flew like a flash,
>   Tore open the shutters and *threw up* the sash.

Psychologist Bruno Bettelheim offers this hope to parents weary of reading the same book: When a child has gotten all he can from the book, or when the problems that directed him to it have been outgrown, he'll be ready to move on to something else.[9]

Parents often are irritated by a child's incessant questions. "My child interrupts the book so often for questions, it ruins the story." First, you need to define the kinds of questions. Are they silly? Are they the result of curiosity or extraneous to the story? Is the child sincerely trying to learn something or just postponing bedtime? You can solve the latter problem if you make a regular habit of talking about the story when you finish, instead of simply closing the book, kissing the child good night, and turning off the light.

In the case of intelligent questions, try to respond immediately if the child's question involves background knowledge ("Why did Mr. MacGregor put Peter's father in a pie, Mom? Why couldn't he just hop out?"), and thus help the child better understand the story. Extraneous questions can be handled by saying, "Good question! Let's come back to that when we're done." And be sure to live up to that promise. Ultimately one must acknowledge that questions are a child's primary learning tool. Don't destroy that natural curiosity by ignoring it. Research (later in this chapter) shows the post-story discussion offers the greatest learning gains.

As boring as repeated readings may be for the adult, they can accomplish very important things within a child. To begin with, he will learn language by hearing it over and over—this is called immersion. Hearing the same story over and over is definitely a part of that immersion process.

The repeated readings also help build children's self-esteem. First, the reader makes the child feel good by granting his wish for a repeat performance. Second, with each repetition the child is better able to predict what will happen next. Very little in a child's life is completely predictable. They never know what you will give them to wear, or to eat, or where you will take them on a given day. And then along comes this book that your repeated readings have made entirely predictable, something at which the young child is suddenly an expert. He can tell you *exactly* what will happen next, word for word, page for page. *Expert*—what a proud merit badge to wear so young. The child feels good about himself and associates that good feeling with reading.

For as long as possible, your read-aloud efforts should be balanced by the outside experiences you bring to the child. Barring cases of bedridden children, it is not enough simply to read to the child. The background knowledge I noted earlier applies to life experience as well. The words in the book are just the beginning. What you as a parent or teacher do *after* the reading can turn a mini-lesson into a sizable learning experience. For example, there is a much-loved children's book about a little girl and a department store teddy bear, *Corduroy* by Don Freeman. The story alone is heartwarming, but the name Corduroy could also be used as a springboard to a discussion and comparison of other common fabrics like denim, wool, cotton, canvas, and felt. And it works in reverse as well: When you find a caterpillar outside, read Eric Carle's *The Very Hungry Caterpillar* inside the house or classroom.

Won't a Video Do as Much Good as a Picture Book?

Film and print are separate art forms that often have a common audience—in this case, the child. On page 17, I showed the difference in vocabulary level between a children's book and TV. But there is another issue to consider, especially for preschoolers or younger: The image on the film moves, but the one on the page is static. Let's see how important that might be.

In a typical video, the image of an insect speeds across the screen at a pace of 24 frames per second. In a two-hour film, that would be more than 170,000 frames—few of which could be studied for details. As soon as you stop the film, the image blurs.

On a page, the insect's image remains in focus and in one place, allowing the child to scrutinize it for details. Because visual literacy comes before print literacy, two-thirds of the questions and comments from young children are about the illustrations.[10] In a study of nine children, ages three to five, 150 hours of parent story-readings were audiotaped and analyzed for the kinds of questions asked by the children.[11] They asked a total of 2,725 questions, the vast majority of which focused on the illustrations. On average, the children asked seven questions per book, and picture queries outnumbered story questions by a two-to-one ratio. Surprisingly, less than 10 percent of the questions concerned letters or sentences (text), and 5 percent were about word meanings.

Handling Story Questions in a Family Is One Thing, but What Do I Do with an Entire Class?

The solution can be found in a study done of different teachers' readings in twenty-five preschool classes for four-year-olds.[12] The readings were filmed, the class and teacher dialogues transcribed and analyzed to establish patterns, and then a representative group of low-income, at-risk students were tested a year later. Three distinct styles of reading were observed, with one being by far the most successful:

1. *The co-constructive classes:* high amounts of talk by both the teacher and students *during* the readings, lots of analyzing, clarifications, amplifications, and talk about characters' emotions; but little talk *before* or *after* the sessions.

2. *The didactic-interactional classes:* limited amounts of talk *during* the story, and very little *before* or *after* the reading; when talk occurred during the story it usually was prompted by the teacher when she called for repeated predictable portions of text from the story; she often called for class responses in order to curtail disruptive or inattentive students; there were only right and wrong answers when she asked questions.

3. *The performance-oriented classes:* little talk *during* the story but some *before* and lots *after;* the pre-story conversation usually came from the teacher's introduction of the book, her feelings about it or reasons for reading it; post-story talk often involved the teacher asking questions that prompted the students to recall portions of the story, thus reconstructing the book in their own words; sometimes the follow-up talk focused on linking the story to events in the children's lives; because the reading was approached as a performance, there were few interruptions during the reading.

The follow-up testing of selected students (now age five) a year later showed the performance-oriented (3) approach to be most effective in supporting vocabulary development and the didactic-interactional (2) to be least successful. In reference to the latter approach, the teachers' book choices often involved highly predictable texts with limited vocabulary and minimal plots, and follow-up analysis showed they did "little to nourish children's literacy-related language growth."

The researchers noted that since the *overall* amount of talk was not related to subsequent learning, "teachers need not feel compelled constantly to stop and discuss books at length," but that discussion before and after are beneficial, with the *post-story* talk being most effective. In other words, when it's time to read the book, don't host a talk show.

How Can Illiterate or Semiliterate Parents Read to Children?

Fifty years ago, this would have been an insurmountable problem, but not now. Two kinds of books and a piece of technology help to save the day. The books are wordless and predictable books and the technology is the tape deck.

Thirty thousand years ago, in a step toward writing, our ancestors used cave drawings to tell stories without words—and wordless books follow that tradition. These books convey a story without using words; pictures (interpreted orally by the reader) tell the whole story—books in pantomime, if you will. The parent who can't read (or can't read English) has little difficulty in looking at the pictures and talking the book to the child. The popularity of this genre has increased in recent years, and there are now more than one hundred wordless books in print, from the simple (like *Deep in the Forest* by Brinton Turkle) to the complex (*The Silver Pony* by Lynd Ward, or *Tuesday* by David Wiesner).[13] (See the Wordless Books listing at the beginning of the Picture Book section of the Treasury.)

Though the "predictable book" form has been around for ages in folk tale and song, only recently have educators discovered how helpful it is in building readers. Because the story line contains phrases that are repeated over and over ("Then I'll huff and I'll puff and I'll . . ."), the child and/or parent can easily predict what's coming and join in on the reading (which enhances comprehension). For example, in Barbara Seulling's *The Teeny Tiny Woman,* the words "teeny tiny" are repeated fifty times throughout the book's thirteen sentences. In addition, predictable books often contain a cumulative sequence, as in *Henny Penny*: "So Henny Penny, Chicken Licken, Turkey Lurkey and Foxy Loxy went to see the king."

Many of these books are available on audiocassette for free at the public library. Illiterate or semiliterate parents can listen to these books on tape, along with the child, and hearing them often enough, will begin to memorize them. Predictable books are not only more accessible for struggling adult readers, they're more inviting and accessible for children as well. In classrooms that have predictable books, such as *We're Going on a Bear Hunt* by Michael Rosen and Helen Oxenbury, beginning readers attempt to read these books twice as often as others during free reading time—largely because they are less intimidating.[14] (See Predictable Books in the Picture Book section in the Treasury.)

However, although predictable, wordless, and controlled-vocabulary books (like Dr. Seuss's *The Cat in the Hat*) build the beginning reader's self-confidence, they have limited value as vocabulary builders, so read-alouds should move beyond that genre. Most libraries (and bookstores) have hundreds of other children's books available on audiocassette, housed with the book in a sealable plastic bag. The illiterate parent and child can sit together and listen to a book, even follow along on the page. They're sharing time and a common story. Is someone else's voice better than the parent's? No, but it's a whole lot better than no story at all. Taking the time to listen beside the child—instead of watching TV or talking on the phone—sends a very loud message to the child about the importance the parent places on books. For parents or teachers of older children, see page 209 in chapter 8 for a discussion of children's novels on audiocassette.

Do the Waldo and I Spy Books Serve Any Purpose?

A first cousin to wordless books are visual-puzzle books like the popular Waldo series by Martin Handford, and Jean Marzollo's I Spy photo riddles, which contain minimal text and no plot. Yes, they're gimmicky, but they are enormously successful with young and often older readers. These books enable a child to make a "pleasure-connection" with print in a book form, and *that* is always more positive than the "pain-connection" made by workbooks and quizzes. Think of such volumes as books with "training wheels."

The Waldo books, which require the reader-viewer to find the peripatetic backpacker amidst thousands of tiny, scurrying figures, hold a similar fascination with young readers, just as crossword puzzles appeal to older readers. But Waldo also builds reading skills. In order to find the Waldo character, the child must: (1) focus on the page; (2) recall what Waldo looks like from the first page; and (3) compare and contrast that memory image with each figure on the page. Thus attention span, recall, and visual discrimination are nurtured—three essential skills in reading.

The same thing holds true with the I Spy series in which hundreds of artifacts are spread across double pages and the reader must find certain objects. Finding the object or Waldo is not terribly far removed from the recall and discrimination necessary to tell the difference between the letters "b" and "d," or between "p" and "q."

Also there are the psychological advantages to such books: (1) They are fun. Never underestimate the power of that three-letter word in attracting and energizing a child's interest; and (2) They can be used by children before they can actually read. Doing so, the child begins to think of himself as a reader (establishing another positive association with books). Most of the books in these two series are listed under *Where's Waldo* in the Treasury.

What Is the Purpose of Fairy Tales?

Before most parents realize it, a growing child is ready, in his own mind at least, to go out and challenge the world. In the last two thousand years, nothing has filled this exploratory need as well as the fairy tale.

I know what you may be thinking. "Fairy tales? Is he kidding? Why, those things are positively frightening. Children see enough violence on television—they don't need kids pushing witches into ovens, and evil spells and poisoned apples."

Stop for a minute and remind yourself how long the fairy tale has been with us—in every nation and in every civilization. Surely there must be something significant here, an insight so important as to transcend time and mountains and cultures to arrive in the twenty-first century still intact. There are, for example, more than seven hundred different versions of *Cinderella* from hundreds of cultures. Nevertheless, they all tell the same story—a truly universal story. (See *Smoky Mountain Rose: An Appalachian Cinderella* in the Treasury.)

What distinguishes the fairy tale is that it speaks to the very heart and soul of the child. It admits to the child what so many parents and teachers spend hours trying to cover up or avoid. The fairy tale confirms what the child has been thinking all along—that it is a cold, cruel world out there and it's waiting to eat him alive.

Now, if that were *all* the fairy tale said, it would have died out long ago. But it goes one step further. It addresses itself to the child's sense of courage and adventure. The tale advises the child: Take your courage in hand and go out to meet the world head on. According to Bruno Bettelheim, the fairy tale offers this promise: If you have courage and if you persist, you can overcome any obstacle, conquer any foe. And best of all, you can achieve your heart's desire. G. K. Chesterton even builds a powerful analogy between fairy tales and the essence of Christianity.[15]

More than a few critics have linked the fairy tale aspect of the Harry Potter books to the series' popularity. Writing in *The New York Times,* Richard Bernstein noted: "What is important in the fairy-tale scheme is that Harry's situation contains many of the inchoate fears of childhood, not just the parental abandonment fear. Harry is skinny and weak and wears glasses patched together with tape, and in this sense he seems to stand in for the vulnerability, the powerlessness that children feel. He lives in a cupboard under the stairs, since his spoiled cousin has both of the children's bedrooms upstairs, so in a sense he is expelled, like Hansel and Gretel, even from the evil home he has."

By recognizing a child's daily fears, appealing to his courage and confidence, and by offering hope, the fairy tale presents the child with a means by which he can understand the world and himself. And those who would deodorize the tales impose a fearsome lie upon the child. J.R.R. Tolkien cautioned, "It does not pay to leave a dragon out of your calculations if you live near him." Judging from the daily averages, our land is filled with dragons.

+ Advocacy groups receive 3 million child-abuse calls each year, with at least 40 percent substantiated.[16]
+ 1,200 children are abused to death each year, and one-half of all abuse victims are under one year of age.[17]
+ Every 12 seconds a man batters his wife, or ex-wife or girlfriend.[18]

To send a child into that world unprepared is a crime.

The older the child, the greater the temptation for adults to choose books that will keep the child forever young, books without problems, conflict, or drama. And then all too soon these same parents are asking why their children have lost interest in books. Of all the things we ask our books to be, few are as important as "believable." Fiction, nonfiction, biographies, fantasies—the good ones work because they are believable. A world that is "forever pink," as author Natalie Babbitt once put it, doesn't work because children eventually realize its fakery.

The warm and fuzzy world of Beatrix Potter has been popular for almost five generations because it is believable. True, rabbits and squirrels don't talk, but there *are* single parents like Peter's mother who daily warn their children of dire consequences, there *are* lost fathers like Peter's, and there *are* Mr. MacGregors out there. And that's why *The Tale of Peter Rabbit* is the best-selling picture book of all time—not just because the illustrations are warm and fuzzy-looking.

Isn't the Fairy Tale's "Prince Charming" a Bit Dated?

If there is one flaw in the fairy tale, it's that many of the more famous tales are top-heavy with heroes and short on heroines. For balance, readers-aloud will want to try these collections of fairy and folk tales focusing on heroines: *Her Stories: African American Folktales, Fairy Tales, and True Tales,* retold by Virginia Hamilton; Ethel Johnston Phelps's two collections, *The Maid of the North* and *Tatterhood and Other Tales*; also *Not One Damsel in Distress,* collected by Jane Yolen; and *The Serpent Slayer and Other Stories of Strong Women* by Katrin Tchana.

Contemporary authors have rendered the women in fairy tales far more completely in some of their retellings. *Ella Enchanted* by Gail Carson Levine gives us a novelized and more believable Cinderella than the ones offered by Perrault and Disney.

For fun, combine Trina Schart Hyman's excellent version of *Sleeping Beauty* with Jane Yolen's *Sleeping Ugly,* or John Howe's *Jack and the Beanstalk* with *Kate and the Beanstalk* by Mary Pope Osborne. And the popular adult novelist Anna Quindlen offers a humorous tomboy spoof on the traditional fairy tale in her picture book *Happily Ever After.*

One of the things that makes the present age a "golden" age of children's literature is the growing number of heroines included in contemporary children's literature. Parents and teachers looking for a treasure map of titles need look no further than Penguin's *Let's Hear It for the Girls: 375 Great Books for Readers 2–14* by Erica Bauermeister and Holly Smith. And to give you an idea of how far we've come with our heroines, check out these three picture books by Emily Arnold McCully about a young French girl: *Mirette on the High Wire*; *Starring Mirette & Bellini*; and *Mirette & Bellini Cross Niagara Falls*; also try these two by Robert D. San Souci: *The Samurai's Daughter* and *Kate Shelley.*

For all of this, there remains a troubling divide between males and females in the world of print, including the diverse ways girls and boys respond to print. Girls are devoted Harry Potter fans, but how many boys would be reading the series if *Harry* had been a *Harriet*?

If We Only Have a Small Amount of Time for Read-Aloud, How Do We Incorporate Discussion?

Steal more time! If that sounds daring, consider the words of education writer Alfie Kohn: "Before a teacher, especially a middle school, high school or college instructor sits down to plan a course, even a unit, or thinks about evaluation, he or she should ask the question, 'What can I reasonably expect that students will retain from this course after a decade?' I know that if I'd been asked that question when I was teaching in high school and college, I would have found it profoundly unsettling, because I knew well, or would have known if I had been brave enough to face the question head-on, that all they would have left was a fact here, a stray theory there, a disconnected assumption or passage from a book. That should lead us to ask what it is we're doing. We sometimes end up making elaborate snow sculptures on the last day of winter."[19]

As I pointed out earlier in this chapter, discussion after the story is of critical importance. Students from classrooms where there were more book discussions tended to score higher in national reading assessments.[20] In chapter 5, I explain the role that discussion played in the success of Oprah's Book Club, which has helped put more than thirty books on *The New York Times* bestseller list. How many books have college professors or high school teachers put there?

Unfortunately, students are seldom invited to the conversation in school. And even when they are, they're not expected to stay very long. Studies reveal most teachers wait only one second or less for answers. But further research showed if they expanded that to three to five seconds before and after the answer, student responses grew more frequent, more logical, and complex thinking skills improved significantly.[21] When 537 K–6 classrooms were observed by practice teachers in 1992, classroom discussion before or after the story averaged less than five minutes.[22]

And things don't get much better as students move up the grade levels. In a 1990 study of 331 students in 15 college classrooms, the students asked only 49 questions in 900 minutes of class time—or 3.3 an hour.[23] Compare that with the nonstop questioning taking place in kindergarten classrooms.

Is There a Natural Transition from Picture Book to Novel?

Thanks to our primal need to find out what happens next, read-aloud is a particularly effective tool in stretching children's attention spans. Just keep in mind that endurance in readers, like runners, is not built overnight; start slowly and build. Start with short picture books, then move to longer ones that can be spread over several days, then to short novels (already broken into convenient chapters), and finally to full-length novels (longer than one hundred pages).

The amount of text on a page is a good way to gauge how much the child's attention span is being stretched. Notice the difference in the amounts of text on the pages in Figures 3.2 and 3.3. When my grandson Tyler was two years old, he regularly heard books with a few sentences on a page (Figure 3.2), but by three and a half he was listening to books that had as much text as Figure 3.3. The transition from short to longer should

Figure 3.2: Angus and the Cat
by Marjorie Flack

Figure 3.3: All About Alfie
by Shirley Hughes

be done gradually over many different books. While you don't want to drown the child in words, you do want to immerse him enough to challenge the mind and memory, enticing him away from a complete dependence on illustrations for comprehension and into more words.

If I had a primary class (or child) that had never been read to (like the ones who spent all of kindergarten filling in blanks and circling letters), I'd start the year with: the repetition of *Tikki Tikki Tembo* by Arlene Mosel; the poignancy of *The Biggest Bear* by Lynd Ward; the mystery of *The Island of the Skog* by Steven Kellogg; the humor of *Here Come the Aliens!* by Colin McNaughton, and the suspense of Paul Zelinsky's retelling of *Rumpelstiltskin*.

Next would be "Red Riding Hood Week," focusing on different versions of that famous red-hooded pilgrim—starting with Trina Schart Hyman's *Little Red Riding Hood,* followed by books chosen from the titles listed with it in the Treasury.

Then I'd schedule several "author weeks," each focusing exclusively on one author's books. I'd start with Kevin Henkes, who uses his mouse tales to read the pulse of childhood so touchingly (see the list of his books accompanying *Lilly's Purple Plastic Purse* in the Treasury). As their attention grew, I'd have a "Bill Peet Week," choosing a week's worth of reading listed with *The Whingdingdilly* in the Treasury. On the day I read *Kermit the Hermit* (about a stingy hermit crab), I'd introduce it with "Hector the Collector" from Shel Silverstein's poetry collection *Where the Sidewalk Ends.* From then on I would begin or end the reading with a poem—not necessarily connected to the reading—and gradually sprinkle poetry throughout the day: waiting for the bell in the morning, between classes, et cetera.

Then I'd move on to a picture book *series,* each volume treated as a chapter in an ongoing book—like Bernard Waber's seven-book Lyle the Crocodile series that begins with *The House on East 88th Street.* (See its Treasury listing for titles in the series.)

Once you've built a child's or class's attention span, it's an easy jump to "chapter books"—either long picture books or short novels of sixty to one hundred pages. These are books that don't have to end with Monday but can be stretched into Tuesday and Wednesday. Preschoolers can enjoy picture books that are divided into chapters, like *Grandaddy's Place* by Helen Griffith; Barbara Brenner's *Wagon Wheels*; and *The Josefina Story Quilt* by Eleanor Coerr. Then I'd do a collection of stories in one volume about one family. One of the best is *All About Alfie* by Shirley Hughes, a collection of four stories about a spirited preschooler and his family. These can be expanded to the other collections about Alfie: *The Big Alfie and Annie Rose Storybook,* and *The Big Alfie Out of Doors Storybook.*

Sometimes you'll encounter a picture book that may be too long for one sitting. Simply divide it into chapters yourself. That works especially well with Rumer Godden's classic Christmas book, *The Story of Holly and Ivy* (you've got to love a book that opens on Christmas Eve in an orphanage).

As for actual short novels, my immediate nominees would be *My Father's Dragon* by Ruth Stiles Gannett; William McCleery's *Wolf Story*; *Lafcadio, the Lion Who Shot Back,* Shel Silverstein's first book and only novel for children; *The Littles,* a series by John Peterson; and Johanna Hurwitz's *Rip-Roaring Russell* (see the Treasury's short novel listings for the other books in the Russell series).

At What Age Can You Begin "Chapter Books"?

Let me give you an idea of how widespread the misunderstanding of listening and reading levels is, as well as the magic that can occur when they are understood. About five years ago I was doing an all-day seminar in a blue-collar community on the Jersey Shore. At lunch, a young teacher named Melissa Olans Antinoff introduced herself and said, "You'd *love* my kindergarten class!" She explained that she read one hundred picture books a year to the class, but also read ten to twelve chapter books. The socioeconomic level of the class had 60 percent of the children on free lunch, and Antinoff was in only her fourth year of teaching.

When the seminar resumed after lunch, I asked how many kindergarten teachers were in the room and learned there were eight. Further investigation showed that Antinoff was the only one who read chapter books to her class. Which of those eight classes will be better prepared for first grade: the ones that heard 150 four-minute picture books, or the one that heard one hundred picture books along with a dozen novels? Which class will have the longer attention spans at the end of the year, and the larger vocabularies? Which class will have exercised more complex thinking, having to recall what happened in Thursday's and Wednesday's chapter in order to understand Friday's chapter?

When I shared that anecdote with teachers elsewhere, several approached me and suggested that I was being too hard on kindergarten teachers, that if I'd been in a more suburban community—not a blue-collar one—I'd have found teachers who understood the differences between listening and reading. Really? Well, let's try the concept in the wealthiest community in America, where I presented six months later.[24]

After the program, a teacher approached me and said, "I'm embarrassed. I've been teaching here for twelve years and, until today, I'd never even thought of doing chapter books with my kindergartners."

This was a teacher who was teaching children who had been on more planes, trains, and cruises, who'd had more distinguished visitors to their homes, whose parents had more print in the house, and more diplomas on the wall, than all the other children in America.

Before I could respond, the teacher behind her, who had overheard the conversation, interjected and said, "Listen, get over the embarrassment and go get the chapter books. Until I heard Jim speak three years ago, I'd never done chapter books with my second-graders. I started the next day and haven't missed a day. It's the best time of the day for all of us."

Could You Read Chapter Books at Preschool Level?

In 1999, my daughter came home for Thanksgiving with a letter she had received from my grandson Connor's preschool teacher at Battery Park City Day Nursery in New York City. "You're going to love this!" she exclaimed as she handed it to me. I've shared it with almost every teacher and parent audience I've had since then. The teacher was a talented young woman with fourteen years' experience working with four- and five-year-olds, and here's what she wrote:

> Dear Parents:
>   Ordinarily, I do not go out of my way to recommend movies to my students' parents, however, there is a movie coming out which could help to extend your child's learning. On December 19th, the movie *Stuart Little* will be opening. It just so happens that we have

just finished reading the book by E. B. White, which the movie is based on.

Throughout the year we will be selecting a few chapter books to read to the children who stay for nap time. Year after year, *Stuart Little* is always my first selection because each chapter of the book is short enough to be read in one sitting and, most especially, I choose it because Stuart is a character that can easily capture the imagination of a young child. You see, Stuart is a young boy who just happens to look like a mouse! Because of his diminutive stature Stuart gets into all kinds of wild and crazy adventures.

Reading chapter books such as *Stuart Little* helps to build a child's visualization skills and helps them to appreciate stories that are told over more than one sitting. By taking your child to the movie, you may be able to initiate a conversation about the similarities and differences between the chapter book and the movie version, as well as the similarities and differences between watching a movie and reading a story. Your child might also enjoy rereading the book with you at home. If you haven't ever read a chapter book to your child, *Stuart Little* might be just the right book for you to get started with.

Happy Reading (& movie-viewing),
Karleen Waldman

For anyone unfamiliar with *Stuart Little,* it's a charming 130-page novel by the same person who wrote the classic *Charlotte's Web.* Karleen Waldman understood that children are ready for chapter books long before most people think they are. Our continued reliance exclusively on four-minute picture books is an insult to their growing minds and attention spans. No, Ms. Waldman didn't begin the year with a novel, nor did she abandon picture books for chapters. She began with picture books and built the children's attention spans. By the end of the year, these same children had also heard *Cricket in Times Square* by George Selden, and *Mr. Popper's Penguins* by Florence and Richard Atwater. I'm not suggesting we abandon picture books. Instead, add a few novel pages and then a daily chapter to the picture books you read to preschoolers.

At What Age Do You Stop the Picture Books?

Although I understand the impatience to get on with the business of growing up, I wince whenever I hear that question. A good story is a good story, whether it has pictures or not. All those pictures in museums don't have a lot of words under them but they still move us, right?

I know nursery school teachers who read Judith Viorst's *Alexander the Terrible, Horrible, No Good, Very Bad Day* to their classes, and I know a high school English teacher who reads it to his sophomores twice a year—first in September and again, by popular demand, in June. A picture book should be someplace on the reading list of every class at every grade level.

Many U.S. high school students were not read to regularly in middle grades and do little or no recreational reading on their own. I remember talking with a remedial class of ninth-graders in California one day. Of the twenty-one students, not one had ever heard of the Pied Piper, none had heard of the Wright brothers, and only two had heard of David and Goliath. Their mainstream cultural references were a bit shallow and ripe for planting.

In sharing an occasional picture book you would give teens a chance at what they missed in primary years—*The Pied Piper of Hamelin,* retold by Robert Holden, and *Sleeping Beauty* and *The Story of Ferdinand* (Munro Leaf's little book that pushed *Gone With the Wind* out of the number-one spot on the bestseller list more than half a century ago). Many of our students are at the doorstep of parenthood. In New York City alone, there are 12,000 kindergarten children with teenage mothers. If they and their friends are ignorant of childhood's stories, how can they share them with their children?

When we go back as adults to the books we enjoyed as children, we bring a perspective that was missing earlier and discover new dimensions. The weight of *The Velveteen Rabbit* by Margery Williams is in direct proportion to our age—the older we are, the more it means to us. Recent years have seen a wave of picture books containing themes sometimes better appreciated by older students than younger, themes that could serve as springboards to deeper classroom discussion with adolescents: aging—*Wilfred Gordon McDonald Partridge* by Mem Fox, and *Old Henry* by Joan Blos; war and peace—*The Butter Battle Book* by Dr. Seuss, *Pink and Say* by Patricia Polacco; *Hiroshima No Pika* by Toshi Maruki, and *Susanna of the Alamo* by Paul Gacon; selflessness—*Kate Shelley: Bound for Legend* by Robert Do San Souci; imperialism—*Encounter* by Jane Yolen; and loneliness—*Somebody Loves You, Mr. Hatch* by Eileen Spinelli. Many upper-grade teachers are now familiar with Jon Scieszka's clever twist on an old story, *The True Story of the Three Little Pigs,* as told by the wolf. If my freshman English prof had had that book, we could have knocked off "point of view" in an afternoon instead of belaboring it for a week.

Since most upper-grade teachers are unfamiliar with the newer picture books, Bette D. Ammon and Gale W. Sherman, two veteran children's literature authorities, have written *Worth a Thousand Words: An Annotated Guide to Picture Books for Older Children*. With its thousands of titles, descriptions, and cross-references, this is an outstanding guide to finding books around a given theme.

Three recommendations to win over anyone who thinks older students will not respond to picture books:

- *Johnny on the Spot* by Edward Sorel (Johnny and his adult neighbor accidentally invent a radio that broadcasts events one day in advance; the conflict arises when Johnny is sworn to secrecy and forbidden to interfere with the future—even if he knows a calamity is about to occur.)
- *The Secret Knowledge of Grown-Ups* by David Wisniewski (The author takes standard rules of behavior imposed by adults—eat your vegetables! don't blow bubbles in your milk with your straw!—and offers intricate, mind-boggling reasons behind the rules. They are the perfect launching pad for further send-ups of family and school rules; for example, the real reason they don't want you to run in the hallways at school is . . .)
- *Don't Go Near That Rabbit, Frank!* by Pam Conrad (Based on an urban legend, usually involving a dog or cat, this story features a prize show rabbit owned by old man Hoover, who warns the new kids next door that he'll shoot their dog if it comes near his rabbit hutch. The rabbit dies of natural causes, the old man buries him in the yard, the dog digs it up that night and brings it home to the kids, who think he killed the rabbit. So they clean up the rabbit and smuggle it back into the hutch so old man Hoover will think it died of natural causes and won't blame their dog. Then the old man comes to clean out the hutch.)

Are There Pitfalls to Avoid in Choosing Long Novels?

The difference between short novels and full-length novels (I use approximately one hundred pages as a demarcation point) is sometimes found in the amount of description, the shorter ones having less detail, the longer ones requiring more imagination on the part of the listener/reader. Children whose imaginations have been atrophying in front of a television for years are not comfortable with long descriptive passages. But the more you read to them, the less trouble they have in constructing mental images. Indeed, research shows us that listening to stories stimulates the imagination significantly more than television or film.[25]

In approaching longer books, remember that all books are not meant to be read aloud—indeed some books aren't even worth reading to yourself, never mind boring a family or class with them. Some books are written in a convoluted or elliptical style that can be read silently but not aloud.

One of the best rules on the difference between *listening* to text and *reading* text was defined by the great Canadian adult novelist Robertson Davies in the preface to a volume of his speeches. He asked readers to remember they were reading *speeches,* not essays: "What is meant to be heard is necessarily more direct in expression, and perhaps more boldly coloured, than what is meant for the reader."[26] This is a fact missed by many speakers, preachers, and professors who write their speeches as if the audience were going to read them instead of listen to them. Be sure to take Davies's advice into consideration when choosing your longer read-alouds. Charles Dickens, whose publisher paid him by the word, also understood the listening-reading differences and edited out the extra adjectives when he read his works aloud during lecture tours.

Another area you should be alert to is subject matter in the novels. With longer books, it is imperative for the adult to preview the text before reading it aloud. The length of such books allows them to treat subject matter that can be very sensitive, far more so than a picture book could. As the reader, you should first familiarize yourself with the subject and the author's approach. Ask yourself as you read it through, "Can my child or class handle not only the vocabulary and the complexity of this story, but its emotions as well? Is there anything here that will do more harm than good to my child or class? Anything that might embarrass someone?"

Along with enabling you to avoid this kind of damaging situation, reading the book ahead of time will enable you to read it the second time to the class or child with more confidence, accenting important passages, leaving out dull ones (I mark these lightly in pencil in the margins), and providing sound effects to dramatize the story line (I'm always ready to knock on a table or wall where the story calls for a "knock at the door").

In reading longer works aloud to students you're preparing them for "dating." No, not the kind you're thinking about, but rather the kind referred to by author Kurt Vonnegut, Jr. Someone had asked him if you could actually teach a person how to write, and he was indignant anyone would doubt it. That, he declared, is the job of an editor. That's the person who teaches the writer how to behave on "a blind date with a total stranger"[27]—the "stranger" being the reader. To borrow that analogy, parents and teachers want students to go on more "blind dates" with authors. And just as the editor must teach the writer how to behave, so too does reading aloud teach the listener how to behave. In listening to the text, the student discovers that we don't always get to know the author's story on the first date/chapter; often we need a couple of dates/chapters before we get comfortable with the book. And as it would be rude to ask too many intrusive questions on the first date, we need to give the author some space to tell his or her story. Hold the questions for a little bit; don't rush the date!

What Makes a Good Read-Aloud?

For infants and young toddlers, the ideal read-aloud floats on its sounds—good rhythm and rhyme, lots of repetition, sounds that are silly or dramatic or exciting, and lots of splashy color, along with plenty of the familiar. Very young children gravitate to the familiar: familiar sounds, people, and things. That's why they want a certain book read over and over. *The Everything Book* by Denise Fleming is perfect for this age.

For a child two and a half to three, the idea of plot begins to creep in, but nothing too complicated: the lost puppy, the lost mitten, the lonely child. Language is still exciting and repetitious, if possible, but with a little more narrative. *Rolie Polie Olie* by William Joyce is a good example, because it has enough of a story to keep the very young interested and pleased when, in the end, the naughty robot (like Max in Maurice Sendak's *Where the Wild Things Are*) is forgiven by his family and all is happily resolved.

When a child is four and older, the plot becomes far more important. What does the story add up to? What happens next? Yes, there is still room for Shel Silverstein and poetry, but the poems that work best are the ones with a strong narrative twist.

As Dickens found when he came to America to read aloud his works to live audiences of 3000, too many words will spoil the listening broth. He condensed his stories in a way that would allow the action and plot to stand in bolder relief.

While we want to be involved with the characters—as in *Where the Red Fern Grows*—we still need to be pulled through the pages by this abstract thing called a plot—the wind beneath the story's wings.

The challenge arrives as the child approaches eight or nine years of age, and the literature written for this level has more of a realistic tone. The plots begin to center on social and emotional issues, many of them growing more severe as the books creep into what is called "young adult" literature: divorce, incest, child abuse, death, substance abuse, and violence. None of those are new issues to literature—Dickens handled them all.

In choosing books that explore such issues, however, we must insure they do so at an appropriate developmental level. What a thirteen-year-old can handle in a story is not appropriate for most nine-year-olds. There is a great advantage to having certain serious issues, like the accident-death in Barbara Park's *Mick Hart Was Here,* shared between an adult and a child or teachers and students. The adult serves as a guide through the pain of the book's events.

But we must also make the distinction, as children grow older, between books that are emotionally appropriate for *hearing* and those for *reading.* The subject matter of some books may be too personal to be shared out loud, especially in a classroom. It would have to be a highly unusual circumstance for me to read aloud to a class of teenagers a book that had incest as its central focus. What you might read one-on-one with a daughter or son could be entirely different when done in a classroom. The more realistic the book's subject, the more likely it may be a read-to-yourself book.

And then there is the issue of fiction versus nonfiction. For example, *The Magic School Bus* is an excellent series, but the myriad details and asides makes it a difficult if not clumsy classroom read-aloud. However, it's easy if you are with just two children who can easily view the pages' details while you're reading to them. Also, if your own child is interested in spiders, you could read a book like *Spider Watching* by Vivian French, but it may not absorb an entire class.

Not every book of nonfiction is written with a strong enough plot to hold the child or class's attention, but here are some that do (*synopsis in Treasury):

A Christmas Tree in the White House by Gary Hines
Eleanor by Barbara Cooney
Graveyards of the Dinosaurs by Shelley Tanaka
Leon's Story by Leon Walter Tillage*
Mary Anning and the Sea Dragon by Jeannine Atkins
The Bobbin Girl by Emily Arnold McCully
The Story of Ruby Bridges by Robert Coles*
*The Tree That Would Not Die** by Ellen Levine
Purple Death: The Mysterious Flu of 1918 by David Getz*
The Last Princess: The Story of Princess Ka'iulani of Hawai'i by Fay Stanley*
The President Has Been Shot! by Rebecca C. Jones
Chibi: A True Story from Japan by B. Brenner and J. Takaya
Alice Ramsey's Grand Adventure by Don Brown
Satchel Paige by Lesa Cline-Ransome
The True Adventure of Daniel Hall by Diane Stanley*
Strange Mysteries from Around the World by Seymour Simon

How Will I Know If the Class or Child Is Ready for Novels?

If the child or class begs for another book, it's a sign the attention span has lengthened enough to try a novel. The kinds of questions asked by the child is another sign: Are they insightful or perplexed? Are the descriptions or characters fascinating or confusing to him?

The first novel I read to Jamie would be my first choice a thousand times over, for almost any child or class—*James and the Giant Peach*. I know a kindergarten teacher who ends her year with this book and I know a sixth-grade teacher who started her September class with it for twenty years. Any book that can hold the attention span and lift the imaginations of six-year-olds as well as eleven-year-olds has to have magic in it. And *James and the Giant Peach* has that.

There's an interesting contrast between what classroom teachers read to themselves as children and what they like to read to their classes today. For several years I surveyed 2,887 teachers in some of my all-day seminars, asking them to list their childhood favorites and today's read-aloud choices. They were mostly elementary teachers (95 percent) with an average of fourteen years' experience in the classroom. As expected, they read more classics and series books to themselves as children than they did to their classes, but they read more award-winners to their students.

Teachers' Favorite Books from Their Own Childhoods *(number of votes in parentheses)*	Teachers' Favorites to Read Aloud to Classes Today *(number of votes in parentheses)*
(226) Nancy Drew (S)	(98) Charlotte's Web (A)
(135) Charlotte's Web (A)	(81) James and the Giant Peach
(123) Heidi (C)	(66) Where the Red Fern Grows
(120) Little Black Sambo	(66) Polar Express (A)
(119) Little Women (C)	(60) Shiloh (A)
(118) Little House on the Prairie (S)	(57) Sideways Stories from Wayside School
(82) The Boxcar Children (S)	(54) Stone Fox
(62) Secret Garden (C)	(40) Summer of the Monkeys
(56) Bobbsey Twins (S)	

(C) classic
(A) contemporary award-winner
(S) series

(53) Black Beauty (C)
(38) Cinderella
(35) Little Engine That Could
(34) Grimms' Fairy Tales
(31) Winnie-the-Pooh
(30) A Wrinkle in Time (A)
(30) Madeline
(29) Where the Red Fern Grows
(29) Poky Little Puppy
(27) Mother Goose
(25) Henry Huggins/Ramona (S)(A)
(23) Wonderful Wizard of OZ (C)
(22) Caddie Woodlawn (A)
(22) Black Stallion (S)
(21) Five Little Peppers (S)
(20) Velveteen Rabbit
(20) Make Way for Ducklings (A)
(17) Tale of Peter Rabbit (C)
(17) Curious George (S)
(16) Pippi Longstocking (S)
(15) Lassie Come-Home

(38) Country Bunny and the Gold Shoes
(36) Giving Tree
(32) Charlie and Chocolate Factory
(31) Tales of a Fourth-Grade Nothing
(30) Henry Huggins/Ramona (A)(S)
(29) The Lion, the Witch, and the Wardrobe (S)
(28) The Indian in the Cupboard (S)
(27) Boxcar Children (S)
(26) Hatchet (A)
(25) Maniac Magee (A)
(23) There's a Boy in the Girls' Bathroom
(22) Trumpet of the Swan
(22) Best Christmas Pageant Ever
(21) True Story of the Three Little Pigs
(21) The Secret Garden (C)
(21) Matilda
(20) The Napping House
(20) Where the Sidewalk Ends
(19) Chicka Chicka Boom Boom
(19) The BFG
(18) Skinnybones
(18) Bridge to Terabithia (A)

Do Children Have to Follow Along in a Book As You Read Aloud?

No, not at all, and usually there aren't enough copies for everyone in the class. But following along in the text has proven to be very effective with remedial students. These students often need repeated readings, which wearies a parent or teacher but coincides perfectly with the recorder's purpose.

Back in the 1970s, a young graduate student named Marie Carbo[28] began recording stories and books for her students who were labeled learning disabled. Eventually she hit upon the idea of recording the stories at different paces—slower for the initial hearings, and faster for subsequent hearings. Students followed along in their own books and, as they became more confident, selected the faster versions.

Describing a particular case, Dr. Carbo wrote: "The greatest gain in word recognition was made by Tommy, a sixth-grade boy reading on a 2.2 level. Prior to working with the tapes he had faltered and stumbled over second-grade words while his body actually shook with fear and discomfort. Understandably, he hated to read. Because a beloved teacher had once read *Charlotte's Web* to him, he asked me to record his favorite chapter from the book. I recorded one paragraph on each cassette side so that Tommy could choose to read either one or two paragraphs daily. The first time that he listened to a recording (five times) and then read the passage silently to himself (twice), he was able to read the passage to me perfectly with excellent expression and without fear. After this momentous event, Tommy worked hard. At last he knew he was capable of learning to read and was willing to give it all he could. The result was a fifteen-month gain in word recognition at the end of only three months. Every learning-disabled child in the program experienced immediate success with her or his individually recorded books."[29]

Ellen Beck of Crosby, Texas, read about Marie Carbo's methods in an earlier edition of *The Read-Aloud Handbook* and thought it might be worth a try. Her librarian at Newport Elementary located a set of the Carbo tapes, and she set up shop with her students. Beck wrote to me:

> I had one student—let's call her Mary—who was officially removed from special education classes by parent request because her mother felt it wasn't benefitting her. She began the new year with me—and struggled. On her initial reading test, she scored only 25 percent. I was mortified and wondered how to help her. Her mother requested that we put her in the third-grade reader so she would be reading the same material as other children in her grade, and I'm forever grateful for that suggestion.
>
> When I told my principal that I wanted to get cassettes and record stories, he suggested I target certain students and do a test run. I selected ten, including Mary. Using the tape approach, Mary scored 60 percent at the end of six weeks; in fact, the scores improved for all the students listening to the tapes. The principal approved buy-

ing two cassette players and five headsets (I'd been borrowing the library's), along with 200 cassettes.

Mary's scores continued to climb. She was up to 70, 75, back to 70, then up to 89. She proudly read to the principal, who was a big encouragement to her, and continued to astound us all. Though other students' scores were improving as well, every child is different, and therefore their needs were different. Mary's needs were sight words. She was highly trained in phonics, but obviously it doesn't always help when you have a strange sight word. The recorded repetition of third-grade vocabulary was the perfect antidote for her problems. On the year-end Texas Assessment of Academic Skills (TAAS) test, she scored 97 percent, missing only one of thirty-six questions, and she did as well the following year.

Needless to say, I'm sold on taped stories, but ten minutes of SSR (with free choice of books) is basic to my classroom, and I read aloud to them daily.[30]

For more on audio books, see chapter 8.

Where Can I Find More Information About Authors?

I don't know of a single lifetime reader who doesn't have favorite authors. We seek them out in books, magazines, and newspapers. For years I bought certain New York newspapers just on the days when my favorite columnists were appearing. Some people only read Mike Royko in the Chicago papers. Until the arrival of literature-based instruction in the 1990s, schools largely ignored authors in favor of "Class, turn to page fifty-two in your reader. . . ." Who remembers the author of a basal reader?

Close behind the schools in ignoring authors were publishers. Even today, how much can you learn about the author from the book's dust jacket or about-the-author page? Almost nothing. Take E. B. White as an example: *Charlotte's Web* has been in print for a half century and still the hardcover publisher hasn't collected a single sentence about him to include in the book. The paperback publisher did a little better, providing a three-paragraph biography, although 90 percent of it is nothing a child would be interested in. Did it tell you if he had a happy childhood, or owned a pet, or lived on a farm, or had any fears? No. (If you want a lovely study on White, check out *E. B. White: Some Writer!* by Beverly Gherman, published by Atheneum.) Most authors don't fare much better than White, even the award-winners: Gary Paulsen in *Hatchet*—three sentences; Roald Dahl in

James and the Giant Peach—three sentences; Jerry Spinelli in *Maniac Magee*—four sentences; Avi in *The True Confessions of Charlotte Doyle*—three sentences. Nor do adult authors fare any better; Alex Haley only received three sentences on the dust jacket of *Roots.*

In recent years, there's been a slight increase in raising author awareness by publishers, part of the Oprah's Book Club's *halo effect,* perhaps. So if you and your class or family wish more information on the author, here are some handy resources.

When I edited my two anthologies of read-aloud stories (*Hey! Listen to This* [for K–4] and *Read All About It!* [for preteens and teens]), I included mini-biographies for each of the nearly fifty authors in each book, most of the time using the common encyclopedic reference resources of my local public library. These led me to other resources, and sometimes even to the author himself. They became like genealogy hunts, and I found so much undiscovered material I created a Children's Author Trivia Quiz for my Web site, www.trelease-on-reading.com/trivia_frame.html.

The best resources for author information are *Something About the Author* and its smaller partner, the Author Autobiography series (both from Gale and found in most large public libraries). The former is a series of more than one hundred volumes containing photos and documentation about almost anyone who has written or illustrated for children in the twentieth century. Other excellent resources: *Fifth Book of Junior Authors and Illustrators* (Wilson); Anita Silvey's *Children's Books and Their Creators* (Houghton); and the *Reader's Guide to Periodic Literature* for articles.

If you are interested in a particular author, write to the children's marketing department at the author's publisher and ask for any author bios, posters, or photos they might have. Many publishers offer inexpensive video visits with authors and illustrators, often filmed in their homes and studios. Also, author interviews may be available on audiocassettes offered by school book clubs.

Back in 1990, a new children's literature journal came onto the scene from the American Library Association—*Book Links*—intended to link books, libraries, and classrooms through common themes and interests. This sixty-four-page bimonthly has succeeded magnificently in that goal, and nothing demonstrates it better than what it has done with authors. Each issue contains at least two extensive author-illustrator studies or interviews. All of *Book Links'* articles, subjects, and themes have been indexed on the Web at www.ala.org/BookLinks. In that index, the subject of "author studies" lists different articles from 1993 to the present; the index also includes publication dates in the magazine for hundreds of full-page author profiles.

Incidentally, should you choose to schedule an author visit to your school, be sure to seek references from previous schools the author has visited. The stories of disastrous author visits are legendary, as are the tales about how poorly prepared some schools are for such events. The latter are described in witty detail in *Author Day* by Daniel Pinkwater, a man who obviously has met his share of the extremes.

Be sure to honor current authors as well as older ones. When author-illustrator Keith Baker visited an elementary school a few years ago, one student asked, "Have you been dead?" When the question-and-answer period was over, Baker quietly asked the child, "Why did you ask me if I had been dead?" The boy replied, "Well—whenever we talk about authors, they're dead!"[31]

Author celebrations in preschool and primary grades usually involve the teacher sharing personal information about the author each day, and then reading one or more of the author's books. Some even go so far as to schedule teleconferences with the author via the phone. I once listened to a wonderful audiotape of a teleconference between twenty-five students in Merry Kahn's school library in Maquoketa, Iowa, and the late Roald Dahl, who was sitting at home in Great Missenden, Buckinghamshire, England.

My favorite author story involves the research I did on Wilson Rawls, author of *Where the Red Fern Grows* and *Summer of the Monkeys.* The dust jacket of Rawls' books contained only a few sentences about him and he had died by the time I began my research. For twenty years he had regularly visited schools and teacher conferences, telling the story of his childhood, out of which grew his two books. Unfortunately, I had never heard him speak, and his speech had never been transcribed into print. But people from his audiences could repeat parts of it almost verbatim. They said one minute you'd be crying over this skinny teenager living in hobo jungles and begging for food on street corners during the Depression, and the next minute you'd be laughing over his efforts to write a book when he had no idea how to spell or punctuate.

I couldn't take people's random recollections as documentation; I needed his exact words. Considering how many times he gave it, I thought *someone* must have a copy of the speech, but every turn led to a dead end—from publishers to professors. Finally I found his widow through the reference room file at the Idaho Falls Public Library, and sure enough, Sophie Rawls had a copy of the speech on tape. It verified everything I'd heard secondhand. (See www.trelease-on-reading.com/rawls.html for information on the audiotape.)

One of the most moving parts of the speech is when he finished rewriting *Red Fern* (he'd burned the original because of the poor grammar and spelling) but couldn't bear to watch his wife's face as she read it (she was far more educated than he was). So he walked the streets of Idaho Falls, waiting for her verdict. In 1996, I gave a speech in the little Idaho Falls Civic Center and told of Rawls's adventures in rewriting his book in the midst of their community. To my surprise, most of the 700 people had no idea this famous book had been written there. They were stunned.

In the audience that evening was Dave Schjeldahl, principal of Temple View Elementary, who was determined that no child would ever again grow up in that town and not know its literary heritage. Schjeldahl initiated a campaign to raise the funds that would erect a life-size statue of a barefoot boy and his dogs. It now stands in front of the Idaho Falls Public Library, reminding passersby of the man who also passed that way and left a mark that will be read and treasured for generations to come.

Is there an author who lives or lived in your community? Has notice been taken in any lasting way? Short of a statue, even stickers inside each of his or her books, noting the connection to the community, would be a step in the right direction.

How Do I Get My Twelve-Year-Old to Sit Still Long Enough for a Story?

Try reading aloud while your child is eating breakfast or dessert. When Jamie and Elizabeth were teenagers, their household responsibilities alternated between setting the table and doing the dishes. And while they did the dishes, I read to them, usually from magazines, newspapers, or anthologies. If I came across an interesting article—maybe an obituary for a rock star or a *Time* magazine essay on hairstyles—that would be the night's reading; *Paul Harvey's The Rest of the Story* collections were also popular.

Whenever I show parent audiences the photograph on the next page of Jamie doing the dishes when he was in seventh grade, I get some strange looks, to which I respond: "Now, if you have a preteen or teen who *doesn't* do the dishes in your home, then the child's IQ is higher than yours. Not a good thing, folks."

As for classroom situations, most of the guidelines suggested for reading to younger students also apply to older ones. Just because they are older doesn't mean they have longer attention spans or that they've been read to previously. Tailor your initial readings to the class situation, win the children's confidence, then broaden the scope and introduce them to times and places other than their own.

While doing the dinner dishes is a perfect time for a teenager to hear a read-aloud.

In choosing novels at elementary and secondary levels, avoid falling into the old book report trap of "thicker is better." There are thousands of children every day who report to the media center and tell the librarian: "My teacher said this book doesn't count for a book report—it's gotta be at least 125 pages." And that's how you kill a reader! There is no connection between thickness and goodness. (Remember: the Gettysburg Address was only two and one-half minutes long, 272 words.)

So read-aloud selections don't even have to be books—short pieces work too. Never mind any misgivings you might have about the title, check out *Uncle John's Great Big Bathroom Reader*. Your class will have a hard time resisting the short but true anecdotes included: thousands of articles covering history, politics, family, death, movies, science, law and order, and myths (www.bathroomreader.com).

In your leisure reading, if you find a magazine article your class would enjoy, save it and read it to them. Reading aloud a newspaper column may turn a student into a daily newspaper reader. You'll know you're on the right track when a student stops you between classes and asks, "Did you read Bob Greene's column yesterday? Wasn't it great?" And if you're looking for a fast-moving novel that will grab even the most reluctant audience, try Avi's *Wolf Rider!*

What Results Should Be Expected from Reading Aloud to Teens?

As the state of Virginia's Standards of Learning imposed more regimen and academic threats on students and faculty, five teachers in one middle school saw negative attitudes developing among their students. In response, they decided to implement daily read-aloud sessions. Even though these teachers came from five different academic disciplines (language arts, math, science, social studies, and special education/family studies) and recognized read-aloud was not a traditional practice among secondary teachers, they decided to try it and, at the same time, measure whatever impact it might have on student attitudes and behavior.[32]

The teachers had sixty-four years of teaching experience between them. The students represented a student body in which 41 percent tested (for general learning) at least one year below grade level, and 14 percent tested four years or more below grade. The teachers' research showed the following:

- 40 percent of their students read at least one book a month, and the best readers were those who read the most.
- When students were asked why people read, pleasure was the first choice, learning was second; only the low-level readers reported "to get a job."
- Only 30 percent reported ever being read to in middle school.
- 49 percent reported they had not been read to at home since third grade.
- 45 percent of high-ability readers read every night for pleasure; low-ability, 3 percent; overall, 60 percent reported *never* reading for pleasure.

As for the daily read-aloud program impacting the students' personal reading behavior:

- Students who read at home for pleasure increased from 40 percent to 75 percent.
- Students who *never* read for pleasure dropped from 60 percent to 34 percent.
- 89 percent responded that they like being read to, though this was less true of high-ability students who could access the books more quickly themselves.
- When asked what teachers should do to help students become better readers, 38 percent suggested requiring the students to read more, and 22 percent recommended more free reading time in class.

Based upon their classroom experiences, the teachers offered these guidelines for a middle school setting:

1. Don't expect immediate large gains in standardized test scores, but do expect changes in attitudes rather quickly.
2. Choose books you personally would enjoy hearing, eventually soliciting titles from the students.

3. Read aloud at the beginning of the class period; the clock frequently cuts off the book when scheduled for the end of the period.
4. Decide ahead of time *exactly* how much time you'll devote to the read-aloud each day.
5. Choose shorter books rather than longer ones.
6. Do lots of book talks about exciting books they could read.
7. Be courageous in book choices, choosing ones not always associated with the class subject, including humorous and even picture books.
8. Provide students who are visual learners with a copy of the book to follow along.
9. Occasionally read above their reading levels, but not too far above.
10. Read ahead, anticipating difficult vocabulary, or a good place to stop for the day.

What About Reading to Students Who Have Serious Discipline Problems?

My resident authority on this subject is Betty Frandsen out in the San Francisco Bay Area. Frandsen used to find it difficult to fall asleep at the end of a day. The day's events—involving her children and her job as an advertising executive in San Francisco—all seemed to collide in her head and keep her awake. Finally she took to using one of those tiny radio earplugs and it helped. Listening to talk radio at night shifted her focus and helped her drift off to sleep.

Ten miles away in Martinez, though, there were no earplugs. The night came every twenty-four hours and it was the worst part of the day for many of the 140 boys and girls locked in the Contra Costa Juvenile Hall, a holding pen for youngsters ranging in age from eight to eighteen. Each had been arrested for committing an adult crime, most already were veterans in the criminal justice system, many came from homes where they were badly abused, and most—though not all—were raised in extreme poverty. There were murderers, rapists, thieves, drug dealers—you name it, they were there.

Betty Frandsen, however, was unaware they existed until the day she saw the newspaper photo (three boys in a cell, two on cots and one sleeping on the floor) that accompanied a story on the institution's crowded conditions. Her own two children were on their own now, and she was looking for something to do with her spare time. "Maybe they could use me there as a volunteer," she thought. As it turned out, they could, assigning her to the "special needs" unit of residents who were too dangerous to have roommates, who often mutilated even themselves. All she would have to do was to play games with them, maybe some cards, and talk.

And before she knew it, they were telling her about the nights, how they hated the nights most of all, when they would lie in bed in the dark, alone, wondering why their parents never came to visit, why they wouldn't even accept their collect calls, thinking about the dreadful things they'd done to someone, and listening to the night noises that come with jails— the cries, the embittered curses, the moans, the pounding of someone's head on the wall.

And that's when Frandsen began to wonder, "If—maybe—bedtime stories might help. What if someone read bedtime stories through the intercom?" It sounded so simple, so childish even, yet so workable. "Here would be something that could help them get through the night, could make them end the day on a happy note, and they might even learn something in the process," she thought.

The authorities agreed to give it a try, and Frandsen rounded up some volunteer readers—a lawyer, a hypnotherapist, an energy consultant, a construction worker—for what they decided to call "The Late Show." The young adult librarian at the county library offered to choose some titles that would appeal to this specialized audience.

For some, it was the first time they had ever been read to, and for most it was their first bedtime reading. And it worked. Officials reported the nights became calmer, and the "special needs" residents were often overheard bragging to newcomers, "And you know what we got here—every night? 'The Late Show.' They read stories, novels and stuff, over the speakers." Several of the "graduates" doing time at the California Youth Authority wanted to know why they couldn't have the show there too. Fresno's Juvenile Hall has picked up on it and now has its own version, and so has the Dade County Juvenile Hall in Miami, Florida.

The fifteen Contra Costa volunteers read three nights a week, each having an audience of forty in the Hall's individual units. One of the Juvenile Hall's probation managers called the program remarkably successful in easing the stress at a critical time of day, and even provoking some of the residents to read. "In the U.S.," the manager noted, "this is looked at as an *innovative* program. Which is shocking. It manifests where we're at in this country—that reading bedtime stories to children is *innovative*!"[33]

Instead of waiting until children end up in juvenile detention centers, professionals in the state of Virginia organized a state-wide-read-aloud campaign in 1999. Read Aloud Virginia has two goals: (1) to motivate all children to develop a passion for reading; and (2) to encourage parents, caregivers, mentors, and teachers to be proactive and strive to develop healthy, resilient, and inquisitive children. They saw reading aloud as an easy and effective way for adults and children to connect.

RAV knows these goals won't be accomplished overnight, so their strategy is a ten-year plan. The brainchild of school psychologist Gary Anderson,[34] RAV was smart enough to build a broad foundation of state and community support that included:

Virginia Academy of Family Physicians
Virginia Chapter of American Academy of Pediatrics
Virginia Academy of School Psychologists
Virginia State Reading Association 3000
Virginia Education Media Association
Virginia PTA
Virginia Library Association
Virginia Board of Education

I Want to Give My High School Students Examples of People Whose Lives Have Changed Because of Reading—Where Can I Find Examples?

Like tens of thousands of other high school English teachers, Jim Burke daily confronted adolescents who found little or no sense in reading, whose preferred source of life and breath was the remote-control device. What Burke did in response a few years ago was most original.

Instead of retiring or becoming bitter, he wrote a letter to the readers of the *San Francisco Chronicle* in which he briefly told of his students' apathy toward books and solicited the readers' responses: How have books played a role in *your* life?

More than 400 letters poured into his Burlingame High School class, from people of all ages and walks of life. They came from second-graders, screenwriters, and lifers at San Quentin. Some were polished and eloquent, others were simply heart felt. The respondents drew upon happy childhoods and horrific ones. What they had in common was a genuine affection and primal need for books and print in their lives.

Burke has taken fifty of those letters and included them in a slim volume called *I Hear America Reading: Why We Read, What We Read*.[35] And in noticing the need for many of his letter-writers to share the names of their favorite books and the constant query from his students, "What's a good book to read?," Burke offers forty usable book lists. Consider: "Ten Books for People Who Think the World Is Absurd," "Ten Books We Should All Read Before Childhood Ends," or "Ten Best Films That Began as Books." (Do you get the feeling right away that *this* is a teacher who reads?)

Reading aloud one of those letters each day for a month will do more to sow the seeds of literacy than a year's worth of tests for your class.

Chapter 4

The Do's and Don'ts of Read-Aloud

Writing begins long before the marriage of pencil and paper. It begins with sounds, that is to say with words and simple clusters of words that are taken in by small children until they find themselves living in a world of vocables. If that world is rich and exciting, the transition to handling it in a new medium—writing—is made smoother. The first and conceivably the most important instructor in composition is the teacher, parent, or older sibling who reads aloud to the small child.

—Clifton Fadiman,
>Empty Pages: A Search for Writing
>Competence in School and Society

Do's

♦ Begin reading to children as soon as possible. The younger you start them, the easier and better it is.
♦ Use Mother Goose rhymes and songs to stimulate an infant's language and listening. Begin with simple black-and-white illustrations at first, and then boldly colored picture books to arouse children's curiosity and visual sense.
♦ With infants through toddlers, it is critically important to include in your readings those books that contain repetitions; as they mature, add predictable books.
♦ During repeat readings of a predictable book, occasionally stop at one of the key words or phrases and allow the listener to provide the word.
♦ Read as often as you and the child (or students) have time for.

♦ Set aside at least one traditional time each day for a story.

♦ Remember: The art of listening is an acquired one. It must be taught and cultivated gradually—it doesn't happen overnight.

♦ Start with picture books, with only a few sentences on the page, then gradually move to books with more and more text, fewer pictures, and build to chapter books and novels.

♦ Vary the length and subject matter of your readings.

♦ To encourage involvement, invite the child to turn pages for you when it is time.

♦ Before you begin to read, always say the name of the book, the author, and illustrator—no matter how many times you have read the book.

♦ The first time you read a book, discuss the illustration on the cover. "What do you think this is going to be about?"

♦ As you read, keep listeners involved by asking, "What do you think is going to happen next?"

♦ Follow through with your reading. If you start a book, it is your responsibility to continue it—unless it turns out to be a bad book. Don't leave the child or students hanging for three or four days between chapters and expect interest to be sustained.

♦ Occasionally read above children's intellectual levels and challenge their minds.

♦ Picture books can be read easily to a family of children widely separated in age. Novels, however, pose a challenge. If there are more than two years (and thus social and emotional differences) between the children, each child would benefit greatly if you read to him or her individually. This requires more effort on the part of the parents, but it will reap rewards in direct proportion to the effort expended. You will reinforce the specialness of each child.

♦ Avoid long descriptive passages until the child's imagination and attention span are capable of handling them. There is nothing wrong with shortening or eliminating them. Prereading helps to locate such passages, and they can then be marked with pencil in the margin.

♦ If the chapters are long or if you don't have enough time each day to finish an entire chapter, find a suspenseful spot at which to stop. Leave the audience hanging; they'll be counting the minutes until the next reading.

♦ Allow your listeners a few minutes to settle down and adjust their feet and minds to the story. If it's a novel, begin by asking what happened when you left off yesterday. Mood is an important factor in listening. An authoritarian "Now stop that and settle down! Sit up straight. Pay attention" doesn't create a receptive atmosphere.

♦ If you are reading a picture book, make sure the children can see the pictures easily. In school, with the children in a semicircle around you, seat yourself just slightly above them so that the children in the back row can see the pictures above the heads of the others.

♦ In reading a novel, position yourself where both you and the children are comfortable. In the classroom, whether you are sitting on the edge of your desk or standing, your head should be above the heads of your listeners for your voice to carry to the far side of the room. Do not read or stand in front of brightly lit windows. Backlighting strains the eyes of your audience.

♦ Remember that even sixth-grade students love a good picture book.

♦ Allow time for class and home discussion after reading a story. Thoughts, hopes, fears, and discoveries are aroused by a book. Allow them to surface and help the child to deal with them through verbal, written, or artistic expression if the child is so inclined. Do not turn discussions into quizzes or insist upon prying story interpretations from the child.

♦ Remember that reading aloud comes naturally to very few people. To do it successfully and with ease you must practice.

♦ Use plenty of expression when reading. If possible, change your tone of voice to fit the dialogue.

♦ Adjust your pace to fit the story. During a suspenseful part, slow down, and lower your voice. A lowered voice in the right place moves an audience to the edge of its chairs.

♦ The most common mistake in reading aloud—whether the reader is a seven-year-old or a forty-year-old—is reading too fast. Read slowly enough for the child to build mental pictures of what he just heard you read. Slow down enough for the children to see the pictures in the book without feeling hurried. Reading quickly allows no time for the reader to use vocal expression.

♦ Preview the book by reading it to yourself ahead of time. Such advance reading allows you to spot material you may wish to shorten, eliminate, or elaborate on.

♦ Bring the author to life, as well as his book. Consult *Something About the Author* at the library, and always read the information on your book's dust jacket. Either before or during the reading, tell your audience something about the author. Let them know that books are written by people, not by machines. You also can accomplish this by encouraging individual children (not the class collectively—many authors hate assembly correspondence) to write and share feelings about the book with the author. *Something About the Author* will provide an address, or you can write care of the publisher. It is important to enclose a self-addressed, stamped envelope *just in case* the author has time to respond. The child should understand from the start that the letter's purpose is not to receive a response. (See *Dear Mr. Henshaw* by Beverly Cleary for more on this touchy subject.)

♦ Add a third dimension to the book whenever possible. For example, have a bowl of blueberries ready to be eaten during or after the reading of Robert McCloskey's *Blueberries for Sal*; bring a harmonica and a lemon to class before reading McCloskey's *Lentil*.

♦ Every once in a while, when a child asks a question involving the text, make a point of looking up the answer in a reference book with the child. This greatly expands a child's knowledge base and nurtures library skills.

♦ Create a wall chart or back-of-the-bedroom-door book chart so the child or class can see how much has been read; images of caterpillars, snakes, worms, and trains work well for this purpose, with each link representing a book. Similarly, post a world or U.S. wall map on which small stickers can be attached to locations where your books have been set.

♦ When children are old enough to distinguish between library books and their own, start reading with a pencil in hand. When you and the child encounter a passage worth remembering, put a small mark—maybe a star—in the margin. Readers should interact with books, and one way is to acknowledge beautiful writing.

♦ Encourage relatives living far away to record stories on audiocassettes that can be mailed to the child.

♦ Reluctant readers or unusually active children frequently find it difficult to just sit and listen. Paper, crayons, and pencils allow them to keep their hands busy while listening. (You doodle while talking on the telephone, don't you?)

♦ Follow the suggestion of Dr. Caroline Bauer and post a reminder sign by your door: "Don't Forget Your *Flood* Book." Analogous to emergency rations in case of natural disasters, these books should be taken along in the car, or even stored like spares in the trunk. A few chapters from "flood" books can be squeezed into traffic jams on the way to the beach or long waits at the dentist's office.

♦ Always have a supply of books for the babysitter to share with the child and make it understood that "reading aloud" comes with the job and is preferable to the TV.

♦ Fathers should make an extra effort to read to their children. Because the vast majority of primary-school teachers are women, young boys often associate reading with women and schoolwork. And just as unfortunately, too many fathers would rather be seen playing catch in the driveway with their sons than taking them to the library. It is not by chance that most of the students in U.S. remedial reading classes are boys. A father's early involvement with books and reading can do much to elevate books to at least the same status as sports in a boy's estimation.

♦ Arrange for time each day, in the classroom or in the home, for the child to read by himself (even if "read" only means turning pages and looking at the pictures). All your read-aloud motivation goes for naught if the time is not available to put it into practice.

♦ Lead by example. Make sure your children see you reading for pleasure other than at read-aloud time. Share with them your enthusiasm for whatever you are reading.

♦ When children wish to read to you, it is better for the book to be too easy than too hard, just as a beginner's bicycle is better too small rather than too big.

♦ Encourage older children to read to younger ones, but make this a *part-time,* not a full-time, substitution for you. Remember: The adult is the *ultimate* role model.

♦ Regulate the amount of time children spend in front of the television. Research shows that after about ten TV hours a week, a child's school scores begin to drop. Excessive television viewing is habit-forming and damaging to a child's development.

♦ When children are watching television, closed-captioning should be activated along with sound. But for older children who know how to read but are lazy about it, turn the volume off and captioning on.

Don'ts

♦ Don't read stories that you don't enjoy yourself. Your dislike will show in the reading, and that defeats your purpose.

♦ Don't continue reading a book once it is obvious that it was a poor choice. Admit the mistake and choose another. Make sure, however, that you've given the book a fair chance to get rolling; some, like *Tuck Everlasting,* start slower than others. (You can avoid the problem by pre-reading at least part of the book yourself.)

♦ If you are a teacher, don't feel you have to tie every book to class work. Don't confine the broad spectrum of literature to the narrow limits of the curriculum.

♦ Don't overwhelm your listener. Consider the intellectual, social, and emotional level of your audience in making a read-aloud selection. Never read above a child's emotional level.

+ Don't select a book that many of the children already have heard or seen on television. Once a novel's plot is known, much of their interest is lost. You can, however, read a book and view the video afterward. That's a good way for children to see how much more can be portrayed in print than on film.

+ In choosing novels for reading aloud, avoid books that are heavy with dialogue; they are difficult reading aloud *and* listening. All those indented paragraphs and quotations make for easy *silent* reading. The reader sees the quotations marks and knows it is a new voice, a different person speaking—but the listener doesn't. And if the writer fails to include a notation at the end of the dialogue, like "said Mrs. Murphy," the audience has no idea who said what.

+ Don't be fooled by awards. Just because a book won an award doesn't guarantee that it will make a good read-aloud. In most cases, a book award is given for the quality of the writing, not for its read-aloud qualities.

+ Don't start reading if you are not going to have enough time to do it justice. Having to stop after one or two pages only serves to frustrate, rather than stimulate, the child's interest in reading.

+ Don't get too comfortable while reading. A reclining or slouching position is most apt to bring on drowsiness. A reclining position sends an immediate message to the heart: slow down. With less blood being pumped, less oxygen reaches the brain—thus drowsiness.

+ Don't be unnerved by questions during the reading, particularly from very young children in your own family. If the question is obviously not for the purpose of distracting or postponing bedtime, answer the question patiently. There is no time limit for reading a book, but there is a time limit on a child's inquisitiveness. Foster that curiosity with patient answers—then resume your reading. Classroom questions, however, need to be held until the end. With twenty children all deciding to ask questions to impress the teacher, you might never reach the end of the book.

+ Don't impose interpretations of a story upon your audience. A story can be just plain enjoyable, no reason necessary, and still give you plenty to talk about. The highest literacy gains occur with children who have access to discussions following a story (see page 70, chapter 3).

+ Don't confuse quantity with quality. Reading to your child for ten minutes, with your full attention and enthusiasm, may very well last longer in the child's mind than two hours of solitary television viewing.

+ Don't use the book as a threat—"If you don't pick up your room, no story tonight!" As soon as your child or class sees that you've turned the book into a weapon, they'll change their attitude about books from positive to negative.

• Don't try to compete with television. If you say, "Which do you want, a story or TV?" they will usually choose the latter. That is like saying to a nine-year-old, "Which do you want, vegetables or a donut?" Since *you* are the adult, *you* choose. "The television goes off at eight-thirty in this house. If you want a story before bed, that's fine. If not, that's fine, too. But no television after eight-thirty." But don't let books appear to be responsible for depriving the children of viewing time.

Chapter 5

Sustained Silent Reading:
Reading-Aloud's Natural Partner

Those who do not develop the pleasure reading habit simply don't have a chance—they will have a very difficult time reading and writing at a level high enough to deal with the demands of today's world.

—Stephen Krashen,
The Power of Reading

AMONG the many purposes of reading aloud, a primary one is to motivate the child to read independently for pleasure. In academic terms, such reading is called SSR—Sustained Silent Reading. Take a book, a newspaper, a magazine, and enjoy it! No interruptions for questions, assessments, or reports; just read for pleasure. The concept operates under a variety of pseudonyms, including DEAR time (Drop Everything And Read); DIRT time (Daily Individual Reading Time); SQUIRT time (Sustained Quiet Un-Interrupted Reading Time); and FVR (Free Voluntary Reading).

This chapter will be devoted to SSR in school as well as at home. I'll also examine a variety of topics associated with silent reading: reading incentive programs (like "Accelerated Reader" and "Reading Counts"); teachers' reading habits; junk versus the classics; and the "dumber in the summer" syndrome. At the moment, the most controversial of those topics is the computerized reading incentive programs that reward (bribe, say the critics) students for reading. Do such programs help or harm? We'll explore the issues.

Because we adults have done this thing called reading for so much of our lives, we take many of its facets for granted. Children do not, as evidenced by the story told to me by Lee Sullivan Hill, of Clarendon Hills, Illinois. Her son Colin came upon her reading silently to herself, and asked, "What are you doing?"

"Reading," she answered.

"Then why aren't you making any noise?"

So she explained how people read *to themselves* as well as to others, like when she reads to him. Hearing that, the light dawned for Colin. "So *that's* what Daddy does!" recalling when he had seen his father reading silently to himself—in fact, practicing SSR. Until it is explained, silent reading is sometimes a mystery to young children.

SSR is based upon a single simple principle: Reading is a skill—and the more you use it, the better you get at it. Conversely, the less you use it, the more difficult it is.[1]

How effective is SSR? When the International Association for the Evaluation of Educational Achievement (IEA) compared the reading skills of 210,000 students from thirty-two different countries, it found the highest scores (regardless of income level) among children:[2]

+ Who were read to by their teachers daily
+ Who read the most pages for pleasure daily

Moreover, the frequency of SSR had a marked impact on scores: Children who had it daily scored much higher than those who had it only once a week. American NAEP assessments found the identical pattern for the nearly twenty-five years NAEP has been testing hundreds of thousands of U.S. students.[3] The evidence for reading aloud to children *and* SSR is overwhelming—yet most children are neither read to nor experience SSR in the course of a school day.

For several years at the end of the 1990s, I surveyed 2,887 teachers from approximately thirty states, in every region of the country. These teachers averaged fourteen years' experience, and 95 percent taught elementary grades—the most critical years for reading. Among the questions I asked: Does their school have any form of SSR in place as a matter of school policy? The response was 60 percent *no*, 40 percent *yes*. This is supported by the 1992 NAEP report showing that more than half of all students have no SSR. While it defies logic, it helps explain why reading scores have stagnated for thirty years and why we have so few lifetime readers.

Between School and Home Time, How Much Do Students Read?

The majority of students don't read very much, a fact conceded by most teachers and unknown to most parents. Even worse, they don't read much when they grow up either, as you'll see later in this chapter.

Two comprehensive investigations of how 155 capable fifth-grade students spend their afterschool time showed that 90 percent of those students devoted only 1 percent of their free time to reading and 30 percent to watching television. Indeed, 50 percent read for an average of four minutes or less a day, 30 percent read two minutes a day, and 10 percent read nothing at all.[4] When students were ranked by reading scores, those in the 90th percentile had read 2.25 million more words than the students in the 10th percentile (see chart).

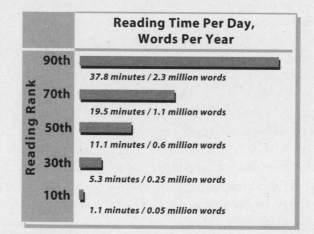

"Well," says the parent, "they may not be reading much outside school but they certainly must be reading during the five hours they're in school!" Nice thought, but not true. The most comprehensive look at the American classroom is John Goodlad's seven-year study, *A Place Called School,* in which he reported that only 6 percent of class time is occupied by the act of reading in the elementary school, 3 percent in the middle school, and 2 percent in the high school.[5] (Yes, there are exceptions to these averages. If your child or school is the exception, consider yourself fortunate.)

If the majority *learn* to read but don't read, we must ask: *Why* are they not reading? The only logical answers are either because they don't like it or because they don't have the time. There are no other major reasons. Eliminate those two factors and you've solved the American literacy dilemma. Reading aloud goes to work on the first factor and SSR attacks the second.

Here is an example reinforcing the "time" factor in reading as an accrued skill. The highly acclaimed KIPP Academies have gained fame and heavy private funding in urban centers because their students—most of whom were initially at-risk—consistently score at the top on standardized tests. What's different about the academies' curriculum? The difference is in amount of *time* they spend in school and reading: 70 percent more time than other students, from 7:30 A.M. to 5:00 P.M. daily, as well as Saturday and summers.[6]

Is SSR a New Idea?

Originally proposed in the early 1960s by Lyman C. Hunt, Jr., of the University of Vermont, SSR received some of its most important support from the research of reading experts Robert and Marlene McCracken.[7] Experimenting with a variety of techniques and schools, the McCrackens recommend the following structures for SSR programs:

1. Children should read to themselves for a *limited* amount of time. Teachers and parents should adapt this to their individual class or family and adjust it with increasing maturity. Ten or fifteen minutes is the common choice for the classroom.
2. Each student should select his own book, magazine, or newspaper. No changing during the period is permitted. All materials must be chosen before the SSR period begins.
3. The teacher or parent must read also, setting an example. This cannot be stressed too strongly.
4. No reports are required of the student. No records are kept.

The single most interesting and comprehensive study ever done on SSR is Dr. Stephen Krashen's compact hundred-page volume *The Power of Reading.*[8] It is inconceivable that anyone could read this book and *not* resolve to incorporate SSR into the school day.

Krashen, graduate professor of education at the University of Southern California, is one of the most accessible, stimulating, intelligent, and entertaining researchers in language and reading—certainly the *only* one who incorporates all of those characteristics in his work. If I could require one professional book to be read by all teachers and librarians, *The Power of Reading* would be my choice. Krashen incorporates all the language-acquisition and reading research he has done over the last twenty years, along with hundreds of studies by others, and builds an unimpeachable case for SSR—which he calls FVR (free voluntary reading).

In examining 41 comparison studies that have been done between SSR students and traditional language-arts students, Krashen found 93 percent of the SSR students did as well as or better than students having no SSR time. His examination of recreational reading's impact on spelling, writing, and language skills may provoke many educators to reassess previous positions.

What Are the Exact Benefits of SSR?

The benefits are many and vary by the individual, but in its simplest form SSR allows a person to read long enough and far enough so the act of reading becomes automatic. If one must stop to concentrate on each word—sounding it out and searching for meaning—then fluency is lost along with meaning. It is also fatiguing. Being able to do it automatically is the goal.[9] To achieve this, the Commission on Reading (*Becoming a Nation of Readers*) recommended two hours a week of independent reading. Where do you find that time? The commission recommended less time be spent on skill sheets and workbooks.[10]

Because it is supposed to be informal and free of grades, SSR also provides students with a new perspective on reading—as a form of recreation. Judging from educated adults who come home each evening and think they can only relax by watching television, there is a critical need for such lessons in childhood.

On the secondary level, SSR may not cause an immediate change in student skills (no "quick fix"), but it can result in positive changes in attitude toward the library, voluntary reading, assigned reading, and the im-

Research clearly shows the more you read the better you read.

portance of reading. This affects the amount students read and thus their facility with the process.[11] A striking example of this is the Lewenberg Middle School, discussed in chapter 1 on page 22.

The speed and ease of student reading has been a matter of growing concern among college faculties in recent years. In a study of college remedial courses, a marked increase was found in the enrollment numbers for such classes, with the students' greatest deficiency being *reading speed* and *comprehension*. Most secondary English teachers are trained to teach not reading skills but literature analysis and interpretation, so if speed and comprehension are not mastered in elementary levels, the deficiency will still be present when the student attempts college-level work.[12] Until students spend more time meeting words in context (reading), there can be no improvement in comprehension or reading speed.

Younger readers, however, show significant improvement in both attitude and skills with SSR.[13] "Poor readers," points out Professor Richard Allington of the State University of New York, "when given ten minutes a day to read, initially will achieve five hundred words and quickly increase that amount in the same period as proficiency grows."

By third grade, SSR can be the student's most important vocabulary builder, more so than with basal textbooks or even daily oral language. The Commission on Reading noted: "Basal readers and textbooks do not offer the same richness of vocabulary, sentence structure, or literary form as do trade books. . . . A diet consisting only of basal stories probably will not prepare children well to deal with real literature."[14] Indeed, about half of the 3,000 most commonly used words are not even included in K–6 basals.[15]

As shown in the chart on page 17, printed material introduces three to six times more rare words than conversation does.

The *1998 Reading Report Card for the Nation and the States*[16] tested more than 20,000 students at fourth-, eighth-, and twelfth-grade levels. When surveyed on how often they were allowed to read books of their own choosing (SSR) on a *daily* basis versus *less than weekly*, the following pattern appeared:

	daily	*less than weekly*
Grade 4	56%	18%
Grade 8	21%	53%
Grade 12	6%	83%

Thus, the higher one goes in school, the less time there is to read for pleasure and the fewer choices one has. Now let's examine the fourth-graders, comparing their reading scores on the NAEP exams with how often they were given free reading time in class:

	daily free reading	once/twice a week	less than weekly
reading score	224	217	208

Clearly, independent reading lifts reading proficiency.

What Would Cause SSR to Fail?

The McCrackens report that most instances where SSR fails are due to:

+ Teachers (or aides) who are supervising instead of reading
+ Classrooms that lack enough SSR reading materials

The McCrackens cite the teacher as a critical role model in SSR, reporting widespread imitation by students of the teacher's reading habits.[17] Students in one class noticed the teacher interrupting her reading to look up words in the dictionary and began doing the same. When a junior high teacher began to read the daily newspaper each day, the class began doing the same.

When teachers talk about what they are reading or describe a spine-tingling section of their book, students are quick to follow suit and share their reaction. By doing this, the McCrackens note, "they are teaching attitudes and skills; they are teaching children that reading is communication with an author, an assimilation of and reaction to an author's ideas." Indeed, they are simply doing what Oprah Winfrey has done so effectively with her book club (see chapter 7).

How Does SSR Help Remedial Readers?

Though poor readers are apt to be the biggest resisters to SSR, they also can be the biggest beneficiaries because of the profound differences between classes for good readers and those for low-level readers. Good readers read three times as many words per day, with 70 percent of their reading done silently, while the poor readers do their 70 percent orally. A study of 14 high- and low-achievement schools showed a negative correlation to the amount of oral reading but a large positive connection to the amount of silent reading. Having to do large amounts of oral reading by poorer readers slows them down and widens the gap between themselves and better readers. This is only exacerbated when the teacher interrupts to make corrections, which happens more frequently with poor readers.[18] SSR offers a welcome respite from the interruptions, assessments, and oral performances. Poor readers will be free to read a book for the purpose for which it was written—to be enjoyed and/or absorbed.

Strangely, the benefits of SSR are seldom advertised to the students. In all the SSR research I've read, that one piece of common sense is missing. When Reni Herda, a graduate education student at the University of Southern California, took a series of substitute teaching days in a small school district, she asked a high school senior why she wasn't reading during the SSR period. "It's a waste of time," the girl griped. "Why do we even do it, anyhow?"

When Herda explained the purpose of SSR, as well as its impact on vocabulary, grammar, and spelling, the girl's attitude changed, and she remarked that they should have explained it that way in the first place. While the majority of seniors were reading, most of the small number who were not reading expressed similar surprise at the underlying purpose for SSR.[19]

While all students should receive an annual explanation for SSR, it is especially important for reluctant teen readers who have been led to believe it is senseless to read for any reason but to attain a grade or to answer questions.

Since even the term Sustained Silent Reading might sound imposing to reluctant readers, perhaps more schools should follow the example of Beverly Holmes, a teacher at Potter-Burns School in Pawtucket, Rhode Island. She calls her SSR time "The easiest time of the day." Each day after recess, she settles behind her desk and asks her second-graders, "What is it time for now?" "The easiest time of the day!" they respond in unison, and then settle into SSR.

Does SSR Work with Learning-Disabled Students?

It does, and let me give you several examples. Martha Efta taught a primary-level class of educable mentally retarded children in Westlake, Ohio. The children, ranging in age from seven to ten, were frequently hyperactive and nonreaders. When she heard of SSR in a graduate course, she was cautious about the idea despite the professor's wholehearted support for it. After all, she thought, the experts were talking about normal children, not the retarded.

With some trepidation, she explained the procedures to her students and reshaped the rules to fit her classroom. Because of their short attention spans, she allowed each student to choose as many as three books or magazines for the period. Students were allowed to sit any way and in any place they chose in the room. Efta initially kept the program to three minutes in length, then gradually increased it to thirteen minutes over a period of weeks. This was the class's limit.

"From the onset [of SSR]," Efta explained, "the students have demonstrated some exciting and favorable behavior changes—such as independent decision-making, self-discipline, sharing . . . and broadened reading interests. The enthusiastic rush to select their day's reading materials following noon recess is indicative of the children's interest and eagerness for SSR. The children seem to delight in the adultlike responsibility of selecting their own reading matter."[20] Efta, who was in my audience ten years ago, told me she still does SSR with her students, as well as reading aloud chapter and picture books to them each day. Ruth Stiles Gannett's series, beginning with *My Father's Dragon,* is a particular favorite of her students. (See the Treasury listing in the short novels section.)

The other example is not a result of classroom SSR but a generic form of it—reading intensively for oneself about a subject of deep personal interest. Dr. Rosalie Fink of Leslie College has done some encouraging research in this area, using extensive interviews with twelve very successful adults, all of whom are *severe dyslexics.* All twelve learned to read about three to four years later than their childhood peers, and all eventually achieved the highest levels of literacy. Not only were all twelve college graduates, most graduated from Ivy League schools, one was a Nobel laureate, three were M.D.s and two were Ph.D.s.[21]

Beyond their dyslexia, the twelve had one thing in common that became the key to overcoming their reading disability. During childhood, each developed a *passionate interest* in a particular subject that required reading to find out more. Fink notes, "By reading in-depth about a single domain of knowledge, each became a virtual 'little expert' about a subject," with some of the subjects eventually leading to careers.

In their extensive reading on the subject, they continually encountered material or words they already knew and had to filter from words they didn't know—which they also encountered. Thus they learned to skim and surmise and conclude. The more they read, the stronger became both their skills and the pleasure they found in the process. This is the same thing accomplished by children who fall in love with a particular series of books (Nancy Drew, Harry Potter, etc.).

In short, find out what interests the learning-disabled child—music, art, sports, dogs, horses, insects—and feed the interest with every book and magazine you can find. The need for intensive reading makes it critically important for the home or classroom library to have a broad cross section of reading materials. It is only by wading into this stream of print that such a child will discover the subject that will pull him deeper into print. But someone must give the student the free time in which to do the exploratory reading. (See also the "home run book" concept later in this chapter.)

What About Summer-School Reading Programs?

Further proof of SSR's benefits is found in the "summer gap." Many parents, especially those whose children are having difficulty with school, see summertime as a school vacation and take it literally. "Everyone needs a vacation, for goodness sake. He needs to get away from school and relax. Next year will be a new start." That attitude can be extremely detrimental, especially to a poor reader.

There is an axiom in education that "you get dumber in the summer." A two-year study of 3,000 students in Atlanta, Georgia, attempted to see if it was true. They found that *everyone*—top students and poor students—learns more slowly in the summer. Some, though, do worse than slow down; they actually go into *reverse*.[22]

Top students' scores rise between the end of one school year and the beginning of the next. Conversely, the bottom 25 percent (largely urban poor) lose most of what they gained the previous school year. Average students (middle 50 percent) make no gains during the summer but lose nothing either—except in the widening gap between themselves and the top students.

When social promotion was ended in many states at the beginning of the millennium, most urban districts tried to use summer school to shrink the large numbers of students who were threatened with retention: Pass summer school and you'll be promoted. This regimen amounts to 120 hours of class spread over five weeks. Chicago's summer-school program, cited by President Clinton as a national model, had only a 56 percent passing rate, and many of those students "were at risk of failure again one year later."[23] It is lunacy, if not fraud, to suggest that students can make up in 120 hours for the thirty-two million words missed in earlier years[24] and years of print deprivation in their homes and classrooms. Ongoing daily SSR, year after year, is equal to or better than an ongoing summer-school reading program. (Incidentally, the original intention of summer school was not to remediate but to keep children out of trouble in urban areas where there were no summer jobs after the passage of child labor laws.)

How to prevent the traditional summer reading gap? The research gives no support to summer *school,* but a great deal to summer *reading*—reading *to* the child and reading *by* the child. Most libraries have summer reading incentive programs, so make sure your child is enrolled and participates. And take your child on field trips—even if you just visit local places like a fire station, the museum, or the zoo, and talk and listen. In that regard, one peculiar piece of information appeared in the "summer gap" research that is worth noting. Among those who suffered little or no summer loss, reading was a prevalent factor, but so also was the availability of a bicycle.[25] Although the research does not expand upon this, I have two immediate reactions:

1. Many libraries would be inaccessible to certain children without a bicycle.
2. In evaluating adults who are unable to read on at least an eighth-grade level, teachers at community learning centers point to a lack of decoding skills and sight vocabulary, and also to a shallow knowledge of the world around them. They know only what they have experienced. In other words, they haven't *traveled* much. There may be a strong connection between children who have the opportunity (via a bicycle) to move beyond the narrowness of their own family or community and the acquisition of new vocabulary and background knowledge.

What If You Let Kids Read Anything and Eased Up on the Tests?

One case offers a dramatic example of learning by simply reading—and maybe the Guinness world record for SSR: that of Robert Allen.[26] Fatherless at birth in 1949 and abandoned by his mother at age six, Allen was raised by his grandfather, three great-aunts, and a great-uncle living in a farmhouse without plumbing in the hills of West Tennessee. There Robert Allen stayed for the next twenty-six years, never attending school, or riding a bicycle or going to a movie theater or having a single playmate his own age.

When he was seven, one of his aunts began reading to him—especially Donald Duck comic books—and soon taught him to read for himself. His grandfather then taught him to write. He began reading the Bible to his blind aunt. Since his relatives were so elderly, one of them was always bedridden, and young Robert's duty was to take care of them. Looking to fill the vacant hours, at age twelve he picked up an old copy of Shakespeare's plays and read it through in one sitting. Soon he was scavenging yard sales for old books, magazines, and comics. Books became his playmates, his escape from the loving but grim reality of where he was.

He read anything and everything until he discovered the county library. There the world's classics awaited him and he waded into them, even teaching himself to read Greek and French, until he read every book in the library. Not surprisingly, the librarian encouraged him to pursue a college education, and in 1981, at age thirty-two, he showed up at Bethel College, a small Presbyterian college just fifteen miles from his farmhouse. His placement test showed he knew more than almost every faculty member, and they had him skip freshman year.

Graduating summa cum laude in three years (only typing kept him from straight A's in his senior year), he went on to Vanderbilt University, where he earned master's and doctoral degrees in English. Today he teaches at the University of Tennessee-Martin. For a guy who came from the Tennessee backwoods, where they weren't exactly speaking the King's English, who missed all those childhood vocabulary tests and book reports, who did no seat work except SSR for twenty-five straight years, and, by my calculations, missed at least 8,000 worksheets, he certainly did all right for himself.

Among the things Dr. Robert Allen's situation might prove, none is stronger than the case it makes for pure, unadulterated, uninterrupted, random, and purposeful reading.

Will SSR Work in the Home as Well?

The same SSR principles apply in the home as in the classroom. Indeed, considering that by the end of eighth grade, a child has spent only 9,000 hours in school compared to 95,000 outside school, it behooves parents to involve themselves in home SSR before they challenge a teacher on "why Jesse isn't doing better in reading this year."

But remember, if the classroom teacher is pivotal, so, too, is the parent; don't tell your child to go read for fifteen minutes while *you* watch television. You can, of course, tailor SSR to fit your family. For children who are not used to reading for more than brief periods of time it is important at first to limit SSR to ten or fifteen minutes. Later, when they are used to reading in this manner and are more involved in books, the period can be extended—often at the child's request. As in the classroom, it is important to have a variety of available material—magazines, newspapers, novels, picture books. A weekly trip to the library can do much to fill this need. The last three decades of NAEP reading research shows that the more kinds of reading material in a home (books, magazines, newspapers, etc.), the higher the child's reading scores in school. (See chart.)[27]

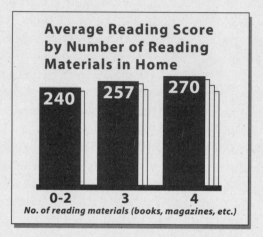

Average Reading Score by Number of Reading Materials in Home

240 — 0-2

257 — 3

270 — 4

No. of reading materials (books, magazines, etc.)

I should also note that the "Three B's" (Books, Book baskets, and Bed lamps) I mentioned earlier (page 43) are invaluable to the success of family SSR.

The time selected for family SSR is also important. Involve everyone in the decision, if possible. Bedtime seems to be the most popular time, perhaps because the child does not have to give up any activity for it except sleeping—and most children gladly surrender that.

Won't Requiring Children to Read Eventually Turn Them Off?

When I'm doing a parent program, I ask: "How many of you have ever *forced* a child to do something—like pick up his room or brush his teeth?" The question receives a positive response from 80 percent of the audience.

I continue, "Yes, we can all concede that it's easier for everyone if the child can be *enticed* into doing those things instead of forced, but sometimes we have neither the time nor the patience.

"Now let's take it further: How many of you think you should ever force a child to *read*?" Fewer hands go up.

The reason parents avoid forcing reading is the fear the child will grow to hate reading and eventually stop. How true is that? Ten-year-olds who are forced to brush their teeth or change their underwear—do they stop doing those things when they grow up? No. So why do we think forcing children to read will kill the love of reading?

Of course, the better word to use here is *require* as opposed to *force*. Nearly all children are *required* to attend school, and all adults are *required* to observe the speed limit, but few end up hating it because of the requirement. The way to take the sting out of the "requirement" is to make the requirement so appealing and delicious as to become a pleasure—and that's where reading aloud comes into play.

In chapter 8, I open with the story of Sonya Carson, a single parent who required her two sons to obtain library cards and read two books a week. Today one is an engineer and the other is a preeminent pediatric brain surgeon. Freak situation? Let's see.

Dr. Michael DeBakey is the most legendary heart surgeon in medical history. Not only did he found the National Library of Medicine (now known as the National Heart, Lung, and Blood Institute), he also invented the Mobile Army Surgical Hospital—the M.A.S.H. unit upon which the movie and TV show were based. DeBakey's parents were self-educated Lebanese immigrants to Louisiana.[28] One *requirement* in the DeBakey home was for each child to visit the library once a week, borrow a book, and read it—one book a week. One day Michael found the best book he'd ever seen, but the librarian wouldn't let him borrow it. When his father learned the *Encyclopedia Britannica* was not for circulation, he bought the family one of its own.

No, I'm not suggesting that requiring children to read will make them all surgeons, but it certainly puts them on the right track. They don't have a chance for higher levels of achievement without high-level reading skills. Where nothing is asked, usually nothing is received. In offices where punctuality is not required, people seldom arrive on time. So how to require reading and keep it pleasure-oriented? First, remember that pleasure is more often caught than taught. Next:

+ Make sure you, the adult role model, are seen reading daily. It works even better if you read at the same time as the child.
+ For young children, looking at the pictures in books and turning pages qualifies as "reading."
+ Allow children to choose the books they wish to read to themselves, even if they don't meet your high standards.
+ Set some time parameters, short at first and longer as children get older and read more.
+ Newspapers and magazines should count toward reading time—their vocabulary is often as sophisticated as that of books (see page 17)

The self-selection, self-interest factor is important here. Let children read what interests them. Those school summer reading lists require them to read what interests the faculty.

If this idea of a reading requirement still puts you off, think about this: If you require a child to pick up his room or brush his teeth but don't require him to read, then it's obvious you think household and personal hygiene are more important than the child's brain.

How Is Required SSR Different from Dreaded Summer Reading Lists?

The difference is the freedom of choice involved in what you read (free reading SSR), versus the book list. There are two schools of thought here:

1. Structure (reading list) provides the undergirding necessary for successful climbing and saves time and effort. If you become interested in paleontology, it would be helpful to have a list of great books on the subject. Lists, however, always work better when accompanied by an enthusiastic endorsement from a living human being. "Class, this is the book that turned my brother from a nonreader into an avid reader!" Summer reading lists unaccompanied by book-talks are like an Oprah book list without Oprah.
2. Unrestricted free reading avoids forced feeding and allows for personal choice (a sense of ownership) and the joy of discovery. It also frees the student from the cultural biases of the faculty or parent, who may choose a narrower and stuffier range of books.

Since a major portion of a school day consists of books that are preselected by the faculty, I side with the second option here—plain old free reading, with the stipulation that the school or classroom library be well stocked with a rich cross section of subject matter that is not restricted to bound volumes. As the chart on page 17 shows, newspapers and magazines often have a richer vocabulary than books, and provide a broader menu of subjects.

On another score, wide-ranging reading is about the only way we'll ever solve the age-old dilemma of students' dismal history scores. Those who think the scores are merely a reflection of "today's watered-down curriculum" should consider the following headlines:

Ignorance of U.S. History Shown
By College Freshmen[29]

America's Students Know Little About
U.S. History, Survey Says[30]

Both headlines appeared in *The New York Times,* in 1943 and 1995, respectively. If it's any consolation, today's history student appears to be just as dumb as yesterday's! (How is this explained by those folks who complain that today's teachers are poorly prepared?) And lest you think the problem is peculiar to American students, try this one:

Winston *Who*? Pupils Cannot Name War Heroes[31]

That one came from the front page of London's *Sunday Times,* 1995, reporting a British study of sixteen hundred students (ages eleven to fourteen) that showed 25 percent couldn't identify Hitler; 60 percent didn't know what the Holocaust was; and 30 percent could not identify Winston Churchill.

Since it is almost universally agreed that awful history textbooks cannot solve the problem,[32] how can a nation follow Churchill's adage, "The farther backward you can look, the farther forward you are likely to see"?

First, understand that a sense of history is not achieved by age twelve or twenty. It arrives over a wide span of years from life experience and wide reading. This is supported by the results of a multiple-choice test consisting of thirty-four high school–level American history questions given to 556 seniors at leading American colleges and universities in 1999.[33] Even with a few give-away questions about contemporary culture (*Who is Snoop Doggy Dog?*), the average score was only 53 percent. The question with the *lowest* number of correct answers was:

What was the source of the following phrase:

"Government of the people, by the people, for the people"?
  a. The speech "I have a dream"
  b. Declaration of Independence
  c. U.S. Constitution
  d. Gettysburg Address

Seventy-eight percent of the college seniors failed to identify (d) as the correct answer. So how would wide-ranging reading solve this problem?

1. I took that history exam when it was reprinted in *The New York Times*[34] and passed it with an 88 percent score. Yet I have not had an American

history course since my senior year of high school (forty years ago), and I took a *single* history course as a college freshman.

2. David McCullough is one of America's most widely recognized historians, author of *Truman* (among others), twice a National Book Award winner for history and biography, a Yale alumnus, and past president of the American Society of Historians. Those aren't bad credentials for someone who *never took a history course after high school.*[35]

Though my humble but more than passing score on the exam should not be mentioned in the same breath with McCullough's achievements, our knowledge of history easily can be attributed to an ongoing relationship with the printed word: daily reading of newspapers, magazines, and books—fiction and nonfiction. A daily reader coming across Lincoln's words ("of the people, by the people . . .") again and again, or seeing recurring references to Churchill in books and magazines, will absorb such words and information, retaining them more easily than if they came from a textbook.

As a passing note, the aforementioned group of college seniors spent more time surfing the Internet than any generation in history, yet suffered from low scores. This does not indicate a low IQ but how little substantive reading they are doing online. Most of their time is spent at entertainment sites—music, games, and chat rooms.

What About Those Computerized "Reading Incentive" Programs?

Twenty years ago when *The Read-Aloud Handbook* was first published, the idea of computerized reading-incentive programs would have sounded like science fiction. Today it is one of the most hotly debated concepts among both educators and parents: Should children read for "intrinsic" rewards (the pleasure of the book) or should they be enticed to read for "extrinsic" rewards—prizes or rewards (or grades)?

Advantage Learning System's *Accelerated Reader*[36] and Scholastic's *Reading Counts,*[37] the two incentive industry leaders, work this way: The school library contains a core collection of popular and traditional children's books, each rated by difficulty (the harder the book, the more points it has). Accompanying the books is a computer program that poses questions after the student has read the book. Passing the computer quiz earns points for the student reader, which can be redeemed for prizes like school T-shirts, privileges, or items donated by local businesses. Both programs strongly endorse SSR as an integral part of their program and require substantial library collections. Although both Accelerated Reader and Reading Counts have expanded their scope beyond "incentives" to include substantial student management and assessment tools, the area that catches the most attention (and heat) is the incentive points.

The response of most children and schools has been overwhelmingly positive, but parents, teachers, and librarians are sometimes divided. Let's first consider some of the positives I've encountered around the nation:

- Students read a significantly larger number of books at all levels as a result of incentives.
- Students tend to choose more complicated books to obtain more points.
- With the increase in usage and demand, the library now contains a larger and newer book collection.
- The critical need for a school librarian is more universally recognized by the faculty and administration.
- More schools use SSR/DEAR time for students to read the books.
- Students discover favorite authors through their expanded reading time and effort.
- The computer test is a fairly accurate measure of whether the child read the book (as opposed to book reports that are easily fudged).
- Because of the increased reading time and print environment, student reading scores improve.

Before considering the negatives, allow me to offer a note about those positives. I've had educators tell me that none of the incentives is necessary if the right things are done by the school and classroom teacher. *Absolutely true!* The aforementioned positives have been accomplished in various places without electronic incentive programs, places where there are first-class school and classroom libraries, where the teachers motivate children by reading aloud to them, give book talks, and include SSR/DEAR time as an essential part of the daily curriculum. And the money that would have gone to the computer tests went instead to building a larger library collection.

Unfortunately, such instances are rare. Where the scores are low, oftentimes so is the teacher's knowledge of children's literature, the library collection is meager to dreadful, and drill and skill supplant SSR/DEAR time. (Consider the blight of empty bookshelves in urban and rural schools noted in chapter 6.)

Another flawed assumption is that teachers themselves are avid readers.

Wrong again. Some aren't even occasional readers, as Jan Lieberman found in January of 2000. It was the height of the Harry Potter craze, when the first three titles were setting a record for sales in the twentieth century and resting at the top of *The New York Times* and *London Times* bestseller lists. Lieberman, a long-time children's literature teacher and librarian in California, did a pre-conference seminar at a prestigious reading conference. Most of the teachers attending the conference paid their own way and gave up a weekend, so one could argue they are among the more motivated educators.

Holding aloft one of the Harry Potter books, Lieberman asked her audience, "How many of you have read at least one of the Harry Potter books?" To her surprise, only two of the forty-two teachers and school librarians raised a hand. In effect, the questions asked by the computer after a child has read a book may be mechanical or electronic in nature, but at least the computer has "read the book." Forty out of forty-two teachers couldn't ask any kind of intelligent question about Harry Potter because they hadn't read it.

In response to the above anecdote, one teacher sent me the following note: "I am one of those who have not read Harry Potter. I have been a voracious reader all my life but I have little interest in reading that series because I don't much care for that type of story. I did buy sets for all our classroom libraries." This is the same person who was arguing against incentive programs because they don't allow for a meaningful dialogue between the teacher and class. How can you talk about what you haven't read? How can you respond to children talking about what they are reading?

Every teacher and librarian ought to read *any* book that has sold more copies faster than any children's novel in publishing history—just to find out what's inside that motivates third- and fourth-graders to *voluntarily* read 400-page books. How could you recommend other books those students might like if you don't know the book they like in the first place?

What Are the Negatives Associated with the Incentive Programs?

They have some serious drawbacks that should be addressed, though most of the negatives come from outside the program. No program is free from abuse. At one time or another, all the world's religions have been misused and abused by various "true believers." Does that mean we should eliminate them? No, but it does mean the congregation must be ever watchful of abuses.

Conceding right up front that I hear ten times more positives than negatives, here are some serious negatives:[38]

♦ Some teachers and librarians have stopped reading children's and young adult books because the computer will ask the questions instead.
♦ Class discussion of books decreases because a discussion would give away test answers, and all that matters is the electronic score.
♦ Students narrow their book selection to only those included in the program (points).
♦ In areas where the "points" have been made part of either the grade or classroom competition, some students attempt books far beyond their level and end up frustrated.
♦ Although the programs discourage it, some districts have made the points part of the child's grade, thus removing the "voluntary" aspect of the program.
♦ Teachers use the points to determine student grades, lightening the teacher's workload by 25 percent.
♦ Where the program is mandatory and grade-associated, some districts even tie the class's total points to the teacher's yearly evaluation.

There is no end to the ways in which a community can warp the goodness of a sane idea. Competitive school athletics is a perfect example. Some districts monitor it and keep it in perspective, while others become "Captain Overboard." Before communities buy into reading-incentive programs, they need to anticipate the pathways and pitfalls. The danger of making the points too important can be found in this report from a professor friend of mine who is also a nationally respected figure in children's literature:

"A parent calls me, all upset. In her daughter's school, the whole reading program is one of these electronic reading-incentive programs. Her gifted fourth-grade daughter wants to please the teacher and asks what book will give her the most points. She's told *Gone With the Wind*. So the child spends much time reading the book and flunks the computer test. In the meantime, her friends have opted for reading lots of little books, making up points by quantity and easier books. The gifted student receives a low reading grade that term (points were tied to grades) and surmises that 'little and easy' is better than 'big and more' difficult."

Where's the problem here? Certainly it's not with the computer program. Who put that level book in the fourth-grade class? Who *encouraged* the child to read it? Who did not *discourage* her from reading it? Why were other children left unscathed by the point system and this one child hurt by it? Was it the competitive nature of the child or family that pushed her to the book? Or did she end up with *Gone With the Wind* out of sheer naiveté?

How the system is managed will determine its effectiveness or damage. For the teacher or librarian not to have forewarned the child, or for the parent not to have involved herself until after the fact, seem to me pivotal points here.

As my friend the professor observed, "I think some librarians and teachers are giving up their professional responsibility for choosing books for their students and conceding the responsibility to the computer programs. That's dangerous!"

Before committing precious dollars to such a program, a district must decide its purpose: Is it there to motivate children to read more or to create another grading platform? Is it there as a weapon to be used on classes, teachers, or even principals?

What's Wrong with Tying the Points to Grades?

The drawback to making the incentive programs and their points part of the grade is that doing so narrows the child's reading horizon. Perhaps only one of Betsy Byars's books is on the point list, but the student liked it so much that he wants to read another one by her. If the program exists to motivate students to read more and expose them to books or authors they'd never have known otherwise, this is the moment for that to happen. But if grading restricts the child to books with points, his choices are narrowed. He can't afford the luxury of reading serendipitously or for fun. How important are free choice and spontaneity? Ask someone who regularly browses bookstores, libraries, or even restaurant menus. Half the fun in reading is the exploration; the freedom to choose, to act on a whim, to wander down unexplored aisles, books, or delicacies.

All in all, I like having the choice of incentives, having them available as options for children who like challenges. But making them compulsory voids many of the gains.

Reasonable anecdotal evidence suggests that incentive programs work best in schools or communities which are low-achieving and where there is a general reluctance to read. In more affluent, high-scoring districts, the points tend to become a distraction. Here's an observation from a media specialist in a community (one of the wealthiest in New England) where an incentive program was in place for grading: "My biggest problem with the program is that repeatedly when I book-talk great books, the first question is always, 'How many points is it worth?' They simply *will not* read a book they will not get 'credit' for!"

Could part of the problem be that grades and points have become more important than the ultimate goal of creating a lifetime reader? If you make the incentive too valuable (and tying to grades in an ultra-competitive community does just that), surely it overshadows the goal and purpose.

In that regard, I'm reminded of the great New York Giants football teams of the 1950s, known for their defense, and led by Sam Huff, Andy Robustelli, and Jim Katcavich. These players were so extraordinary at stopping the opposing quarterback before he could get off a play, they inspired the NFL to begin keeping track of quarterback "sacks" for the first time. Why this sudden passion for sacks on the part of the Giants?

Robustelli explained it this way: One day the team owner approached the defensive unit with this offer: He'd give five dollars to anyone who sacked a quarterback. To stars who were earning $30,000 a year (low by today's standards), the money was insignificant enough for them to donate it to charity each week. What *was* significant was that their accomplishment was being *officially recognized* by the team owner. That recognition is terribly important.

On the other hand, if the five dollars had been $1000, it could very easily have become a distraction and corrupted teamwork. (Anyone connected with today's professional athletes will tell you the high salaries and incentive clauses have done serious damage to the chemistry of many teams.) The same kind of distraction can occur in communities that make the incentive program's rewards too important.

What Does Research Say About Using "Rewards" in Education?

There are mixed findings, but the most powerful argument against rewards is offered by Alfie Kohn, a widely respected educator who has backed up his arguments with strong evidence in his book *Punished by Rewards*.[39] He, of course, is not without opposition.[40]

The National Reading Research Center sided with Kohn and found that "intrinsic motivations" enhance *long-term* relationships between students and reading while "extrinsic motivations" have only a positive *short-term* effect on student reading and ultimately the relationship turns negative.[41] In other words, reading the Ramona Quimby books for the pure pleasure they were written to give will create a long-term positive relationship between reader and print; conversely, reading Ramona for points will have an initial positive impact that will last for only a short time—or as long as the points are offered.

Does anyone besides me see a flaw in that finding? First, it suggests that Ramona isn't good enough to overcome the point spread, that child readers won't find anything strong enough to lure them into the rest of the series. If Ramona's contents work for the intrinsic reader, why not the extrinsic reader? But *nothing* will work unless we can get the student to read the book.

But there's an even stronger flaw in the anti-rewards position: If pure intrinsics is so successful, where has it been all these years? What was working so well *before* the incentive programs? How effective were the intrinsics if 60 percent of students found no pleasure in reading and didn't read much?

There is ample evidence that many children do not like to read and find it boring, to say the least. They haven't discovered the intrinsic rewards of print. If they were only first-graders, you could argue for patience. But many of these students are in secondary schools—they've had seven to twelve years' worth of "intrinsics" and it hasn't worked. The "dead writers and poets" haven't turned them into lifetime readers. Maybe by reading for points the student—first-grader or ninth-grader—will get good enough at reading to find it a pleasure. The pleasure, in turn, may bring forth the intrinsics.

Yes, there are isolated schools or classrooms with high scores in response to good teaching and the availability of books. Unfortunately, they're exceptions, not the norm. Because not every teacher is an avid reader and a motivater, and not every school has sustained silent reading, and good school and classroom libraries, incentives are worth a try.

Aren't the Incentive Programs Nothing More Than "Bribery"?

The outrage over students reading for points instead of pleasure (or to "enrich the mind, spirit, or personality," as Harold Bloom[42] would assert) is a false alarm. If you surveyed human beings on the reasons for reading, the answers would include: money; competitiveness; grades; degrees/diplomas; escape; curiosity; filling time; pleasure; and enrichment of the spirit—depending on the person's circumstances on a given day.

There are many books and articles I read *only* because they are associated with my job; many are boring, but as an educator and author I read them to stay abreast professionally. Wouldn't this be considered reading for money? I hope my physician does the same. Most of the books college students read in school aren't for intrinsic reasons—and we all know it. How different is that from reading for *points*?

If the grownups can have their frequent flyer and traveler points, why can't the kids accumulate their reading points? Furthermore, isn't the report card the original "point" program?

One can make an analogy between the points in these incentive programs and the audience's applause for a musician or artist. The cynic calls it bribery, the optimist calls it encouragement.

My favorite reward story is that of little Orville and his grandmother. One would have expected Orville's grandfather, the founder and president of the Sherwin Williams Paint empire, to be the big influence in the boy's life, but not so. It was his grandmother who offered him a five-dollar "bribe" if he would learn to read—the equivalent of eighty dollars today. Orville's eventual success was based on a two-part formula. The first part was the *extrinsic* five-dollar reward, which led him to the second part—the *intrinsic* reward—the pleasure he found as a beginning reader in the stories of Thornton W. Burgess, one of the first (and often scorned) "series" writers at the beginning of the 1900s. Reading steered Orville Prescott away from the family paint business and eventually to *The New York Times,* where he was the paper's literary critic for nearly a quarter of a century. But he always credited Grandma and her bribe for his start in the business.[43]

If the story of Prescott and his grandmother sounds too good to be true, then you'll never believe the next "bribery" story. Walter and Nancy Behrens had sold off their three motels and were settled into retirement near the Oregon coastline in Lincoln County. That's when they read about the budget cuts in county schools and wondered if they could help. As always, reading was the biggest problem. Taft Elementary exemplified the woes; of its 490 students, 75 percent were on reduced or free lunch, highly transient, often absent, and had low reading scores.

Around the same time, then–Speaker of the House Newt Gingrich was proclaiming the merits of "paying" children to read.[44] That caught the eye of Walter Behrens, who had come to the United States as a nine-year-old, grew up in the hardscrabble of Brooklyn, and never forgot the motivating power of money. After hearing Taft principal David Phelps explain the complications of raising reading scores for children who come from at-risk homes where reading is not valued, Behrens countered with, "Suppose we pay 'em to read."

Phelps winced and said, "You'd meet a lot of criticism on that one."

"I don't care. Would it work?" Behrens asked. Phelps was willing to give it a try, and the Behrens were willing to commit $25,000 to cover four elementary-level schools in the county. A key ingredient would be to involve the parents, which they did by calling a meeting to describe the project and its serious implications. To everyone's relief, the parents liked it. Students in kindergarten through second grade would earn two dollars for every thirty-page book they heard or read (parents would need to sign a form). Grades three through five would receive two dollars for every hour of reading, along with a very brief written summary of the book (again approved by the parent).

After a short trial at the end of the 1996 school year, the program was put into place and was still thriving in 2000. "It really lit a pilot light for parent involvement," Phelps told me. "Many who were never involved before suddenly saw how important reading was to the schools." Student reaction was so positive, the administrators had to put some ceilings on how much they could earn. From a monthly limit of fifty dollars, they've scaled it back to thirty and then fifteen dollars because many children were reading so many books. Monthly reading rallies are held in school, and the names of all the students who have participated in the program are announced, but no dollar amounts are ever publicized. "We try to downplay that as much as possible," Phelps said.

When the monetary incentive plan began, approximately 63 percent of the district's third-graders were passing the state's reading benchmark exams; four years later, that rate had climbed to 87 percent.

Can You Cite an Example Where SSR and an Incentive Program Worked?

Tatum (Texas) Primary School offers pretty convincing evidence. Consisting of 360 pre-K to grade-three students, the school is 21 percent bilingual, 49 percent free lunch, and received school-wide Title 1 status in the 1997–98 school year. With those socioeconomic levels, it would be expected to have low scores.

In the 1995–96 school year, Tatum adopted both SSR (fifteen minutes daily) and a computerized reading-incentive program. The year's library circulation was a disappointing 2,693 books, and some attributed that to the fact only 25 percent of the library collection was on the incentive program's list. But maybe there were more important factors.

Part of the formula for becoming a better reader is the "time" one must spend reading. The following school year, 1996–97, Tatum made a significant change in its program. It increased the amount of daily SSR from fifteen minutes to *sixty* minutes. Library circulation that year climbed from 2,693 to 28,271. Granted, more books from the incentive core list were now in the library.

In the 1997–98 school year, yet another change was made, perhaps the most important one of all. Jill O'Farrell, the school's media supervisor, added "flextime" to the library schedule; this allowed a student to visit the library as often as deemed necessary (instead of once a week), and he or she could check out ten books (instead of the previous two books). In a primary school where most of the students were reading picture books and had sixty minutes a day of SSR, a policy of only two books a week would cripple growth. That year the library's circulation climbed to 46,680 books, and in the 1999–2000 school year it rose to 56,686 books.

After four years of the program, Tatum's primary students were each borrowing an *average* of 160 books a school year. And the incentive points are not tied to Tatum students' grades. It is purely independent reading.

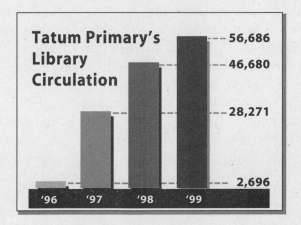

Tatum Primary's Library Circulation

56,686
46,680
28,271
2,696

'96   '97   '98   '99

If you get better at reading by reading, then the proof should be in Tatum's scores. On the Texas standards exam (TAAS), Tatum's passing rate rose from 84 percent in 1998 to 96 percent in 1999 and 94 percent in 2000. How does that compare with other Texas schools? The highly celebrated, selective, and deeply funded KIPP Academy in Houston had a passing rate of 98 percent on the TAAS test but its students had to spend 70 percent more time in school than did Tatum's.[45]

While some would argue the incentive points should be wearing off after four years, the opening day of school in August 2000 found Tatum students standing in line at the library door even before the first hour of classes. By the end of the second day of school, 600 books had circulated.

Tatum Primary demonstrates that incentive programs, if used judiciously with ample amounts of SSR and a well-stocked library, can motivate and enrich. As the first year of the program showed, points alone are *not* enough of an incentive. Tatum's "flextime" policy clearly proves the arguments offered in chapter 6—greater access to print results in more reading and higher scores.

How Do I Stop Them from Reading "Junk" During SSR?

I will address part of the "junk" issue in chapter 7 with the history of "series" books, but there is another aspect that fits into SSR—what Krashen calls "lite" reading. Series books usually fit this category because they're accessible, having both simple sentence structure and simple plots.

With that in mind, Krashen and graduate student Kyung-Sook Cho decided to try series books with adults for whom English is a second language (ESL).[46] They selected four immigrant women, three Korean and one Hispanic, whose ages were thirty, twenty-three, thirty-five, and twenty-one. Their average residency in the U.S. was 6.5 years. The oldest of the four was a thirty-five-year-old Korean who had majored in English in college and had taught it for three years in a high school. None of them, however, felt confident enough with English to speak it unless it was required, and most did little or no recreational reading in English.

Wishing to combine the women's low reading levels with interesting text, they chose the grade-two level of the Sweet Valley High series, called *Sweet Valley Kids* (seventy pages). After being given some background information about the series and characters, the women were simply asked to read the books during their free time for several months. Occasional discussions took place between one of the researchers and the women, to answer any questions they might have, but for the most part they were comprehending what they read.

The response was just as anticipated. "All four women became enthusiastic readers. Mi-ae reported she read eight Sweet Valley Kids books during one month, Su-jin read 18 volumes in two months, Jin-hee (the English major) read 23 in a little less than a month, and Alma (Hispanic) read 10 volumes over a two-week period. Two of the women read as many words per month as would a native-born student."

All became very fond of the series. "This is the first experience in which I wanted to read a book in English continuously," said one woman. The one who had taught English in high school said, "I read the Sweet Valley series with interest and without the headache that I got when reading *Time* magazine in Korea. Most interestingly, I enjoyed reading the psychological descriptions of each character." She went on to read thirty Kids volumes, along with seven of the Twins series and eight of the Sweet Valley High books. All of the women reported an involvement with the characters in the books that served to bring them back for more.

All displayed greater proficiency not only in their reading but in speaking English as well. And all demonstrated increased vocabulary development.

Krashen and Cho noted: "Our brief study with these four women also supports the value of 'narrow' reading—reading texts in only one genre or by only one author—for promoting literacy development. Narrow reading allows the reader to take full advantage of the knowledge gained in previously read text."

This study is one of many that demonstrate the powerful role that recreational "lite" reading—series books and comic books—plays in developing good and lifetime readers. Is it classic literature? Of course not. Does it have a better chance of creating fluent readers than the classics would? Definitely. And can it eventually lead to the classics? Yes, and certainly sooner than would *The Red Badge of Courage*.

My Son Loves Comic Books—Is That Good or Bad?

Comic books are a frequent childhood choice of people who grow up to become fluent readers.[47] The reasons for their popularity and success are the same as for series. And anyone questioning their success in creating readers should consider this: In the IEA assessment of more than two hundred thousand children in thirty-two countries, Finnish children achieved the highest reading scores. And what is the most common choice for recreational reading among Finnish nine-year-olds? Fifty-nine percent read a comic almost every day.[48]

I am not recommending comic books as a steady diet for reading aloud, but as an introduction to the comic format. Young children must be shown how a comic "works": the sequence of the panels; how to tell when a character is thinking and when he is speaking; the meaning of stars, question marks, and exclamation points.

Adults who provide a wide variety of reading materials for the child need not fear that the child or class will develop a "comic-book mentality." One study showed that more top students (nearly 100 percent) in all grades read comics or comic books than did lower-ranking students.[49] The most recent studies of comic book reading among seventh-graders showed boys were far bigger comic readers than girls (half the girls never read them), middle-class students read them as often as Title I students, and nearly 80 percent read them at least once a week. Students who read more often for pleasure also read more comic books. In comparing "gifted" students with regular students, there was no difference in their preferences for comic books, nor did comic reading affect the amount of book reading done by students.[50]

In recent years, comic books have experienced a revival and revolution, to the point where many communities now have whole stores devoted exclusively to comics. Unfortunately, the revolution has included new lines of comics with heavy strains of sex and violence. (Need I say this is not peculiar to comics? Books and film have similar woes.) So the days of giving a young child the money for a comic and sending him or her off to the corner convenience store are a thing of the past. As with television, videos, and books, parents must stay aware and awake.

In *The Power of Reading,* Krashen gives an extensive overview of the research on children and comic book reading, including a chart of readability levels for nineteen of the most popular comics. What do you think the difference in reading level is between the following comic books: *Archie, Batman,* and *Spiderman?*[51] He also shows the positive effect on library traffic and non-comic library circulation when comics are included in a school's non-circulating library collection.

On the basis of my personal experiences and the research available, I would go so far as to say if you have a child who is struggling with reading, connect him or her with comics. If an interest appears, feed it with more comics.

As a child, I had the largest comic collection in my neighborhood, as did Stephen Krashen, Cynthia Rylant, John Updike, and Ray Bradbury in their neighborhoods. There is, of course, the old saw that comics will corrupt a child's moral fiber. Heated Congressional hearings were devoted to this comical subject back in the early 1950s, when people were convinced that eliminating comics would eradicate juvenile delinquency. In response to such folderol, I offer this reflection from a Nobel Peace Prize winner, South Africa's Bishop Desmond Tutu: "My father was the headmaster of a Methodist primary school. Like most fathers in those days, he was very patriarchal, very concerned that we did well in school. But one of the things I am very grateful to him for is that, contrary to conventional educational principles, he allowed me to read comics. I think that is how I developed my love for English and for reading."[52]

If you're looking to challenge a child's mind and vocabulary with comics, then I suggest *The Adventures of Tintin*. If you looked closely at Dustin Hoffman while he was reading to his son in *Kramer vs. Kramer*, you would have noticed he was reading Tintin. Or if you read the list of favorite read-alouds offered by historian Arthur Schlesinger, Jr., in *The New York Times Book Review*, you would have found Hergé's Tintin between *Huckleberry Finn* and the Greek myths.[53]

Begun as a comic strip in Belgium in 1929, Tintin now reaches, in comic-book form, thirty countries in twenty-two languages and is sold only in quality bookstores. The subject is a seventeen-year-old reporter (Tintin) who, along with his dog and a cast of colorful and zany characters, travels around the globe in pursuit of mad scientists, spies, and saboteurs.

Two years were spent researching and drawing the seven hundred detailed illustrations in each issue. But Tintin must be *read* in order to be understood—and that is the key for parents and teachers. Each issue contains 8,000 words. The beautiful part of it is that children are unaware they are reading 8,000 words. (See *Tintin in Tibet* in the picture book section of the Treasury.)

How Much Do Teachers Read?

Throughout this book I've offered research showing the impact of parent role models on children's reading habits. Though they have less impact than parents, teachers should be reading role models as well—especially for those children whose parents cannot or will not do the job. The trouble, however, is most teachers are seldom seen reading for pleasure. Reading for work, from the text, from lesson plans, yes. But sitting back and savoring a book for its own sake or talking about a book they read last night? Seldom.

Research with teachers shows that in schools where their administrators talk about books and professional journals, the teachers read more on their own.[54] (See page 172 in chapter 7.) So why wouldn't the same be true for students if *their* instructional leaders talked more about books? In other words, the teacher stands before the class and daily gives mini–book talks based on the classroom library.

The fly in this ointment is that book talks work only when the person talking has actually read the book. And the harsh reality here is most teachers don't read much.

That's not a speculative comment but one based on both research and personal experience. One study of 224 teachers pursuing graduate degrees showed the teachers read few or no professional journals that included research.[55] (Suppose your doctor only read *Prevention* magazine?) More than half said they had read only one or two professional books in the previous year, and an additional 20 percent said they had read nothing in the last six months or one year. What did they read beyond professional material?

♦ 22 percent read a newspaper only once a week.
♦ 75 percent were only "light" book readers—one or two a year.
♦ 25 percent were "heavy" readers (three to four books a month). This means that teachers don't read any more often than adults in the general population.[56]

More recently (1998), in a national survey of 666 academic *high school* teachers, almost half reported not reading one professional journal or magazine.[57] The 51 percent who did such reading regularly were also more apt to belong to professional associations linked to their teaching area. The survey group averaged fifteen years of teaching, with 63 percent holding graduate degrees. Science teachers led all disciplines, with 61.8 percent reading at least one journal, while social studies trailed the faculty at 36.4 percent.

If the Child Isn't an Avid Reader by Age Thirteen, Is There Any Hope?

Just as few jobs or marriages are set in stone, so, too, children can change their minds about reading. Many are just waiting for their "home run book." Clifton Fadiman once wrote an essay about his days as a child reader, attributing his early start at age four to one book: *The Overall Boys.*[58] It was so perfect to him that he never stopped reading until blindness overtook him when he was well into his nineties. Along the way, his reading made him one of the guiding lights of American literature and culture in his roles as the book editor for *The New Yorker* and a founding father of the Book-of-the-Month Club.

The important thing here is a small observation Fadiman made in the course of his essay: "Everything after *The Overall Boys* has been anticlimax. One's first book, kiss, home run, is always the best." Could it be, I wondered, that most lifetime readers can look back on one particular book as a launching pad for reading? For aliterates, young or old, is it the absence of a "home run" book that's holding them back?

One day I mentioned this to my brother Brian, a voracious reader and successful businessman today but a late bloomer in the classroom. "Absolutely true," he answered. "In fact, I had *two* home run books. Until those, it was pretty much sports magazines." Then he challenged me, "I'll bet you can't name the two books." Since I'd read them first and then tossed them his way, I easily met his challenge: Gerald Green's *The Last Angry Man,* a 1950s bestseller about a besieged inner-city physician, and *A Distant Trumpet,* a 629-page historical novel written by Paul Horgan, who won two Pulitzer Prizes for history. Neither of Brian's favorites was written for children or even adolescents, but they were the right pitch to the right reader in the right inning of his life. (We both still own copies of these two books and will never part with them.) For late bloomers like my brother, it's terribly important that parents and teachers not stop trying to serve up the right pitch/book that the child will connect with.

In two studies[59] built around the idea of "home run books," the majority of avid student readers could name favorite books that inspired them to keep reading, while those who disliked reading complained that it was "boring" and were unable to name a favorite book. Plainly, the bored readers haven't yet found the right book. This is still another reason to incorporate SSR across the grades. Just as you can't hit a home run if you're not in the lineup, you can't discover a "home run book" if you're not reading, or if *no one thinks it's important enough to give you time to do it.*

The idea of waiting for that "home run book" coincides with the research of Dr. G. Kylene Beers,[60] who spent one year observing and interviewing two classes of seventh-graders. Her conclusion: the vast majority of teenagers know *how* to read but choose not to read. But the aliterates can be divided into three groups: dormant; uncommitted; and unmotivated.[61]

The "dormant" readers actually like to read but presently are too busy or stressed to do it very often. The "uncommitted" readers don't read because they find no pleasure in it, but they respect those who do read, almost wishing they had the skill. They also leave the door open to one day becoming a reader, maybe. The "unmotivated" readers also view reading as meaningless for themselves—it's just words on a page—but additionally are resolved they will *never* like it. They often have difficulty connecting visually and emotionally to the plots and characters in books.

Beers also found profound differences in the early childhood experiences of these distinct groups of aliterate teens.

- Avid and dormant readers recalled being read to at home as children and connected the experience to pleasure and fun; they owned library cards.
- Uncommitted and unmotivated readers were never or seldom read to as children, and did not connect reading with anything resembling entertainment. They had never belonged to summer reading groups, clubs, and *not one had ever owned a library card.*

Certain factors had positive results with the three groups of seventh-grade aliterates:

+ Giving them personal choice in what they read
+ Nonfiction
+ More illustrations in the book
+ Movies—they prefer to see the movie first, then read the book
+ Read an entire book aloud to them
+ More magazines

Granted, none of this is going to rival *Lord of the Flies,* but it (1) is better than nothing; and (2) may eventually lead to bigger and better things. The social commentator Fran Lebowitz once observed that because magazines often lead to books, they should be regarded by the prudent as the "heavy petting" of literature.

Do Students Really Need to Write Something Every Time They Read?

They wouldn't if I were the teacher. But here's my slant on the so-called reading-writing connection—which doesn't always win me friends in some circles.

Writing is an integral part of any good reading and language-arts curriculum. For many years, the classroom obsession with worksheets resulted in severe writing neglect. But beginning in the 1980s, that changed. Writing became a major focus, as schools hired writing consultants who taught teachers how to write, and then how to teach writing to children. Good so far.

Writing became the new buzzword in schools. Students began to spend more time writing. When some teachers read the research that showed worksheets had no impact on children's reading skills, they began to look at writing as the new "crowd control" device. It would cover language arts, keep the class busy and focused, and give the teachers something they could put grades on. Writing became the new "weapon of choice." Soon, many students were spending more time writing than reading. Not good.

An exaggeration? A few years ago, in a small Michigan community outside Detroit, a parent presented me with a set of documents that outlined the requirements for eighth- and ninth-grade language-arts students in her district. According to the rules, all reading had to be "logged." That is, a student had to read twenty to thirty minutes at a time, and then write a response to what he read: one written page merited a D, two pages a C, three pages a B, and four pages an A. As if that were not labor enough, once a week the student had to solicit a response to the journal entries from a teacher, parent, or student.

I shudder to think how little most of us would read—magazines, newspaper, or books—if we had that much labor attached to the experience.

The assignment for incoming ninth-graders was no less pain-oriented. Response journals had to be kept for summer readings, all of which would be collected the first day of school in September. The required response included:

♦ Read the title and predict what the story will be about from the title. (If you'd never read *Moby-Dick, The House of the Seven Gables, Gone With the Wind,* or *The Wind in the Willows,* would the titles offer even the barest clue? Does the clarity of the title make any difference in how good a book it is?)
♦ Read the first few paragraphs. Now predict what you think will happen by the end of the story, and what will happen next.
♦ Read the first chapter and predict what will happen next. (Who has time to read if you have to make all these predictions? There are people who read the *Daily Racing Form* who don't make this many predictions, and they're trying to make a living at it!)

Is it any wonder that some people have begun to ask: Isn't all this writing taking an awful lot of time away from reading? Certainly writing is important, but of the four language arts (listening, speaking, reading, and writing), the art of writing is the one *least* used in the work day of an average adult.

This is not to say writing is unimportant or that we shouldn't have *any* writing experiences connected to reading. There is real value in writing as an exercise in mental discipline because it requires us to collect our thoughts in a coherent fashion—unlike the randomness of conversation. And writing gives the individual a rare sense of inner focus, an opportunity for self-examination. In that respect, there is research to show writing makes the writer more intelligent.[62] So for all of those reasons, writing should never be ignored to the degree it was in the 1950s, '60s and '70s. But it is *not* as important as reading!

Writing does not build vocabulary as effectively as reading,[63] nor does it teach grammar, spelling, or reading skills as well; it doesn't offer the writer as much knowledge or information as reading, and it doesn't even teach writing as well as reading does. And research (as well as common sense) confirms *each* of those points.[64]

What About the "Classics"?

Now that I have made such a strong case for "lite" reading, some may be wondering where the "classics" fit into this. An interesting thing happened to the classics: About the only people in this country who read them are teenagers—and only because they have to.

Don't misunderstand me: I am awed by the great minds and great writing. I read and revere the classics, but everything I've seen in the last thirty-five years indicates we are misusing them in schools, to the point that we are undoing much of the good they were created to accomplish. We've got ninth-graders reading books like *The Great Gatsby* before they're old enough to bring a frame of reference to them. And to make things worse, the books are dissected until every trace of appeal has been lost.

When I look at most high school reading lists, I have to wonder: Has anyone on the faculty read anything *new* in the last half century? Additionally, most of the books were originally written for an adult audience. (No wonder the faculty likes them!)

Susan Ohanian, my favorite education writer, once interviewed then–Secretary of Education William Bennett, a man who is especially fond of lists, particularly lists of classic books that should be read by children. Knowing this predilection, Ohanian asked if he would be so kind as to recommend a single book that had been published *in this century,* or least since *Heidi*? Bennett paused, and then confessed he could not.[65]

By almost every gauge available, the teaching of the classics or serious literature in American schools has been a gigantic failure. The most comprehensive evaluation of U.S. adult reading habits is found in *Who Reads Literature?* by Nicholas Zill and Marianne Winglee, and is based upon 1982 and 1985 national surveys sponsored by the National Endowment for the Arts and conducted by the U.S. Census Bureau with 30,929 people.

In terms of general novel reading, that is, books never included in the secondary curriculum (mysteries, romances, thrillers, etc.), 30 percent of the adult population can be described as regular readers. Serious contemporary literature (authors like William Styron, John Updike, and Alice Walker) is read by only 11 percent of the population; classics are read by only 7 percent. (Serious and classic book sales account for only 1 percent of bookstore sales.) Only 4 percent of adults read poetry. (Poetry magazines and journals have circulations in the low thousands and often only hundreds.) And only 3 percent report reading a play in the last year.[66]

In other words, about 80 percent of the adult population never reads what they were taught to read in high school. Isn't there something wrong here? If we spent twelve years teaching children to brush their teeth and then 80 percent of them grew up and never brushed their teeth, shouldn't we conclude that we were doing something wrong?

There is no greater plum for the guidance department of any school than to land a student at Harvard. It is the image of Harvard—and its brother/sister Ivies—that looms largest in high school advanced-placement classes, justifying the stacks of classics and student papers in the sophomore, junior, and senior years of high school.

What is the cumulative effect of all those papers on the classics? Sven Birkerts had taught six years of expository writing at Harvard when he wrote the following for *Harvard Magazine*: "Almost none of my students reads independently." On the first day of class Birkerts asked them to write a reading autobiography—what they read, how much, when, where. "The responses are heartbreaking. Nearly every student admits—some of them sheepishly, others not—that reading is a problem. 'Too busy!' 'I wish I had the time.' 'I've always had a hard time with books that are supposed to be good for me.' And then, proudly, 'If I have time, I like to relax with Stephen King.' I can't tell you how many of my best and brightest have written that sentence."

If a three-to-four-year diet of high school classics and paperwork creates high scores but turned-off readers and poor writers, shouldn't we reevaluate the process? At some point, it might be helpful for secondary English departments to define the goal of their curriculum: Is it to create future English professors or future readers? Most junior high and high school English classes are structured with future English professors in mind, yet the last thing 99 percent of their graduates would like to be is an English professor.

If Not the Classics, What Else Should They Be Reading?

Back in 1984, a writer for *School Library Journal* surveyed the English departments at the Ivy League and Seven Sister colleges (Harvard, Yale, Radcliffe, Smith, etc.), seeking a list of books high school librarians should have on the shelf.[67] Some responded with lists but no one title made all lists.

Professor Arthur Gold, then chair of the English department at Wellesley, came the closest to the "lite" reading proposition I offer in this chapter. He preferred that teachers and librarians simply encourage wide reading and not bother themselves with specific titles. "I'd have secondary-school teachers weigh books on a scale and award letter grades for reading done by the pound," Gold declared. "My general sense is that memory needs to be stored at an early age," he argued, "that people need a good supply of anecdote, gossip, and emotional experience, and that the appropriate time for sorting things out comes after we have acquired a stock of information. Helter-skelter, chaos, putting first things last and last things first, not worrying whether one hasn't read what everyone should have read—these seem to me the appropriate terms and principles for a secondary-school approach to reading."

Gold argued *against* including Shakespeare, Greek mythology, modernist poetry, and Robert Frost, and says, "High school's the time for Thomas Wolfe, Vachel Lindsay, Jack London, Kipling, Robert Service, Vonnegut, and whatever's in fashion on the national scene."

Gold sounded iconoclastic, but at least rational. Why not try Gold's "by the pound" formula? English by the pound? Could we be worse off than we are right now?

Chapter 6

Libraries: Home, School, and Public

The best of my education has come from the public library . . . my tuition fee is a bus fare and once in a while, five cents for an overdue book. You don't need to know very much to start with, if you know the way to the public library.

—Lesley Conger

IN the wake of the Internet's success, recent years have seen a heated debate about the role of libraries in schools and communities. This chapter offers some ammunition that might be used in such debates. Not all of what I share here is complimentary to libraries, but that just shows there's always room for improvement.

Nothing explains the importance of any library—home, classroom, school, or public—the way the "Israeli hockey syndrome" does. Every four years, Israel, like dozens of other countries, sends a team of skiers and skaters to the Winter Olympics, and every four years they lose. No contest! While many countries would suffer national shame at such poor showings, Israel has none of that. No outcry for the prime minister to resign, the coaches to be fired, the athletes to be dismissed. Everyone in Israel knows it's not the personnel—it's the climate! Too much sand, not enough snow and ice.

If Israel were located just north of Sweden, it would be a major hockey powerhouse! Climate immediately affects sports scores. On the opening day of baseball season in 1998, there were eight players on major league rosters from San Pedro de Macoris (Dominican Republic),[1] a city of 130,000 people, while the entire state of Maine (1.3 million) had only two players. How come? In Maine you can play baseball ninety days a year, but in San Pedro, 365 days a year—ask Sammy Sosa.

Similarly, climate plays a key role in reading scores—in this way: Just as there would be higher skiing scores in Israel if there were more blizzards, there are always higher reading scores where there are more books. Strangely, most so-called education "experts" have yet to make the connection between print climate and reading scores. Instead, they blame the teachers, curriculum, or students for the low scores, which would be like the Israelis blaming the coaches, players, and equipment for poor hockey scores. Unlike the geophysical climate, the encouraging thing about the print climate is *we can change it.*

The last decade's research by respected researchers like Krashen,[2] Mc-Quillan,[3] Allington,[4] and Lance[5] unmistakably connects access to print with high reading scores and, conversely, lack of access with lower scores. The high NAEP reading scores can be found in states with better libraries, more bookstores, more print in the home, and more free or independent reading.[6] Elley's 1992 study of 210,000 students in thirty-two countries found similar results: The better the print climate—that is, the larger the school and classroom libraries—the higher the students' reading scores.[7]

In two significant studies conducted by Library Service Center of the Colorado State Library at the beginning and end of the 1990s, a strong correlation was found between the caliber of the school library and student scores, even when pupil-teacher ratio, community demographics, and teacher qualifications were factored in.[8] Among 850 schools in Colorado, Pennsylvania, and Alaska, higher caliber library facilities improved scores by 10 to 15 percent. The more time students and teachers spent visiting the library and consulting with *qualified* librarians, the higher the scores, especially in reading. Additionally, more individual students visiting the media center also meant higher scores. Pennsylvania, Alaska, and California are among the states not requiring qualified library personnel in their schools; in fact, during the 1990s, California had a higher librarian-to-patron ratio in its schools (1:5,496)[9] than it did in its prisons (1:815).[10]

What makes the school's print climate so essential is that children with the fewest books at home meet the fewest books in school. When researchers compared libraries in six poverty-level schools with six affluent ones, the poverty schools had 50 percent fewer books, and many (if not most) of those had thirty-year-old copyrights—older than the students' parents. In addition, library visits were more restricted in the poverty schools, and several schools prohibited books from being taken home from school, while none of the affluent schools had such a restriction. While 500 books is a recommended amount for classroom libraries, no poverty school met that goal, and the classrooms in the poorest school averaged between twenty-five and fifty books per room.[11]

The most dramatic example of the impact of the print climate on school scores is the one involving three California communities, twenty miles apart on the map but worlds apart in other ways. Dr. Stephen Krashen and colleagues at USC did a print inventory of homes, classrooms, and libraries in the three communities[12]—Beverly Hills, Watts, and Compton. In Beverly Hills, high scores send 93 percent of its high school students to college, while relatively few go to college from Watts and Compton. In 1999, Compton's state-appointed administrator reported that barely one in ten students was performing at grade level. One look at the chart below clearly shows the print desert surrounding urban children, versus the rich print climate surrounding others.

Average Print Climate in Three California Communities

	Books in Home	Books in Class	Books in School Library	Books in Public Library
Beverly Hills	199.0	392	60,000	200,600
Watts	.4	54	23,000	110,000
Compton	2.7	47	16,000	90,000

Krashen's evidence[13] was presented to a state commission revising California's language-arts curriculum after the state tied Louisiana for last in the nation in reading. Holding one of the nation's largest child-poverty populations, and lowest support for school and public libraries, including school library collections in which the average nonfiction book was almost thirty years old,[14] the politicians responded with $195 million for increased phonics instruction.[15] Giving phonics instruction to children who don't have books is like giving oars to people who haven't got a boat.

I don't wish to imply that California education has a corner on craziness; in education politics, there's more than enough of that to go around. In 1999, while announcing that 67 percent of New York City's fourth-graders had failed the new state standards exam in reading and writing, the state education commissioner reminded parents that every child should be reading twenty-five books a year. That rankled the nerves of a New York reporter, who filed a report detailing the dreadful condition of the city's school libraries,[16] noting that New York State annually allotted four dollars per pupil for books, when the average hardcover cost $16.60. New York City's school budget allotted $30.41 per child for drug-abuse programs, but only $14.81 per child for books *and* librarians. At Public School 108, an average school in

South Ozone Park, Queens, 68 percent of the 1,500 students failed the state reading test. Its book-to-student rate is two books to every child, versus the national average of nineteen books per child.

Why Don't Poor People Understand That Books Are a Necessity?

Poor people are human—they worry more about putting bread on the table for their children than books on a shelf for their children. Books may be a necessity to well-fed people, but to those who wonder where the next meal is coming from, they're a *luxury.* Thus students coming from the lowest income families have access to the fewest books. In the ongoing study of 22,000 U.S. kindergartners, only 37 percent of incoming kindergartners with high school–educated parents had fifty or more books in their homes, whereas 71 percent with college-educated parents had that number.[17] The end result can be seen in a half century of annual SAT scores in which the higher the parents' education, the higher the student's scores. As the Israeli study below indicates, the print climate immediately affects the number of books and words a child is exposed to during the first five years of life— giving favored students a head start while severely delaying others. This is something the high-stakes testing folks haven't been able to grasp yet.

A study of 102 Israeli kindergartners in 34 schools[18] turned up the same evidence: The 51 children from affluent homes had an average of 54 books per home, while children in schools with low achievement levels averaged 4.6 books, and 61 percent didn't have any. Naturally, the lack of print affected how often these children were exposed to the language of print: 94 percent of the affluent children were read to every day (45 percent for a half hour or more), while 60.8 percent of the lower SES children received no read-alouds.

The print climate also affects the age at which a child is exposed to print. The Israeli study showed that 49 percent of the affluent children were being read to regularly before age two, while none of the low-income children received read-alouds before age four (15.7 percent).

Since the vocabulary of children's books is three times more complex and rich (thirty rare words per thousand words) than parent-child conversation (ten rare words per thousand), this two-to-three-year head start gives affluent children a gigantic advantage at the start of school. Unless the print environment of the affluent child suffers a serious draught, it's unrealistic to expect the low-income child to catch up simply by going to school (annually 900 hours in class vs. 7500 hours at home), nor can it be made up in 120 hours of summer school.

Will Access to Print in Class Help At-Risk *Preschoolers*?

In an experiment to see if "flooding" books into the classrooms of at-risk three- and four-year-olds would make much of a difference, Dr. Susan Neuman initiated the Books Aloud project. It was also decided that professional training would have to be included with the books since urban child-care centers are often staffed by people lacking professional credentials, and sometimes with only high school diplomas. Few people outside the day-care world realize the extensive turnover of staff at these centers, ranging from 23 to 300 percent.[19]

At a cost of $2.1 million, Books Aloud delivered 88,960 books to 337 nonprofit day-care centers serving 17,675 children.[20] Many of the centers were located in dangerous parts of the inner-city, often under guard. In a 100-classroom sample before the project's start, only 25 had bookshelves, with most books in tattered condition. There were 30 TV's in the one hundred classrooms. After the arrival of the books and staff training, 83 of 100 classrooms made significant improvements in the children's access to print, and the number of literacy encounters between a teacher and child doubled, from 5 to 11 per day.

The importance of reading aloud to children was the focal point of the professional training given to the center staffs and was reflected in the dramatic change that resulted. Where previous daily routines included read-alouds (usually once a day, though 20 percent never had read-alouds), the daily literacy schedules were usually organized around skills-based instruction. After Books Aloud, daily read-alouds increased significantly. In the control group classes (not in the Books Aloud program), only 11 percent of classrooms had read-alouds as often as four times a day, while 21 percent of Books Aloud classes included them that often.

Six months later the follow-up evaluation of the program's impact on children's literacy skills showed the Books Aloud children significantly outdistanced the control groups in four of six measures.

How Do I Build a Good Home Library?

Long before children are introduced to the public library, books should be a part of their home lives. Begin a home library as soon as the child is born. If you can provide shelving in the child's room for such books, all the better. The sooner children become accustomed to the sight of the covers, bindings, and pages of books, the sooner they will begin to develop the concept that books are a part of daily life.

If you have children under the age of four, divide your books into two categories: expensive and inexpensive. The higher-priced or fragile books should be placed on shelves out of the reach of sticky fingers, dribbles, and errant crayons. While out of reach, they should still be within sight—as a goal. On lower shelves and within easy reach should be the less expensive and, if possible, more durable books. If the replacement price is low enough, you'll have fewer qualms about the child "playing" with the books. This "playing" is an important factor in a child's attachment to books. He must have ample opportunity to feel them, taste them, and see them.

Your home (and classroom) library should contain not only books the child will immediately relate to, but also those he or she will grow into—like encyclopedias. Someone had told me of a young osteopath, Dr. Charles Allen Holt, who preached the doctrine of read-aloud to the undereducated, poor parents he met during his internship at Cardinal Glennon Memorial Hospital for Children in St. Louis. Curious about his background, I finally found him living in Indianapolis and asked if he could spare a minute to tell me how he came to be a reader and proponent of reading aloud.

He told me that during his childhood in Jefferson City, Missouri, his parents read to him all the time, that television viewing was controlled in his home, and that books were available even before he could read. Dr. Holt also explained, "I remember my [schoolteacher] mother placing a *World Book Encyclopedia* on the floor in front of me to peruse in my leisure hours. By the time I was in kindergarten, I could find something within one minute in the encyclopedia on any topic you could suggest."

With the arrival of the encyclopedia on CD, the days of the expensive hardbound $1,000 encyclopedia are gone. Unfortunately, young children need to *feel* books, they need the opportunity to browse and scrutinize things in a setting beyond the desktop computer. (Ever try to use one of those in bed?) In the Treasury, on page 222, I've listed some children's reference volumes that are worthy substitutes for the old encyclopedia.

As I noted in earlier chapters, until about two years of age, your child's reading interest is usually better served by a few books that he sees and hears regularly than by dozens and dozens with which he never develops a working familiarity. However, as his attention span and interests grow, that home library should expand if your family budget permits.

Twenty years ago, most of the books in my family library were bought secondhand at garage sales, the Salvation Army thrift shop, and used bookstores. I think my children were nearly ten years old before they realized that not all books came with scribble marks and somebody else's name crayoned inside the cover. Given the choice, I guess we all prefer the qualities of a brand-new book—its bright, crisp pages, its fresh smell. But struggling young families and teachers don't always have the money. If it's any consolation, barring damage, a "used" copy of *Charlotte's Web* has the same words in it as a "new" copy but at a fraction of the price. Young families should tap the resources of the Salvation Army and Goodwill thrift shops, check out the library discard table and annual used-book sale, and never pass up the book table at a yard sale.

With the Internet in Place, What's the Role of Libraries?

As I note in chapter 7, the Internet's unrestrained growth and unverifiable offerings are a *long* way from replacing libraries. The biggest threat to libraries is—libraries. A sure sign of life is change and growth. Dead things don't change. Unless libraries are willing to change in the next decade or two, their existence *will* be endangered.

This doesn't mean the state of reading is dying. Far from it. Think back fifteen years to when video stores were blooming on nearly every corner, the number of cable channels was mushrooming, library branches were closing or shortening hours, and the doomsayers were forecasting the end of reading in America.

Back in those days, if you walked into the typical American bookstore:

- There was a sign on the door: No food and beverage beyond this point.
- There was no place to sit down.
- There was no place to buy coffee or snacks.
- Loitering was discouraged.
- The book store closed at 9 P.M. or earlier.

In less than fifteen years, all of that changed. The "No Food" sign has been replaced by an advertisement for the store's cafe; stuffed chairs, comfortable sofas, and study tables are sprinkled throughout; information kiosks have been added; and closing time is 11 P.M., later than many video stores. The result: Mega-bookstores dominate the industry and are so crowded on weekends they practically have to announce a bomb threat to clear the store for closing.

As we entered the year 2000, the book scene was described this way:

"The . . . superstore is to this generation's avid readers what an Andrew Carnegie Library was to those of an earlier era: community center, reading room and, of course, repository of thousands of books. The carefully calculated lounge-and-browse ambiance is so relaxing—so free from petty distractions of commerce—that a Manhattan customer died at the Broadway and 82nd Street branch, nestled in an overstuffed chair and left to slumber undisturbed until closing." (*The New York Times Magazine*)[21]

"(The new bookstores) have become cultural magnets for a fragmented society that no longer gathers on the front porch or at the corner store. Bookstores have become one of the last public places where people feel safe and mentally enriched and where cost-free loitering *without* intent is accepted as browsing." (*USA Today*)[22]

At a time when reading was supposed to be dead, the bookstores made themselves "user-friendly" and woke the dead. Granted, it's taken half a millennium, but someone finally publicly admitted that we humans like to sit comfortably when we read, preferring to nibble and sip while we do so. The booksellers sensed that if you build it comfortable and tasty, "they will come." And come they have, in numbers that should make librarians green with envy.

There is a powerful message here for the school and public librarians. Are they listening? How long before we have juices, fruit, and sodas in libraries? What about public libraries with coffee shops attached? How about soft chairs and convenient hours? What percent of a week's sales is done by the mega-bookstores on Saturday and Sunday? Forty-two percent. Not surprising, when you consider those are the days when most people have the most time to read and shop or peruse. But what days are public libraries open the fewest hours? Saturday and Sunday.

If it takes another 200 years before our schools and libraries are as user-friendly as the bookstores have become, they'll be fossils. Still, around the nation, some libraries have begun to catch the scent of the times. The first hints of change occurred in the early 1990s when new library branches began to open in shopping malls. The Roseville Public Library, outside St. Paul, Minnesota, now has a coffee shop. The coffee is on, the circulation is up, and the patrons are happy. On a grander scale, when the Duxbury (Massachusetts) Free Library opened its new quarters in November 1997, it was minutes from local schools and the town pool, had plenty of computers, a phone-home lounge with free local calls, and a French cafe. It's now an after-school hot-spot with teens—in other words, user-friendly.

On the other hand, others resist the movement, fearing it will corrupt the purpose of a library. (I once read the posting of a college librarian on an Internet bulletin board in which she declared she has a hard enough time getting her students to wash their hands before using the books, never mind serving food.) A library doesn't exist to exist; its purpose should be to serve, and if no one is there, how much service is possible?

What follows is "a tale of two cities"—Fort Collins, Colorado, and Long Beach, California, and how two very different public schools modeled their libraries on those mega-bookstores and became user-friendly. But it took two imaginative and unorthodox school librarians—Charli O'Dell and Helen Cox—to bring the dead back to life. Let's look at how they did it.

Charli (Charline) O'Dell and the Boltz Junior High Library

Charli O'Dell is the media specialist at Boltz Junior High, population 990 students. Set in an affluent community less than an hour north of Denver, the school leads the district in Iowa test scores and its hub is the school library. But that was not always the case. O'Dell was a science teacher for twelve years and regularly used the library with her students; in other words, she knew the library's potential and recognized when it wasn't meeting the students' needs. Having grown up working in a family-owned grocery store, O'Dell knew first-hand the importance of meeting every customer's needs and how different each might be. She also saw the importance of marketing.

Waiting for the former librarian to retire, O'Dell took a master's degree in educational technology and media, then moved into the position when it opened. Her first job was morphing the "ugliest room I have ever seen" into something attractive. "Decorated in the 1970s in screaming oranges, electric blues, and brilliant yellows, it provided the perfect playground for students who didn't want to engage in academics," she explains today. Through fund-raisers and just plain begging, she organized a $35,000

Charli O'Dell

facelift for the room. Gone were the layers of duct tape from the ripped carpets, off came the computer-generated posters and signs from the walls.

With the change in decor came a change in attitude. O'Dell removed the sign at the library's entrance: "The library closes at 3 o'clock sharp!" In its place was a new sign, "Welcome to the Boltz Media Center," along with a listing of the expanded hours. Recalling how her grocer parents had made their customers feel special, O'Dell carried that over into her approach to library customers. She mounted a bulletin board displaying photos of the library "regulars" with the caption: "We like it here!" Naturally, everyone wanted *their* photo on the board. "Good libraries," she explains, "cater to a number of basic human needs: belonging, power, importance—and yes, they're also great places to find books and information."

But nothing demonstrates O'Dell's golden touch with PR better than her "Thanks-A-Latte Day!"[23] After visiting one of those ubiquitous bookstores with a built-in coffee shop, she reasoned that if food and beverages changed the way many adults think about bookstores, they just might change some minds about school libraries. So she came up with a special event to celebrate the library.

She rounded up thirty volunteer media moms and supplies (packets of instant cappuccino, hot chocolate, hot cider, etc.), and promoted the event to the hilt. Not only was there 100 percent staff/class participation, the day-long event resulted in 1,000 drinks being sold for a profit of $700. Complete with music in the background, the Latte Day served as a showcase for the school's 400 new books and initiated enough interest in the media center to boost library visitors to four times the norm before school the next day. The following year, two Latte Days were scheduled—at the request of students and staff. Joining the students were other district librarians and administrators, school board members, Rotarians, and others. (For those worried about junior high students adding caffeine to their already precarious hormonal balance, O'Dell points out that the Swiss Miss cappuccino packet contains half the caffeine of a can of Coke.)

Helen Cox and the Lindbergh "Reading Room"

Like Charli O'Dell, Helen Werner Cox[24] was positive there were better ways to market the love of reading than the previous approach at Lindbergh Middle School in North Long Beach, California. *Anything* would be better, she thought.

What could be less tempting to teenagers than thousands of dusty, untouched books that dated back as far as 1913? Maybe the thousands of creaky volumes that contained an all-vanilla cast of characters when the

Helen Cox

student body was brown and tan and black. To make matters worse, the books were stuffed into a room that was dingy, contained three teachers' desks and dozens of brown hard-backed chairs and desks, and was overseen by a discolored WPA mural.

Small wonder Lindbergh students and staff preferred going anywhere but the library. But Cox was just an art teacher in the school, albeit one who loved books and reading. What could she do about the library?

Adding to her difficulties, most of the 1,400 students at Lindbergh Middle School, a Title I school with 80 percent of its students on the free-lunch program, came from homes that contained few if any books, magazines, or newspapers, and had the least access to public libraries.

The plight of Lindbergh's students is more common than rare in California, a state that ranks at or near the bottom of the nation in library support (public and school). Where the national average of books-per-pupil is 19:1, California's is 11:1. In urban centers like Los Angeles or New York City, the ratio drops as low as 6:1; Lindbergh's was 4:1.

So when Lindbergh's librarian retired in 1994, Cox drew up a proposal that included the progressive changes she would make in the facility, changes that would make it look more like a Barnes & Noble than a California school library. Her principal bought into the idea.

Primary among its needs was a paint job, something that often takes large urban districts more than a year to accomplish. Unless, of course, there are volunteers—including someone whose husband works for a paint company, as was the case at Lindbergh. The volunteers immediately attacked and conquered the dingy walls, though hardly to the pleasure of the district painters, who protested the job should have been theirs.

Next came a massive weeding of the out-of-date collection, to the dismay of some faculty—many of whom had avoided the room for years. There were armloads of books that hadn't been touched or circulated since 1969. But when decades' worth of *National Geographic,* coated with a quarter inch of dust, were labeled by the new librarian as disposable, protesting groans rose from the traditionalists. "Are you crazy? Those things are worth thousands of dollars!"

If that's the case, maybe I can get something for them, Cox thought. Six used-book stores told her they were useless, until one finally offered to give her $300 worth of children's books in trade for them.

Then came a massive clean-up of the remaining books, nearly all of which had had their dust jackets removed years ago. (The jackets eventually were discovered in one of the many file cabinets in the library.) Cox and a team of student aides took each book, sandpapered the edges of the pages to remove the grit that had settled on most of them, cleaned the bindings, and put on laminated dust jackets.

Around the same time, several apartments in her condominium were foreclosed and the abandoned, nearly-new furniture placed out on the street. Cox offered to cart it away, scrubbed it, and placed it in her library, which was now renamed the "Lindbergh Reading Room," carrying a less threatening label than "library" for its student visitors.

Four years later, the Reading Room is the pride of the school and the comfort zone is filled with soft chairs, sofas, hassocks, rugs, and a dozen stuffed animals (yes, middle school kids still cuddle with them as they read—though not in a crowd). Circulation has doubled and climbs every year. Cox writes grants and continues to make improvements (including a morning Literati Cafe on the school patio, weather permitting), but the book budget is still constrained.

After the initial reluctance to accept the change and the subsequent switch to year-round scheduling (which resulted in a healthy exodus of old faculty blood and an influx of new), Cox receives great support from the faculty. In order for a student to be designated a Distinguished Scholar, he or she must spend three thirty-minute periods a week in the library doing intensive reading, as well as a research project.

Does Lindbergh's Reading Room rank with the finest of suburban situations, like Fort Collins's Boltz Junior High? No, but it's light-years from what it used to be and improving every year. There was an 11 percent increase in students applying for Distinguished Scholar status in the 1998–99 school year. What did it all take? Someone who truly loved books, who possessed a creative mind, who saw the obvious rather than the obstacles, who understood children, and an administration that was willing to risk change.

As I drove away from my visit to Lindbergh, one thought poked through many positive impressions: Why had it taken an art teacher on the faculty to recognize the problem and its solutions? Where were the principals, English teachers, and science or social studies teachers for all those decades of decay? Why had they remained silent and uninvolved for so long? Was it possible they themselves didn't love reading enough to raise a protest or solution? Or didn't they know the connection between print climate and school scores?

How Do I Make My Library More Successful on a Limited Budget?

In 1996, *The New York Times* ran an article on supermarkets and the keys to their success.[25] The author noted there originally was only one rule for supermarkets: Put the milk at one end of the store and bread at the other—to get people to walk through the entire store. That rule still applies: The more they see, the more they buy. But the Universal Price Code scanner that sits at the checkout has allowed the industry to make other observations, including some we might apply to libraries:

- Only 31 percent of grocery patrons bring a shopping list (more than half of adult library patrons arrive without a book in mind; even more so for children).
- Two-thirds of purchases are unplanned (very similar to book choices).
- Specialty items (like ice cream sprinkles) sell best when placed near the checkout line (books displayed near the circulation desk always move faster).
- Ninety-five percent of customers who take a sample will end up buying the product (this coincides with the research on kindergarten children's choices for SSR after they've heard a story read aloud—they most often choose to read a book they've "tasted" through read-aloud).
- Products placed at the optimum level (15 degrees below eye level) sell 8 percent better (clear or weed spaces at eye level for displaying books).

Few grocery customers know that food companies pay nine billion dollars for shelf space ("slotting fees"), accounting for one-half of stores' annual profits. In simple terms, they're renting shelf space. Paying that kind of money, the manufacturer makes sure its product is displayed on the shelf to its best advantage—that is, face-out. This visibility is so connected to sales, the low-paying companies receive the worst seats in the house—the top and bottom shelves.[26]

Grocery stores thrive on "face-out" display, but most libraries ignore it.

The reason companies want each product face-out is simple: It's the cover that most often influences our choices—the picture of the cookie, cereal, cake mix, or magazine. Any magazine editor can tell you immediately the names of the persons whose images will immediately boost newsstand sales (once it was Diana, now it's Oprah).

Compare that successful marketing approach with what we do with books and children. I often get the feeling that if most librarians were brought in as consultants for the grocery industry, the first thing they'd suggest would be to turn all the boxes and bags sideways to squeeze more of them onto the shelf.

What does the spine of the book tell you? The title, author, publisher, and Dewey decimal number. Since 60 percent of the people going into a bookstore or library don't have a particular book (or author or publisher) in mind, it's the cover that will move the book, not the spine. The majority of public and school libraries I see in my travels are clueless when it comes to these principles. Many don't have a single book shelved cover-out. The power of face-out works even at the lowest levels of literacy. When researchers observed a kindergarten classroom library for one week, 90 percent of the books that children chose had been shelved with the covers facing out.[27] The photograph above of the children's room of a public library is typical of what I find in 90 percent of libraries (school and public) around the U.S. (Yes, I know there are exceptions to this rule, and the reason they stand out is because they're *exceptions*.)

Another factor worth considering is how often students are allowed to visit the library. This is not only part of the print access concept, it addresses what could be the most cost-effective way of lifting circulation and reading scores. In chapter 5, I described Tatum (Texas) Primary School's library program and how its annual circulation rose from 28,271 books to more than 56,000 when the frequency of student visits was increased (from once a week to unlimited), as was the number of books they could borrow (from two to ten).

Where Do I Get the Library Shelf Space for Face-Out Books?

I'm not talking about positioning *every* book face-out. Bookstores don't place every book face-out, but the ones they really want to move—the new arrivals, the bestsellers—always go face-out. Unlike most educators and librarians, publishers know the cover sells the book, so not only do they work extra-hard designing the right cover, many pay the book chains as much as $750 a month per book to have the cover showing.[28] *That's* how important the cover is.

Nonetheless, classroom teachers have even less room than libraries for this approach. In response to the space challenge, a few years ago a teacher (whose name I wish I had jotted down) told me how she'd solved the problem by installing rain gutters in the dead spaces throughout her classroom: the space between the chalk ledge and the floor, the two-foot space between the closet and the chalkboard. Then another teacher sent me photographs of the rain gutters she'd installed.

The rain gutters they were talking about were purchased at the local hardware store for about three dollars per ten-foot strip, and were made of enameled, reinforced plastic. As plastic, they were easily cut to any size, and were supported by plastic brackets that could be screwed into almost any wall, including concrete blocks (see below). And they hold a *lot* of books—face-out.

After I mentioned the concept at an all-day teacher workshop, Mike Oliver, then the principal of Alma Elementary in Mesa, Arizona,[29] approached me at the break. "We could do this at my school!" he exclaimed with great enthusiasm. "We could do it in every classroom. I know we could." I could see the images dancing in his head as he spoke to me. I could also see an inner-city principal who understood that reading is more than just teaching the basics, more than drill and skill.

That summer, Oliver spent nearly $3,000 on rain gutters (I now call Mike the "Martha Stewart" of rain gutters!), and recruiting volunteers from parents and faculty, Mike installed the shelving throughout the school, including his own office. The impact was immediate and positive. (Other photos can be seen at www.trelease-on-reading.com/whats_nu_raingutters. html.) Whereas the trophy cases in some school foyers often send ambiguous messages, visitors to Alma Elementary had no trouble determining the

*Mike Oliver in his office (left),
and fifth-grade class (right).*

most important subject in the school. The walls of every classroom proudly declared it.

Rain gutters alone aren't going to solve a school's reading problems. They're merely a piece of a marketing strategy. But without marketing, few products get off the ground, no matter how good their design.

Besides Face-Out, How Do We Guide Students to the Better Books?

One of the prime reasons given by preteens and teens for reading series books is they are easier to find (they're all shelved together) and they're predictable (you know the author and characters going in). If this ease-of-use factor is so important, what would happen if you applied it to good books in a library? A few years ago, Dr. Kylene Beers shadowed two classes of seventh-graders, monitoring their classes, conversations, and library visits. Some of what she learned about aliterate students was discussed on page 137, but she also tried an experiment that she wrote about afterward in *School Library Journal*.[30]

THE "GOOD BOOKS" SOLUTION

By Dr. Kylene Beers

After one library visit, I told the school librarian I wanted to try something new. I asked her to gather together about thirty "drop-dead–great books" and put them in a box labeled "Good Books" for our next class visit.

When the students returned, the aliterate readers went directly to the couches or wandered their normal path about the stacks. Then one student noticed the "Good Books" box near the librarian's desk.

"What are these?" Kii asked.

"Good books," the librarian replied, continuing her work.

"So these are the good ones?" she asked, with awe in her voice.

Eventually the other uncommitted readers found their way over to the box. By the end of the visit, all of the students checked out a book and, more important, all of them read their book before our next visit.

What happened the following week was equally unexpected. As the students came in, those who had taken their books from the "Good Books" box refused to put them in the book drop; instead, they carried them to the librarian to be returned to the box. Then one student asked, "Do you have any more good books?" "Sure do," the librarian replied, pointing him to a second box she had labeled "More Good Books." Students chose books from this box, checked them out, and read them.

This pattern of reading from the two boxes continued until one student returned his book and announced, "This was not a good book!"

Without missing a beat, the librarian said, "Really?" Then she pulled out another empty box and labeled it "Not Good Books." She didn't argue with him, tell him the book was one of her favorites, suggest he reread it, or show him glowing reviews to prove its merit. Instead, she accepted his response as valid. As she placed the book in the "Not Good" box, another student walked by, watched what was happening, and reported she had read the book and "It was, too, good." Soon these two students, who six weeks earlier never checked out or read any books, were discussing what made this book good and bad. A third student snatched the book and declared, "I'll read it and tell y'all next week if it's good or not."

When I asked one student why he liked the box approach, he had a ready answer:

"It's like when they made Foley's at the mall bigger. It was so big that when I'd go in, I didn't know where anything was and I never bought anything. So I started shopping at the Gap. It's a lot smaller and I can find anything. I come [to the library], and I feel like I'm in Foley's—I can't find anything."

Other students expressed the same frustration with the library. They didn't know authors, didn't know genres, and didn't know where to look for the proverbial "good book." Narrowing the choice allowed them to "shop" in a smaller place and still feel independent in their selection.

Where Do We Get the Money for All These Improved Libraries?

Libraries are expensive, far more expensive than phonics kits, but if we know there is a direct connection to higher scores, the resolution is simple: Pay now or pay later.

♦ Do we pay now to create a print-rich classroom for those children coming from print-poor homes?

or

♦ Do we pay later to house those coming from print-poor homes when they are sentenced to prison? (The largest single common denominator in American prisons is school dropout: 82 percent.)

For what it costs to house an inmate ($27,500 annually), it's much cheaper to create print-rich schools. When children come from food-poor homes, schools create food programs in school to fill that gap—a humane and intelligent thing to do. Children learn better on full stomachs. So, too, when children come from print-poor homes, we should create print-rich schools. They learn better with a full head.

While communities and states save money initially with cheap libraries, eventually the penny-pinching exacts a heavy toll. California, with the nation's largest prison population, built twenty-one prisons between 1988 and 1998, but only one university. During the same period the state laid off 10,000 university personnel but hired the same number of prison guards.[31] Bound by Proposition 13, the state could not afford both to educate and to punish. It chose its prison system, which tends to replenish itself with high recidivism rates (California spends only $300 a year per prisoner on education). At our present rate, America will soon have more people in prison than in college.[32]

Do Magazines Count as Reading?

In spite of the research and the fact that adults themselves read enormous numbers of magazines, the latter still appear to some parents as a threat to child literacy. More than a few mothers have said to me, "I just don't know what to do with my thirteen-year-old. He hates to read."

When I asked one mother what her son's interests were, she replied, "Sports." But when I suggested a subscription to a sports magazine, she said, "Oh, he already gets *Sports Illustrated*. He reads it cover to cover."

"Excuse me, but I thought you said he hates to read?"

The woman looked puzzled for a moment and responded, "Well I didn't think *Sports Illustrated* counted." I quickly explained to her that it did count, that I had read (and saved) every issue of *Sports Illustrated* from the time I was thirteen until I was eighteen and that was where I had first encountered Faulkner, Hemingway, and J. P. Marquand.

For those educators inclined to look down their noses at magazine reading as being less than complex, I refer you to a paragraph pulled at random out of old clippings in a file drawer, and I confidently declare that most, if not *all,* textbook publishers would reject it as too complex for American high school students. The magazine was *Sports Illustrated*; the subject was the former Yale President Bart Giamatti, soon to become baseball commissioner and too soon thereafter to die; the author was Frank Deford:

"So it was, this April Fool's Day, that the man who stood with God at the helm at Yale became the man who stands with the child in all our selves on behalf of baseball. *Quo vadis?* Giamatti, in his new book, quotes an apocryphal memo he supposedly wrote and released to 'an absent and indifferent' university community upon assuming the presidency at Yale: 'In order to repair what Milton called the ruin of our grandparents, I wish to announce that henceforth, as a matter of University policy, evil is abolished and paradise is restored.' "[33]

Look at those literary allusions, the figurative writing, the vocabulary, the complex and compound sentences. Please don't tell me those wouldn't challenge college-bound readers or any adolescent with a brain.

If you are a parent or teacher looking to build a collection of sports books in the home or classroom, here are some authors who may have turned more boys on to reading than all the textbooks combined. Take their names to the library or bookstore:

- Matt Christopher, the most popular sports author for grades one through four
- Alfred Slote, grades five through seven (see page 291)
- Thomas J. Dygard, grades seven through ten (see page 309)
- John R. Tunis, a writer from the 1930s to 1960s, whose stories still hold up, grades five through ten
- And keep an eye on two rising stars: Carl Deuker and John H. Ritter, grades seven through twelve

How Do I Find Out About Good New Children's Books?

What children read is less important than *that* they read, but most adults want the best for their money. This handbook, with its list of a thousand read-alouds in the Treasury, should solve at least part of the problem of what to buy; the list here is also updated monthly at my Web site, www.trelease-on-reading.com. If you are fortunate enough to have in your community a bookstore that specializes in children's books (or a general bookstore that gives more than cursory attention to children), by all means tap them as a resource. Many have free newsletters to keep you abreast of new titles in children's books.

In addition, your neighborhood library subscribes to several journals that regularly review children's books, including *The Horn Book, Kirkus Reviews, Booklist,* and *School Library Journal.* These will give you an idea of what's new, good and bad, in children's publishing. The latest arrival on the scene, though, may just be the most accessible: *Book Links,* published bimonthly by the American Library Association. This slim magazine is aimed at teachers and librarians, but devoted read-aloud parents will love it too. Each issue's six or seven articles include author profiles and interviews, as well as reviews of books grouped by subject or theme for a variety of grade levels.

Here are some more resources:

+ The American Library Association and its national board of reviewers offer an extensive listing each year that includes the best of children's books, videos, and audios. The lists can be found at your local public library or on the Web at www.ala.org/parents/.
+ Publishers annually ask 10,000 students and teachers to vote on their favorite books published in a given year, tabulating the votes into lists called "Children's Choices." There are three components to the vote: children (elementary); young adults (teens); and teachers. Copies can be obtained by either mail (send a nine-by-twelve-inch self-addressed envelope plus $1.00 for postage and handling to International Reading Association, 800 Barksdale Road, P.O. Box 8139, Newark, DE 19714-8139) or on the Web at www.reading.org/choices/.
+ *Booklist* is the major reviewing organ for the American Library Association, with reviews of children's literature that are reliable and highly regarded. Its Web site, www.ala.org/booklist/, contains a list of outstanding titles published in the last year, broken into three age groups.

♦ *School Library Journal*'s "Best Books of Year" can be found at www.slj. com/articles/articles/articlesindex.asp.

♦ A complete list of all the books used on the hundreds of *Reading Rainbow* episodes can be found at its excellent Web site, gpn.unl.edu/ rainbow.

♦ The Center for the Study of Books in Spanish for Children and Adolescents; directed by Isabel Schon, Ph.D., at California State University San Marcos, San Marcos, CA; tel: (760) 750-4070; Web site coyote. csusm.edu/campus_center/csb/english.

♦ The International Reading Association offers a comprehensive guide to children's magazines and their subjects, *Magazines for Children* (U.S. $5.25). Order from IRA, Order Department, P.O. Box 8139, Newark, DE 19714-8139.

♦ Published each fall, winter, and spring, *T'N'T* (*Tips and Titles of Books for Grades K–6*) is a newsletter for busy parents and teachers that covers more than a hundred books each year. Written by Jan Lieberman, a librarian and former elementary teacher who truly understands children and their reading appetites, each issue covers a cross section of literature with creative tips on related activities. Subscribers are free to make copies for faculties and PTA groups at no extra charge. Send three self-addressed, stamped envelopes (legal size) with $1.00 in cash or stamps to: Jan Lieberman, T'N'T, 121 Buckingham, Apt. 57, Santa Clara, CA 95051.

If you are just looking for a guide to good books, not necessarily new ones, your child's teacher (if she regularly reads to classes) may have a list of choices she can't possibly get to in the course of the year. At your next parent-teacher conference, ask for recommendations. Your community children's librarian also can be a good resource. And here are two volumes with excellent lists of children's books:

♦ *What Else Should I Read? vol. 1, 2* by Matt Berman (Libraries Unlimited). These two volumes aren't inexpensive but they're worth the price if you're in the position of being asked by children, "What else should I read?" Former classroom teacher and children's book critic Matt Berman offers comprehensive "bookwebs" that connect the student who, for example, loved *The Indian in the Cupboard* to forty-seven related titles.

♦ *Black Books Galore! Guide to Great African American Children's Books* by Donna Rand, Toni T. Parker, and Sheila Foster (Wiley). This is a collection of 500 book recommendations (from picture books to novels) involving black characters, history, culture, or authors.

How Can I Find a Copy of a Favorite Book from My Childhood?

If you're earnestly searching for a childhood favorite, you will need the name of either the book or the author. "It was about either a gray or a black kitten that slept in an abandoned car" isn't enough information for a book search. Next, check the reference *Books in Print* to see if it's still available. Sometimes a bookstore will carry *Books in Print*; otherwise, telephone your local library reference room. If it's still in print, you can order a copy from the store.

If the book is out of print (OP), you used to have only one choice (other than scouring used-book stores), but now you've got at least two options:

1. If you just want to read (not own) the book, ask your public library to do a computer search of its system. If this comes up empty, they can check the OCLC database, which has computer connections to national libraries, some of which house collections of more than 300,000 children's books. Your library can borrow the book from any public library that owns it.

2. To own a copy, go to the World Wide Web and consult one of the following sites that are linked to used-book stores around the world. You simply type in the name of the book or author and wait for the list of bookstores that own that title to appear. It'll then be up to you to pursue it further, if you wish.

   ♦ BookFinder
     www.bookfinder.com
   ♦ Bibliofind www.bibliofind.com
   ♦ ALibris www.alibris.com
   ♦ Advanced Book Exchange
     www.abebooks.com
   ♦ The Big Link www.booksearch.com/

But even if a search does produce your childhood favorite, it is unlikely you'll equal the adventure of Stanley Woodworth. Growing up in Massachusetts during the Depression, Woodworth spent long hours devouring childhood classics like *The Merry Adventures of Robin Hood* and *Treasure Is-*

land, but none had the emotional hold on him of *Porto Bello Gold* by Arthur D. Howden Smith—an obscure volume of pirate tales.

Somewhere between childhood and adulthood, Woodworth and his beloved book parted company. Perhaps it was lost, maybe worn out—he never knew. But he did remember it fondly and often found himself searching for his old friend on the dusty shelves of used-book stores—to no avail. For forty years Woodworth taught ancient and foreign languages, English, and philosophy at The Cate School in Carpinteria, California, living on the school grounds and becoming a beloved campus figure. All the while, he built his personal library.

And then one day he was browsing the shelves of Bart's Books, a legendary used-book store in nearby Ojai, and there it was—*Porto Bello Gold,* for just $2.50. "I was so excited," he said later, "I would have paid $250 for it." And yet, when he got it home, he was afraid to open it, never mind read it, for fear it would be too much of a disappointment after sixty years. But finally he did and what he found was beyond even his wildest expectations. There, following the title page, was a child's scribbled signature— *Stanley Woodworth.*

What he had found was the original volume from his childhood shelf. The boy and his book finally had been reunited.[34]

Can You Ever Have "Too Many" Books in a Classroom?

Despite the research included in this chapter about "print climate," consider the circumstances of my friend Jim Jacobs. In 1991, Dr. Jacobs took a sabbatical from his job as associate professor of elementary education and teaching children's literature at Brigham Young University. "My teaching credentials were in secondary education, but most of my college students were elementary majors. So I decided to get my elementary credentials and prove to myself that *I* could do what I tell *them* to do," Jacobs told me. So he secured a fourth-grade teaching job in Germany with the Department of Defense DODDS program. It took him an entire year to build a classroom library of trade books, but by the start of year two, his scrounging and personal investments had created a collection of fifteen hundred titles for his incoming fourth-graders.

"I thought, 'These kids are going to walk in here the first day of school, take one look at this magnificent collection of books, and say, "Wow! This Mr. Jacobs is great!"' But it didn't happen," Jacobs related. "These weren't book readers to begin with. I knew that, but compared to the previous year when the class was so book poor, I believed just having access to the books would make all the difference. Wrong. Without a book background, 1,500 titles were overwhelming, not exciting—even with reading aloud and SSR every day."

Six weeks into the year, he added a daily routine of book talks, selecting twenty to twenty-five titles out of the fifteen hundred and giving brief talks about them through the course of the day. "What I learned is that we (teachers) don't have a clue as to what will turn a kid on to a book or which book will reach them. There was a girl in the class, very giddy, and the very last student I would expect to be interested in a biography of Hitler. And what happened? She devoured it, every page!

"If I had it to do over again, I'd cover all the bookcases with brown wrapping paper for the start of the year. And then each day, I'd uncover fifteen books, giving book talks on each. And gradually build the interest through the year. And that way," Jacobs cautioned, "they wouldn't be overwhelmed by the choices and numbers."

Can Pediatricians Help to Reach At-Risk Families with the Reading Message?

I see two valuable but largely dormant links to better family literacy in America. One is clergy, and the other is pediatricians.

Churches have a proud history of support for family reading. Unfortunately, it is largely *ancient* history; in Colonial America church elders regularly inspected homes and businesses to ensure that children and servants were being taught to read. Since church theology held that only those who read the Bible could be saved, those who impeded that opportunity would be held accountable.[35]

In a strange turn of events, today's reading connection with churches seems to be more negative than positive, with churches often focused on the banning of books. Indeed, organized religion could be doing a whole lot more for literacy. Family is still the centerpiece in most congregations, and since few experiences tighten family ties and strengthen the minds of future generations the way reading does, why is the subject addressed so seldom in the nation's pulpits? In much the same way that black churches are stepping in to try to heal the damage to black family life in the wake of desertions, teenage parenthood, and economic despair, so too can American clergy attempt to repair the ravages of illiteracy and aliteracy.

Librarians and educators must work together to provide materials and reminders for the clergy to disseminate—so that a year doesn't pass without clergy reminding parents of the importance of reading aloud within the family, the ease of obtaining a library card, and the dangers of over-viewing television.

With the deterioration of the extended American family, pediatricians have become a prime resource for teaching the business of parenting, providing the common sense formerly passed along by grandparents. As new parents, my wife and I didn't see the pediatrician's words as suggestions or even recommendations—they were commandments carved in stone and handed down from the mountain!

Imagine, therefore, the impact they could have on a nation's literacy if their message included the need for parents to read to their child and control family television viewing. Pediatricians tell me they are never approached by teachers or librarians to work in concert.

The most encouraging aspect of pediatrics and literacy can be found in Reach Out and Read (ROR—formerly ROAR), the brainchild of pediatrician Robert Needlman (the son of an early childhood educator) working at Boston City Hospital in the 1980s. Needlman and colleague Barry Zuckerman had seen enough at-risk children and families to know the future looked pretty bleak for them all unless something changed in the print environment of the child and family.

Then one day they were discussing the disappearance of books from the clinic waiting room, obviously taken home by patients' families. "Maybe that's a good place for them—at home with the kids," commented Zuckerman. That spontaneous observation launched a series of suppositions. They wondered if it would make a difference if:

♦ At every well-child checkup, the pediatrician encouraged parents in at-risk families to read aloud to the child, and offered meaningful suggestions

♦ Pediatricians gave the child (from ages six months to five years) an appropriate book to keep

♦ Volunteer readers in clinic waiting rooms demonstrated the importance of reading aloud by reading to the children

Follow-up research showed disadvantaged children who would otherwise have been at high risk for language delay were manifesting near normal language development, and mothers associated with ROR were four times more likely to read to their children than women of similar socioeconomic circumstances but without ROR. The response from the pediatric community was so enthusiastic, ROR could boast the following statistics in just a *decade*:

+ 744 sites in forty-eight states and the District of Columbia
+ 1.3 million children served annually
+ 2.6 million new books given annually[36]
+ 6,000 pediatricians trained

For more information, go to www.reachoutandread.org, or write to Reach Out and Read National Center, 2 Charlesgate West, Boston, MA 02215; tel: (617) 638-2280.

Chapter 7

Lessons from Oprah, Harry, and the Internet

It is wondrous indeed that you know where to find all the themes you've carefully arranged on the shelves around you. But it would be good, for once, to hear you tell the story of your favorite novels to the visitors who've lost their way in the forest of potential reading. Just as it would be good if you'd regale them with memories of your favorite books.

—Daniel Pennac, *Better than Life*

I N 1982 when the first Penguin edition of *The Read-Aloud Handbook* was published, Oprah Winfrey was an unknown doing a local talk show in Baltimore, the Internet was a U.S. Defense Department network, Harry Potter hadn't been conceived yet in the mind of Joanne Rowling, and the Department of Education was preparing a scathingly critical report on the sorry state of American education, much of it hastened by alarms over reading scores.[1]

Twenty years later, Oprah has put more books on *The New York Times* bestseller list than all the college professors in the last century; people are making funeral arrangements for books and newspapers while forecasting that we'll all be reading off the computer screen soon, so there's no need to stock libraries with books; and a 734-page book about an English child-wizard named Harry Potter has sold more copies in a week than any book—adult or children's—in the history of publishing.

Can we learn anything from these phenomena that will help children and those who work with them in homes, classrooms, and libraries? Let's see.

Five Lessons from Oprah

How Did Oprah Make TV into a "Pro-Reading" Experience?

Television has long had a relationship with print, stealing many of its early reporters and analysts from newspapers and magazines. Local and network news departments still swipe a large amount of their material from daily newspapers, put a new tread on it, and peddle it a few hours later as their own. For decades, authors and writers have been mainstays on television, from panelists on the early quiz shows (Clifton Fadiman, Bennet Cerf) to today's guests on the *Today Show, Good Morning, America, Larry King Live,* and the daily talk shows. But those authors have nearly always been writers of nonfiction—an exposé of the Kennedys, a biography of Sinatra, the ubiquitous self-help books.

Then along came Oprah Winfrey. In 1996, after ten years of sleaze and self-help as a show menu, her staff tentatively suggested that she do a "book club." Oprah herself was a big reader, and had been since age five, growing up with her grandmother. Reading three books in a weekend (her normal diet) would give her an enormous advantage over nearly everyone in the television industry, as well as most teachers who don't read that many books in a *month.*

It is Oprah's reading appetite that drives the curriculum of her book club. There is no supervisor or syllabus telling her what she should like and not like. This will only work if the teacher is a devoted reader, like Oprah. Does she get recommendations from staff and friends? Yes, but this only means she surrounds herself with staff who are readers. That's not something that could be said of every school faculty (see page 135). But in the end, the final choice is Oprah's.

Lesson No. 1: *Oprah's Book Club could never have succeeded if she herself hadn't been an avid reader.* You can't give someone a cold if you don't have one, and you can't give a child the love of reading if you yourself don't have it.

What Does Oprah's Book Club Have to Do with a Class of Fifth-Graders Who Hate to Read?

Let's look at who is watching television at ten in the morning or two in the afternoon, when Oprah's show is aired in a lot of places: not the valedictorians, or honor graduates, or the former gifted and talented students. They're all working. Oprah's "class" often consists of the laid-off, the laid-back, and the lying-down crowd, people who haven't read a book in twenty years, people who quit reading because they got tired of reading dead poets they couldn't understand back in high school.

It should also be noted that Oprah and her producers were smart enough at the very start not to use the word I used in the above paragraph: *class*. They knew very well the connotations carried by that word with many in their audience: requirements, demands, and tests. So they used the word "club," which suggests belonging, membership, invitation, even *exclusivity*.

Demonstrating the subtle power of the word "club," Dr. G. Kylene Beers at the University of Houston found in the writings of W. S. Hinchman in 1917 that when students at the Groton School (Massachusetts) were offered the choice between a reading club or a literature class, their usual choice was the club and they ended up reading more.[2]

Lesson No. 2: *Book* **Club** *works better than Book* **Class.**

If Oprah's Audience Is So Reluctant, How Did She Motivate Them?

Having selected a book, Oprah simply walks out to her audience of 22 million in 119 countries and talks about the book she's selected. She *talks* about the book, animatedly, passionately, and sincerely. No writing, no tests, no dumb dioramas to make, just good old-fashioned enthusiasm for something she's read. Further, she brings the author before the audience (which eliminates all those "dead authors" from consideration) and there's more *talk*.

Since her audience already trusts her, they buy in—to the tune of at least 500,000 copies for every book she mentions. Finally, she selects four letter-writers from the 10,000 viewers who apply and invites them to dinner with her and the author, where they *talk* even more about the book.

What can we apply from this to our work with children? Well, let's eliminate not all but *much* of the writing they're required to do whenever they read. ("The more we read, the more we gotta write, so let's read less and we can work less, right?") We adults don't labor when we read, so why are we forcing children to? It hasn't created a nation of writers or readers.

Instead, let's schedule more time to talk animatedly about what we're reading, including some Socratic coaching from the teacher-Oprah figure. Let's read books that are "good reads" and let the college professors take care of the classics. After all, most classics were written for adults, not thirteen- or sixteen-year-olds. F. Scott Fitzgerald must turn over in his grave at the thought of *The Great Gatsby* being assigned to ninth-graders.

In a study of eleven- and twelve-year-olds' reading habits,[3] researchers found the children often selected series books because they didn't know about the better books. When they did choose higher-level books, 68 percent of the time they did so as a result of hearing the book discussed by peers and teachers. People want "information" about a book before committing themselves to buying it or reading it. This may be the exact quandary that faced Oprah's audiences until she came along to prime them with information.

We're an oral species first.

Lesson No. 3: *More talk, less writing; more open discussion without right or wrong answers.*

How Can the Faculty Imitate Oprah?

The love of reading in a community should start at the top, with the school superintendent. Education, like a bike, always rolls better from the top to the bottom. Witness the case of Superintendent Bob Tebo of Michigan's Britton-Macon Area school district, a 500-student district. In 1998, Tebo's wife bought him a copy of *Tuesdays With Morrie* by Mitch Albom. This bestseller explores the emotional bond between a professor and a former student as the old mentor is dying. Because his own father was gravely ill, Tebo let it sit on the shelf, unread.

Then in the summer of 1999, Tebo's father died, and ten days later his father's brother died. They'd married sisters and were each other's best friend. It was an emotionally trying period for Tebo, so afterward he took the book on vacation and read it. When he finished it, he called his secretary and asked her to order thirty copies for the district.

On the opening day of school, he addressed the staff and bared his soul over the book—the same thing Oprah does with her books. He spoke of the powerful messages that lifted him in an hour of need, the things that were clarified for him—as a human being and as an educator. Pointing to the thirty books, he told the staff, "All I ask is, if you like it, share it with someone else."

The book was an unqualified hit. Throughout the year, teachers thanked him for sharing it, and one high school English teacher asked if he could have a set to use with his class (the answer was yes). It was one of Bob's teachers who told me about him when she attended one of my workshops.

There are several points to ponder here: (1) How many teachers can recall a superintendent talking publicly about the emotional impact of a book? (2) Notice that Tebo didn't *require* anyone to read it or write about it. He just talked about it, passionately. (3) There are summer reading lists for students, but where are the lists for faculty and parents? Many of the education journals, like *The Reading Teacher* or *Phi Delta Kappan,* have recommended summer titles. School districts should follow suit, listing the teacher's or administrator's name beside the book that he or she recommends.

Lesson No. 4: *Good readers make better leaders.*

Can the Oprah Lessons Be Applied in the Home?

Although book discussion clubs have long been a part of the public and private library scene, they had fallen on hard times in the last four decades, many fading away like front-porch gatherings. When Oprah's Book Club began in 1996, there were approximately 250,000 book discussion clubs. Three years later there were 500,000.[4]

One of the first to recognize the moment's potential was Shireen Dodson, assistant director of the Center for African American History and Culture at the Smithsonian Institution and the mother of an eleven-year-old daughter. In 1996, Dodson founded a book discussion group that eventually led to the publication of her popular handbook on the subject. *The Mother-Daughter Book Club: How Ten Busy Mothers and Daughters Came Together to Talk, Laugh and Learn Through Their Love of Reading* (Harper). Along with bringing the mother-daughter relationships closer, the club provoked greater class participation by the girls, broadened their reading interests, and provided platforms for open discussion of issues both parent and child had avoided previously.[5] Dodson's guide book is simply but elegantly organized and includes a thousand book titles recommended by successful men and women across America. Also check out Dodson's follow-up volume, *100 Books for Girls to Grow On* (Harper), and *Let's Hear It for the Girls: 375 Great Books for Readers 2–14* by Erica Bauermeister and Holly Smith (Penguin).

As soon as Margie McPartland of Greenwich, Connecticut, saw Dodson's book in 1997, she knew she had to start a mother-*son* book club (which may have been the country's first; we're still waiting for a *father*-son book club). Many of her mom-friends were anxious about their sons starting middle school, so she had no trouble collecting a dozen mothers with eleven-year-olds in tow for two hours a week (usually a Saturday or Sunday, depending on sports schedules). "Our first book was Lois Lowry's *The Giver* and we almost fell off our chairs at the discussion that ensued," McPartland told me. By and large, the mothers let the boys carry the discussion, limiting themselves to providing the lists of books to choose from each month, and refreshments.

McPartland explained, "We were careful to match the books to the school workload, so lots of the books were pretty short, which the boys seemed to appreciate. They really ran the discussions themselves and did an amazingly great job. It was nice to see other kids talk about books and also to see your own child in a group like that. It was like having kids ride in the backseat of the car; if the moms kept quiet long enough, the boys would forget we were there and just talk. As one of five daughters, it was very interesting to watch the emerging adolescent male mind in operation! But we could never forget to have lots of cookies, chips, and plenty of time for basketball or some other physical outlet!"

The monthly meetings were successful enough to last all the way through the boys' eighth grade, and then began anew when McPartland's second son started sixth grade in 2000.

MOTHER–SON BOOK GROUP READING LIST (GR. 6–8)

The Giver by Lois Lowry
Across Five Aprils by Irene Hunt
The Rifle by Gary Paulsen
Building Blocks by Cynthia Voight
The Voyage of the Frog by Gary Paulsen
When the Tripods Came by John Christopher
Who Was That Masked Man, Anyway? by Avi
Walk Two Moons by Sharon Creech
The Shadow of the Bull by M. Wojciechowski
The Lemming Condition by Alan Arkin
Twenty and Ten by Claire H. Bishop
Adem's Cross by Alice Mead
Tunes for Bears to Dance To by R. Cormier
Wringer by Jerry Spinelli
Rules for the Road by Joan Bauer

Black Like Me by John Griffen
And Then There Were None by Agatha Christie
Gifted Hands by Ben Carson
Wait Til Next Year by Doris Kearns Goodwin
The Hessian by Howard Fast
Holes by Louis Sachar
Rascal by Sterling North
Within Reach, My Everest Story by Mark Pfetzer
Harry Potter I, II, III by J. K. Rowling
The Lord of the Flies by William Golding

A few last thoughts on Oprah's Book Club: There is a tendency for the elite to demean her success because she's not doing the traditional classics. True, but she has included among her many unknown writers some of the decade's finest: Toni Morrison, Ernest Gaines, Mary McGarry Morris, and Barbara Kingsolver—all widely praised before chosen by Oprah. If anything, Oprah's selections have elevated her audience's playing field: There isn't a single Harlequin romance in the lot. And the halo effect of it is affirmed by bookstore owners, who report that when people buy an Oprah selection, they almost always buy another book as well.

Anyone who sees the club as a commercial enterprise for Oprah or her syndicate should think again. No one in her company makes a dime from any choice, and the publisher of each selection is required to donate 10,000 copies to public libraries. Further, nearly all the books chosen have been available in paperback, which means they are more affordable for a broad base of reader/viewers. The Oprah Club knows what the number crunchers in schools don't understand:

Lesson No. 5: *If you're going to change reading habits for the better, you'd better change the print climate in the community and home* (see chapter 6 for proof of this).

Lastly, consider the range of high-profile people and intellects who have held sway on television through the decades—from Jack Paar, Steve Allen, Edward R. Murrow, and Walter Cronkite to Barbara Walters, Diane Sawyer, Mike Wallace, Alistair Cooke, Bill Cosby, Larry King, Phil Donahue, and Ted Koppel. It's interesting that it wasn't one of them who started a televised book club. Instead it was a woman from impoverished Kosciusko, Mississippi—a state with one of the worst literacy rates in the country—who would lead millions of people to good books and reading, often for the first time in their lives. One Stanford professor even declared she'd done more for reading habits than anyone since Samuel Johnson.[6] Never mind cloning the sheep; let's clone Oprah for every school district in America.

Eight Lessons from Harry Potter

Every decade seems to produce reading material that provokes the wrath of parents, teachers, and librarians, all of whom are absolutely certain these books will corrupt children's reading and souls to the core. Back in the 1940s and 1950s it was comic books. In the 1980s it was the Baby-Sitters Club and Sweet Valley High books, in the 1990s the Goosebumps, and now it's Harry Potter in 2000.

How Is Harry Potter Different from Other "Series" Books?

There are two kinds of series books:

1. The quick-and-easy commercial kind like Nancy Drew, Goosebumps, and The Baby-Sitters Club
2. The more sophisticated series like Cleary's Ramona books, Lewis's The Chronicles of Narnia, Banks's *The Indian in the Cupboard,* and Rowling's Harry Potter.

The quick-and-easy series are often mass-produced, sometimes written by more than one author, and churned out at a pace of more than one a year; the books in a more sophisticated series are always written by one person, published a year or more apart, and characterized by richer text, plot, and characterization.

Along with its excellent imagery, what especially sets Harry Potter books apart from nearly all other series books is the amount of text. Consuming that many words, students are getting prodigiously better at reading—many for the first time—and *enjoying* it.

Some critics have complained that J. K. Rowling's language is not classical. True, her sentences are largely unadorned and, except for proper nouns, there is less for the reader to *stumble over.* And that's good. Stumbling over text is a discouragement for young readers, not an incentive. And while classics like *Heidi* have heavier, more adorned text, when was the last time you saw a kid reading *Heidi* in the airport? I saw five kids reading the fourth Harry Potter book in airports on July 10, 2000. A classic that is unread is like an unheard concert. In order for medicine to do any good, it must be absorbed. To get a lot better at reading, children must read a lot of words.

Before someone exclaims, "I've read *Heidi* and Harry's no *Heidi,*" I'm not talking about the book's literary style or imagery, not even its emotional levels—just the number of words a child must traverse in order to reach the end. Here's a word count I did on some books, including a few classics:

Goosebumps: 8 words per sentence; 22,450 words in book.

Heidi: 19.6 words per sentence; 93,600 words in book.

The Hobbit: 18 words per sentence; 97,470 words in book.

The Hunchback of Notre Dame: 15 words per sentence; 126,000 words in book.

Harry Potter and Goblet of Fire: 13 words per sentence; 181,000 words in book.

Lesson No. 1: *Harry Potter has children willingly reading books that are eight times longer than* **Goosebumps** *and twice as long as* **Heidi.**

Is Harry Potter a Classic?

"Classic" has about as many definitions as there are tastes. Classics have been variously described as: the wisest of counselors; the telescopes and charts by which we navigate the dangerous seas of life; the keys to the palace of wisdom; and the means by which we elevate the mind.

I'm not sure Harry fits any of those definitions, though he certainly keeps children's minds and vocabularies from sinking. But there's a definition of a classic I like best of all, perhaps because it's more democratic. It comes from Columbia's legendary professor of English, Mark Van Doren: "A classic is a book that stays in print."[7]

That is, if it continually meets people's needs, generation after generation, regardless of whether the critics liked it or not, and they keep buying it, publishers keep it in print. Only time and sales will tell if Harry is a classic—or they issue a *Cliffs Notes* for it.

In the debate over whether Harry Potter is a classic, one thing that has been ignored is Harry's competition. I have to wonder how many classics could have survived what Harry faced at the turn of the millennium:

♦ 98 percent of homes have a television, most offering thirty cable channels or more.

♦ 50 percent of children's bedrooms have a TV.
♦ Annual video sales outnumber book sales.[8]
♦ More and more teens have cellular phones and pagers.
♦ Internet use is doubling every one hundred days.[9]
♦ Shopping malls are open seven days and six nights a week.

Lesson No. 2: *Children will choose a book over TV if the book is interesting enough.*

Why Are the Potter Books So Popular?

The fantasy is rich and the cheeky humor (with a dollop of Roald Dahl thrown in) is very appealing, but there's something else, too. Shortly after Harry's initial success, and while many adults were pondering his fortune (the *Horn Book,* the distinguished children's literature journal, wouldn't give Harry a starred review), a Texas library professor made a simple but insightful observation: The Harry Potter books are entirely "plot-driven."

This isn't to say such a condition is good or bad, but it may account for many children's reactions to the series. When we adults want to enjoy ourselves with print, relax on the beach, or in front of a roaring fire on a winter afternoon, many of us choose a novel that will have us turning pages, forgetting what time it is, and reading into the wee hours. In such circumstances we don't want issue-driven novels or complex studies of human character. We want a good, plot-driven book when we read for pleasure.

But what do the adults foist on students? Issue- or character-driven novels, awarded prizes for their complexity and character study. This is not to say such volumes are either bad or ill-chosen, but where in the name of Uncle Newbery are the plot-driven books on the award lists? (I might point out, the most popular Newbery winners are the ones with strong plot lines.[10]) It's okay for adults to read such books, but children should be reading for learning, enrichment, and insight—not for the pure pleasure of turning pages to find out what happens next. As Harry might say, "Oh, those stupid muggles!"

Lesson No. 3: *Children want page-turners, just like grown-ups do.*

At What Age Can I Read Harry Potter to My Child?

There is a difference between "can" and "should," and the latter is what's more appropriate. When the Potter books first arrived in the U.S., talk-show host Rosie O'Donnell declared her everlasting love for Harry (terrific, I thought) and announced she'd just finished reading it to her four-year-old son (I shuddered).

Many of the concepts in the Potter books—class rivalries, sibling rivalries, child abuse, orphanhood, and generational inheritance—are beyond the grasp of very young children. Why not wait until the child is old enough to bring a frame of reference and maturity to the book so it can be fully enjoyed instead of just wondered at?

Furthermore, the realistic fantasy in the books can be frightening to any child too young to make the distinction between fantasy and reality. The author herself didn't feel it appropriate to read Harry to her daughter until she was almost seven years old.

Lesson No. 4: *Unlike Beanie Babies, Harry Potter books are not for all ages.*

Are the Potter Books Really a Threat to Children's Souls?

The writer Anna Quindlen once wisely noted, "There is nothing so wonderful in America that someone can't create a Calvary out of it." So when thirty-five million children lay down their Walkmans, cell phones, remotes, and Gameboys to read 400-page books (Harry Potters), the doomsayers shout, "It's the Devil wearing the Messiah's clothes!"

Anything new, popular, or magical becomes the anti-Christ—which is not peculiar to our time or place. The furor over the Potter books reminded me of a similar one in 1847, when Sir James Young Simpson introduced pain-killing anesthetics to the maternity ward. He was immediately accused by church leaders of circumventing God's will (If God imposes pain in childbirth, who is man to nullify it?). Today, Simpson's innovative practices are commonly used in both Christian and secular hospitals throughout the world.

The issue of censorship and children's books is greater than we have space for here (see my essay at www.trelease-on-reading.com/censor1. html), so for now, suffice it to say: Since the arrival of the Potter books, violent crime is at a record thirty-year low,[11] there's been no increase in juvenile crime, and none of the boys who murdered their classmates and teachers in recent years were reading the Potter books. Additionally, the thousands of midnight Potter-parties in bookstores on July 8, 2000, were marked by nothing but orderly, good-humored behavior on the part of the children and their parents—something that probably couldn't have been said about a similar gathering of 100,000 children and parents at a thousand midnight Little League games.

What's Wrong with Series Books in the First Place?

That question is best answered by the award-winning research[12] of Dr. Catherine Sheldrick Ross, acting dean of graduate studies and professor of library and information science, at the University of Western Ontario, Canada.

Ross found "series books" to be the uncontested favorite of young readers for the last one hundred years, but acknowledges they have long been the object of scorn by the cultural gatekeepers—teachers and librarians. That long-term antagonism is worth exploring if you wish to understand children's reading patterns.

According to Ross, around the time of the Civil War and coinciding with significant revolutions in printing and delivery services (like the railroads), there appeared a new kind of reading material: cheap fiction called the "story papers" and "dime novels." Printed on inexpensive pulp paper, these stories of adventure-bound heroes and heroines appealed to the servant and labor classes—the very people ignored by traditional publishers. Immediately these newfound appetites for reading were scorned by the upper classes and attacked as dangerous.

The papers, fictional forerunners of today's daily and supermarket tabloids, contained serialized adventure tales. With their "blood and thunder" tales of cowboys and Indians, pirates, outlaws, and triumphant orphans, the papers and dime novels were published bi-weekly, became national sensations, and annually sold into the millions. Instead of rejoicing at the idea of millions of unlettered citizens beginning the reading habit, social critics denounced the trend and predicted disaster.

The offspring of the dime novel was the "series book" for young read-

Years of research among graduate students showed their childhood favorites to be "series" books.

ers, conceived by Edward Stratemeyer in the late 1890s. Aimed at the preteen and teen reader, the series books eventually included Nancy Drew, The Hardy Boys, The Bobbsey Twins, The Motor Boys, The Rover Boys, Tom Swift, and the Outdoor Girls. The stories were adventure- or family-oriented, written nonstop by a large syndicate of writers, all using pseudonyms.

Just as social critics condemned dime novels, librarians and teachers denounced the series books. Franklin K. Mathiews, chief librarian of the Boy Scouts of America, wrote in 1914: "I wish I could label each one of these books: 'Explosive! Guaranteed to Blow Your Boy's Brains Out.' . . . [A]s some boys read such books, their imaginations are literally 'blown out,' and they go into life as terribly crippled as though by some material explosion they had lost a hand or foot."[13]

Fifteen years later, the elitists were so certain Nancy Drew would corrupt girls' minds (as sixty years later they would think Goosebumps would turn every child into a serial killer), H. W. Wilson Company, the largest U.S. manufacturer of library supplies, refused to print the index cards for the card catalog for Nancy Drew, and even published a list of nearly sixty authors who should not be circulated by libraries, all of them authors of series like Tom Swift and the Bobbsey Twins.

Coupled with the elitism was the widely held belief that fiction was something to be fed to children in only small, controlled doses. They believed children only learned from *facts*; therefore, fiction was useless. And the worst fiction of all would be the sensational fiction of series books. Here's a quote from 1850: "No part of education . . . is of greater importance than the selection of proper books . . . No dissipation can be worse than that induced by the perusal of exciting books of fiction . . . a species of a monstrous and erroneous nature."[14]

What made the series books especially evil for children was that they were "addictive." Children weren't content to read just one; they'd read the first, then the second, then the third, and so on. Unfortunately, moaned the experts, the whole time they're reading that junk, they're *not* reading the wonderful nonfiction book on sponges that just arrived in the library!

Lesson No. 5: *The fear that Harry and series books will corrupt the soul is at least as old as the Bobbsey Twins.*

Why Don't Kids Read the Classics Anymore?

If you think America's children were huddled in corners with their classics until television arrived in the 1950s, you're wrong. They were reading, but not the classics. Way back, they were reading those infamous "Frank Merriwell" dime novels cranked out weekly by William Gilbert Patten under the pen name of Burt L. Standish. For all her imagination, J. K. Rowling still has a way to go to equal the stamina of Patten: He wrote 776 of the titles, and sales often reached as high as 125,000 copies a week.

How much damage these mindless adventure stories might do was hotly debated, but not by young Jacques, who was fresh off the boat from France and soaking up every Merriwell novel he could find. Nor was he ashamed years later to admit the profoundly positive influence the books played in his reading development and acclimation to America, except by then he was well on his way to becoming America's best known humanities scholar—Jacques Barzun (who turned ninety-six in 2000 and celebrated by producing a bestseller on the history of world culture).

If you think today's best writers were all reading the classics as children, guess again. A few years ago at an event at the Museum of the City of New York, two men were huddled together talking. There were perhaps no two people in the room more disparate than they.

One was Louis Auchincloss, son of a corporate lawyer and one himself, a Yale graduate, novelist, biographer, essayist, and president of the Museum of the City of New York. He's been described as the closest thing this age can offer in the way of Henry James, Edith Wharton, and Anthony Trollope.

His partner in conversation was Pete Hamill, eighteen years his junior, son of impoverished Irish immigrants, college dropout, a sheet-metal worker, advertising designer, journalist, and New York newspaper editor. While Auchincloss spent much of his life writing about boardrooms and bankers, Hamill won awards for writing about the Bowery and boozers. Yet here they were, deep in conversation. About what? If you'd been close enough to eavesdrop, you'd have heard them discussing the fact that Auchincloss had just found a used copy of *Bomba the Jungle Boy at the Death Swamp,* the favorite series from both of their childhoods.[15]

On the other hand, if you think the adults were all home reading books when TV arrived, a Gallup poll in 1952 reported only 18 percent of the adults were presently reading a novel when surveyed, and in 1963 less than half the adults had finished a book in the last year. By contrast, in 1999 that figure had climbed to 84 percent.[16]

Lesson No. 6: *They really weren't reading all that much in the good old days (but they sure are now, thanks to Harry, Oprah, and user-friendly bookstores).*

Do Series Books Actually Do Any Good or Just Take Up Kids' Time?

Certainly series books make a "pleasure" connection with the child. As we saw in chapter 1, humans seldom do something over and over unless it brings repeated pleasures. Pleasure is the "glue" that holds us to a particular activity.

As I pointed out in the Oprah section, a study of eleven- and twelve-year-olds' reading habits[17] showed they chose series books because they were easier to find and they already knew something about the book (its characters and setting). With this advance knowledge, they had a head start on the reading. Ross's research[18] shows that young readers frequently complain about the difficulty in starting a new book, getting through the early chapters and meeting the characters. In a familiar series, this difficulty is averted. This "instant start" instead of frustration plays a large role in luring some students into regular reading.

And finally, Ross points to the large chunks of reading done by the series reader as examples of what Margaret Meek called "private lessons." That is, these daily readings teach the child the rules about skimming and inferring, about where one must slow down to decipher the clues, about the importance of chapter titles or of character and setting. The adage that "the more you read, the better you get at it" is not only true, but it should be the slogan of series books.

It's amazing that the critics of series books have never caught on to the simple biblical message that forbidden fruit is often that much more appealing. But they also don't understand that some of the very best readers are produced by such books, and eventually graduate on to better books. In 1926, the American Library Association asked 36,750 students from thirty-four cities to name their favorite books. Ninety-eight percent listed one of the mass-produced Stratemeyer series books (The Rover Boys; The Motor Boys; Tom Swift; and the Bobbsey Twins), with the high-IQ students reading twice as many of the series books.[19]

Updating that to the present, as part of its annual "Read Across America" promotion, the National Education Association asked student participants to name their favorite books. From the 8,100 titles they nominated, the NEA culled the top 100, which ran from No. 1 (Harry Potter) to No. 100 (*Sarah Plain and Tall* by Patricia MacLachlin). Among the top 100 titles, 35 percent were series books, including Potter, Goosebumps, Arthur, the Berenstain Bears, and American Girls. It's worth noting that the books were nominated by the readers, not the "I-hate-reading" kids.

Over a five-year period, I surveyed 2,887 teachers, with an average of fourteen years' teaching experience (see page 86). When asked to name the favorite books from their own childhoods, 30 percent named a series book as their personal childhood favorite. Since a recent study shows teachers' literacy skills to be the equal of their college classmates, and 50 percent of the teachers' skills exceed 80 percent of the general population's,[20] it should be obvious that series books do not impede literacy.

The most conclusive evidence of series books' ability to produce *better* readers can be found in the thirty years of research done by Professor G. Robert Carlson. Each semester he asked his graduate students to write their "reading autobiographies," recollections of their early years with reading—what they loved and what they hated. As he reports in *Voices of Readers: How We Come to Love Books,* the majority of these students had strong relationships with series books in their early years. Did it stunt their intellectual growth? Well, if they made it all the way to graduate school, apparently not.[21]

Lesson No. 7: *Series books are avidly read by the best readers, without impeding their skills.*

So I Should Read Series Books to My Class?

That depends on which kind you're going to read. The cheap commercial ones are best left to the children to find on their own—and they will. No one needed to read Goosebumps to their classes. Kids walk into second grade already knowing about them. There is a built-in magnet between kids and junk; they can find each other in the dark—junk food, junk clothes, junk music, junk hairstyles.

The real job of the parent and teacher is to get the child ready for the magic moment. And the magic moment occurs when, after reading the thirty-fifth book in a series, the child turns to a best friend and confides, "Do you ever get the feeling it's like reading the same book, over and over?" At that point, they're ready to move up. But if they don't know there is an "up" to move to, they're stuck in a rut. So while they're reading Goosebumps or Baby-Sitters to themselves, you're reading aloud to them from better literature.

I do think the *quality* series, like Harry Potter or Indian in the Cupboard—and the Magic Treehouse for kindergartners—are fine for reading aloud. Reading aloud the first book in such a series is a very good way of whetting their appetites to go and read the rest of the series on their own if they are capable of doing that.

Lesson No. 8: *When reading aloud, avoid the "junk" series; the kids will find those on their own.*

Four Lessons from the Internet

Ten years ago, the only time parents or teachers mentioned computers was in conjunction with how much time kids spent playing video games on them. Not only has that issue faded greatly, a larger, more ominous issue has arisen: the Internet. Many school districts and communities are wrestling with how to squeeze both books and bytes (computers) into their budget, and if both can't fit, shouldn't technology be favored since that's the future—isn't it?

There are the technocrats who say the world's children can be turned into millions of hitchhikers on the "information highway" who surf their way to achievement heights beyond anyone's estimation.

Conversely, the traditionalists point out books are more permanent, portable, and far more verifiable than computer bytes. Moreover, what children are largely visiting on the Internet is fun and games; much of the content is violent, and very little of it nurtures intellectual muscle.

For what it's worth, I offer my slant on the matter, but first I confess my biases: I am a fan of computers, own five Apple Macs, built my Web site myself, and use the Internet regularly for research and shopping. Having admitted that, I am free to declare: In its present state, the difference between the Web and the library is the difference between a microwave oven and a full-fledged, four-burner stove and oven. Which will give you a better meal? No contest.

What Should Be the Balance Between Print Literacy and Computer Literacy?

If anyone is qualified to weigh in on that issue, it would be Dr. Michael L. Dertouzos, director of the Laboratory for Computer Science at the Massachusetts Institute of Technology. Not only did Dertouzos accurately forecast (in the 1970s) the wide home use of computers, but it also was in his laboratory that Tim Berners-Lee invented the World Wide Web. According to him, the presence alone of computers and wiring to the Internet are not enough. Without education, computers are useless. As he explained to *The New York Times*:

"A while ago, I had this naive assumption that I could go to Nepal, obtain computers and training for the Nepalese and get them to have a 20 percent jolt in the G.N.P. But here's what I found: Only 30 percent of the Nepalese are literate. Of that 30 percent, only 10 percent speak English. Even if I got someone to provide every one of them with a computer with communications, what could they do with them? They have no skills to sell. To get people to do this, I would have to educate them, and people don't get educated overnight." He reasoned it would take at least fifteen years "from this and other experiences, I've concluded that the information revolution, if left to its own devices, will mean that the rich are going to buy more computers, be more productive and become richer, and the poor will not be able to do that and will stand still."

Substantial and meaningful education must precede the computer if the computer is to be used effectively. When Benjamin Netanyahu, then prime minister of Israel, told Dertouzos that he needed funding to connect the 300,000 five-year-olds in his country to the Internet, Dertouzos scoffed at the idea, declaring that the "jury is still out" on the effectiveness of computers with the very young and in education.

If this most renowned of computer scientists is unsold on technology's effectiveness with children, how can any principal or school-board member empirically declare it to be "more essential than books"? Further downgrading the "essential" nature of computer literacy skills is the fact that nearly all software is outdated within three to five years.

Lesson No. 1: *Wiring the home or school is a long way from wiring the brain.*

Then Why Do They Call It the "Information" Highway?

Because it's loaded with information, totaling 550 *billion* pages in 2000, but only one billion has been catalogued—the rest is made up of what one wag called "the stuff you find on your refrigerator door."[22] Nonetheless, those one billion pages contain a huge amount of information. At least fifteen of the research papers referenced in this book were downloaded via the Internet. These were papers that would have taken at least *weeks* to obtain by mail; I obtained them in thirty minutes. *But I would never have known about them had I not read about them in journals or newspapers first.* And it would have taken me twice as long to read them off the screen as it did to download them and print them out on paper.

In order to build my Web site, I had to learn both the language of hypertext (html) and the methods of Adobe Photoshop (to create the graphics).

To accumulate that knowledge, I read forty-nine pounds of print (twenty-six books, each averaging three hundred pages). Only about 25 percent of that information was readily available on the Internet. The real power of the Internet is in the hands of those who know how to use or control it. And nearly all that know-how is found in *print,* not on-line.

The Internet's growth is so vast (doubling every one hundred days) that after four years it reached an audience (50 million people) that it took radio thirty years and television thirteen years to reach.[23] But the growth is largely unbridled and therefore often unorganized. A study of 200 million Web sites (one fifth of the total in 2000) found that most of the essential "links" connecting the user to the next step actually went nowhere. It showed:

- Connecting to information using links will fail 75 percent of the time.
- 26 percent of the Internet is solidly connected to the rest of the Web, the rest is weak or completely isolated—a dead end.[24]

This is the equivalent of looking for books in the library catalog, then finding 75 percent of them are missing from the shelves. For all the information on the Web, finding it is sometimes like looking for a pixel in a haystack. The reason can be attributed to the Web's unrestrained growth—7.3 million pages a day.

Lesson No. 2: *A good library reference room is far better organized and quicker for research than the Internet.*

There is also the issue of shallowness. Here's a quote from the wonderful folks who designed and created the Web site for Sun Microsystems, one of the world's leading computer companies: "[Web] Users don't want to read: reading speeds are more than 25 percent slower from computer screens than from paper, but that does not mean that you should write 25 percent less than you would in a paper document. You should write 50 percent less!"

Reading and comprehension are more difficult when done from a screen. Reading is 25 percent slower because computer screens use a technology that renders lettering at a resolution of 72 dpi (dots per inch), compared to 600 dpi for most books or laser printers. This makes the computer screen six times less clear than book text.[25] In a comparative study of college undergraduates reading from both a computer screen and printed material, the comprehension level was significantly lower from the computer screen.[26] Students admitted to printing out Web material because of the difficulty both in reading it and comprehending text on the screen. No less an authority on computers than Microsoft's Bill Gates is on record as stating, "Reading off a screen is still vastly inferior to reading off of paper. . . . When it comes to something over four or five pages, I print it out and I like to have it to carry around with me and annotate."[27]

Want another point of view on Internet depth? Here's one from Mark Holmes, the man in charge of *National Geographic*'s Web site: "People hate to read on a computer screen. Whatever I put on a site, it's got to be short or broken into digestible chunks." So much for the information highway going into depth or building a focused attention span.

If those Web leaders and designers constitute the prevailing mindset, the Internet shouldn't replace the library very soon.

Lesson No. 3: *Reading from a computer screen is proven to be slower and harder work than reading from paper.*

Will You Concede That *Some* Important Information Is on the Web?

Yes, but most students are *unwilling to dig for it.* "Ninety percent of people reading a Web page don't scroll down," reports Jack Powers, director of the International Informatics Institute, a New York think tank. In other words, they don't go too deep.

How close to the mark is that observation? In an interview with *Phi Delta Kappan,*[28] Stephen Jay Gould spoke of the highly skilled former high school valedictorians he meets while teaching Harvard graduate and undergraduate courses. (Gould is president of the American Association for the Advancement of Science, a biology professor at New York University and geology professor at Harvard.) He contrasts the common image of the Internet as "information highway" with its reality: "What you get is a pretty picture, a paragraph, a song, and directions for how to dig deeper, which most people are disinclined to do."

He describes his Harvard students as generally unwilling to look deeply into references "because they're not used to doing that." If Harvard students, products of the most advanced placement classes, can be categorized that way, what can be inferred about their lower-achieving peers?

Because of the Internet's explosive growth, searching for something like "dyslexia" might give you links to 5,000 possible sites, unless you were capable of using the right kind of search tools and phrasing (see www. searchenginewatch.com for an excellent prep course in searching, as well as links in Appendix B, page 345). Another handy guide for both educators and families (including students in grades four and up) is *Homework*

Help on the Internet by Marianne J. Dyson (Scholastic), a sixty-four-page paperback with valuable searching tips and links to helpful sites in the major school subjects.

Nonetheless, the good old public library still offers the best organized and most efficient resources for academic inquiry (as opposed to "looking up"). Indeed, the peripatetic nature of the Internet hardly produces the kind of discipline necessary for true scholarship. Diane Ravich, former U.S. Department of Education official and now historian of education at New York University, explains, "The Internet encourages browsing, jumping around, surfing, sampling—much like clicking the dial for TV but with millions of unfiltered choices. It does not teach concentration, effort or stick-to-itiveness."

If Students Aren't Doing Research on Their Laptops, What *Are* They Doing?

One of the cyberworld's "dirty secrets" was aired publicly by Nate Stulman, a sophomore at Swarthmore College, in an essay for *The New York Times* Op-Ed page, "The Great American Goof-Off Machine."[29] Although his highly ranked college is not your run-of-the-mill institution, Stulman found Swarthmore students using their computers and modems in the same way millions of others do at lesser schools.

Walking through the residence halls, he noted the majority "are playing Tomb Raider instead of going to chemistry class, tweaking the configurations of their machines instead of writing the paper due tomorrow, collecting mostly useless information from the World Wide Web instead of doing a math problem set—a host of other activity that has little or nothing to do with traditional academic work." And they spend endless hours searching for and downloading more music files than they could listen to in a month. His conclusion is that many students are too immature to handle the distractions and temptations of the Internet, a fact largely unaddressed by those who think the "goof-off machines" will make books obsolete.

His observations meshed perfectly with the arrival months later of the Napster software application that allowed users to download copyrighted popular music easily without paying royalties. Its use became so pervasive on college campuses, it strangled campus computer networks, forcing two-hundred schools to ban it.[30]

Things aren't much better in the faculty room. Patrick Welsh, a Virginia high school English teacher and member of *USA Today*'s board of contributors, recalled how each of the 165 teachers at his school received laptops. After four years, he estimated that half of the teachers didn't even use them, and 95 percent of school computer usage comprises silly e-mail and clerical tasks formerly handled by the photocopy machine.[31]

Lesson No. 4: *Most students and families use their computers not to learn, but in the same way they use the VCR: as entertainment.*

Is There a Proven Connection Between Computer Use and Children's Improved Scores?

It's true that students with computers in their homes have higher scores, but students who have their own bathrooms have higher scores, too. Did the bathroom plumbing cause the higher scores or did the computer? Neither. It was the family situation (income)—all the travel, family education, parenting skills, lack of emotional stress, good prenatal nutrition, and abundance of printed material in the home. However, there is this to ponder, a finding from the National Assessment of Educational Progress history exam:[32]

♦ "The use of computers in social studies or history classrooms, which was more common for the fourth-graders than the eighth-graders, was associated with lower scores on the history test for both grades.
♦ "Fourth-graders who reported using computers almost every day scored an average of 8 points below those who did so once or twice a month and 14 points below those who used them a few times a year. Similarly, eighth-graders who said they never used computers or did so a few times a year scored 18 points higher than those who used them almost every day."

When Montclair Kimberly Academy, a New Jersey independent school, investigated the learning advantages of student laptops, they found a wealth of research (68 studies) but none reported learning results. So they decided to do their own investigation into whether equipping a group of sixth-graders with laptops would enhance their learning, specifically writing skills. The outcome: "There was no discernible difference in writing between the students in the laptop class and their peers who had approached writing in a more traditional way."[33]

There is a severe line of demarcation between computer use with secondary students and those in *preschool* and *elementary* levels. With the latter group, where there is growing pressure from government, school board, and parent factions to increase technology time and equipment, there are numerous red flags being waved by experts.

The most damning accumulation of evidence against the overuse of this technology with *preschool* and *elementary* students is found in the Alliance for Childhood's 2000 report, *Fool's Gold: A Critical Look at Computers in Childhood*.[34] Endorsed by prominent social and medical scientists, as well as child development experts, the document offers reasoned and substantial evidence that computer education does not comply with proven and effective teaching methods that are developmentally appropriate for children. Furthermore, it poses serious health risks to children, including eye strain and repetitive stress syndrome, and deprives them of the physical and emotional contact with caring adult teachers that is necessary for balanced human beings. Among the report's important and troubling findings:

- "Treating young children like small scholars and overwhelming them with electronic stimuli that outstrip their sensory, emotional, and intellectual maturity may actually be a form of deprivation." They found this to be reminiscent of the failed experiments in the 1960s in which preschoolers were pushed to learn to read and write, only to burn out by middle school and fall behind those students who were not pushed.
- Technology emphasizes analytic and abstract thinking at a time when very young children are both incapable of achieving such, and deeply in need of physical, emotional, and social experiences that computers ignore.
- The ergonomic issue of very young children spending multiple stationary hours staring at lighted screens under poor lighting conditions (classrooms are far too bright to view computer screens correctly) is "a time bomb waiting to go off."
- More than 60 percent of preteens and teens using laptops report physical discomfort due to musculoskeletal issues: if the keyboard is low enough to use correctly, the screen is too low; if the screen is high enough to view, the keyboard is too high.
- Developmental experts are increasingly concerned about the possible connection between children involved with electronic media for long periods of daily time and the rise in attention disorders.
- Social scientists point to the serious threat to children's emotional stability by exposure for long periods of time to cyberspace, which leaves them less able to separate the living from the inanimate, and contributes to escapism and a lack of security.

♦ Very young children (in the elementary grades and worldwide) developmentally need an environment that has a controlled amount of information in order to focus on key concepts, whereas the Internet offers an infinite and overwhelming number of links to "information that is outside their experience," and beyond their ability to absorb it.

♦ President Clinton's Committee of Advisors on Science and Technology (1997) conceded that the quality of research on the impact of computers on academic achievement is low and largely anecdotal, that no one has established how to use technology in ways that actually improve education, that there is a dearth of high-quality software for K–12 schools, and that educational software and technology must be updated every three to five years, thus making it difficult to completely train faculties in its use.

None of that research means computers must be *eliminated* among young children. Used in a limited way, much the way television watching should be controlled, computers pose no apparent danger to the child's development. The optimal amount appears to be no more than one hour a day, and this should be monitored by a caring adult.

Won't All the E-Mail Use Help to Improve Writing?

Most of what passes for e-mail is the equivalent of conversation at the drinking fountain or voice-mail messages—short, disjointed, and shallow. Would anyone recommend *that* as a model for elocution lessons?

No research indicates an improvement in writing, grammar, or imagination since professional writers began using computers or word processors instead of typewriters or pens. True, the writing and editing are faster, but faster is not better. Because your voice can now travel from east coast to west coast in one second doesn't make the conversation more intelligent than in the days when the journey took five seconds.

What About Computerized Books for Pre- and Beginning Readers?

So far the research shows that children enjoy such books; I know my grandsons do. But they also grow bored with the special effects and eventually tune in only to the story, clicking less and less often on the sounds.[35] But you're still paying for those sounds—the ones that are no longer used.

More than half the computerized book's cost is money down the drain. Buy the print version and save that money.

Isn't It Better for My Child to Be in Front of a Computer Than in Front of TV?

Anything can be overdone—food, basketball, gambling, religion, even books. When such overuse interferes with a person meeting with other persons in a meaningful way—especially for children whose social skills are still unformed—then the medium can easily become addictive. It is extremely easy to become addicted to the instant gratification of pushing a single computer key. For the introverted child (or adult), the computer offers an escape from reality, and that can lead to social dysfunction.

If the state universities of Maryland, Texas, Michigan, and Washington were concerned enough to set up either monitoring systems to watch for overuse or counseling programs for addicted students,[36] then parents should be *very* concerned about the "overuse" of computers. They warrant as much attention as the TV. Just as pediatric experts warn against putting a TV in a child's bedroom, they also recommend the computer in an area of the home that receives plenty of family traffic, and not in the isolation of the child's room.

Along with the *Fool's Gold* report mentioned earlier, I recommend two excellent books: *The Child and the Machine: How Computers Put Our Children's Education at Risk* by Alison Armstrong and Charles Casement,[37] and *Failure to Connect: How Computers Affect Our Children's Minds—for Better and Worse* by Jane M. Healy.[38]

Chapter 8

Television

I believe television is going to be the test of the modern world, and that in this new opportunity to see beyond the range of our vision we shall discover either a new and unbearable disturbance of the general peace or a saving radiance in the sky. We shall stand or fall by television—of that I am quite sure.

—E. B. White,
"Removal from Town,"
Harper's (October 1938)

MODERN technology, if we use it instead of abusing it, can actually help us create lifetime readers. This chapter covers both the positive and negative aspects of the technology—from television and video to books on audiocassette. What helps and what hurts? I'll also describe a pair of devices, one that automatically limits a child's viewing and another that teaches vocabulary with your favorite shows. As for programs, I'll tell you what the research shows to be the best kind for children.

But this chapter is neither a hermit's nor luddite's complaint. I own two television sets and a VCR, have favorite shows (*60 Minutes* and *Late Night with David Letterman*), watch videos with my grandsons, and enjoy being entertained.

Nothing exemplifies my television thesis better than the following story, which I've shared with every parent audience I've addressed in the last decade.

It begins with a woman named Sonya Carson, trying to raise two sons in inner-city Detroit as a single parent. One of twenty-four children, Mrs. Carson had only a third-grade education. A hardworking, driven woman, she worked as a domestic or child care-giver for wealthy families—sometimes working two or three jobs at a time to support her sons. Sometimes

she worked so hard that she had to "get away to her relatives for a rest."
Only years later did her sons discover that she was checking herself into a
mental institution for professional help for depression.

Her sons, on the other hand, were not working *themselves* into any kind
of frenzy. Both were on a slow ship to nowhere in the classroom. Bennie,
the younger one, was the worst student in his fifth-grade class. The two
brothers had done fine previously in a church school in Boston, but the
change to Detroit public schools revealed the low standards of the earlier
institution. As if raising two sons in one of the most dangerous cities in
America were not enough, Mrs. Carson now had a new challenge—the
boys' grades. She met it head-on. "Bennie—you're smarter than this report
card," she declared, pointing to his math score. "First thing, you're going to
learn your times tables—every one of them!"

"Mom, do you know how many there are? It would take me a whole
year!" he replied.

"I only went through the third grade and I know them all the way
through my twelves," his mother answered. "And furthermore, you are not
to go outside tomorrow until you learn them."

Her son pointed to the columns in his math book and cried, "Look at
these things! How can anyone learn them?"

His mother simply tightened her jaw, looked him calmly in the eye, and
declared, "You can't go out until you learn your times tables."

Bennie learned his times tables—and his math scores began to climb. His
mother's next goal was to get the rest of his grades up. Her intuition
pointed to the television that never seemed to be off when the boys were
home. "From now on, you can only watch three television programs a
week!" A week! (What Sonya Carson lacked in book sense she made up
for with common sense—that would be vindicated nearly thirty years later
when major research studies showed a powerful connection between
"over-viewing" and "underachievement.")

She next looked for a way to fill the free time created by the television
vacuum: She said, "You boys are going to the library and check out two
books. At the end of each week you'll write me a report on what you've
read." (Only years later did the boys discover she couldn't read well enough
to understand any of the reports.)

They didn't like it, of course, but they didn't dare refuse. And in reading
two books a week, then talking about them to his mother, Bennie raised
his reading scores. And because the entire curriculum is tied to reading, the
rest of the report card began to improve. Each semester, each year, the
scores rose. And by the time he was a senior in high school he was third in
his class, scoring in the ninetieth percentile of the nation.

Dr. Ben Carson

With colleges like West Point and Stanford waving scholarships in his face but only ten dollars in his pocket for application fees, Bennie let his choice fall to whichever school won the *College Bowl* television quiz that year (Yale). He spent four years majoring in psychology at Yale, then went on to the medical schools at the University of Michigan and Johns Hopkins. Today, at age fifty, Dr. Ben Carson is one of the world's premier pediatric brain surgeons. When Johns Hopkins named him head of pediatric neurosurgery he was, at age thirty-three, the youngest in the nation.

Ask Dr. Carson to explain how you get from a fatherless inner-city home and a mother with a third-grade education, from being the worst student in your fifth-grade class, to being a world-famous brain surgeon with a brother who is an engineer. Again and again, Ben Carson points to two things: his mother's religion (Seventh-Day Adventist) and the pivotal moment when she limited their television viewing and *ordered* him to start reading. (For the "complete" story, read *Gifted Hands: The Ben Carson Story* by Ben Carson [HarperCollins/Zondervan].)

I have people in my audiences with three times the education of young Mrs. Carson and ten times her income—but not half her common sense when it comes to raising children. They can't bring themselves to "raise" children—they can only "watch them grow up," and most of the watching occurs from the couch in front of a television set.

There are two important factors to remember from the Carson family's story: (1) Mrs. Carson didn't trash the set—she *controlled* it; and (2) she had high expectations of her children and demanded appropriate behavior from them. (The idea of *requiring* children to read is often debated by parents; my slant can be found on page 118.)

What Exactly Is So Wrong with Television?

Nothing. There has never been a single TV set that caused brain damage or committed a crime. Critics who assault TV as a nemesis of society are looking in the wrong corner of the room. People control it and use it; it is the *over-viewing* of television that causes the problem.

This chapter is largely a plea to control the *amount* of television viewed within the home, not a petition to eliminate it. While there is no evidence to support the elimination of TV, there is some research to support the premise that students who have *no* television in their homes perform no better in school than those who watch a *moderate* amount. Moderation and the choice of programming appear to be significant factors, along with the age of the child. The American Academy of Pediatrics recommends children under two years of age should not watch TV *at all* and older children should not have sets in their bedrooms (more on that later). Part of the recommendation on babies was based on research that indicates developing brains need live interaction with people and objects, not passive viewing of TV.[1]

The Academy has called for a child limit of 10 hours of TV a week. This was based on a research analysis of 23 TV-learning studies involving England, Japan, Canada, and five areas of the U.S., with 87,025 children, in a time period from 1963 to 1978.[2] The study's findings showed no detrimental effects on learning (and some positive effects) from TV viewing *up to 10 hours a week,* after which the scores begin to decline. It also found the most negative effects of heavy TV viewing occurred among girls and students of high IQ. Since the average child watches at least twice the recommended dosage, the research team cited that as "clearly a matter of concern."

What Else Does Research Show About "Over-Viewing" of TV?

Scientific analyses of television and its impact on children over the last forty years still leave many questions unanswered. We know for a fact that children who watch the most TV also have the lowest school scores, but why? To date no one has uncovered a biological explanation. It's definitely not brain or cognitive damage.[3]

One frequent argument is that television viewing takes away from reading and homework time and thus lowers grades. The flaw in that reasoning is: Would those same children in those same homes and families have been reading and doing homework if TV were not available? No research comes close to answering that one way or another. Conversely, children who watch little TV and do well in school usually watch educational TV and spend larger amounts of time with print and educational experiences. Were they doing that because TV was limited or would those parents have been actively involved in the children's lives anyway and provided an abundance of print in the home? More evidence points to parent behavior than to TV as the reason.

The only constant in the pros and cons of television is *time*. Those who watch the most achieve the least in school. For more than three decades, the National Assessment of Educational Progress (NAEP) has tested American (and foreign) school children in major subject areas, thus giving us our only reliable "national report card."[4] Taking the home patterns they found in the scores of thousands of students over the last three decades, the U. S. Department of Education compared the scores of thirteen-year-old math students, based upon how much TV they watched. As shown in the chart below, they found a clear correlation between over-viewing of television in the home and underachievement in the classroom.[5]

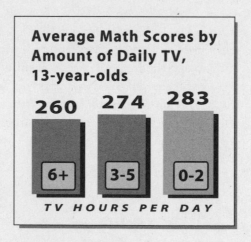

Average Math Scores by Amount of Daily TV, 13-year-olds

260	274	283
6+	3-5	0-2

TV HOURS PER DAY

Is it the fault of TV viewing or the fault of families that allow children to waste that much time in front of a plastic box? That's someone else's call. All I can do is raise a warning flag: If you allow your child to watch too much TV, you're asking for academic trouble, and there's ample evidence to prove it.

A 1996 study of 2,420 Asian and Latin American immigrants to California's San Diego area showed that eighth- and ninth-graders with the highest ratios of homework-to-television-viewing hours had the highest grade-point averages. Asian students did the most homework and Latin Americans did the least. The more TV viewed by the student, the lower his grades and the lower his aspirations for the future.[6] Did the home cause it or TV?

If Time Is the Problem, What Are the Current Dosages?

We can get a quick gauge on the time problem by examining the rise in total daily viewing per household:

+ 1950—four hours, thirty-five minutes
+ 1987—seven hours
+ 1999—seven hours, twenty-four minutes[7]

A further sign of growth (or addiction) is the increase in the number of channels now available to households: sixty-two, double that of 1988.[8]

The Henry J. Kaiser Family Foundation issues an annual media usage report that examines the media environment of 3,155 children ages two through eighteen, representative of the U.S. child population.[9] The 1999 report shows that media usage usually fell along demographic lines: Children of higher-educated parents watched thirty minutes less TV each day, and children from higher-income levels watched an hour less than lower-income peers. While more than half of households watch TV during meals, less than half of college-educated parents allowed the practice. (Awareness of the TV dangers apparently comes with more education, thus widening the education gap between haves and have-nots.)

+ 60 percent of households have three or more TV's
+ 58 percent have 2 VCRs
+ 58 percent have TV on during meals
+ 50 percent have no TV rules
+ two-to-seven-year-olds average 2 TV hours daily
+ eight-to-eighteen-year-olds average 2¾ TV hours daily
+ two-to-eighteen-year-olds average 29 video minutes daily
+ 53 percent of children have a TV in their bedroom

The 1999 report expressed serious concerns about the last item on the list and the isolated environment in which many children now experience media. It conceded that while past forms of media (print, film, radio) have had an impact on children, it usually was in the presence of others.

The new forms (TV, VCR, computers) are having their impacts on children in private, thus lessening the chance of an adult or parent filtering what the media is streaming into the child's mind. As the Kaiser Foundation Report notes, this greatly enlarges the media power over the child.

A separate study involving the TV's presence in a child's bedroom suggested part of the learning difficulties of children who watch large amounts of television may be caused by sleep deprivation. In 1999, sleep researchers working with parents and teachers of 495 students, kindergarten through fourth grade, found that those with televisions in their bedrooms (25 percent) were far more apt to have difficulty falling asleep and woke up more often during the night. This made them more prone to sleepiness during the day, impeding their school performance. The study was prompted by the number of children visiting the Hasbro Children's Hospital Pediatric Sleep Disorder Clinic who had televisions in their bedrooms. The researchers strongly urged the rooms be cleared of both TVs and computers, especially if there are sleeping problems.[10]

The issue of TV demographics is explored further in a largely silent but smoldering issue in American education—the white-black test score gap—that appears to have a solid link to TV viewing, among other causes. Although there were considerable scoring gains made by African-American students following integration and the civil rights struggle, that upward movement hit a ceiling in the 1980s. During the 1990s it was an issue administrators worried over, but did so silently because of the issue's sensitive racial overtones.

A turning point came at decade's end when the standards movement demanded high-stakes testing and an end to social promotion, forcing national and state agencies to release students' scores to the public. The issue became the center of heated debate and then, finally, the subject of careful study in numerous communities throughout the nation.[11]

Although low-income families nearly always project lower scores for students, black children of parents with at least one graduate degree still score 191 points below their white counterparts in similar family circumstances.[12] A number of reasons are offered, based on research to date:

1. Their parents are the first generation of high education (college) and may not be seen studying or reading as often as they should be.
2. The grandparents of these children (an important support group in families) are still working class.
3. Middle-class black children watch twice as much TV as their white counterparts.

The aforementioned TV finding came from a study of an academically oriented high school in the middle-class white-black community of Shaker Heights, Ohio. Done by Harvard's Ronald F. Ferguson, the study showed black middle-class students made up only 9 percent of the top 20 percent of their classes and 83 percent of the bottom 20 percent. Ferguson's research shows this first generation of children of black achievers watches twice as many hours of TV as their white classmates: three hours a day compared to one and a half hours. The Kaiser Family Foundation study in 2000[13] showed national results almost identical to Ferguson's study, but also found black children were far more likely to have TVs in their bedroom, including ones with premium cable services.

Don't Kids Need the Entertainment Break That TV Offers?

Of course they do, and so do I—even the mindless kind. As I wrote earlier, it's the number of TV hours filling a child's time that causes a problem. And I'm not even addressing the subject of what they're watching; the bigger issue is what are they *not* doing while they watch TV.

Paul Copperman, author of *The Literacy Hoax,* saw the interruption in these terms: "Consider what a child misses during the 15,000 hours [from birth to age seventeen] he spends in front of the TV screen. He is not working in the garage with his father, or in the garden with his mother. He is not doing homework, or reading, or collecting stamps. He is not cleaning his room, washing the supper dishes, or cutting the lawn. He is not listening to a discussion about community politics among his parents and their friends. He is not playing baseball or going fishing, or painting pictures. Exactly what does television offer that is so valuable it can replace these activities that transform an impulsive, self-absorbed child into a critically thinking adult?"[14]

Based on the figures in the studies listed earlier, the average child will view 1,200 hours of television and video this year. If that's a hard figure to comprehend, then think of 1,200 hours as the equivalent of watching "Gone With the Wind" 307 times *this* year. Television has become an electronic pacifier for entire families, putting them into states of semi-wakefulness.

Now let's compare a diet of sit-com watching with the experience of the family of Mike and Sally Hard of Sarasota, Florida. They had four children, including a Down's Syndrome son named Jacob, who was eighteen. The others were ages thirteen, ten, and six. In 1989, Mike and Sally came to hear me speak at a local college, and as I spoke, Mike began to hear the echoes of his eighth-grade teacher, Miss Marie Hunt, back in Metropolis, Illinois, as she read to the classes every day for twenty minutes. "We'd hurry to class so we wouldn't miss the next part of the story," Mike recalls. Coupling those powerful memories with my remarks about the need to control television viewing in the family, Mike and Sally made a resolution: No TV on school nights. Instead the family would read aloud together.

That's not an easy thing to do with four children, especially Jacob. But within three weeks, the reading-aloud had become both a habit and a magnet. Jacob would hurry through the dishes and bring them the book to hear the next chapter.

Mike also spent those evenings teaching his youngest, Andrew, how to play chess. Six years later, Andrew tied for first in the Florida Scholastic Chess Championship, and the family credited the long hours of listening to stories for his remarkable concentration in chess tournaments. But even more credit must be given to two parents who were intelligent and determined enough to control their TV before it controlled their children's futures.

Isn't TV the Same as Reading: Stories Made out of Words?

There are distinct differences between reading and TV viewing, including:

1. *Television is the direct opposite of reading.* In breaking its programs into eight-minute segments (shorter for shows like *Sesame Street*) it requires and fosters a short attention span. Reading, on the other hand, requires and encourages longer attention spans in children. Good children's books are written to hold children's attention, not interrupt it. Because of the need to hold viewers until the next commercial message, the content of television shows is almost constant action. Reading also offers action but not nearly as much, and books fill the spaces between action scenes with subtle character development.

   The use of the remote control only exacerbates the attention span problem: The average family "zaps" once every three minutes and twenty-six seconds, versus those who have no remote (once every five minutes and fifteen seconds); and higher-income families zap three times more often than poorer families.[15]

2. *For young children television is an antisocial experience, while reading is a social experience.* The three-year-old sits passively in front of the screen,

oblivious to what is going on around him. Conversation during the program is seldom if ever encouraged by the child or by the parents. On the other hand, the three-year-old with a book must be read to by another person—parent, sibling, or grandparent. The child is a participant as well as a receiver when he engages in discussion during and after the story.

3. *Television deprives the child of his most important learning tool: questions.* Children learn the most by questioning. For the more than twenty hours a week that the average five-year-old spends in front of the set (usually alone or with siblings), he neither asks a question nor receives an answer.

4. *Television interrupts the child's most important language lesson: family conversation.* Studies show the average kindergarten graduate has already seen nearly 6,000 hours of television and videos before entering first grade, hours in which he engaged in little or no conversation. And with 58 percent of families watching TV during dinner and 53 percent of preteens and teenagers owning their own sets (and presumably watching alone in their rooms), the description of TV as "the great conversation stopper" has never been more appropriate.

5. *Television encourages deceptive thinking.* In *Teaching as a Conserving Activity,* Neil Postman pointed out that implicit in every one of television's commercials is the idea that there is no problem that cannot be solved by simple artificial means.[16] Whether the problem is anxiety or common diarrhea, nervous tension or the common cold, a simple tablet or spray solves the problem. Instead of encouraging us to think through our problems, television promotes the "easy way." The cumulative effect of such thinking is enormous when you consider that between ages one and seventeen the average child is exposed to 350,000 commercials (four hundred a week) promoting the idea that solutions to life's problems can be purchased.

6. *The vocabulary of television is lower than nearly all forms of print,* from comic books to children's books and newspapers and magazines. A study of the scripts from eight programs favored by teenagers showed a sentence averaged only seven words (versus eighteen words in my local newspaper).[17] Since TV is a picture medium, a fair comparison would be with children's picture books:

   ♦ 72 percent of the TV scripts consisted of simple sentences or fragments.
   ♦ In *Make Way for Ducklings* by Robert McCloskey, only 33 percent of the text is simple sentences.

♦ In *The Tale of Peter Rabbit* by Beatrix Potter, only 21 percent of the text is simple sentences.

Thus one can say even good children's *picture* books contain language that is *at least* twice the complexity of television's. Imagine how much more complex the novels are.

How Can Parents Cope with the TV Problem?

My family's restricted viewing began in 1974, at about the time I'd begun to notice a growing television addiction in my fourth-grade daughter and kindergarten-age son. (They are now thirty-six and thirty-two.) Even our long-standing read-aloud time each night had begun to deteriorate because, in their words, it "took too much time away from the TV."

One evening while visiting Marty and Joan Wood of Longmeadow, Massachusetts, I noticed their four teenage children went right to their homework after excusing themselves from the dinner table.

I asked the parents, "Your television broken?"

"No," replied Marty. "Why?"

"Well, it's only six forty-five and the kids are already doing homework."

Joan explained, "Oh, we don't allow television on school nights."

"That's a noble philosophy—but how in the world do you enforce it?" I asked.

"It is a house *law*," stated Marty. And for the next hour and a half, husband and wife detailed for me the positive changes that had occurred in their family and home since they put that "law" into effect.

That evening was a turning point for my family. After hearing the details of the plan, my wife, Susan, agreed wholeheartedly to back it. "On one condition," she added.

"What's that?" I asked.

"*You* be the one to tell them," she said.

After supper the next night, we brought the children into our bedroom, surrounded them with pillows and quilts, and I calmly began, "Jamie . . . Elizabeth . . . Mom and I have decided that there will be no more television on school nights in this house—forever."

Their reaction was predictable: They started to cry. What came as a shock to us was that they cried for four solid months. Every night, despite explanations on our part, they cried. We tried to impress upon them that the rule was not meant as a punishment; we listed all the positive reasons for such a rule. They cried louder.

The peer group pressure was enormous, particularly for Elizabeth, who said there was nothing for her to talk about during lunch at school since she hadn't seen any of the shows her friends were discussing. There was even peer pressure on Susan and me from neighbors and friends who thought the rule was needlessly harsh.

As difficult as it was at first, we persevered and resisted the pressure on both fronts. We lived with the tears, the pleadings, the conniving. And after three months we began to see things happen that the Woods had predicted. Suddenly we had the time each night as a family to read aloud, to read to ourselves, to do homework at an unhurried pace, to learn how to play chess and checkers and Scrabble, to make plastic models that had been collecting dust in the closet for years, to bake cakes and cookies, to write thank-you notes to aunts and uncles, to do household chores and take baths and showers without World War III breaking out, to play on the parish sports teams, to draw and paint and color, and—best of all—to talk to one another, ask questions and answer questions.

Our children's imaginations were coming back to life again.

For the first year, the decision was a heavy one, but with time it grew lighter. Jamie, being younger, had never developed the acute taste for television that Elizabeth had over the years, and he lost the habit fairly easily. It took Elizabeth longer to adjust.

Over the years the plan was modified until it worked like this:

1. The television is turned off at suppertime and not turned on again until the children are in bed. Monday through Thursday.
2. Each child is allowed to watch one school-night show a week (subject to parents' approval). Homework and chores must be finished beforehand.
3. Weekend television is limited to any two of the three nights. The remaining night is reserved for homework and other activities. The children make their selections separately.

We structured the diet to allow the family to control the television and not the other way around. Perhaps this particular diet won't work for your family, but any kind of control is better than none. Those parents who feel restrictions are "cruel and unusual punishment" might ponder the research mentioned earlier, the examples of Mike and Sally Hard and Mrs. Carson, or even the privileged Park Avenue childhood that produced executive Michael Eisner, who has headed ABC, Paramount, and now the Disney empire. "For every hour of television I watched, I had to read for two hours," Eisner recalls, and his movie viewing was so limited he didn't see his first Disney movie until several years after college.

Is There a Mechanical Device
That Will Limit TV Viewing?

Until recently the only option working parents had for controlling the TV was to play video cop and incur the wrath of their children, something few had the courage (or wisdom) to endure. At some point, almost every parent has exclaimed, "If only there were some way to put a lock on that thing!" (I once knew a woman who would surreptitiously remove tubes from the back of the set, claiming "the set must be broken again.") And now, thanks to the same technical wizardry that gives you sixty channels on a single cable, you can indeed limit your children's television "dosage" each week—without guilt or even much effort.

TV Allowance (tel: 800 231-4410) is a digital device that limits the amount of time each child (or the entire family) spends watching television, videos, or playing Nintendo. The television is plugged into the device, and the device into the wall. Using TV Allowance, parents assign a password or number to each child and then enter the number of weekly TV hours for that child.

From that point on, the child must punch in the password or number in order to activate the television. The device's inner clock keeps track of the time used. When the assigned hour is reached, the set darkens, and the child is unable to activate it for the rest of the day or week. The device also allows parents to block out certain hours of the day or night during which children are unable to *ever* activate the set.

Reports to date indicate that with these devices in place children: (1) watch less television; (2) become more discriminating in how they spend their television allowance; and (3) seldom leave the room with the set still on.

The device is currently priced at $99. (I have no connection with the company, other than that they love this chapter in my book.)

These devices may not win any popularity points with kids, but they do eliminate the role of "video cop" from a parent's job list while simultaneously preventing the child's mind and skills from atrophying in front of a plastic box for twenty hours a week.[18]

Does "Closed Captioning" Really Help
Children's Reading?

Thanks to former president George Bush, every television sold in the U.S. since July 1993 is equipped with a computer chip allowing "closed captioning" (subtitles) to appear at the bottom of the screen. Initially invented to make television and film accessible for the hearing-impaired, the captions reach all but the blind, and a recent federal law requires that all TV programming be captioned by 2006.

Because of its newness, research is just beginning with captioned TV, but there are enough data to indicate significant gains in comprehension and vocabulary development (especially among bilingual students) when receiving instruction with educational television that is captioned.[19] Since we know children easily learn to read words from pages or product labels when they see the words and simultaneously hear the parent say the words, it appears that reasonable doses of captioned television can do no harm and most likely help with reading.

Research among nine-year-olds in Finland appears to confirm this. These children are the highest-scoring young readers in the world, but they also spend more time watching TV than reading. "However, there is a special feature in Finnish TV programs and also those of other Nordic countries," reports Pirjo Linnakylä, a Finnish national research coordinator. "Many programs have subtitles, and watching these programs seems to motivate and enhance reading among young students." In fact, almost 50 percent of Finnish television consists of foreign TV programs and movies that must be read—and read quickly—in order to be understood. Finnish nine-year-olds want to learn to read in order to understand TV and therefore watch a moderately heavy amount. By age fourteen, however, the situation reverses itself and Nordic children who watch a light amount of TV outscore the heavy viewers.[20]

And a final aspect of captions you might wish to consider: For children who already are competent but lazy readers and prefer watching television to reading, turn the sound off and the captioning on; this requires children to *read* their shows instead of just watching them. With the sound off, there are no vocabulary gains, but with achieving readers, that's not your goal: It is to keep the child's mind from turning to mush and discourage TV overdosing. Reading the captions prevents *mindless* viewing.

Is There Any Difference Between Educational TV and the Rest?

I've often said that educational TV is television from the neck up, while the rest is from the neck down. Parent fans of PBS can take heart from numerous studies indicating I'm not far off the mark in my assessment—that PBS programs have a positive impact on children's intellect, and other programming (particularly cartoons and sitcoms) leaves a negative impression if consumed in heavy amounts. In small amounts, commercial programming is benign entertainment.

In a two-year study of 326 five- and seven-year-olds, viewing of educational television had a positive effect on children's reading, while noninformative shows (situation comedies) had a detrimental effect.[21] That same long-term project concluded that the biggest influence on children's reading development and skills was parent attitudes about reading and the availability of books in their homes. A follow-up study seven years later confirmed the original findings and showed the intellectual gains for at-risk children were long-lasting .[22]

One of the things I respect about PBS is that it learns from its mistakes (something seemingly beyond the grasp of other network and cable channels) and keeps improving its educational programs. For example, *Sesame Street,* as popular as it is, does not qualify as a great literacy lesson. When researchers studied ten episodes of *Sesame Street* in 1995, they counted 350 segments, of which 184 were literacy related and overwhelmingly related to letter *sounds,* not *context.*[23] Of those 184 segments, only 21, included print "in context," as in signs, labels, posters, or logos. Even the impact of "role modeling" was missing most of the time in "Sesame's" instruction; only nine times in the ten hours were characters actually seen reading, and always to themselves. Not once in 350 segments did anyone read aloud to children or Muppets.

Recognizing the limitations of *Sesame Street's* format, PBS created two literacy shows targeting specific literacy issues—*Reading Rainbow* and *Between the Lions.*

Reading Rainbow, the award-winning PBS series on children's books, shows what can be accomplished when the industry sets its mind to educate and entertain. It is presently the most used television program in elementary classrooms, with more than four million students tuning in regularly. Once a book is spotlighted on the show, libraries and bookstores report an immediate positive response among children and their parents. It is not unusual for a book that normally sells twelve hundred copies to sell twenty thousand after being featured on *Reading Rainbow.* A complete list of books used on the hundreds of *Reading Rainbow* episodes can be found at http://gpn.unl.edu/rainbow/parents/mainlib.htm.

Between the Lions is a highly praised children's television program that is aimed at promoting reading skills and based on solid classroom and early childhood research. It's truly the best of its kind ever on national TV.

With the show's extensive Web site, www.pbskids.org/lions, PBS has shown that it is possible to marry TV to the Web in a meaningful way for families. Most of the entertainment industry's Web sites are intended purely to sell, seldom to educate, and never do either intelligently. This site's parent index points parents to ways they can teach literacy using story time, bath time, made-up stories, warning labels, television, food, errands, songs, newspapers, the dictionary, and airport or train signs. Each category offers almost ten simple literacy activities.

Do Audio Books Count as Reading?

As educational TV demonstrates, technology and literacy are not mutually exclusive. It all depends on the people in charge. When parents ask me if stories on tape are okay, I respond: "If they're used as a full-time substitute for a literate parent, no, they're not okay. But used to *supplement* your readings or used by children whose parents are illiterate or unavailable, they are excellent!"

As Americans spend more and more time in their cars (average commute time is now more than forty-five minutes), audio recordings have become a major player in the publishing industry, with 1,000 publishers producing more than 55,000 audio titles each year.[24]

Salespeople are driving across the land listening to books they never got around to reading; family car trips have grown noticeably calmer with children's stories in the tape deck. All are examples of how technology can be used to make us a more literate nation.

For family or classroom use, audiocassettes are a big plus. And while it lacks the immediacy of a live person who can hug and answer a child's questions, a story on tape can fill an important gap when the adult is not available or is out of breath. Even when the cassette is used as background noise while a child is playing, its verbal contents are still enriching his vocabulary more than television would with its abbreviated sentences. So by all means begin building your cassette library with songs, rhymes, and stories. Community libraries and bookstores now have a growing assortment for all ages. You might even consider recording the stories yourself.

While a story on tape is almost never as good for the child as having someone read it aloud in person, it *is* better than nothing at all. At Santa Clara (CA) Public Library, whoever does Saturday morning duty in the children's room also records a story to be used on the library's telephone story-line. In the course of a week, they receive from 120 to 175 calls on this line. Asian Americans who have not mastered English sometimes record the story off the phone and then borrow the book from the library so their child can hear *and* see the book. But for other children, like Sarah, that story on the telephone is much more. Here is ten-year-old Sarah's letter (complete with her invented spellings) to librarian Jan Lieberman:

"Dear Mrs. Leaberman:

I moved to Santa Clara when I was 5, and I lessend to the storys of the library over and over again. But when I herd your storys it was different. More sarcasem and exprechon! I'm having problems at home because my dad just died so sometimes I need something to help me get to sleep at night so I push 241-1611 and hug my teady bear and lessen!

Thanks,—Sarah"

Which Is Better: Abridged or Unabridged Recordings?

The unabridged version is preferable, by far. Taking a 400-page book and reducing it to two cassettes is usually an insult to both the writer and to the listener's attention span. On the other hand, many books are only available in abridged format, which is better than nothing. I once took a two-day trip through rural Georgia. In a manner of speaking, at the start of the trip I picked up a hitchhiker in a bookstore. His name was Dr. Samuel DeWitt Proctor, theologian, college president, distinguished professor, Kennedy Peace Corps administrator, and Harlem pastor.

For two days, Dr. Proctor's audio book, *The Substance of Things Hoped For,* informed, inspired, admonished, and entertained me. I had never met this distinguished African American, but at the end of our two days together, as he finished his life story, I felt I had made a new friend who widened my world. With this kind of technology at our fingertips, even the most humble of families can have the most distinguished visitors to their homes or dinner tables. And the audio department of the public library has the "guest list."

There was a time when the only people who listened to recorded books were the blind. In those days, federal law decreed that only the blind could take advantage of these recordings funded by federal moneys. With the arrival of audiocassettes and portable tape decks, a new industry was born. One of the early, and sometimes current, fears is that audio books will make readers "print lazy," similar to the anxieties the Greeks had about writing—that it would shrivel the memory muscles.

If you're wondering about those folks who have the time to listen to unabridged books, Helen Aron of Union College (NJ) did a random survey of 1000 renters of unabridged audio books, and the results were quite revealing.[25] Renters proved to be among the most educated, literate, affluent citizens in America. The average respondee rented 11 audio books a year while personally reading an average of 12 books. Other findings included:

♦ Men outnumbered women, 55 percent to 45 percent.
♦ The majority of renters were in their forties and fifties.
♦ 47 percent also borrow tapes from their local library.
♦ 75 percent were college graduates.
♦ 41 percent had postgraduate degrees.
♦ 80 percent had an annual family income of $51,000 or higher.
♦ 86 percent read at least one newspaper daily.
♦ 95 percent read at least one magazine monthly.
♦ 21 percent read at least 25 books a year.
♦ 80 percent usually listened while driving, only 7 percent while exercising.

For adults who are poor readers themselves, audio books can serve several purposes:

♦ They provide a common ground upon which you and your family or class can listen to literature.
♦ Since the readers are professional performers, they offer excellent role models for how to read aloud with the right expression and pace.
♦ For families embarking on long car trips, audio books serve as peacekeepers as well as entertainers.

Your local library may be your cheapest resource for audio books and will often search area libraries for titles it doesn't have. Wondering if your favorite book is available on audiocassette? Your library should have R. R. Bowker's *On Cassette,* listing almost 50,000 titles and their data.

My personal preference for unabridged audio books is Recorded Books (for both children's and adult titles) because of its huge catalog of titles and its superior stable of reader/narrators. The ultimate success of an audio book is determined by the reader, his timing, range of voices and emotions—and Recorded Books has the best. In 1999, the company won eight "notable" awards from the American Library Association, more than any other audio book publisher.

Titles listed with Recorded Books are for rent or for sale, with individuals usually choosing to rent and institutions like libraries and schools purchasing (unabridged books often have as many as eight to ten cassettes, boosting the purchase price upwards of $60). If you call for the juvenile catalog, it lists their hundreds of titles, but with only purchase prices. To get the rental price for a particular title (approximately $12 for thirty days), call (800) 638-8070, or check the title and rental price at their Web site, www.recordedbooks.com.

Listening Library (part of Random House Audio) has a good catalog of unabridged children's books, but its shining moment was winning the rights to the U.S. audio for the Harry Potter books. If anything comes close to matching the magic of Potter author J. K. Rowling, it might be the performance of Britain's multi-talented Jim Dale in these unabridged recordings. Got a long family car trip ahead? For children who are eight or older, Dale's readings will keep the peace while building the suspense. Each of the first three books lasts approximately eight hours, while the fourth (*Goblet of Fire*) lasts 20.5 hours and required Dale to create 125 different voices. The latter sold 150,000 copies in two weeks, an audio industry record.

What About Using Audio Books in Classrooms?

In Dr. Kylene Beers's ongoing research to find out what makes teenagers into readers or nonreaders (see page 137), she stumbled across a Colorado middle school teacher who had successfully incorporated audio books into her class.[26]

The teacher had been working with a class of difficult eighth-graders, including two who were pregnant and a host of others with criminal or drug-related records. They had trouble in every subject but they *really* hated reading.

The teacher tried everything from assembling a library of young adult books to book talks and classroom pillows, but nothing worked until she gave up and read to them. Fifteen minutes into Joan Lowery Nixon's *The Seance,* she experienced the year's first attention-span moment. They were actually listening. So she read all that class period, and the next and the next. Days later, when she finished the book, they spontaneously erupted into a book discussion. A week later, when she finished Lois Duncan's *Killing Mr. Griffin,* they earnestly compared and argued about the two books.

Though she'd finally found the key that unlocked her most difficult class, she also knew her vocal cords wouldn't last the year. That's when the school librarian suggested audio books. She matched each tape to its book, gathered as many tape players and headphones as she could find, and set up her class. They'd listen and follow along in their books three days a week, write and talk about what they were listening to on the fourth day, and devote the fifth day to book talks to help them find their next book.

"It was incredible. By February some of the kids were wanting to take the books home at night so they could keep reading to see what was happening. By the end of the year, all twenty-three of the kids in that reading skills class had come up about two grade levels in their reading and all had better attitudes toward reading. Audio books made the difference for those kids."

Chapter 9

How to Use the Treasury

The success we have in helping children become readers will depend
not so much on our technical skills but upon the spirit we transmit of
ourselves as readers. Next in importance comes the breadth and depth
of our knowledge of the books we offer. Only out of such a ready
catalogue can we match child and book with the sort of spontaneous
accuracy that is wanted time and again during a working day.
                              —Aidan Chambers, "Talking About Reading,"
                              The Horn Book

AN essential element in reading aloud is *what* you choose to read
aloud. Not all books are worth reading aloud. (Some aren't even worth
reading to yourself, if you want to be candid about it.)

The style of writing—if it's convoluted or the sentence structure too
complex for the tongue or ear—can make your read-aloud choice unsuccessful. And reading aloud a boring book induces the same results as reading it silently. Boring is boring. Therefore, the aim of the Treasury is to list
books whose subject matter, style, and structure make successful read-
alouds.

There are two ways to use the Treasury. One way offers hundreds of ti-
tles and synopses; the second way, however, will triple the number of titles.
For example, when you look up *Dinosaur Bob and His Adventures with the
Family Lazardo,* you will find this citation:

Dinosaur Bob and His Adventures with the Family Lazardo
BY WILLIAM JOYCE
PreS.–2nd   *30 pages*   *Harper, 1988*
In this dinosaur fantasy book, the Lazardo family brings a dinosaur home
from Africa and it proves to be the ultimate pet for home and commu-

nity—after some initial misgivings by the police department. Also by the author: *George Shrinks*; *Rolie Polie Olie*; *Santa Calls*; and *The World of William Joyce Scrapbook*. On the Web: www.harperchildrens.com/williamjoyce. For related dinosaur books, see *Dinosaurs! The biggest, baddest, strangest, fastest* (p), and *How Do Dinosaurs Say Goodnight?* (p).

Under the title and author/illustrator you'll find a *listening level* by grade for the book; in this case, PreS.–2nd; this means the book can be understood when read aloud to most children preschool through grade 2. There will be many first-graders who couldn't read it on their own but can certainly comprehend it when it is read to them. But I must emphasize these grade recommendations are meant to be flexible guidelines, not rules.

The listening level is followed by the number of pages and publisher information. Next is a synopsis of the book's plot (including any warnings, such as "This is not recommended for timid children"). Following that are listings of other books by the author, related books, and any information for author studies, or a Web site (if available).

Notice in the listing cited here, the related books have the designation "(p)" after the titles. This means there is a primary listing and synopsis for that particular book in the Picture Book section of the Treasury. There are five different categories that will appear this way throughout the Treasury, including:

+ Picture Books (p)
+ Short Novels (s)
+ Novels (n)
+ Poetry (po)
+ Anthologies (a)

All books in the respective categories are listed alphabetically by title. The Author/Illustrator Index to the Treasury at the end of the book will also help you locate books.

In the synopses, I occasionally note "for experienced listeners" to indicate those books I feel would be poor choices for children just beginning the read-aloud experience. These books should be read aloud only after the children's attention and listening spans have been developed with shorter books and stories.

What is the difference between those titles given main entries and the "related" titles listed after the synopsis? Many times there is only a small difference, sometimes none. The problem in compiling the Treasury is there isn't enough room to give every book a main entry and synopsis.

Of the more than 4,800 children's books published each year, about 60 percent could be categorized as "fast food for the mind," and of minimal lasting value. Only about 10 percent of the year's crop could be rated Grade A.

This is not to say that fast-food books are worthless. On the contrary, they sometimes serve as hors d'oeuvres and build appetites (to say nothing of reading skills) for more nourishing books later. The reader-aloud, however, offers an alternative for the child, allowing him to sample the "Grade A" books that may be beyond either his reading skills or his surface appetites.

The Treasury is meant to guide the parent or teacher to the best read-alouds, while avoiding poor choices.

Therefore, in reading aloud we should concern ourselves primarily (though not exclusively) with books that will stimulate children's emotions, minds, and imaginations, stories that will stay with them for years to come, literature that will serve as a harbor light toward which a child can navigate.

Few parents and teachers have the time or opportunity to wade through the vast numbers of newly published books, not to mention the previous year's volumes. Librarians and booksellers can help in this chore, especially when they know the patron's needs and preferences. But not everyone has access to such professional services before they visit a bookstore, and it is my hope the Treasury will help in that regard.

I fully recognize the danger in compiling any book list. There will always be those who see it as exclusive ("If it's not mentioned in *The Read-Aloud Handbook*'s Treasury, it can't be that good!"). As well intentioned as such thinking may be, it is wrong. If Harvard and Stanford can't agree on which classics constitute the core curriculum, how could *I* come up with

the ultimate list? And with nearly five thousand new children's books being issued *this year,* the best of those will already be missing from this revision and must wait for the revision five years from now. (In the meantime,
I post reviews of the newer books at my Web site between editions of *The
Handbook.*)

I make no boast of the Treasury being a comprehensive list. It is intended only as a starter and time-saver. (I'd be willing to wager, in fact, that
I've left your all-time favorite off the list.) One thing to keep in mind as
you look through the list is that these are *read-aloud* titles, which eliminates
some titles that are difficult to read aloud or, because of the subject matter,
are best read silently to oneself—like Robert Cormier's *The Chocolate War*
(subject) or Mark Twain's *Tom Sawyer* (dialect).

I have tried to make the collection as balanced as possible between
classic, traditional, and contemporary titles. It's easy to focus on the time-
tested books like *Charlotte's Web* or *The Tale of Peter Rabbit,* but the drawback is you will miss the wonderful new books—like *Lilly's Purple Plastic
Purse* by Kevin Henkes. So my hope is the Treasury will do at least two
things: (1) introduce the standards to new parents and teachers; and (2) introduce new titles to old parents and teachers.

I have tried to select only those books that are still in print, mindful how
frustrating it is to have someone recommend a book, only to find it's out
of print. As for locating those out-of-print titles, see pages 164–65 to find
out how you can search the Web for them.

In listing the publishers, it is impossible to stay abreast of the changes in
the publishing industry as one publisher absorbs another, or as a book goes
into paperback or out of print. So I've only listed the original hardcover
publisher (or paperback if that is the only format available). As this goes to
my editor, everything is still in print—but changes occur monthly.

Happy reading!

Treasury of Read-Alouds

Treasury Contents

WORDLESS BOOKS   *Page 219*

PREDICTABLE BOOKS   *Page 220*

REFERENCE BOOKS   *Page 222*

PICTURE BOOKS   *Page 223*

SHORT NOVELS   *Page 270*

FULL-LENGTH NOVELS   *Page 284*

POETRY   *Page 323*

ANTHOLOGIES   *Page 327*

FAIRY AND FOLK TALES   *Page 330*

AUTHOR-ILLUSTRATOR INDEX   *Page 395*

ABBREVIATIONS USED IN THE TREASURY
(f) fairy tales (p) picture book (po) poetry
(s) short novel (n) novel (a) anthology

Wordless Books

These books contain no words; the story is told entirely with pictures arranged in sequence. Wordless books can be "read" not only by pre- and beginning readers, but also by adults (even illiterate or semiliterate) who want to "read" to children. They "tell" the book, using the pictures for clues to the emerging plot. Books marked with an * are described at length in the Picture Book section of the Treasury.

Ah-Choo! by Mercer Mayer (Dial, 1976)
The Angel and the Soldier Boy by Peter Collington (Knopf, 1987)
Ben's Dream by Chris Van Allsburg (Houghton, 1982)
A Boy, a Dog, and a Frog by Mercer Mayer (Dial, 1967)
Changes, Changes by Pat Hutchins (Macmillan, 1971)
Clown by Quentin Blake (Holt, 1996)
Deep in the Forest by Brinton Turkle (Dutton, 1976)*
Frog Goes to Dinner by Mercer Mayer (Dial, 1974)
Frog on His Own by Mercer Mayer (Dial, 1973)
Frog, Where Are You? by Mercer Mayer (Dial, 1969)
Good Dog Carl by Alexandra Day (Green Tiger, 1985)
The Grey Lady & the Strawberry Snatcher by Molly Bang (Four Winds, 1980)
The Hunter and the Animals by Tomie dePaola (Holiday, 1981)
The Midnight Circus by Peter Collington (Knopf, 1993)
Noah's Ark by Peter Spier (Doubleday, 1977)
Pancakes for Breakfast by Tomie dePaola (Harcourt, 1978)
Peter Spier's Christmas by Peter Spier (Doubleday, 1982)
Peter Spier's Rain by Peter Spier (Doubleday, 1982)
Rainy Day Dream by Michael Chesworth (Farrar, 1992)
Rosie's Walk by Pat Hutchins (Macmillan, 1968)
Sector 7 by David Wiesner (Clarion, 1997)
The Silver Pony by Lynd Ward (Houghton Mifflin, 1973)*
The Snowman by Raymond Briggs (Random House, 1978)
Time Flies by Eric Rohmann (Crown, 1994)
Tuesday by David Wiesner (Clarion, 1991)

Predictable Books

These picture books contain word or sentence patterns that are repeated often enough to enable children to predict their appearance and thus begin to join in on the reading. Books marked with an * are described at length in the Picture Book section of the Treasury.

All Join In by Quentin Blake (Little, 1991)
Are You My Mother? by P. D. Eastman (Random House, 1960)
Ask Mister Bear by Marjorie Flack (Macmillan, 1986)
Bearsie Bear and the Surprise Sleepover Party by Bernard Waber (Houghton, 1997)
The Big Sneeze by Ruth Brown (Lothrop, 1985)
Brown Bear, Brown Bear, What Do You See? by Bill Martin, Jr. (Holt, 1983)
The Cake That Mack Ate by Rose Robart (Atlantic, 1986)
Can I Help? by Marilyn Janovitz (North-South, 1996)
Cat Come Back, illustrated, retold by Bill Slavin (Whitman, 1992)
The Cat Sat on the Mat by Alice Cameron (Houghton, 1994)
Chicka Chicka Boom Boom by Bill Martin, Jr. & John Archambault (Simon & Schuster, 1989)
Chicken Soup With Rice by Maurice Sendak (Harper, 1962)
Do You Want to Be My Friend? by Eric Carle (Putnam, 1971)
Drummer Hoff by Barbara Emberly (Prentice-Hall, 1967)
Duck in the Truck by Jez Alborough (Harper, 2000)
The Flea's Sneeze by Lynn Downey (Holt, 2000)
Froggy Gets Dressed by Jonathan London (Viking, 1992)*
The Gingerbread Boy by Paul Galdone (Clarion, 1975)
Good Night, Gorilla by Peggy Rathmann (Putnam, 1994)
Goodnight Moon by Margaret Wise Brown (Harper, 1947)*
The Gunnywolf by A. Delaney (Harper, 1988)
Hattie and the Fox by Mem Fox (Simon & Schuster, 1987)
Henny Penny by Paul Galdone (Clarion, 1968)
The House That Jack Built by Jeanette Winter (Dial, 2000)
If You Give a Moose a Muffin by Laura Numeroff (Harper, 1991)
I Know an Old Lady Who Swallowed a Pie by Alison Jackson (Dutton, 1997)
If You Give a Mouse a Cookie by Laura Numeroff (Harper, 1985)*
If You Give a Pig a Pancake by Laura Numeroff (Harper, 1998)
If You Take a Mouse to the Movies by Laura Numeroff (Harper, 2000)

The Important Book by Margaret Wise Brown (Harper, 1949)

Is It Time? by Marilyn Janovitz (North-South, 1994)

It Looked Like Spilt Milk by Charles Shaw (Harper, 1947)

Let's Go Home, Little Bear by Martin Waddell (Candlewick, 1993)

The Little Black Truck by Libba Moore Gray (Simon & Schuster, 1994)

The Little Old Lady Who Was Not Afraid of Anything by Linda Williams (Crowell, 1986)

Millions of Cats by Wanda Gag (Putnam, 1977)

Mrs. McNosh Hangs Up Her Wash by Sarah Weeks (Harper, 1998)

My Little Sister Ate One Hare by Bill Grossman (Crown, 1996)

The Napping House by Audrey Wood (Harcourt, 1984)*

No Jumping on the Bed by Tedd Arnold (Dial, 1987)*

No, No, Jo! by Kate and Jim McMullan (Harper, 1998)*

Old Black Fly by Jim Aylesworth (Holt, 1992)

Over in the Meadow by Olive Wadsworth (Viking, 1985)

Owl Babies by Martin Waddell (Candlewick, 1992)*

Pierre: A Cautionary Tale by Maurice Sendak (Harper, 1962)

The Pig in the Pond by Martin Waddell (Candlewick, 1992)

Polar Bear, Polar Bear, What Do You Hear? by Bill Martin, Jr. (Holt, 1991)

Rolie Polie Olie by William Joyce (Harper, 1999)*

She'll be Coming 'Round the Mountain, adapted by Tom and Debbie Birdseye (Holiday, 1994)

Simpkin by Quentin Blake (Viking, 1994)

Sitting in My Box by Dee Lillegard (Dutton, 1992)

Small Brown Dog's Bad Remembering Day by Mike Gibbie (Dutton, 2000)

The Teeny Tiny Woman by Barbara Seuling (Puffin, 1978)

That's Good! That's Bad! by Margery Cuyler (Holt, 1993)

This Is the Bear by Sarah Hayes (Candlewick, 1993)

This Is the Bread I Baked for Ned by Crescent Dragonwagon (Macmillan, 1989)

Three Blind Mice by John Ivimey (Clarion, 1987)

Tikki Tikki Tembo by Arlene Mosel (Holt, 1968)*

The Tree in the Wood, adapted by Christopher Manson (North-South, 1993)

The Very Hungry Caterpillar by Eric Carle (Philomel, 1969)*

We're Going on a Bear Hunt by Michael Rosen (Atheneum, 1992)*

What Baby Wants by Phyllis Root (Candlewick, 1998)

The Wheels on the Bus by Maryann Kovalski (Little Brown, 1987)

Where's Spot? by Eric Hill (Putnam, 1980)

Who Is Tapping at My Window? by A. G. Deming (Puffin, 1994)

Reference Books

The DK Children's Illustrated Encyclopedia

ANN KRAMER, SENIOR ED.

Reference 625 pages DK, 1998

This is the most comprehensive single-volume reference book for the primary grades. No one organizes and illustrates this kind of book the way DK does. More than 400 entries and 3,500 illustrations fill this book and yet it never feels crowded. It speaks the language of children and is up-to-date enough to include a section on Desert Storm.

The DK Nature Encyclopedia

Reference 300 pages DK, 1998

For pre-readers, there is a wealth of pictures; and for readers there is enough text to provide information without "overload." This is a precursor to a real encyclopedia, where "in-depth" information is still to be found.

In the Beginning: The Nearly Complete History of Almost Everything

BY BRIAN DELF AND RICHARD PLATT

Reference 75 pages DK, 1995

Ambitious as the title sounds, it's pretty close to the mark: From buildings, clothing, medicine, weapons, measures, writing, industry, transportation, and everyday life—they are all here in gloriously detailed drawings. For example, the subject of bridges is spread over two large pages, from clapper bridges in 2000 B.C. to a six-mile network of bridges today in Japan.

Richard Orr's Nature Cross-Sections

BY RICHARD ORR AND MOIRA BUTTERFIELD

Reference 30 pages DK, 1995

Double-page cross sections detail the workings of nature—from beehives to beaver lodges—with all climates represented, on land and sea.

The World in One Day: Incredible Comparisons

BY RUSSELL ASH

Grades 2–5 32 pages DK, 1997

Children often need concrete comparisons in order to understand abstract concepts. This book uses such visual comparisons to make sense of our planet, plants, animals, human body, world population, and daily food consumption. For example, the amount of wheat eaten by the world *in one day* is represented by the weight of three Empire State Buildings. This book will fascinate all age groups.

Picture Books

Aesop's Fables

BY JERRY PINKNEY

Grades 2–5   85 pages   *North-South, 2000*

Aesop's fables offer us not only wisdom but also an introduction to the characters, ideas, and images that turn up again and again in the literary tradition. This volume offers more than 60 of Aesop's most famous tales. The most economical collection is *Aesop's Fables*, selected and adapted by Jack Zipes; smaller collections: *Anno's Aesop: A Book of Fables by Aesop* by Mitsumasa Anno; and *Fables* (contemporary) by Arnold Lobel. For an off-beat satire on Aesop, see *Squids will Be Squids: Fresh Morals for Beastly Fables* by Jon Scieszka. *Aesop and Company* by Barbara Bader, includes historical background information on Aesop and his times.

Alexander and the Terrible, Horrible, No Good, Very Bad Day

BY JUDITH VIORST; RAY CRUZ, ILLUS.

K and up   34 pages   *Atheneum, 1972*

Everyone has a bad day once in a while but little Alexander has the worst of all. Follow him from a cereal box without a prize to a burned-out nightlight. Sequels: *Alexander Who Used to Be Rich Last Sunday*, and *Alexander, Who's Not (Do you hear me? I mean it!) Going to Move*. Also by the author: *If I Were in Charge of the World and Other Worries* (po). Related book: *Some Things Are Scary* by Florence Parry Heide.

All About Alfie

BY SHIRLEY HUGHES

PreS.–1st   128 pages   *Lothrop, 1998*

This handy collection features preschooler Alfie in four of his most popular stories (published individually over the years). Though set in England, the stories radiate the feeling of children everywhere—from facial expressions and clothing to the crises that really matter to young children (birthday party companions). With spare text and glorious illustrations, the plots hold young children. Other books about Alfie's family: *The Big Alfie Out-of-Doors Storybook*; *The Big Alfie and Annie Rose Storybook*; and *Rhymes for Annie Rose*; also *Dogger*; for other children: *The Lion and the Unicorn* (p).

Amelia Bedelia

BY PEGGY PARISH; FRITZ SEIBEL, ILLUS.

K–4   24 pages   *Harper, 1963*

America's most lovable housekeeper since "Hazel," Amelia is a walking disaster—thanks to her insistence on taking directions literally, causing her to: "dust the furniture" with dusting powder; "dress the turkey" in shorts; and "put the lights out" on the clothesline. She makes for a hilarious exploration of homonyms and idioms. There are now more than a dozen Amelia sequels, with the late Peggy Parish's nephew carrying on the writing. Related books: *The King Who Rained* by Fred Gwynne, and Harry Allard's zany "Stupids" series beginning with *The Stupids Step Out*.

Angus and the Ducks

BY MARJORIE FLACK

PreS.–K   32 pages   *Doubleday, 1930*

Angus, the Scotch terrier, represents all inquisitive young children exploring and confronting their surroundings. Created more than sixty years ago, this tale and its two sequels—*Angus and the Cat*, and *Angus Lost*—are timeless. Also by the author: *The Story About Ping* and *Ask Mr. Bear*.

Arthur's Chicken Pox

BY MARC BROWN

PreS.–1st   28 pages   *Little, 1994*

Long before he was discovered by PBS, there was Arthur in print, a series of wildly popular stories about an aardvark family's warm and often hilarious adventures at home, at school, and in the neighborhood. There are numerous books to choose from, and children can relate to Arthur. In this adventure, he's got a case of chicken pox, along with all its lifestyle complications for the entire family.

Aunt Minnie McGranahan

BY MARY SKILLINGS PRIGGER; BETSY LEWIN, ILLUS.

K–2   30 pages   *Clarion, 1999*

Everyone in the small Kansas farm town thought Aunt Minnie had lost her mind when she took in nine orphaned nieces and nephews in 1920. Based on the true story of one of the author's relatives, the tale describes Minnie's sometimes whimsical adventures with the children as they adjust to farm life and she adjusts to all of them. Related books: *Brothers of the Knight* by Debbie Allen; *Nine for California* (p); and *Saving Sweetness* (p).

Baby in a Basket

BY GLORIA RAND; TED RAND, ILLUS.

K–2   36 pages   *Dutton, 1997*

With the winter of 1917 approaching Fairbanks, Alaska, Marie Boyer bids good-bye to her postmaster husband, bundles her three-year-old and four-month-old daughters in fur skins, and boards a large sleigh for the ten-day trip to warmer and safer Seattle. But a ferocious winter storm strikes the travelers, spooking the horses and dumping the sleigh's contents into the snow and river. How they survived and the miraculous river rescue of the baby in the basket make this true story a great read-aloud. Related books: *The Bear That Heard Crying* by Natalie Kinsey-Warnock; *Mailing May* (p); *Marven of the Great North Woods* (p); and *Tim and Charlotte* by Edward Ardizzone.

The Biggest Bear

BY LYND WARD

K–3   80 pages   *Houghton, 1952*

Johnny adopts a bear cub fresh out of the woods and its growth presents problem after problem—the crises we invite when we tame what is meant to be wild. Also by the author: *The Silver Pony* (p). Related books: *Capyboppy* by Bill Peet; *Faithful Elephants* by Yukio Tsuchiya; *Harry's Pony* by Barbara Ann Porte; *The Josefina Quilt Story* by Eleanor Coerr; *The Polar Bear Son* by Lydia Dabcovich; and *Rikki-Tikki-Tavi* (p).

Big Jabe

BY JERDINE NOLEN; KADIR NELSON, ILLUS.

Grades 1–4   30 pages   *Lothrop, 2000*

Some saw him as a Moses figure, others as John Henry, but everyone agreed that Big Jabe did wondrous things on the plantation—things no other slave ever dreamed of doing, including saving many of his people. The illustrator, Kadir Nelson, is the single best talent I've seen in children's books in the last five years and this book radiates with his art. Also by the author: *Harvey Potter's Balloon Farm*; also by the illustrator: *Brothers of the Knight* by Debbie Allen; and *Salt in His Shoes* by Deloris and Roslyn Jordan.

The Boy Who Wouldn't Go to Bed

BY HELEN COOPER

Tod–PreS.   36 pages   *Dial, 1996*

An exploration of fantasy and bedtime resistance, this book follows with amusement and tenderness the nocturnal path of a little boy's adventures with his bedroom playmate-dolls and toys, until they are all too tired to continue their struggle. Related bedtime books: *Barn Dance!* by Bill Martin, Jr., and John Archambault; *Bedtime for Frances* by Russell Hoban; *Edward and the Pirates* (p); *How Do Dinosaurs Say Good Night?* by Jane Yolen; *In the Night Kitchen* by Maurice Sendak; *Ira Sleeps Over* (p); *May We Sleep Here Tonight?* (p); *No Jumping on the Bed* (p); and *The Very Noisy Night* by Diana Hendry.

Brave Irene

BY WILLIAM STEIG

K–5   28 pages   *Farrar, 1986*

When Irene's dressmaker mother falls ill and cannot deliver the duchess's gown for the ball, Irene shoulders the huge box and battles a winter storm to make the delivery. For other books by this great artist-storyteller, see *Sylvester and the Magic Pebble* (p). Related books on courage: *The Butterfly* by Patricia Polacco; *The Bravest of Us All* by Marsha Diane Arnold; *Dandelions* by Eve Bunting; *The Heroine of the Titanic* by Joan W. Blos; *Kate Shelley: Bound for Legend* by Robert San Souci; *Mirette on the High Wire* (p); *This Time, Tempe Wick?* (p); and *When Jessie Came Across the Sea* (p).

Brown Bear, Brown Bear, What Do You See?

BY BILL MARTIN, JR.; ERIC CARLE, ILLUS.

Tod–K   24 pages   *Holt, 1983*

This classic predictable book follows the question through various animals and colors. Sequel: *Polar Bear, Polar Bear, What Do You Hear?* Also by the author: *Barn Dance*; *Chicka Chicka Boom Boom*; *The Ghost-Eye Tree*; and *Knots on a Counting Rope*. For other predictable books, see list on page 220–21.

By the Dawn's Early Light: The Story of the Star-Spangled Banner

BY STEVEN KROLL; DAN ANDREASEN, ILLUS.

Grades 3–8   34 pages   *Scholastic, 1994*

In this book about the origin of the U.S. national anthem, we see how a picture book can be used to explain complicated or little-known historical moments, and can be used across grade levels. Related book: *Purple Moun-*

tain Majesties: The Story of Katharine Lee Bates and "America the Beautiful" by Barbara Younger—the song some people call the "other" national anthem.

Call Me Ahnighito

BY PAM CONRAD

K–3   32 pages   *Harper,* 1995

When Admiral Peary explored the North Pole at the turn of the century, his party discovered a giant meteorite, so large it would take nearly seven years to transport it to New York's Museum of Natural History. Pam Conrad imagined what it might have been thinking (if meteorites could think) through the numbing cold and the long wait for a home. If only all museum objects could be so gloriously brought to life for children's understanding. For other books by the author see: *My Daniel* (n). Related book: *Mr. Popper's Penguins* (n).

Captain Abdul's Pirate School

BY COLIN MCNAUGHTON

Grades 1–5   32 pages   *Candlewick,* 1994

Hoping to toughen up their children, parents send them off to pirate school—something like a contemporary military or prep school. With tongue-in-cheek humor (some of it scoundrel-crude), the kids shape up and then turn against the pirates. Prequel: *Jolly Roger: And the Pirates of Captain Abdul.* Also by the author: *Here Come the Aliens* (p); *Making Friends With Frankenstein.* Other pirate books: *Andy's Pirate Ship* by Philippe Dupasquier; *Edward and the Pirates* (p); *Everything I Know about Pirates* by Tom Lichtenheld; and *Maggie and the Pirates* by Ezra Jack Keats.

A Chair for My Mother

BY VERA B. WILLIAMS

K–3   30 pages   *Greenwillow,* 1982

This is the first book in a trilogy of tender stories about a family of three women: Grandma, Mama, and daughter Rosa (all told in the first person by the child). In this book, they struggle to save their loose change (in a glass jar) in order to buy a chair for the child's mother—something she can collapse into after her waitressing job. In *Something Special for Me*, the glass jar's contents are to be spent on the child's birthday present. What an important decision for a little girl to make! After much soul-searching, she settles on a used accordion. In *Music, Music for Everyone*, the jar is empty again. With all the loose change going for Grandma's medical expenses now, little Rosa searches for a way to make money and cheer up her grandma. Also by the author: *More, More, Said the Baby.*

Chato and the Party Animals

BY GARY SOTO; SUSAN GUEVARA, ILLUS.

K–2   28 pages   *Putnam, 2000*

When Chato, the original party animal (cat), discovers that his friend Novio Boy came from the pound and thus doesn't even know his own birthday, he decides to schedule one for him and invites everyone in the barrio. The problem: He forgets to invite Novio Boy. When he doesn't show up and can't be found, everyone assumes he's died or been kidnapped. When he finally shows up, there is a great *pachanga*. An excellent celebration of Latino culture. Prequel: *Chato's Kitchen*. Also by the author: *Baseball in April* (s).

Chewy Louie

BY HOWIE SCHNEIDER

PreS.–K   32 pages   *Rising Moon, 2000*

My three-year-old grandson never laughed so hard at a book as he did with this one, the tale of a new puppy with a gigantic need to *chew*. Louie devours everything in sight, from food bowls, tables, chairs, toys, the vet's pants, to the family car. Will they have to give Louie up to save their home? And then comes the wonderful ending! As much as he understands dogs, Schneider also understands kids and where their funny bones are. Also by the author: *No Dogs Allowed*. Related pet books: *The Biggest Bear* (p); *Capyboppy* by Bill Peet; *Harry's Pony* by Barbara Ann Porte, and *Mush, a Dog from Space* by Daniel Pinkwater.

Cloudy with a Chance of Meatballs

BY JUDI BARRETT; RON BARRETT, ILLUS.

PreS.–5th   28 pages   *Atheneum, 1978*

In the fantasy land of Chewandswallow, the weather changes three times a day, supplying all the residents with food out of the sky. But suddenly the weather takes a turn for the worse; instead of normal-size meatballs, it rains meatballs the size of basketballs, and pancakes and syrup smother the streets. Something must be done! Sequel: *Pickles to Pittsburgh*. Also by the author: *Animals Should Definitely Not Act Like People*, and *Animals Should Definitely Not Wear Clothing*.

The Complete Adventures of Peter Rabbit

BY BEATRIX POTTER

PreS.–1st   96 pages   *Warner, 1982*

Here are the four original tales involving one of the most famous animals in children's literature—Peter Rabbit. In a vicarious way children identify with his naughty sense of adventure, and then thrill at his narrow escape from the clutches of Mr. MacGregor. Although all the Potter books come in a small format that is ideal because young children feel more comfortable holding that size (3" x 5"), this larger volume is the most *affordable* choice, and still retains the Potter illustrations. The original story of Peter was contained in a get–well letter Potter wrote to a child; the story of that child and his letter is explored in the picture book *My Dear Noel* by Jane Johnson, and can be used as low as kindergarten level. Author studies: a children's biography, *Beatrix Potter: The Story of the Creator of Peter Rabbit* by Elizabeth Buchan; and *Beatrix Potter* by Alexandra Wallner. On the Web: www.peterrabbit.co.uk/index2.html.

Corduroy

BY DON FREEMAN

Tod–2   32 pages   *Viking, 1968*

In this beloved story, a teddy bear searches through a department store for a friend. His quest ends when a little girl buys him with her piggy–bank savings. Also by the author: *A Pocket for Corduroy*; *Beady Bear*; *Bearymore*; *Dandelion*; *Mop Top*; and *Norman the Doorman*. For related books see *Ira Sleeps Over* (p).

Curious George

BY H. A. REY

PreS.–1st   48 pages   *Houghton, 1941*

One of the classic figures in children's books, George is the funny little monkey whose curiosity gets the best of him and wins the hearts of his millions of fans. Among the more than twenty books in the series: *Curious George and the Dump Truck*; *Curious George Flies a Kite*; *Curious George Goes to a Restaurant*; *Curious George Goes to the Hospital*; *Curious George Plays Baseball*; and *Curious George Rides a Bike*.

The Cut-Ups Cut Loose

BY JAMES MARSHALL

K–2   30 pages   *Viking, 1987*

Armed with rubber snakes, spitballs, and stink bombs, Spud and Joe are the quintessential neighborhood and school cut-ups, and every reader/ listener will love their antics in battling Mr. Spurgle—who not only lives in their neighborhood but is their school principal too. Also in the series: *The Cut-Ups*; *The Cut-Ups at Camp Custer*; *The Cut-Ups Carry On*; and *The Cut-Ups Crack Up*. For humorous books about school, see *Rotten Teeth* (p).

A Day's Work

BY EVE BUNTING; RONALD HIMLER, ILLUS.

K–4   *30 pages*   *Clarion, 1994*

A young Mexican-American boy seeks work for his newly arrived grand-father who speaks no English. In persuading a man that his grandfather knows how to garden, the boy tells a small lie that ends up causing them twice as much work. The lesson in truthfulness is apparent, but just as important is the tender relationship of the child with an old man who needs help in a frightening new land.

Deep in the Forest

BY BRINTON TURKLE

PreS.–2nd   *30 pages*   *Dutton, 1976*

A wordless book reversing the conventional Goldilocks and the Three Bears tale. This time the bear cub visits Goldilocks's family cabin, with hilarious and plausible results. Also by the author: *Thy Friend, Obadiah*; *Do Not Open*. For a list of other wordless books, see the list on page 219. Related books: *Goldilocks Returns* by Lisa Campbell Ernst; *May We Sleep Here Tonight?* (p); *Somebody and the Three Blairs* by Marilyn Tolhurst; and *The Three Bears* by Paul Galdone.

Dinosaur Bob and His Adventures with the Family Lazardo

BY WILLIAM JOYCE

PreS.–4th   *30 pages*   *Harper, 1988*

In this dinosaur fantasy book, the Lazardo family brings a dinosaur home from Africa and it proves to be the ultimate pet for home and community—after some initial misgivings by the police department. Also by the author: *George Shrinks*; *Rolie Polie Olie*; *Santa Calls*; and *The World of William Joyce Scrapbook*. On the Web: www.harperchildrens.com/williamjoyce. For related dinosaur books, see *Dinosaurs! The biggest, baddest, strangest, fastest* (p), and *How do Dinosaurs Say Goodnight?* (p).

Dinosaurs! The biggest, baddest, strangest, fastest

BY HOWARD ZIMMERMAN

PreS.–5th   *60 pages*   *Atheneum, 2000*

Carefully researched and magnificently illustrated by a group of today's most talented graphic artists, this is one of the more dramatic books on dinosaurs. Along with a much-needed pronunciation guide, it has up-to-date research findings, and a handy guide to dinosaur sites listed on the World Wide Web! *Warning*: The illustrations frequently picture them in bloody combat or defending themselves against vicious predators, so this book may not be for the faint-of-heart child.

Related books: *The Big Book of Dinosaurs: A First Book for Young Children* by Angela Wilkes; *On the Trail of Incredible Dinosaurs* by William Lindsay (for older children, this traces the fossil route followed by the great "bone detectives" at the beginning of this century); *Asteroid Impact* by Douglas Henderson (Did a gigantic asteroid cause the end of the dinosaur age? Here's the theory, in vivid, detailed illustrations, based on the latest scientific theories); *Graveyards of the Dinosaurs* by Shelley Tanaka; *Mary Anning and the Sea Dragon* by Jeannine Atkins; *Scholastic Question and Answer Series: Did Dinosaurs Live in Your Backyard?* by Melvin and Gilda Berger; for students in grades four and older, see *My Daniel* (n).

Disaster! Catastrophes That Shook the World
BY RICHARD BONSON AND RICHARD PLATT
Grades 1–6   36 pages   *Dorling Kindersley, 1997*
This book takes us on a breathtaking tour of thirteen of the world's worst disasters. From Vesuvius and the Black Plague to the *Titanic* and a 1974 cyclone in Australia, this is irresistible reading and viewing. Each event is illustrated in detailed schematics (in the tradition of Stephen Biesty's Cross-Section books) that enumerate the hows and whys, as well as consequences of such events. Even non-readers will be fascinated by the illustrations here. Related book: *Nature's Fury* by Carole G. Vogel provides eyewitness reports on thirteen major natural disasters to strike the U.S. in the last century, accompanied by outstanding photographs.

Don't Go Near That Rabbit, Frank!
BY PAM CONRAD; MARK ENGLISH, ILLUS.
Grades 4 and up   48 pages   *Harper, 1998*
First—do *not* read this to the lower elementary grades. The humor of the situation will elude them entirely and the story could bother them. But it's perfect for older grades—the older the better. It's based on an urban legend that usually involves a dog. In this case, it's a prize show rabbit owned by old man Hoover, who warns the new kids next door that he'll shoot their dog if it comes near his rabbit hutch. The plot is: The rabbit dies of natural causes, the old man buries him in the yard, the dog digs it up and brings it home to the kids, who think he killed the rabbit. So they clean it up in the tub and smuggle it back into the hutch so old man Hoover will think it died of natural causes and won't blame their dog. When the old man comes to clean out the hutch . . . *Note:* This book was erroneously listed in some editions of *Books in Print* as *Old Man Hoover's Dead Rabbit.* More ur-

ban legends (for fourth grade and up): Jan Brunvand's collections—*Too Good to Be True: The Colossal Book of Urban Legends*; *The Big Book of Urban Legends*; *The Vanishing Hitchhiker*; *The Choking Doberman*; *The Mexican Pet*; and *Curses! Broiled Again.*

Dreamland
BY RONI SCHOTTER; KEVIN HAWKES, ILLUS.
K–2   32 pages   Orchard, 1996
While everyone in Theo's family toils in the family's tailor shop, Uncle Gurney dreams of what could be—much to the dismay of his hardworking relatives. Everyone, that is, except little Theo, who is a dreamer like his uncle. When Gurney heads west to seek his fortune, Theo gives him his marvelous invention drawings as a going-away gift. What his uncle does with those drawings is a tribute to both of them and to "dreamers" everywhere. Related books: *Applemondo's Dream* by Patricia Polacco; *Cloud Nine* by Norman Silver; *Edward and the Pirates* (p); *The Flying Dragon Room* by Audrey Wood; *Incredible Ned* by Bill Maynard; *The Silver Pony* (p); and *Weslandia* by Paul Fleischman.

Edward and the Pirates
BY DAVID MCPHAIL
PreS.–K   28 pages   Little, Brown, 1997
Edward has learned to read and reads everything, elaborating on the books through his imagination. One night, while he is reading *Lost Pirate Treasure*, the pirates visit his bedroom in hopes of stealing that book. Edward refuses to give it up (it's a library book!) and is about to walk the plank when his mom and dad come to the rescue as only storybook heroes can. All is happily resolved for the pirates when Edward agrees to read the book *to* them (since pirates can't read!). This is a sequel to *Santa's Book of Names*. Related pirate books: *Captain Abdul's Pirate School* (p); related books on children's wild imaginations, see *Dreamland* (p) and *The Magic Paintbrush* (p).

Encounter
BY JANE YOLEN; DAVID SHANNON, ILLUS.
Grades 3–7   30 pages   Harcourt, 1992
In observance of the 500th anniversary of Columbus's arrival in the Western Hemisphere, Yolen views the arrival through the eyes of a Taino Indian boy on San Salvador who has a foreboding dream about the newcomers. Portrayed in hauntingly beautiful illustrations, the boy's warnings are rejected by the tribe's elders. A thought-provoking book on imperialism and colonialism. Related reading: *Time* article, "Before Columbus," October

19, 1998, pp. 76–77, detailing recent archeological discoveries about the Taino tribe in Caribbean digs. Some of our most common words come from this tribe: *barbecue, canoe, hurricane, hammock,* and *tobacco.*

Erandi's Braids

BY ANTONIO HERNANDEZ MADRIGAL; TOMIE DEPAOLA, ILLUS.

PreS.–2nd   30 pages   *Putnam, 1999*

It was once the custom for women in poor Mexican villages to sell their hair, which was then used for wigs and fancy embroidery. In this tale, Erandi's mother has decided to sell her hair in order to pay for a much-needed fishing net. The barber refuses, saying hers is too short, but that he would gladly take the child's braids. It is now the child's difficult decision to make. Related books: *The Legend of the Bluebonnet* (p); *The Hunter* by Mary Casanova; the sacrifices that parents make are explored in these books: *The Babe and I* by David A. Adler, and *I Remember Papa* by Helen Ketteman.

The Everything Book

BY DENISE FLEMING

Inf–Tod   64 pages   *Holt, 2000*

After Mother Goose, all new parents should have this terrific book that truly is about everything important to a child—animals, shapes, colors, rhymes, finger games, food, faces, letters, traffic, and toys. The art is a rainbow feast for the eyes, but done in a style very young children can easily absorb. Related book: *My First Word Book* by Angela Wilkes.

Fairy Tales (see page 330)

The Foot Book

BY DR. SEUSS

Tod–PreS.   28 pages   *Random House, 1968*

Most of Dr. Seuss's books are aimed at kindergarten and older, but here is one of the more accessible ones for toddlers, mainly because the subject is so near (eighteen inches away) to the child's heart: feet! No plot but lots of repetition, rhyme, and Seussian illustrations. Also by the author: *If I Ran the Zoo* (p). For a list of Seuss books, see the Web sites www.randomhouse. com/seussville/ and klinzhai.iuma.com/~drseuss/seuss/.

Fans of Dr. Seuss will enjoy the books of Bill Peet—see *The Whing-dingdilly* (p). For Seuss author studies: "Oh, the Places You've Taken Us: RT's Tribute to Dr. Seuss," in the May 1992 issue of *The Reading Teacher*; and *Dr. Seuss and Mr. Geisel: A Biography* by Judith and Neil Morgan (Random House), the definitive book on his life.

Frederick

BY LEO LIONNI

PreS.–2nd   28 pages   *Pantheon, 1966*

Frederick is a tiny gray field mouse. He is also an allegorical figure representing the poets, artists, and dreamers of the world. While his brothers
and sisters gather food against the oncoming winter, Frederick gathers the
colors and stories and dreams they will need to sustain their hearts and
souls in the winter darkness. Also by the author: *Alexander and the Wind-Up
Mouse*; *The Biggest House in the World*; *Fish is Fish*; *Frederick's Fables: A Leo
Lionni Treasury of Favorite Stories*; *Little Blue and Little Yellow*; *Nicholas, Where
Have you Been?*; *Swimmy*; *Tillie and the Wall*. Other mice books, see *Lilly's
Purple Plastic Purse* (p).

Frog and Toad Are Friends

BY ARNOLD LOBEL

PreS.–2nd   64 pages   *Harper, 1970*

Using a simple early-reader vocabulary and fable-like story lines, the author-
artist developed an award-winning series that is a must for young children.
Generous helpings of humor and warm personal relationships are the
trademarks of the series, each book containing five stories relating to
childhood. As an author-illustrator, Arnold Lobel did it all. Sequels: *Days
with Frog and Toad*; *Frog and Toad All Year*; and *Frog and Toad Together*; also:
Mouse Soup; *Mouse Tales*; *Owl at Home*; and *Uncle Elephant*.

Froggy Gets Dressed

BY JONATHAN LONDON; FRANK REMKIEWICZ, ILLUS.

PreS.–K   32 pages   *Viking, 2000*

Young Froggy is so excited about the first snowfall, he rushes outside to
play with his friends before realizing he's forgotten to get dressed! Out of
breath and back outside after all that dressing, his mother shouts to remind
him he's forgotten his long *underwear*! This popular series includes: *Let's Go
Froggy!*; *Froggy Learns to Swim*; *Froggy Goes to School*; *Froggy's First Kiss*; *Froggy
Plays Soccer*; *Froggy's Halloween*; *Froggy Goes to Bed*; and *Froggy's Best Christmas*.

The Gardener

BY SARAH STEWART; DAVID SMALL, ILLUS.

K–4   32 pages   *Farrar, 1997*

In the midst of the Depression, Lydia Grace is sent to stay temporarily with
her uncle in the city. Told in a series of short letters, this gentle tale re-

counts her life in the city and her efforts to cheer her overworked uncle and to find a place to plant a garden where it seems only cement can grow. Her success on both counts is a joy. Also by the author–illustrator team: *The Money Tree* and *The Library*. Related books: *Aunt Minnie McGranahan* (p); and *The Babe and I* by David A. Adler.

A Gift for Tia Rosa

BY KAREN T. TAHA; DEE DEROSA, ILLUS.

K–4   36 pages   *Bantam, 1991*

Carmela's elderly Hispanic neighbor, Tia Rosa, is teaching her how to knit. Carmela loves her dearly and is grief-stricken when the woman dies. As saddened as she is by the loss, Carmela is even sadder because she didn't have a chance to tell her how much she loved her. And then she discovers a way. A sensitive example of families and neighbors supporting each other in times of loss. Other picture books treating death and loss include: *The Accident* by Carol Carrick; *The Big Red Barn* by Eve Bunting; *Everett Anderson's Goodbye* by Lucille Clifton; *The Log Cabin Quilt* by Ellen Howard; *My Grandson Lew* by Charlotte Zolotow; *Nana Upstairs & Nana Downstairs* by Tomie dePaola; *The Tenth Good Thing about Barney* by Judith Viorst; for older students, see the novels listed with *A Taste of Blackberries* (s).

The Gingerbread Boy

RETOLD BY RICHARD EGIELSKI

PreS.–1st   30 pages   *Harper, 1997*

A Caldecott-winning artist gives us this traditional tale in a modern setting— New York City, with the gingerbread boy racing from brownstone apartments to subways, through construction sites, and into Central Park, where the fox awaits him. Related titles: *The Bee Tree* by Patricia Polacco; *Clay Boy* by Mirra Ginsburg; *Red's Great Chase* (p); and *The Story of Little Babaji* (p).

Goodnight Moon

BY MARGARET WISE BROWN; CLEMENT HURD, ILLUS.

Tod–PreS.   30 pages   *Harper, 1947*

This modern classic is based on a bedtime ritual, sure to be copied by every child who hears it. Also by the author: *The Important Book*; *The Runaway Bunny*; and *Sailor Dog*. Related bedtime books for infants and toddlers: *Can't You Sleep, Little Bear?* by Martin Waddell; *Good Night, Gorilla* by Peggy Rathman; *Go to Bed!* by Virginia Miller; *How Do Dinosaurs Say Good Night?* (p); *Max's Bedtime* by Rosemary Wells; *The Napping House* by Audrey Wood; *Ten, Nine, Eight* by Molly Bang; and *The Very Noisy Night* by Diana Hendry.

Grandaddy's Place

BY HELEN GRIFFITH; JAMES STEVENSON, ILLUS.

K–3   36 pages   *Greenwillow, 1987*

On her first visit to her grandaddy's rural Georgia cabin, a young city girl is frightened by its strangeness. Soon, however, the old man's quiet charm begins to work its magic and a new world opens for the child. The book is divided into short, six-page chapters. Sequels: *Georgia Music*; *Grandaddy and Janetta*; and *Grandaddy's Stars*.

Other grandparent books: *The Crack-of-Dawn Walkers* by Amy Hest; *A Day's Work* (p); *Grandma's Promise* by Elaine Moore; *Grandma Summer* by Harley Jessup; *Grandpa's Song* by Tony Johnston; *Knots on a Counting Rope* by Bill Martin, Jr., and John Archambault; *Little Cliff and the Porch People* by Clifton Taulbert; *The Log Cabin Quilt* by Ellen Howard; *Mailing May* (p); *The Midnight Eaters* (p); *Music, Music for Everyone* by Vera B. Williams; *Not the Piano, Mrs. Medley* (p); *Tales of a Gambling Grandma* by Dayal Kaur Khalsa; *Tom* by Tomie dePaola; *What's Under My Bed?* (p); *When Grandma Came* by Jill Paton Walsh; *When Jessie Came Across the Sea* (p); also these novels: *Anna, Grandpa, and the Big Storm* (s); *Stone Fox* (s); and *The War with Grandpa* by Robert K. Smith.

Gulliver's Adventures in Lilliput

BY JONATHAN SWIFT, RETOLD BY ANN KEAY BENEDUCE; GENNADY SPIRIN, ILLUS.

Grades 2 and up   32 pages   *Philomel, 1993*

This is an abridged children's version of Swift's classic visit to the Lilliputians that retains much of his adventure and insight. And surely there were never better illustrations to match the story's fantasy.

Harry in Trouble

BY BARBARA ANN PORTE; YOSSI ABOLAFIA, ILLUS.

K–2   48 pages   *Greenwillow, 1989*

This "Harry" easy-reader series is about people as real as the folks next door—grade-schooler Harry, his widower father, and their relatives, neighbors, friends, and teachers. In this book, Harry loses his library card for the *third* time. Also in the series: *Harry's Dog*; *Harry's Mom*; *Harry Gets an Uncle*; *Harry's Visit*; and *Harry's Pony*.

Haunted House Jokes

BY LOUIS PHILLIPS; JAMES MARSHALL, ILLUS.

K–5   57 pages   *Viking, 1987*

Joke books give beginning readers a sense of both accomplishment and satisfaction. From the joke-meister himself, here's a wonderful collection of horror-ible jokes, knock-knocks, and riddles about vampires, ghosts, werewolves, Frankenstein, skeletons, and mummies. Example: What do ghosts drink in the summer?: Ghoul-ade! Also by the author: *Keep 'em Laughing*, and *Wackysaurus Dinosaur Jokes*. Other popular joke books: Joan Eckstein's and Joyce Gleit's two super joke books—*The Best Joke Book for Kids* and *The Best Joke Book for Kids #2*; *Buggy Riddles* by Katy Hall and Lisa Eisenberg; *The Carsick Zebra and Other Animal Riddles* by David Adler; and *Halloween Howls: Riddles That Are a Scream* by Giulio Maestro.

Heckedy Peg

BY AUDREY WOOD; DON WOOD, ILLUS.

K–5   30 pages   *Harcourt, 1987*

A determined mother outsmarts a witch who has captured and bewitched her seven children. Also by the author: *The Napping House* (p). Related books: *The Whingdingdilly* (p); *The Pumpkinville Mystery* by Bruce Cole; and *The Widow's Broom* by Chris Van Allsburg.

Here Come the Aliens!

BY COLIN MCNAUGHTON

PreS.–2nd   26 pages   *Candlewick, 1995*

A spaceload of horrific-looking aliens is en route to earth, and they're loaded down with McNaughton's usual helping of "gross" appetites, noises, and faces. Earthlings are forewarned to beware. And then the hideous creatures catch a glimpse of what awaits them on earth and they retreat into space. What frightened them? The class picture from a preschool group of four-year-olds! Also by the author: *Captain Abdul's Pirate School* (p), and *Making Friends with Frankenstein*. Related titles: *Company's Going* by Arthur Yorinks; *Dogzilla* by Dav Pilkey; and *Mush, a Dog from Space* by Daniel Pinkwater.

The House on East 88th Street

BY BERNARD WABER

PreS.–3rd   48 pages   *Houghton, 1962*

When the Primm family discovers a gigantic crocodile in the bathtub of their new brownstone home, it signals the beginning of a wonderful picture book series. As soon as the Primms overcome their fright, they see him as your children will—as the most lovable and human of crocodiles. Sequels (in this order): *Lyle, Lyle, Crocodile*; *Lyle and the Birthday Party*; *Lyle Finds His Mother*; *Lovable Lyle*; *Funny, Funny Lyle*; *Lyle at the Office*; and *Lyle at Christmas*. Also by the author: *Ira Sleeps Over* (p).

How Do Dinosaurs Say Good Night?

BY JANE YOLEN; MARK TEAGUE, ILLUS.

PreS.–K   *30 pages*   *Scholastic, 2000*

In this popular bedtime book for little dinosaur fans, the author uses nine different dinosaurs as humorous examples of good and bad bedtime behavior. Related fiction books on dinosaurs: *Can I Please Have a Stegosaurus, Mom? Can I Please?* by Lois G. Grambling; *Little Grunt and the Big Egg: A Prehistoric Fairy Tale* by Tomie dePaola; *Sammy and the Dinosaurs* by Ian Whybrow; for older children: *Dinosaurs Before Dark: Magic Treehouse series* (short novel), by Mary Pope Osborne. For nonfiction dinosaur books, see *Dinosaurs! The biggest, baddest, strangest, fastest* (p).

100th Day Worries

BY MARGERY CUYLER; ARTHUR HOWARD, ILLUS.

Grades 1–3   *30 pages*   *Simon & Schuster, 2000*

Jessica is a big-time worrier, and now she has the biggest worry ever. Her class is observing the 100th day of school by having everyone bring in a collection of 100 things. She can't think of anything to bring and time is running out! That's when her family comes to the rescue. An excellent math concepts book. Related books: *If You Hopped Like a Frog* by David M. Schwartz is a picture book introduction to the concept of ratio, using children's bodies in comparison to the abilities of animals; and *Rotten Teeth* (p).

The Hunter

BY PAUL GERAGHTY

PreS.–3rd   *26 pages*   *Crown, 1994*

A lost African girl, finding a baby elephant orphaned by poachers, leads it safely past dangers in the bush to another herd. Along the way, she loses her ambition to become a hunter. Related books: *Elephant Quest* by Ted and Betsy Lewin, and *The Gnats of Knotty Pine* by Bill Peet; for related books on courage, see *Brave Irene* (p).

If You Give a Mouse a Cookie

BY LAURA NUMEROFF; FELICIA BOND, ILLUS.

PreS.–K   *30 pages*   *Harper, 1985*

In a humorous cumulative tale that comes full circle, a little boy offers a mouse a cookie and ends up working his head off for the demanding little creature. Sequels: *If You Give a Moose a Muffin*; *If You Give a Pig a Pancake*; and *If You Take a Mouse to the Movies*. For other cumulative stories, see Predictable Books on pages 220–21.

If I Ran the Zoo

BY DR. SEUSS.

PreS.–4th   54 pages   *Random House, 1950*

Little Gerald McGrew finds the animals at the local zoo pretty boring compared with the zany, exotic creatures populating the zoo of his imagination (just like a little lad imagined things while walking to and from school in Seuss's first book for children, *And To Think That I Saw It on Mulberry Street*). Be sure to tell your listeners that Dr. Seuss's father, Theodor E. Geisel, was the zoo director for thirty-one years in Seuss's hometown of Springfield, Massachusetts. For a listing of all Seuss books and Web site information, see *The Foot Book* (p). Fans of Dr. Seuss also will enjoy the books of Bill Peet—see *The Whingdingdilly* (p).

Ira Sleeps Over

BY BERNARD WABER

K–6   48 pages   *Houghton, 1972*

This is a warm, sensitive, and humorous look at a boy's overnight visit to his best friend's house, centering on the child's quandary whether or not to bring his teddy bear. It makes for lively discussion about individual sleeping habits, peer pressure, and the things we all hold on to—even as grownups. In the sequel, *Ira Says Goodbye*, the two best friends experience a childhood pain when Reggie moves away. Waber is also the author of the popular Lyle the Crocodile series that begins with *The House on East 88th Street* (p). Related books: *Corduroy* (p); *I Lost My Bear* by Jules Feiffer; and *Where's My Teddy?* (p).

Highly recommended: the award-winning record/cassette *Unbearable Bears* by Kevin Roth (Marlboro Records, Kennett Square, PA) for a collection of favorite teddy bear songs.

The Island of the Skog

BY STEVEN KELLOGG

PreS.–2nd   32 pages   *Dial, 1973*

Sailing away from city life, a boatload of mice discover the island of their dreams, only to be pulled up short by the appearance of a fearful monster already dwelling on the island. How imaginations can run away with us and how obstacles can be overcome if we'll just talk with others are central issues in this tale. Also by the author: four retellings of American legends—Johnny Appleseed; Mike Fink; Paul Bunyan; and Pecos Bill; also *The Mysterious Tadpole* (p); *Pinkerton, Behave!*; *Prehistoric Pinkerton*; *A Rose for Pinkerton*; and *Tallyho, Pinkerton!*

Jack and the Beanstalk

RETOLD BY JOHN HOWE

K–3   30 pages   Little, 1989

The classic tale of a boy's battle to outwit the giants atop the beanstalk is retold and illustrated magnificently here with the ultimate in ferocious giants. A tongue-in-cheek sequel can be found in *Jim and the Beanstalk* by Raymond Briggs, along with the parody *Jack and the Giant* by Jim Harris. Other "giant" stories: *Christopher: The Holy Giant* by Tomie dePaola; *Clay Boy* by Mirra Ginsburg; *David and Goliath*, adapted by Leonard Everett Fisher; *David's Father* by Robert Munsch; and *Diane Goode's Book of Giants and Little People* by Diane Goode.

Johnny on the Spot

BY EDWARD SOREL

Grades 1–4   28 pages   Simon & Schuster, 1998

Young Johnny and his adult neighbor accidentally invent a radio that broadcasts events one day in advance. The conflict arises when Johnny is sworn to secrecy and forbidden to interfere with the future—even if he knows a calamity is about to occur. Created by one of America's premiere political artists, the tale is both adventure and morality tale. Also by the author: *The Saturday Kid*. Related titles: *A Day's Work* (p); and *The Real Thief* by William Steig.

The Last Princess: The Story of Princess Ka'iulani of Hawai'i

BY FAY STANLEY; DIANE STANLEY, ILLUS.

Grades 2–6   36 pages   Simon & Schuster, 1991

The story of the last princess is also the story of America's last state—Hawaii. It is a tragic but important story, showing the proud heritage of the Hawaiian people and one of America's dark historical chapters. Related book: *Encounter* (p); for other Diane Stanley nonfiction books, see *The True Adventure of Daniel Hall* (p).

The Legend of the Bluebonnet

RETOLD BY TOMIE DEPAOLA

PreS.–4th   30 pages   Putnam, 1984

Here is the legend behind the bluebonnets that blanket the state of Texas—the story of the little Comanche Indian orphan who sacrificed her only doll in order to end the draught that was ravaging her village. Related books: *The Legend of the Indian Paintbrush* by Tomie dePaola; also *Erandi's*

Braids (p); and *The Hunter* by Mary Casanova. A complete listing of books by Tomie dePaola can be found at: www.bingley.com. Many of his books are autobiographical or based on relatives, including: *The Art Lesson; Nana Upstairs & Nana Downstairs; Now One Foot, Now the Other; Oliver Button Is a Sissy; Tom;* and *Tony's Bread.* Recently, he has written a series of acclaimed autobiographical chapter books (in order): *26 Fairmont Street; Here We All Are;* and *On My Way.* For author studies: *Tomie dePaola: His Art and His Stories* by Barbara Elleman.

Lilly's Purple Plastic Purse

BY KEVIN HENKES

PreS.–1st   30 pages   Greenwillow, 1996

Few writers for children have as firm a grip on the pulse of childhood as does Kevin Henkes. His mice-children experience all the joys and insecurities of being a kid, but he manages to maintain a light touch throughout his stories. In this case, Lilly loves school and her teacher—until the day her antics distract the class and the teacher must temporarily confiscate her precious new plastic purse. Shattered, she's uncertain how to handle this small rebuke and seeks ways to show her hurt. With the help of her family, Lilly overcomes her embarrassment and hasty behavior, writes an apology, and soars on the good feelings that come from doing the right thing. Lilly also stars in: *Chester's Way*, and *Julius, the Baby of the World.* Also by the author: *Chrysanthemum; Sheila Rae, the Brave; Owen; Wemberly Worried;* and *A Weekend with Wendell.* Related book: *Rotten Teeth* (p).

The Lion and the Unicorn

BY SHIRLEY HUGHES

Grades 1–4   58 pages   DK, 1999

Young Lenny is one of the thousands of lonely, frightened children evacuated from London during the German bombings of WWII. But the children in the village where he is sent are far from sympathetic, especially when they discover he wets his bed at night. Just when he thinks he can't stand it any longer, he meets the local hero, an amputee, who confesses to having had many of the same fears, including a bedwetting problem. His advice sustains Lenny until his mom arrives. This is one of Hughes's finest and deepest picture books; it is longer than most, but well worth the time. In a related book, a young girl poses as a boy to sail with her father in the dramatic rescue of British soldiers at Dunkirk in *The Little Ships* by Louise Borden; see also: *The Bravest of Us All* by Marsha Diane Arnold; and *Molly's Pilgrim* (p).

Little Bear

BY ELSE HOLMELUND MINARIK; MAURICE SENDAK, ILLUS.

PreS.—1st   54 pages   *Harper, 1957*

This series of books uses the simple but important elements of a child's life (clothes, birthdays, playing, and wishing) to weave poignant little stories about a child-bear and his family. The series has won numerous awards and is regarded as a classic. A former first-grade teacher, the author uses a limited vocabulary without sacrificing the flavor of the story. The series includes: *Little Bear*; *A Kiss for Little Bear*; *Father Bear Comes Home*; *Little Bear's Friend*; and *Little Bear's Visit*. Also by the author: *No Fighting, No Biting!* Related books: *All About Alfie* (p) and *Frog and Toad Are Friends* (p).

A Little Excitement

BY MARC HARSHMAN; TED RAND, ILLUS.

Grades 1—4   28 pages   *Dutton, 1989*

Even though his grandmother has cautioned him against wishing for things he might not be prepared for, young Willie wishes for a little excitement to break the monotony of winter farm days. His wish comes true when his father makes a mistake in banking the stove one night, nearly setting the house afire. The excitement of helping family and neighbors fight the impending fire isn't quite what Willie had in mind, but it makes for a touching and dramatic story. Ted Rand's watercolors bring to life the frigid winter night and family warmth in an unforgettable fashion. Also by the author: *Snow Company*. Related book: *Baby in a Basket* (p).

The Little House

BY VIRGINIA LEE BURTON

PreS.—3rd   40 pages   *Houghton, 1942*

This Caldecott Medal winner uses a little turn-of-the-century house to portray the urbanization of America. With each page, the reader/listener becomes the little house and experiences the contentment, wonder, concern, anxiety, and loneliness that the passing seasons and encroaching city bring. Many of today's children who daily experience the anxieties of city life will identify with the little house's eventual triumph. Other books by the author: see *Mike Milligan and His Steam Shovel* (p) and *Katy and the Big Snow*. Related books: *Farewell to Shady Glade* and *Wump World* by Bill Peet; *Just a Dream* by Chris Van Allsburg; *The Little Black Truck* by Libba Moore Gray; and *The Mountain That Loved a Bird* by Alice McLerran.

The Little Old Lady Who Was Not Afraid of Anything
BY LINDA WILLIAMS

PreS.–1st   28 pages   *Harper, 1988*

Walking through the dark woods toward home, the little old lady is approached by a succession of scary articles of empty clothing—gloves, hat,
shoes, trousers, etc. She refuses to allow them to frighten her, until the last
one—which sets her running. In the end, however, she solves the problem
by making all the items into a scarecrow. Other scary but non-threatening
books for young children: *Here Come the Aliens!* (p); *The Lost Boy and the
Monster* (p); *May We Sleep Here Tonight?* (p); *Red's Great Chase* (p); *Some
Things Are Scary* by Florence Parry Heide; *The Teeny Tiny Woman* by
Arthur Robins; *There's a Nightmare in My Closet* by Mercer Mayer; and
Watch Out! Big Bro Is Coming! by Jez Alborough.

Little Red Riding Hood
RETOLD BY TRINA SCHART HYMAN

PreS.–3rd   32 pages   *Holiday, 1983*

It's hard to imagine a better illustrated version of this famous tale. The artist
has given us a child and grandma who are every child and grandmother and
a texture so rich you can almost smell the woods. Other versions of Little
Red Riding Hood: *Flossie and the Fox* by Patricia McKissack (African-
American version); *The Gunnywolf,* retold by A. Delaney; *Little Red Cowboy
Hat* by Susan Lowell; *Little Red Riding Hood: A Newfangled Prairie Tale* by Lisa
Campbell Ernst; *Liza Lou and the Yeller Belly Swamp* by Mercer Mayer; *Lon
Po Po* by Ed Young (Chinese version); and *Ruby* by Michael Emberly.

Little Tim and the Brave Sea Captain
BY EDWARD ARDIZZONE

K–2   46 pages   *Lothrop, 1936*

Between 1936 and 1977, this popular British illustrator created a wonderful series of adventure books around the seaside lives of three children, all
of whom are called upon to exhibit bravery, contrition, and perseverance
as they confront great obstacles in their seaside community. Sequels: *Tim in
Danger; Tim and Ginger; Tim's Friend Towser; Tim and Charlotte;* and *Tim to
the Rescue.* Related book: *Brave Irene* (p).

The Lost Boy and the Monster

BY CRAIG KEE STRETE; STEVE JOHNSON AND LOU FANCHER, ILLUS.

PreS.–K   24 pages   *Putnam, 1999*

When a lost Native American child is trapped by a tree monster, he is rescued by a snake and scorpion repaying the kindness he extended to them
earlier. Though an original tale, it features art based on Indian artifacts and
cave dwellings. Related Native American tales, see *The Lost Children* (p).

The Lost Children

RETOLD BY PAUL GOBLE

Grades 1–5   30 pages   *Simon & Schuster, 1993*

This is the Blackfeet cautionary tale about six boys who were neglected by
their family and village. In despair, the boys left the earth and became
bunched stars in the heavens—what we call the Pleiades—and their lights
today are reminders that children are the Great Spirit's greatest gift, to be
treasured always. Other books by Paul Goble include: *Crow Chief; Death of
the Iron Horse; Dream Wolf; The Girl Who Loved Wild Horses; Iktomi and the
Berries; Iktomi and the Boulder; Iktomi and the Buzzard; Iktomi and the Ducks;
Love Flute;* and *Star Boy.*

Other American Indian books: *Annie and the Old One* by Miska Miles;
The Boy Who Lived With the Seals by Rafe Martin; *Daily Life in a Plains Indian Village, 1868* by Michael Bad Hand Terry; *Doesn't Fall Off His Horse*
by Virginia A. Stroud; *The First Strawberries: A Cherokee Story* by Joseph
Bruchac; *Knots on a Counting Rope* by Bill Martin, Jr., and John Archambault; *The Legend of the Bluebonnet* (p); *The Lost Boy and the Monster* (p); *Nine
for California* by Sonia Levitin; *The Rough-Face Girl* by Rafe Martin (Indian
Cinderella); *The Story of the Milky Way* by Joseph Bruchac and Gayle Ross;
Uncle Smoke Stories: Nehawka Tales of Coyote the Trickster by Roger Welsch;
and *Where the Buffaloes Begin* by Olaf Baker.

See also these novels: *Return to Hawk's Hill* by Allan W. Eckert; *Thunder
Cave* (n); *Sign of the Beaver* (n); *Sing Down the Moon* (n); and *Weasel* (n).

The Lucy Cousins Book of Nursery Rhymes

ILLUSTRATED BY LUCY COUSINS

Inf—PreS.   64 pages   *Dutton, 1989*

Because it is vibrantly illustrated in primary colors with boldly outlined
images (of multi-ethnic characters), this collection of sixty-four Mother
Goose rhymes is especially for infants and toddlers to view. Cousins also has
a set of small board books based on this book. Also by Lucy Cousins: *Maisy*
(p). Other Mother Goose collections include: *The Random House Book of*

Mother Goose; *Tomie dePaola's Mother Goose*; and *Whiskers and Rhymes* by Arnold Lobel; see also *The Everything Book* (p) and *Rhymes for Annie Rose* by Shirley Hughes.

Madeline

BY LUDWIG BEMELMANS
K–3   30 pages   *Viking, 1939*
This series of six books features a daring and irrepressible girl named Madeline and her eleven friends, who all live together in a Parisian boarding school. The author's use of fast-moving verse, daring adventure, naughtiness, and glowing color keep it a favorite in early grades year after year. Other books in the series: *Madeline and the Bad Hat*; *Madeline and the Gypsies*; *Madeline in London*; *Madeline's Rescue*; and *Madeline's Christmas*. Related books: *The Three Robbers* and *Zerlada's Ogre*, both by Tomi Ungerer.

The Magic Paintbrush

BY ROBIN MULLER
Grades 1–5   32 pages   *Viking, 1990*
Nib is an illiterate street orphan with the ambition but not the money to become a great artist. When he comes to the aid of an old man being robbed in an alleyway, he is rewarded with a magic paintbrush that will bring to life whatever he paints. This enchantment will bring both fame, misery, mystery, and finally fulfillment to the young lad. Related books: *Dawn* and *Tye May and The Magic Brush*, both by Molly Bang; *The Art Lesson* by Tomie dePaola; *The Boy Who Drew Cats*, retold by Arthur A. Levine; *The Legend of Slappy Hooper*, retold by Aaron Shepard; and *Pumpkin Light* by David Ray.

Mailing May

BY MICHAEL O. TUNNELL; TED RAND, ILLUS.
PreS.–2nd   36 pages   *Greenwillow, 1997*
The year is 1914 and five-year-old May wants to visit her grandmother in Idaho. All that stands between them is seventy-five miles of treacherous, roadless mountains and the exorbitant cost of a train ticket. Her wish is finally fulfilled when she agrees to let her parents *mail* her to Idaho. Posted with stamps, she boards the train's mail car and heads for Grandma's. Based on a true story. Related books: *Baby in a Basket* (p); *Grandaddy's Place* (p); *Marven of the Great North Woods* (p); and *Nine for California* (p).

Maisy Drives the Bus

BY LUCY COUSINS

Tod–PreS.   *20 pages*   *Candlewick, 2000*

Maisy is a tiny mouse character who does a lot of the things very young children like to do or wish they could do. Drawn in primary colors, the animal characters are outlined in bold black lines, making the illustrations easily seen and absorbed by the youngest of children, who sometimes are confused by finely detailed art in books. The story line is simple but boldly portrayed in large type, another advantage for toddlers who might be noticing letters. Other books in the ongoing series: *Happy Birthday, Maisy; Maisy at the Farm; Maisy Dresses Up; Maisy Goes to School; Maisy Goes to the Playground; Maisy Makes Gingerbread; Maisy Takes a Bath; Maisy's ABC; Maisy's Bedtime;* and *Maisy's Pool.* Also by the author: *The Lucy Cousins Book of Nursery Rhymes* (p).

Make Way for Ducklings

BY ROBERT MCCLOSKEY

PreS.–2nd   *62 pages*   *Viking, 1941*

In this Caldecott Award–winning classic, we follow Mrs. Mallard and her eight ducklings as they make a traffic-stopping walk across Boston to meet Mr. Mallard on their new island home in the Public Garden. Also by the author: *Blueberries for Sal; Burt Dow, Deep-Water Man; Lentil; One Morning in Maine;* for older students: *Homer Price* (n) and *Centerburg Tales.* Related books: *Chibi: A True Story from Japan* by Barbara Brenner and Julia Takaya, the true story of a nest of ducklings in modern Tokyo and how they caught the attention of thousands as they survived a terrible typhoon.

Marven of the Great North Woods

BY KATHRYN LASKY; KEVIN HAWKES, ILLUS.

K–4   *36 pages*   *Harcourt Brace, 1997*

In 1918, one of history's worst flu epidemics was sweeping across the world, killing tens of thousands. The Lasky family believed their ten-year-old son's chances of escaping the plague would be greater if he spent the winter far from the city of Duluth, Minnesota. So they packed Marven's bags and sent him by train to a logging camp in the great North woods. There he spends the winter as the camp's paymaster, as well as the backup human alarm clock for the giant loggers who fail to wake for breakfast. A true story of courage, history, and the warm friendship between a small Jewish city boy and a French-Canadian giant, told by the boy's daughter. Related books: *Mailing May* (p) and *Wagon Wheels* (n).

Matthew's Dragon

BY SUSAN COOPER; JOSEPH A. SMITH, ILLUS.

K–3   30 pages   *Atheneum, 1991*

After Matthew's mother turns out the light, the dragon in his book comes alive to take him on a thrilling ride through the night sky—but first there's a dramatic escape from a hungry cat. You'll have a wide-eyed audience for this tale every time. Also by the author, for older students: *Over Sea, Under Stone*. Related books: *Andy and the Lions* by James Dougherty; *Edward and the Pirates* (p); *Where the Wild Things Are* (p); and *The Littles* (s).

May We Sleep Here Tonight?

TAN KOIDE; YASUKO KOIDE, ILLUS.

PreS.–K   32 pages   *S&S, McElderry, 1981*

This is a fabulous read-aloud for preschoolers! One by one, small animals lost in the fog stumble upon what they think is an empty cabin. Each fearfully knocks and enters, raising the suspense for the earlier visitors who are now tucked into bed. The bed grows more and more crowded until finally there are loud footsteps outside and something *huge* enters without knocking. It's the bear who owns the cabin, and as a twist on *Goldilocks*, he gladly serves everyone a hot meal. Related books: *Red's Great Chase* (p) and *Where's My Teddy?* (p).

Max

BY BOB GRAHAM

PreS.–K   26 pages   *Candlewick, 2000*

Little Max is the son of two superheroes, Captain Lightning and Madam Thunderbolt, but he's a late bloomer at flying, not quite ready for prime-time heroics, can't even hover. As an ordinary kid in superhero clothes, he worries his folks and amuses his classmates. Finally, when the occasion warrants—a baby bird falling from its nest—Max flies. Here is a heroic triumph for young listeners. Also by the author: *Benny: An Adventure Story*. Related book: *Leo the Late Bloomer* by Robert Kraus.

Max's Dragon Shirt

BY ROSEMARY WELLS

PreS.–K   22 pages   *Dial, 1991*

As a tuned-in author-parent who has never forgotten the child she used to be, Rosemary Wells writes books that are equipped with built-in enjoyment. In this first book in the series, rabbit Max and his bossy sister Ruby set off to buy him some pants, only to have hilarious circumstances intervene, so that Max ends up with a dragon shirt instead. Also in the series: *Hooray for Max*; *Max's Bath*; *Max's Breakfast*; *Max's Birthday*; *Max's Chocolate Chicken*; *Max's New Suit*; and *Max's Ride*.

Mike Mulligan and His Steam Shovel
BY VIRGINIA LEE BURTON
K–4   42 pages   *Houghton, 1939*
This is the heartwarming classic about the demise of the steam shovel and how it found a permanent home with driver Mike. Also by the author: *Choo-Choo*; *The Emperor's New Clothes*; *Katy and the Big Snow*; *The Little House* (p); and *Maybelle the Cable Car*. Related books: *The Caboose Who Got Loose* and *Smokey*, both by Bill Peet; *Isaac the Ice Cream Truck* by Scott Santore; and *The Little Black Truck* by Libba Moore Gray.

The Minpins
BY ROALD DAHL; PATRICK BENSON, ILLUS.
K–4   47 pages   *Viking, 1991*
This is one of Dahl's final and most sensitive and dramatic works. When a small boy disobeys his mother and enters the dark forest, he meets not only the monster she predicted but also tiny matchstick-size people who inhabit all the trees. The tiny creatures enable his escape and help destroy the monster. For other books by the author, see *James and the Giant Peach* (n).

Mirette on the High Wire
BY EMILY ARNOLD MCCULLY
K–2   30 pages   *Putnam, 1992*
One hundred years ago in a small boarding house in Paris, there appeared a stranger seeking solitude. He is the Great Bellini, the daredevil tightrope walker who has lost his confidence. In the weeks that follow, the innkeeper's daughter becomes enchanted with rope walking and is able to restore the man's lost confidence while becoming a star herself. Winner of the Caldecott Medal, the book is followed by *Starring Mirette and Bellini* and *Mirette & Bellini Cross Niagara Falls*. Also by the author: *The Bobbin Girl*; *Hurry!*; *Little Kit, or The Industrious Flea Circus Girl*; and *An Outlaw Thanksgiving*. Despite the confines of the picture book format, McCully is able to create highly developed characters, plot, and a strong sense of history.

Miss Nelson Is Missing

BY HARRY ALLARD; JAMES MARSHALL, ILLUS.

PreS.–4th   *32 pages*   *Houghton, 1977*

Poor, sweet Miss Nelson! Kind and beautiful as she is, she cannot control her classroom—the worst-behaved children in the school. But when she is suddenly absent, the children begin to realize what a wonderful teacher they had in Miss Nelson. Her substitute is wicked-looking, strict Miss Viola Swamp, who works the class incessantly. Wherever has Miss Nelson gone and when will she return? Sequels: *Miss Nelson Is Back* and *Miss Nelson Has a Field Day*. Also by the author: *The Stupids Step Out*. Related school book: *Rotten Teeth* (p).

Molly Bannaky

BY ALICE MCGILL; CHRIS K. SOENTPIET, ILLUS.

Grades 3–8   *32 pages*   *Houghton, 1999*

Benjamin Banneker was one of the first black American scientists, wrote the first black almanac, and was part of the federal panel that planned Washington, DC, but the story behind the man was his grandmother. She came to America as a white indentured servant, having narrowly escaped the English gallows by proving she could read the Bible. In America, she served her seven years of servitude, later bought a farm and then bought a newly arrived slave, whom she grew to love and married. For the story of her famous grandson, see: *Dear Benjamin Banneker* by Andrea D. Pinkney. Related books on slavery: *Amistad Rising: A Story of Freedom* by Veronica Chambers; *A School for Pompey Walker* (p); *Slavery Time When I was Chillun* by Belinda Hurmence; *The Strength in These Arms: Life in the Slave Quarters* by Raymond Bial; and *The Wagon* by Tony Johnston.

Molly's Pilgrim

BY BARBARA COHEN

Grades 1–4   *41 pages*   *Morrow, 1983*

Molly, an immigrant child and target of her classmates' taunts, discovers she is more a part of America's Thanksgiving tradition than anyone in the class. This book was the basis for the 1985 Academy Award–winning best short film of the same title. Related books: *The Lion and the Unicorn* (p); *N. C. Wyeth's Pilgrims* by Robert San Souci; *An Outlaw Thanksgiving* by Emily Arnold McCully; *Thanksgiving at the Tappletons'* by Eileen Spinelli; and *The Thanksgiving Story* by Alice Dalgliesh.

Monster Mama

BY LIZ ROSENBERG; STEPHEN GAMMELL, ILLUS.

K–2   30 pages   *Philomel, 1993*

Patrick Edward's mother is truly monstrous-looking. She cares dearly for her little boy, but avoids others so as not to frighten them. When three bullies pick on her son, she comes out of hiding and proves that looks can be deceiving. Related books: *Crow Boy* by Taro Yashima; *David's Father* by Robert Munsch; and *Pumpkin Time* by Jan Andrews.

Mother Goose (see *The Lucy Cousins Book of Nursery Rhymes*, page 244)

Mrs. Toggle's Zipper

BY ROBIN PULVER; R. W. ALLEY, ILLUS.

PreS.–2nd   28 pages   *Simon & Schuster, 1990*

When the early primary teacher Mrs. Toggle loses the toggle on the zipper of her winter coat en route to school one day, her class, the school nurse and the principal all fail to get her out of the coat—until the custodian comes to the rescue. Sequels: *Mrs. Toggle and the Dinosaur* and *Mrs. Toggle's Beautiful Blue Shoe*. Also by the author: *Nobody's Mother Is in Second Grade*. Related school book: *Rotten Teeth* (p).

The Mysterious Tadpole

BY STEVEN KELLOGG

PreS.–4th   30 pages   *Dial, 1977*

When little Louis's uncle in Scotland sent him a tadpole for his birthday, neither of them had any idea how much havoc and fun the pet would cause in Louis's home, classroom, and school swimming pool. The tadpole turns out to be a direct descendant of the Loch Ness Monster (but what a cuddly monster this is!). For other books by the author, see *Island of the Skog* (p).

　　Related books about unusual pets: *The Boy Who Was Followed Home* by Margaret Mahy; *Chewy Louie* (p); *Dinosaur Bob and His Adventures With the Family Lazardo* (p); *Harry's Pony* by Barbara Ann Porte; and *The Salamander Room* by Anne Mazer.

The Napping House

BY AUDREY WOOD; DON WOOD, ILLUS.

Tod–PreS.   28 pages   *Harcourt, 1984*

One of the cleverest bedtime books for children, this simple tale depicts a cozy bed on which are laid in cumulative rhymes a snoring granny, dreaming child, dozing dog, and a host of other sleeping characters until a sudden awakening at daybreak. The subtle lighting changes on the double-page illustrations show the gradual passage of time during the night and the clearing of a storm outside. Also by the author: *Heckedy Peg* (p). On the Web: www.AudreyWood.com/. Related books: *The Flea's Sneeze* by Lynn Downey; other bedtime books, see *The Boy Who Wouldn't Go to Bed* (p).

Nicholas Pipe
BY ROBERT D. SAN SOUCI; DAVID SHANNON, ILLUS.
Grades 1–4   30 pages   *Dial, 1997*
When a young maiden falls in love with a merman, her father forbids her to have anything to do with him. Since the merman is also the protector of the village, this leads to near disaster. In the end, their determined love for each other saves the village. Compare this tale with a similar one that has a very different ending: *Blue Willow* by Pam Conrad. Related book: *The Sea Man* by Jane Yolen.

Nine for California
BY SONIA LEVITIN; CAT B. SMITH, ILLUS.
K–3   30 pages   *Orchard, 1996*
When Mama decides to take her five children to California via stagecoach, the other three passengers are in for a lively twenty-one days that include outlaws, a buffalo stampede, threatening Indians, and hours and hours of endless boredom. But each crisis is solved with Mama's "sack." An ingenious, humorous historical picture book. Related titles: *Aunt Minnie McGranahan* (p) and *Saving Sweetness* (p).

No Jumping on the Bed
BY TEDD ARNOLD
PreS.–2nd   30 pages   *Dial, 1987*
Warned that he mustn't jump on his bed or he might crash through the floor into the apartment below, Walter can't resist the temptation. The exaggerated results are hilarious, and just when you think he dreamed it all . . . Also by the author: *Green Wilma*; *No More Water in the Tub*; and *Parts*. Related bedtime books, see *The Boy Who Wouldn't Go to Bed* (p).

No, No, Jo!
BY KATE AND JIM MCMULLAN
Tod–PreS.   12 pages   *Harper, 1998*
Jo, the family kitten, tries to be helpful but with unsuccessful results, provoking the urgent and constant response from family members: "No, no, Jo!"

Not the Piano, Mrs. Medley

BY EVAN LEVINE; S. D. SCHINDLER, ILLUS.

PreS.–3rd   26 pages   *Orchard, 1991*

Grandmothers like to be prepared, but Max's grandma takes it to new limits when she and Max schedule a day at the beach. The number of items she intends to bring grows and grows, until pure zaniness breaks through. It's a book you immediately wish had a sequel. Related book: *A Perfectly Orderly House* by Ellen Kindt McKenzie and *Pigsty* by Mark Teague. For other grandparent books, see *Grandaddy's Place* (p).

Owl Babies

BY MARTIN WADDELL; PATRICK BENSON, ILLUS.

Tod—PreS.   30 pages   *Candlewick, 1992*

Three young owls awaken to find their mother missing, and their ensuing hours are spent thinking, worrying, imagining, talking, and wishing for her return. And, of course, she returns, to their great relief and delight. Related books: *Are You My Mother?* by P. D. Eastman; and *Stellaluna* (p).

The Pied Piper of Hamelin

RETOLD BY ROBERT HOLDEN; DRAHOS ZAK, ILLUS.

K and up   28 pages   *Houghton, 1998*

The consequences of breaking your word are dramatically portrayed here in this 700-year-old tale of enchantment when the Pied Piper rids Hamelin of its rat infestation but is denied his reward. Other versions: *The Irish Piper* by Jim Latimer; *The Pied Piper of Hamelin* by Robert Browning, revised by Terry Small; for older students: *What Happened at Hamelin*, a novel by Gloria Skurzynski. Related books about mysterious strangers: *The Hero of Bremen*, retold by Margaret Hodges; *Old Henry* by Joan Blos; *The Paper Crane* by Molly Bang; *The Selkie Girl*, retold by Susan Cooper; *The Stranger* and *The Wreck of the Zephy*, both by Chris Van Allsburg; and *The Wish Giver* (s).

Pink and Say

BY PATRICIA POLACCO

Grades 3 and up   48 pages   *Philomel, 1994*

Based on an incident in the life of the author-illustrator's great-great grandfather, this is the tale of two fifteen-year-old Union soldiers—one white, one black. The former was wounded while deserting his company, the latter has been separated from his black company and stumbles upon the left-for-dead white soldier. The pages that follow trace this sad chapter in American history about as well as it's ever been told for children, beginning

with a visit to the black soldier's mother, who is living on a nearby plantation ravaged by the war. There the wounded boy is nursed to both health
and full courage, while discovering the inhumanity of slavery. Patricia
Polacco is one of the most popular and productive author/illustrators creating for children. A complete list of her books can be found on the Web:
www.patriciapolacco.com.

Related books: *Christmas in the Big House, Christmas in the Quarters* by Pa-
tricia and Fredrick McKissack; *Thunder at Gettysburg* by Patricia Lee
Gauch; a Newberry Honor–winning Civil War novel, *The Perilous Road* by
William O. Steele; for mature readers; *Nightjohn* by Gary Paulsen.

The Poppy Seeds

BY ROBERT CLYDE BULLA

K–2   34 pages   *Puffin, 1994*

A selfish old man who scorns the friendship and needs of his neighbors is
finally reached through the kindness of a Mexican child who attempts to
plant poppies in the man's yard. Related book: *Old Mother Witch* by Carol
Carrick.

The Principal's New Clothes

BY STEPHANIE CALMENSON; DENISE BRUNKUS, ILLUS.

K–4   40 pages   *Scholastic, 1989*

In this modern-day version of the classic tale, a nattily dressed school principal is tricked. The faculty and older students cannot bring themselves
to tell him the bad news, but the youngest are happy to oblige. Related
book: *The Emperor's New Clothes* by Hans Christian Andersen, translated
by Naomi Lewis; illustrated by Angela Barrett. Other clothing stories: *The
Five Hundred Hats of Bartholomew Cubbins* by Dr. Seuss; *Froggy Gets Dressed*
(p); *The Mitten*, adapted by Jan Brett; *Mrs. Toggle's Beautiful Blue Shoe* and
Mrs. Toggle's Zipper (p), both by Robin Pulver; *The Purple Coat* by Amy
Hest; and *Thomas' Snowsuit* (p).

Red's Great Chase

BY SIMONE LIA

PreS.   28 pages   *Dutton, 1999*

A little girl, Red, is afraid of monsters in the cellar, and suddenly a blue
one jumps out and starts chasing her. Through every conceivable terrain,
from mountains and skyscrapers to jungles and outer space, the monster
pursues her. The illustrations are non-threatening and heighten suspense,
not fears. When the monster finally catches her, it takes off a mask to reveal the child's mom, who says it's now Red's turn to chase *her*! It's all been

a grand game. Related titles: *The Little Old Lady Who Was Not Afraid of Anything* (p); *The Lost Boy and the Monster* (p); *We're Going on a Bear Hunt* (p); and *Where the Wild Things Are* (p).

Regards to the Man in the Moon

BY EZRA JACK KEATS

PreS.–3rd   32 pages   *Four Winds, 1981*

When the neighborhood children tease Louie about the junk in his back-yard, his father shows him how imagination can convert rubbish into a spaceship that will take him to the farthest galaxies. The next day, Louie and his friend Susie hurtle through space in their glorified washtub and discover that not even gravity can hold back a child's imagination. The settings for Ezra Jack Keats's books are largely the inner-city but the emotions are those of all children. On the Web: www.lib.usm.edu/~degrum/keats/main.html. Related books on children's imaginations, see *Dreamland* (p).

Richard Wright and the Library Card

BY WILLIAM MILLER; GREGORY CHRISTIE, ILLUS.

Grades 2–5   32 pages   *Lee & Low, 1999*

Growing up in segregated Mississippi in the 1920s, young Richard Wright had an insatiable hunger for print that only a library card could satisfy. Unfortunately, his skin color prevented him from owning one. So as a young janitor, the future author of *Native Son* and *Black Boy* conspired with a white man to beat the system. Also by the author: *Zora Hurston and the Chinaberry Tree* and *Frederick Douglass: The Last Day of Slavery*. Related books for younger students: *Tomás and the Library Lady* by Pat Mora, the childhood story of Tomás Rivera, the son of migrant workers who became chancellor of the University of California, Riverside. Also, *The Library* by Sarah Stewart; *Red Light, Green Light, Mama and Me* by Cari Best; *A School for Pompey Walker* (p); and for older readers: *The Library Card* by Jerry Spinelli.

Rikki-Tikki-Tavi

BY RUDYARD KIPLING; ADAPTED AND ILLUSTRATED BY JERRY PINKNEY

K–4   44 pages   *Morrow, 1997*

Rikki is a fearless little mongoose, adopted by a family in India to protect their child. In no time, he is tested by the cunning cobra snakes that live in the garden. Made famous by Kipling a century ago, this tale features a ferocious fight between the mongoose and snakes and is not for the timid.

Rolie Poli Olie

BY WILLIAM JOYCE

Tod–PreS.   40 pages   *Harper, 1999*

The author's simple rhyming prose and witty illustrations follow a happy robot family through the day, doing chores, eating, dancing, playing, and even
getting into trouble for being too rambunctious. While there's no great plot
here, the book has a lyrical simplicity that attracts toddlers and preschoolers.
They especially identify with the happy resolution to the boy-robot's naughtiness at the end and the use of the word "underpants." Sequel: *Snowie Rolie*.
For other books by the author and Web site information, see *Dinosaur Bob
and His Adventures with the Family Lazardo* (p).

Rotten Teeth

BY LAURA SIMMS; DAVID CATROW, ILLUS.

K–3   30 pages   *Houghton, 1998*

Melissa is the smallest, quietest person in first grade. And she's never
brought anything for show and tell—until today! Direct from her father's
dental lab comes a bottle of *Rotten Teeth*, extracted from her father's patients. To the disgusted astonishment of her teacher, Melissa puts a rotten
tooth on each classmate's desk. No one has *ever* brought anything like this
for show and tell, and suddenly Melissa is a class star! One of the most original creative artists in the children's field today is David Catrow, who illustrated the book. As good as the story is, Catrow adds new dimensions with
his zany art. Be sure to check out these books illustrated by Catrow: *The
Emperor's Old Clothes* and *She's Wearing a Dead Bird on Her Head!*, both by
Kathryn Lasky; *The Long, Long Letter* by Elizabeth Spurr; and *Over the River
and Through the Wood* by Lydia Child.

   Other fun books about school: *100th Day Worries* (p); *Author Day* by
Daniel Pinkwater; *The Frightful Story of Harry Walfish* by Brian Floca; *The
Lost and Found* and *The Secret Shortcut*, both by Mark Teague; and *Lunch
Money and Other Poems About School* by Carol D. Shields.

The Samurai's Daughter

BY ROBERT D. SAN SOUCI; STEPHEN T. JOHNSON, ILLUS.

Grades 2–6   30 pages   *Dial, 1992*

In this retelling of an ancient legend, a Japanese knight is banished to a far-
away island by his emperor. The Samurai's daughter, displaying her family's
courage and boldness, sails to the island and battles a ferocious sea serpent
to win her father's release. Related heroine books: *The Courage of Sarah Noble* (s) and *The Serpent Slayer and Other Stories of Strong Women* (f).

Saving Sweetness

BY DIANE STANLEY; G. BRIAN KARAS, ILLUS.

K–2   28 pages   *Putnam, 1996*

When feisty little Sweetness can't tolerate any more of the orphanage and
its matron of cruelty, Mrs. Sump, she runs away, only to be pursued by the
dumbest sheriff with the biggest heart in the West. Both end up facing
dangerous Coyote Pete. In the end, Coyote Pete marries his parole officer
(Mrs. Sump) and the sheriff adopts Sweetness and the other seven orphans.
In the sequel, *Raising Sweetness*, the children find the sheriff's long-lost girlfriend and arrange a mother for themselves. This is rib-tickling fun! On a
more serious but still relevant note, *Train to Somewhere* by Eve Bunting follows fourteen children as they head west on the orphan train in the late
1800s. Related book: *Little Kit* by Emily Arnold McCully.

A School for Pompey Walker

BY MICHAEL J. ROSEN; AMINAH B. ROBINSON, ILLUS.

Grades 2–8   44 pages   *Harcourt, 1995*

A ninety-year-old man, addressing the students at the school named for
him, recounts his life story, from his days as a slave child to the day he won
his freedom, including the great deceit he and his white friend pulled on
slave owners that enabled him to earn the money to build the school. Although the character is largely fiction, the book is based on a small newspaper account. The memories the old man shares provide remarkable
images of what slavery was like for families and children. Despite the heavy
subject, the author has imbued the character with wonderful wit, and the
story with a feeling of great warmth and triumph. For experienced listeners. Related titles, see *Mary Bannaky* (p).

The Secret Knowledge of Grown-ups

BY DAVID WISNIEWSKI

Grades 6 and up   48 pages   *Morrow, 1998*

The author has taken standard rules of behavior imposed by adults—Eat
your vegetables! or Don't blow bubbles in your milk with your straw!—and
offers the "top secret" intricate, humorous, and mind-boggling reasons behind the rules. This book is the perfect launching pad for readers and listeners to devise further send-ups of family and school rules; for example,
the *real* reason they don't want you to run in the hallways at school is . . .

The Secret Shortcut

BY MARK TEAGUE

PreS.–K   *32 pages*   *Scholastic, 1996*

Wendell and Floyd are in trouble with their teacher for being late for school every day. She doesn't understand how hard they're trying: every shortcut they take to save time is a turn for the worse: they meet pirates one day, a plague of frogs the next, even space men. It's their last secret shortcut—the jungle route—that turns out to be the best and muddiest of all. In the sequel, *The Lost and Found*, they meet Mona Tudburn outside the principal's office and begin a journey to the depths of the lost and found bin. Also by the author: *Pigsty*. Related books: *Cloud Nine* by Norman Silver; *Edward and the Pirates* (p); *The Flying Dragon Room* by Audrey Wood; *Regards to the Man in the Moon* (p); and *Rotten Teeth* (p).

The Seven Silly Eaters

BY MARY ANN HOBERMAN; MARLA FRAZEE, ILLUS.

K–3   *38 pages*   *Harcourt, 1997*

There are seven children in the Peters family and, unfortunately, each has a different favorite food that must be specially prepared or the child will not eat. Mrs. Peters is at her wit's end and worn to a frazzle trying to cook these specialties three times a day. When her birthday arrives, she's certain her children won't remember it—but she's wrong. They're up all night scheming and their birthday present accidentally solves her cooking dilemma forever. Also by the author/poet: *A House Is a House for Me* and *Fathers, Mothers, Sisters, Brothers: A Collection of Family Poems*. Other food-related books: *A Bad Case of Stripes* by David Shannon; *Heckedy Peg* (p); and *Zak's Place* by Margie Palatini.

The Shrinking of Treehorn

BY FLORENCE PARRY HEIDE; EDWARD GOREY, ILLUS.

Grades 3–8   *60 pages*   *Holiday, 1971*

When a young boy mentions to his social-climbing parents that he's begun to shrink, he's ignored. When he calls it to the attention of his teachers, his words fall on deaf ears. Day by day he grows smaller and day by day the adults continue to talk around him and his problems. Finally he must solve it himself. Also by the author: *Some Things Are Scary*. Related books: *Max* (p); and *Wallace Hoskins: The Boy Who Grew Down* by Cynthia Zarin.

The Silver Pony

BY LYND WARD

PreS.–4th · *176 pages*   *Houghton, 1973*

A classic wordless book (and the longest published for children), this is the heartwarming story of a lonely farm boy and the flights of fancy he uses to escape his isolation. His imaginative trips take place on a winged pony and carry him to distant parts of the world to aid and comfort other lonely children. Also by the author: *The Biggest Bear* (p). List of wordless books on page 219.

Sleep Out

BY CAROL CARRICK; DONALD CARRICK, ILLUS.

K–4   30 pages   *Clarion, 1973*

Christopher and his dog achieve that one great triumph that all children dream of accomplishing: They sleep out alone in the woods one night. This is the first in a series of eight books about Christopher and his family. While the books can be enjoyed separately, they work best when read in sequence. After *Sleep Out*, they include: *Lost in the Storm*; *The Accident*; *The Foundling*; *The Washout*; *Ben and the Porcupine*; *Dark and Full of Secrets*; and *Left Behind*.

Smoky Mountain Rose: An Appalachian Cinderella

BY ALAN SCHROEDER; BRAD SNEED, ILLUS.

K–5   30 pages   *Dial, 1997*

Cinderella is the most frequently told children's tale, with more than 750 different versions defined through the centuries, all the way back to A.D. 850. Here is s homespun American version set in Appalachia, complete with colorful dialect.

Other *Cinderella* versions: *Cinderella* by Charles Perrault, illustrated by Loek Koopmans (the standard version); *Cindy Ellen: A Wild Western Cinderella* by Susan Lowell; *Cinder-elly* (rap version) by Frances Minters; *The Golden Sandal: A Middle Eastern Cinderella Story* by Rebecca Hickox; *The Irish Cinderlad* by Shirley Climo; *Iron John*, adapted by Eric A. Kimmel; *Moss Gown* (southern version) by William H. Hooks; *Mufaro's Beautiful Daughters: An African Tale* by John Steptoe; *The Persian Cinderella*, by Shirley Climo; *Princess Furball*, by Charlotte Huck; *The Rough-Face Girl* (North American Indian version) by Rafe Martin; *The Way Meat Loves Salt: A Cinderella Tale from the Jewish Tradition* by Nina Jaffe; and *Yeh-Shen* (Chinese version), retold by Ai-Ling Louie.

The novel *Ella Enchanted* by Gail Carson Levine is the most original of all the retellings of fairy tales in recent years, offering us a psychological yet very plausible view of Cinderella and her strange family, both before and after the stepmother's appearance.

Somebody Loves You, Mr. Hatch

BY EILEEN SPINELLI; PAUL YALOWITZ, ILLUS.

K and up   *30 pages*   *Simon & Schuster, 1991*

A definitive book on friendship, it introduces us to a lonely little man, Mr. Hatch, who has no friends. And then one day a box of Valentine chocolates is delivered to him by mistake, changing his life forever. Also by the author: *Thanksgiving at the Templetons'*. Related friendship picture books: *Chester's Way* by Kevin Henkes; *The Poppy Seeds* by Robert Clyde Bulla (p); *Teammates* by Peter Golenbock; and *Uncle Jed's Barbershop* (p).

Spot's Touch and Feel Book

BY ERIC HILL.

Inf–Tod   *10 pages*   *Putnam, 2000*

In a book reminiscent of *Pat the Bunny* but far more reflective of today's culture, the perennial favorite Spot enjoys touching a variety of textures through the ten pages, including burlap, plastic, tree trunk, and wool.

Beginning with the first book in the series back in 1980 (*Where's Spot?* [p]), this has become one of the most popular "interactive" series of the last fifty years. Infants and toddlers are encouraged to lift the flaps (which are reinforced and fairly sturdy) to find Spot and his friends. The series has grown to include various teaching concepts like sounds, shapes, colors, numbers, letters and holidays. Other lift-the-flap books allowing active involvement between child and book: *I'm a Little Mouse* by Noelle and David Carter, and *Where Are Maisy's Friends?* by Lucy Cousins (series).

Stellaluna

BY JANELL CANNON

K–5   *44 pages*   *Harcourt, 1993*

Separated accidentally from its mother, a baby bat lands in the nest with three baby birds where it must adapt to bird-ways of resting, sleeping, flying, and (ugh!) eating. Gradually a bond of friendship grows, one that will last when Stellaluna is reunited with her mother. An award-winning celebration of differences and friendship, with a whimsical touch of Mowgli. Related books: *Are You My Mother?* by P. D. Eastman; and *Owl Babies* (p).

The Story of Ferdinand

BY MUNRO LEAF; ROBERT LAWSON, ILLUS.

PreS.–2nd   *68 pages*   *Viking, 1936*

This world-famous tale of a great Spanish bull who preferred sitting peacefully among the flowers to fighting gloriously in the bullring is a children's classic. Illustrated in a simple black-and-white style, it was the first children's book to make *The New York Times* bestseller list—pushing *Gone With the Wind* out of first place. Related books: *Crow Boy* by Taro Yashima; *Oliver Button Is a Sissy* by Tomie dePaola; and *William's Doll* (p).

The Story of Little Babaji

BY HELEN BANNERMAN; FRED MARCELLINO, ILLUS.

Tod–K   *68 pages*   *Harper, 1996*

Reset in India (where it originally was written in 1899), redrawn with Indian characters (instead of the African grotesques it degenerated into), and with the offending name removed, this is nearly word-for-word the original story of *Little Black Sambo*. The original version rightly fell from favor in the 1950s, but this retelling corrects the earlier offenses and allows children to enjoy the battle of wits between the child and the boy-eating tigers. Related books: *The Gingerbread Boy* (p); and *Red's Great Chase* (p).

The Story of Ruby Bridges

BY ROBERT COLES; GEORGE FORD, ILLUS.

Grades 1–5   *26 pages*   *Scholastic, 1995*

From the pen of a Pulitzer Prize–winning research psychiatrist comes the true story of six-year-old Ruby Bridges, one of four black children selected by a federal judge to integrate the New Orleans public schools in 1960. Escorted to the school doors by federal marshals, Ruby had to pass through a gauntlet of curses and spittle. Whispering prayers and backed by her parents' love, the child withstood the daily attacks without bitterness. Rarely can we teach American history using a six-year-old; usually history is peopled by adults—explorers, kings, queens, generals, and inventors. Here is a powerful exception. Ruby Bridges herself expands on Coles's work in *Through My Eyes*, updating the story, including photographs taken during and after the integration conflict. For related books, see listing with *Roll of Thunder, Hear My Cry* (n).

Sylvester and the Magic Pebble

BY WILLIAM STEIG

PreS.–4th   *30 pages*   *Simon & Schuster, 1969*

In this contemporary fairy tale and Caldecott Medal winner, young Sylvester finds a magic pebble that will grant his every wish as long as he holds it in his hand. When a hungry lion approaches, Sylvester wishes himself into a stone. Since stones don't have hands, the pebble drops to the ground and he can't reach it to wish himself normal again. The subsequent loneliness of both Sylvester and his parents is portrayed with deep sensitivity, making all the more real their joy a year later when they are happily reunited. Also by the author: *The Amazing Bone*; *Brave Irene* (p); *Caleb and Katie*; *Doctor De Soto*; *Doctor De Soto Goes to Africa*; *Pete's a Pizza*; *The Toy Brother*; and *Zeke Pippin* (p); for older students: *The Real Thief* (s).

The Tale of Peter Rabbit (see *The Complete Adventures of Peter Rabbit*, page 228)

The Tale of Thomas Mead

BY PAT HUTCHINS

K–3   *32 pages*   *Morrow, 1980*

When all the other children were learning to read, Thomas Mead chose not to. "Why should I?" he asked defiantly. The ensuing farcical misadventures with signs, elevators, rest rooms, doors, traffic signals, and the police more than answer that question for him. Related books about reading: *Andy and the Lion*, by James Dougherty; *Arthur's Prize Reader*, by Lillian Hoban; *Aunt Lulu*, by Daniel Pinkwater; *Aunt Chip and the Great Triple Creek Dam Affair*, by Patricia Polacco; *More Than Anything Else*, by Marie Bradby; *Thank You, Mr. Falker* (p); *Tomás and the Library Lady* (p); and *Santa's Book of Names*, both by David McPhail.

Thank You, Mr. Falker

BY PATRICIA POLACCO

Grades 1–5   *36 pages*   *Philomel, 1999*

Continuing her highly successful formula of drawing on her childhood family and neighborhood experiences, Polacco offers the powerful story of her own illiteracy. Unable to read until fifth grade, she was the daily object of classroom taunts and torment. Finally a sensitive young teacher (Mr. Falker) discovered her dark secret and resolved to bring her out of the darkness. Many children will identify with Polacco's plight and take comfort in her triumph. This story is a natural sequel to her earlier *Bee Tree*. For more about the author, see *Pink and Say* (p).

Related books: *The Art Lesson* by Tomie dePaola; *The Hundred Dresses* by Eleanor Estes (s); *The Library* by Sarah Stewart and David Small; *The Library Card*, a novel by Jerry Spinelli; *More Than Anything Else* (Booker T. Washington learns to read) by Marie Bradby; and *Richard Wright and the Library Card* (p).

This Time, Tempe Wick?
BY PATRICIA LEE GAUCH; MARGOT TOMES, ILLUS.
Grades 2–4   44 pages   Putnam, 1974
When George Washington's unpaid, poorly clad colonial troops mutiny during their winter encampment, they figure to take advantage of the local citizens. But they meet their match in a tough, nervy local girl named Tempe Wick. Based on fact and legend. Related books: *Brave Irene* (p); *The Courage of Sara Noble* (s); *A Lion To Guard Us* (s); and *Toliver's Secret* (s).

Thomas' Snowsuit
BY ROBERT MUNSCH; MICHAEL MARTCHENKO, ILLUS.
PreS.–4th   24 pages   Annick, 1985
Thomas hates his new snowsuit, much to the dismay of his mother, teacher, and principal—all of whom find him a most determined fellow. But children will find the situation just plain funny! Robert Munsch is as popular with Canadian children as Shel Silverstein (see *Where the Sidewalk Ends* [po]) is in the U.S. Also by the author: *The Boy in the Drawer*; *David's Father*; *50 Below Zero*; *I have to Go!*; *Moira's Birthday*; *Mortimer*; *Mud Puddle*; and *The Paper Bag Princess*. For related clothing stories, see *The Principal's New Clothes* (p).

The Three Robbers
BY TOMI UNGERER
PreS.–1   34 pages   Atheneum, 1962
Take three fierce, dark-of-night thieves, one charming little girl, a black cave, trunks of gold, carts and carts of abandoned children, and one majestic castle—what do you have? A tale that will rivet young listeners. Also by the author: *Zerlada's Ogre*.

Tikki Tikki Tembo
BY ARLENE MOSEL; BLAIR LENT, ILLUS.
PreS.–3rd   40 pages   Holt, 1968
This little picture book tells the amusing legend of how the Chinese people stopped giving their first-born sons incredibly long first names and started giving all children short names. Related books with Asian settings:

Beautiful Warrior: The Legend of the Nun's Kung Fu by Emily Arnold Mc-Curry; *Blue Willow* by Pam Conrad; *The Boy Who Drew Cats*, retold by Arthur A. Levine; *Crow Boy* by Taro Yashima; *The Emperor and the Kite* by Jane Yolen; *The Hunter* by Mary Casanova; *The Journey of Meng* by Doreen Rappaport; *The Rainbow People* by Laurence Yep; *The River Dragon* by Darcy Pattison; *The Samurai's Daughter* (p); *The Seven Chinese Brothers* by Margaret Mahy; and *The Voice of the Great Bell* by Lafcadio Hearn.

Tintin in Tibet (comic book)
BY HERGÉ
Grades 2–4   62 pages   *Little, 1975*
When you've been in print for more than sixty years, translated into twenty-two languages, and praised in *The Times* of London and *The New York Times*, you must be special. Tintin is just that. He's the boy detective who hop-scotches the globe in pursuit of thieves and smugglers. Loaded with humor, adventure, and marvelous artwork (700 pictures in each issue), Tintin's special appeal for parents who want to assist their child in reading is the fact that each Tintin contains more than 8,000 words. Having heard Tintin read aloud, children will want to obtain his other adventures and read them by themselves, oblivious to the fact that they are reading so many words in the process. Because of the size of the pictures, Tintin is best read aloud to no more than two children at a time. Furthermore, a comic should be read aloud to the child only a few times—to show the child how a comic works. This is similar to the concept of a model train: the parent shows the child how, then turns it over to the youngster to use. Beginning in 1994, Tintin's American publisher began issuing hardcovers, three comics to a volume. You'll find a complete listing of Tintin comics on the Web at www.du.edu/~tomills/tintin.htm.

The Tree That Would Not Die
BY ELLEN LEVINE; TED RAND, ILLUS.
Grades 1–4   30 pages   *Scholastic, 1995*
This is the true story of a famous tree in Austin, Texas—the Treaty Oak—that has witnessed much of American history—some good, some shameful—and its survival from a near-fatal poisoning, thanks to good citizens who cared deeply.

The True Adventure of Daniel Hall
BY DIANE STANLEY
Grades 1 and up   40 pages   *Dial, 1995*
Based on the memoirs of a fourteen-year-old boy in the 1850s, this is a no-holds-barred account of serving on a whaling ship that includes dealing

with an abusive sea captain, whaling life, escaping to the coast of Siberia, surviving a winter in isolation (at forty degrees below zero), and eventually being rescued. For experienced listeners. Diane Stanley has become one of the most versatile of writers/illustrators, with an award-winning series of picture book biographies that include: *Leonardo da Vinci*; *Bard of Avon: The Story of William Shakespeare*; *Cleopatra*; *Charles Dickens: The Man Who Had Great Expectations*; *Michelangelo*; and *Shaka, King of the Zulus*. Also by the author: *Saving Sweetness* (p).

The True Story of the Three Little Pigs

BY JOHN SCIESZKA; LANE SMITH, ILLUS.

K and up   28 pages   *Viking, 1989*

For 200 years, we've taken the word of the three little pigs as "gospel truth." But when the author presents the infamous wolf's side of the story, we get an implausible but entertainingly different point of view. Also by the author: *The Stinky Cheeseman*; *Squids Will Be Squids*; *Fresh Morals for Beastly Fables*; and the Time Warp series of short, zany novels—*The Good, the Bad, and the Goofy*; *Knights of the Kitchen Table*; *The Not-So-Jolly Roger*; *See You Later, Gladiator*; *Summer Reading Is Killing Me!*; *Tut Tut*; *2095*; and *Your Mother Was a Neanderthal*. On the Web: www.chucklebat.com.

Other fairy tale parodies include: *Beware of Boys* by Tony Blundell; *Cinder-Elly* by Frances Minters; *The Cowboy and the Black-eyed Pea* by Tony Johnson; *Happily Ever After* by Anna Quindlen; *Jim and the Beanstalk* by Raymond Briggs; *The Jolly Postman* by Janet and Allan Ahlberg; *Little Red Riding Hood: A Newfangled Prairie Tale* and *Goldilocks Returns*, both by Lisa Campbell Ernst; *The Principal's New Clothes* (p); *Ruby* by Michael Emberley; *Sleeping Ugly* by Jane Yolen; *Somebody and the Three Blairs* by Marilyn Tolhurst; and *A Telling of the Tales: Five Stories* by William J. Brooke.

Truman's Aunt Farm

BY JAMA KIM RATTIGAN; G. BRIAN KARAS, ILLUS.

PreS.–2nd   30 pages   *Houghton, 1994*

When little Truman's aunt sends him an ant farm, it turns out to be an "aunt" farm—dozens of swarming aunts who cannot do enough to help him. Overwhelmed but pleased by all the affection and attention, Truman is fast running out of room when he hits upon a solution. See also *The King Who Rained* by Fred Gwynne, and *Pigsty* by Mark Teague. Other books about relatives: *Aunt Minnie McGranahan* (p); *The Go-Between* and *The Purple Coat*, both by Amy Hest; *The Lemon Drop Jar* by Christine Widman; *My Great-Aunt Arizona* by Gloria Houston; *Nana's Birthday Party* by Amy Hest;

and these novels about aunts: *The Lost Flower Children* by Janet Taylor Lisle; *Shoeshine Girl* (s); *The Trolls* (n); and *Understood Betsy* (n).

Uncle Jed's Barbershop

BY MARGAREE K. MITCHELL; JAMES RANSOME, ILLUS.

K–4   30 pages   *Simon & Schuster, 1993*

In the segregated South of the 1920s, Uncle Jed was the only black barber in the county, riding horseback from one sharecropper to the next. His dream was to own a barbershop, but every time he had enough money saved, another neighbor's crisis proved more worthy of the money. Finally his dream comes true! Related books: *From Miss Ida's Porch* by Sandra Belton; *Leon's Story* (s); *A School for Pompey Walker* (p); *The Story of Ruby Bridges* (p); and the novels: *Francie* (n) and *Roll of Thunder, Hear My Cry* (n).

The Very Hungry Caterpillar

BY ERIC CARLE

Tod–1   38 pages   *Philomel, 1969*

What an ingenious book! It is, at the same time, a simple, lovely way to teach a child the days of the week, how to count to five, and how a caterpillar becomes a butterfly. First, this is a book to look at—bright, bright pictures. Then it is something whose pages beg to be turned—pages that have little round holes in them made by the hungry little caterpillar. And as the number of holes grow, so does the caterpillar. Other books by the author: *The Grouchy Ladybug*; *The Hole in the Dike*; *The Very Busy Spider*; *The Very Clumsy Click Beetle*; *The Very Lonely Firefly*; and *Eric Carle's Treasury of Classic Stories for Children* (a). For other books by the author, see his Web site: www.eric-carle.com.

Wagon Wheels

BY BARBARA BRENNER; DON BOLOGNESE, ILLUS.

PreS.–3rd   64 pages   *Harper, 1978*

In four short chapters, this story can be read either as a long picture book or as an introduction to chapter books. Three young black brothers follow a map to their father's homestead on the western plains. The trio braves storms, fires, and famine to reach their goal. Other historical fiction picture books: *Araminta's Paint Box* by Karen Ackerman; *Charlie's House* by Clyde R. Bulla; *The Drinking Gourd* by F. N. Monjo, a story of the underground railroad; *From Miss Ida's Porch* by Sandra Belton; *The Josefina Story Quilt* by Eleanor Coerr; *The Log Cabin Quilt* by Ellen Howard; *The Lucky Stone* by Lucille Clifton; *Minty: A Story of Young Harriet Tubman* by Alan Shroeder; *Molly Bannaky* (p); *The Wagon* by Tony Johnston; and *Watch the Stars Come Out* by Riki Levinson.

We're Going on a Bear Hunt

BY MICHAEL ROSEN; HELEN OXENBURY, ILLUS.

Tod–K   32 pages   Atheneum, 1992

A family hunts a bear through field, river, swamp, forest, snowstorm (with predictable, appropriate sounds and movement). When they find him, he hunts them back home via the same route and sounds. See list of predictable/cumulative books on page 220. Related books: *Red's Great Chase* (p); and *Where's My Teddy?* (p).

What's Under My Bed?

BY JAMES STEVENSON

PreS.–2nd   30 pages   Greenwillow, 1983

In this ongoing series, Stevenson gives us an endearing combination: Two innocent but slightly worried grandchildren turn again and again for reassurance to their grandfather, who concocts imaginative tales about his childhood that makes their worries pale by comparison. They've yet to invent the superhero who can equal the hilarious heroics and hair-raising escapades of Grandpa as a child. Also in the series: *Could Be Worse!*; *Grandpa's Great City Tour*; *The Great Big Especially Beautiful Easter Egg*; *No Friends*; *That Dreadful Day*; *That Terrible Halloween Night*; *That's Exactly the Way It Wasn't*; *We Can't Sleep*; *Worse Than Willy!*; *We Hate Rain!*; and *Will You Please Feed Our Cat?*

When Jessie Came Across the Sea

BY AMY HEST; P. J. LYNCH, ILLUS.

Grades 1–5   32 pages   Candlewick, 1997

The courageous and bittersweet story of American immigration is told in the story of a Jewish orphan girl from Eastern Europe who receives a one-way ticket to America from the village rabbi. This great opportunity is tempered by the fact she must leave her grandmother—the only relative she has in the world. The girl's courage in the new world and her eventual reunion with her grandmother make this an inspiring story. Related book: *Coming to America: The Story of Immigration* by Betsy Maestro; *Street of Gold*, retold by Rosemary Wells; and the novel about a Mexican child who is smuggled across the border, *Lupita Mañana* (n).

Where the Wild Things Are

BY MAURICE SENDAK

K–3   *28 pages*   *Harper, 1963*

This is the 1963 Caldecott winner that changed the course of modern children's literature. Sendak here creates a fantasy about a little boy and the monsters that haunt and fascinate children. The fact that youngsters are not the least bit frightened by the story, that they love it as they would an old friend, is a credit to Sendak's insight into children's minds and hearts. Also by the author: *In the Night Kitchen*; *Maurice Sendak's Really Rosie*; *The Nutshell Library* (which includes *Alligators All Around*; *Chicken Soup with Rice*; *One Was Johnny*; *Pierre*).

For a listing of books about bedtime antics, see *The Boy Who Wouldn't Go to Bed* (p). For more monster chases: *Clay Boy* by Mirra Ginsburg; *Dogzilla* by Dav Pilkey; *Here Come the Aliens!* (p); *The Lost Boy and the Monster* (p); *Red's Great Chase* (p); and *The Teeny Tiny Woman* by Arthur Robins.

Where's My Teddy?

BY JEZ ALBOROUGH

PreS.–K   *24 pages*   *Candlewick, 1997*

Alborough has created three popular books in this series about little Eddie and the giant bear who lives in the park. In their first encounter (*Where's My Teddy?*), Eddie mistakenly ends up with the bear's teddy and the bear has his. Though each is equally afraid of the other, they both finally end up with the right teddy. In the second book (*It's the Bear!*), Eddie's mother is a non-believer until she and the bear come face-to-face (reminiscent of Robert McCloskey's *Blueberries for Sal*). In the third book (*My Friend Bear*), their fear of each other is happily resolved when each realizes how much they have in common—including a needless fear of each other and a love of their teddies. Related books: *I Lost My Bear* by Jules Feiffer; and *May We Sleep Here Tonight?* (p).

Where's Waldo?

BY MARTIN HANDFORD

PreS.–4th   *26 pages*   *Little, 1987*

Waldo is a hiker on a worldwide trek who plays hide-and-seek with the reader-viewer, who has to find him as he threads his way through thousands of people who populate a dozen different landscapes. Children will spend hours searching the pages for Waldo and the list of more than 300 items checklisted at the end of the book. Also note that in each scene Waldo loses one of his twelve personal items. Books like this stretch children's attention spans while polishing visual discrimination. (They should also be required equipment for anyone taking a child under six to a restaurant or church.) Sequels: *Where's Waldo? The Wonder Book; Where's Waldo Now?; Where's Waldo? The Fantastic Journey; Where's Waldo? In Hollywood.*

Related books: Writer Jean Marzollo and photographer Walter Wick have created a sensational series of photo-puzzle books: *I Spy: A Book of Picture Riddles; I Spy Christmas; I Spy Fantasy; I Spy Fun House; I Spy Gold Challenger; I Spy Mystery; I Spy School Days; I Spy Spooky Night;* and *I Spy Super Challenger.* Also, the long-running "hidden pictures" feature from *Highlights for Children* magazine has been collected in: *The Jumbo Book of Hidden Pictures; The Second Jumbo Book of Hidden Pictures;* and *The Super Colossal Book of Hidden Pictures.*

The Whingdingdilly

BY BILL PEET

PreS.–5th   60 pages   *Houghton, 1970*

Bill Peet should be declared either a national treasure (along with Dr. Seuss) or a modern Aesop. Using animals to make his points, Peet has given us more than thirty wonderful picture books in the last forty years, with nary a one going out of print. Typical is this book: Discontented with his life as a dog, Scamp envies all the attention given to his beribboned neighbor—Palomar the wonder horse. But when a backwoods witch changes Scamp into an animal with the feet of an elephant, the neck of a giraffe, the tail of a zebra, and the nose of a rhinoceros, he gets more attention than he bargained for: He ends up a most unhappy circus freak. But all ends well, and tied into the ending is a subtle lesson for both Scamp and his readers: Be yourself!

Among Peet's most popular titles are: *Big Bad Bruce; The Caboose Who Got Loose; Eli; Encore for Eleanor; Farewell to Shady Glade; Fly, Homer, Fly; How Droofus the Dragon Lost His Head; Kermit the Hermit; Randy's Dandy Lions;* and *Wump World.* Also, *Bill Peet: An Autobiography* is a 180-page autobiography (Caldecott Honor winner) with an illustration on every page.

William's Doll

BY CHARLOTTE ZOLOTOW; WILLIAM PÈNE DU BOIS, ILLUS.

PreS.–3rd   32 pages   *Harper, 1972*

William's father wants him to play with his basketball or trains; William, to the astonishment of all, wishes he had a doll to play with. "Sissy," say his brother and friends. But William's grandmother says something else—

something very important—to William, his father, and his brother. One of the most prolific and successful authors for children, Charlotte Zolotow is also one of the most beloved. She writes quiet little books with simple sentences, and her work is always illustrated by the best artists. You'll have no trouble finding the many Zolotow books in your library—she has almost the entire "Z" shelf to herself.

A partial listing of her most popular books includes: *Big Sister and Little Sister*; *But Not Billy*; *Do You Know What I'll Do?*; *A Father Like That*; *The Hating Book*; *I Know a Lady*; *Like to Be Little*; *If It Weren't for You*; *If You Listen*; *Janey*; *May I Visit? Mr. Rabbit and the Lovely Present*; *My Grandson Lew*; *Over and Over*; *The Quarreling Book*; *Some Things Go Together*; *Something Is Going to Happen*; *The Storm Book*; *The Summer Night*; *Timothy Too!*; *When I Have a Little Boy*; and *When I Have a Little Girl*.

The Wretched Stone
BY CHRIS VAN ALLSBURG
Grades 2–7   30 pages   *Houghton Mifflin, 1991*
When the crew of a clipper ship, sailing tropical seas, discovers a deserted island, they also find a large gray stone, luminous and with one smooth side. When it is brought on board, an eerie change begins to envelop the ship. Fascinated by the rock, the crew gradually deserts its work and leisure activities, spending more and more time gazing in silent numbness at the rock—despite the protestations of their captain. In the hands of one of today's most important and thought-provoking author-illustrators for children, this is a powerful allegory about the effects of television on society.

Van Allsburg's other books include: *Ben's Dream*; *The Garden of Abdul Gasazi*; *Jumanji*; *Just a Dream*; *The Mysteries of Harris Burdick*; *The Polar Express*; *The Stranger*; *The Sweetest Fig*; *Two Bad Ants*; *The Widow's Broom*; *The Wreck of the Zephyr*; and *The Z Was Zapped* (an unusual alphabet book). On the Web: www.eduplace.com/rdg/author/cva/index.html.

Zeke Pippin
BY WILLIAM STEIG
PreS.–3rd   28 pages   *Harper, 1994*
Zeke the pig finds a magic harmonica in the street. It puts everyone to sleep who hears its beautiful sounds. Although Zeke doesn't realize its magic immediately (he thinks people are bored by his playing), he eventually uses it to overcome robbers and wolves, and then to bring great solace to his community. Steig again proves he is one of the century's great writers for children. For other Steig books, see *Sylvester and the Magic Pebble* (p).

Short Novels

Anna, Grandpa, and the Big Storm
BY CARLA STEVENS

PreS.–1st   64 pages   *Puffin, 1985*

It is March 1888, and seven-year-old Anna absolutely *must* get to school for the spelling bee finals, even if it is snowing. Entrusted to the care of her grandfather, Anna sets off. The storm worsens and the pair is stranded on the elevated train with other passengers, waiting to be rescued by fire fighters, but not before Anna leads the frightened adult passengers in a game of Simon Says. This exciting story of the great Blizzard of '88, with its short chapters and abundant illustrations, makes an excellent introduction to chapter books. Related storm books: *Baby in a Basket* (p); *Blizzard!* by Jim Murphy; *Chibi: A True Story from Japan* by Barbara Brenner & Julia Takaya; *Kate Shelley: Bound for Legend* by Robert San Souci; and *An Outlaw Thanksgiving* by Emily Arnold McCully.

Baseball in April
BY GARY SOTO

Grades 6 and up   107 pages   *Harcourt, 1990*

One of the freshest voices in children's books, Soto is a product of the Latino community in Fresno, California, who grew up with a cement factory across the street, a junkyard next door, and a raisin factory at the end of the street. This collection of eleven short stories is largely based on his early teen years, filled with the bittersweet laughter and tears found in all adolescent lives. Also by the author: *Chato and the Party Animals* (p); *Living Up the Street*; *Local News*; *Pacific Crossing*; *The Pool Party*; *The Skirt*; *Taking Sides*; and *Too Many Tamales*.

The Bears' House
BY MARILYN SACHS

Grades 4–6   82 pages   *Dutton, 1987*

A perfect vehicle for a classroom discussion of values, this novel portrays a ten-year-old girl whose mother is ill and can no longer care for her family after the father deserts them. The girl decides to tend to the family, while suffering the taunts of classmates because she sucks her thumb, wears dirty clothes, and smells. To escape, she retreats to the fantasy world she has created in an old dollhouse in her classroom. Sequel: *Fran Ellen's House*. Related books: *The Great Gilly Hopkins* by Katherine Paterson; *The Hundred Dresses* (s); and *Tyler, Wilkin, and Skee* by Robert Burch.

The Best Christmas Pageant Ever
BY BARBARA ROBINSON
Grades 2–6   80 pages   *Harper, 1972*
What happens when the worst-behaved family of kids in town comes to
Sunday school and muscles into all the parts for the Christmas pageant? The
results are zany and heartwarming; a most unusual Christmas story. Sequel:
The Best School Year Ever. Related novel: *Sideways Stories from Wayside School* (n).

A Blue-Eyed Daisy
BY CYNTHIA RYLANT
Grades 4–8   99 pages   *Simon & Schuster, 1985*
This is the warm yet bittersweet year in the life of an eleven-year-old girl
and her family in the hills of West Virginia as she experiences her first kiss,
has a brush with death, comes to understand her good but hard-drinking
father, and begins to grow into the person you'd love to have as a relative.
Also by the author: *But I'll Be Back Again* (her autobiography for older students); *Best Wishes* (her autobiography for younger children); and *A Couple of Kooks* (s). On the Web: www.rylant.com. Related books: *Because of
Winn-Dixie* (n); and *Ida Early Comes Over the Mountain* (n); and for teen
readers: *Rocket Boys* by Homer Hickam, Jr., a memoir by a NASA engineer
growing up in Coaltown, West Virginia, not unlike the community Rylant
writes about here.

Call It Courage
BY ARMSTRONG SPERRY
Grades 2–6   94 pages   *Macmillan, 1940*
Set in the South Seas before the traders or missionaries arrived, this Newbery winner describes the struggle of a boy to overcome his fear of the sea,
which tragically took his mother. The taunts of his peers drive him to confront his fears and demonstrate his courage by going alone to the sea in a
canoe. Related books: *The Cay* (n); *Toliver's Secret* (n); *The True Adventure of
Daniel Hall* (p); and *The Wreck of the Zanzibar* by Michael Morpurgo.

Cam Jensen and the Mystery of the Dinosaur Bones
BY DAVID ADLER
Grades 1–3   56 pages   *Puffin, 1997*
Thanks to her photographic memory, little escapes the notice of Cam
Jensen in this easy mystery series that now comprises more than twenty
books. You might say she's a grade-school Nancy Drew, but with far fewer
pages per book. In this volume, when Cam's class visits the museum's dino-

saur room, she quickly notes that three of the skeleton's bones are *missing*! For a complete series list: www.penguinputnam.com. This is an excellent introduction to the mystery genre.

Chocolate Fever

BY ROBERT K. SMITH

Grades 1–5   94 pages   *Dell, 1978*

Henry Green doesn't just *like* chocolate—he's *crazy* about it. He even has chocolate sprinkles on his cereal and chocolate cake for breakfast. He thus is a prime candidate to come down with the world's first case of "chocolate fever." Funny, with a subtle message for moderation. *Jelly Belly*, also by the author, uses humor and insight to describe the self-image problems of an overweight child. In *Jelly Belly*, as well as in *The War With Grandpa*, Smith paints a powerful picture of the relationship between child and grandparent. Also by the author: *Bobby Baseball* and *Mostly Michael*. Related book: *The Chocolate Touch* (n).

The Courage of Sarah Noble

BY ALICE DALGLIESH; LEONARD WEISGARD, ILLUS.

K–3   54 pages   *Atheneum, 1986*

At the beginning of the eighteenth century, an eight-year-old girl journeys into the Colonial wilderness with her father. With her family's instructions—"Keep up your courage!"—ringing in her ears, she faces the dangers of the forest while her father builds their new cabin. Just when she feels she has confronted all her fears, her father asks her to stay in the nearby Indian village while he returns for the rest of the family. Based on a true incident, the story is an excellent introduction to the historical novel in a short form. Also by the author: *The Bears on Hemlock Mountain*; *The Silver Pencil* (an autobiographical novel). Related book on the Colonial period: *Colonial Times* by Joy Masoff, part of Scholastic's Chronicle of America series that uses photographs from America's living history museums to illustrate this excellent forty-eight-page reference volume.

Related picture books on courage: *The Bear That Heard Crying* by Natalie Kinsey-Warnock and Helen Kinsey; *Brave Irene* (p); *The Bravest of Us All* by Marsha Diane Arnold; *The Butterfly* by Patricia Polacco; *The Cabin Key* by Gloria Rand; *The Hunter* (p); *Kate Shelley: Bound for Legend* by Robert San Souci; *Katie's Trunk* by Ann Turner; *The Samurai's Daughter* (p); *Tea with the Old Dragon* by Jane Yolen; *This Time, Tempe Wick?* (p); *Wagon Wheels* (p); and *When Jessie Came Across the Sea* (p).

Dinosaurs Before Dark (Magic Tree House series)

BY MARY POPE OSBORNE

K–2   76 pages   *Random House, 1992*

In this first book of the popular time-travel series (with three- to four-page chapters), young Annie and Jack discover a treehouse that transports them back in time to the age of dinosaurs. The journey is filled with fantasy adventure while exploring scientific, cultural, or historic places and events. Web site: www.randomhouse.com/kids/magictreehouse/books/books.html.

The Friendship

BY MILDRED TAYLOR

Grades 4 and up   53 pages   *Dial, 1987*

The Logan children (from *Roll of Thunder, Hear My Cry*) witness the searing cruelty of bigotry during this story set in 1933 in rural Mississippi, where two men (one white, one black) see their one-time friendship destroyed by violence when the black man dares to call the other by his first name. Readers should be aware of racial epithets in the context of the story. In the paperback edition, this book is combined with *The Gold Cadillac* in a single volume. For other books by the author and related titles, see listing with *Roll of Thunder, Hear My Cry* (n).

Frindle

BY ANDREW CLEMENTS

Grades 3–6   105 pages   *Simon & Schuster, 1996*

This book will have you laughing out loud by paragraph five and wanting to adopt the main character (a fifth-grade boy) by the end of the first chapter, nodding in affirmation of its wisdom throughout, and wiping the tears away at its end. The story is what education, family, and relationships are supposed to be about, never mind what a good book can do for the reading appetite. And—it's fall-down funny. Oh, yes, it's about the dictionary, too. It was overlooked for the Newbery Award but it keeps winning kids' votes in the state awards. Also by the author: *The Landry News* (how a fifth-grade girl's classroom newspaper changes her teacher and school); and *The Janitor's Boy* (life in fifth grade if your father is the school custodian).

The Half-A-Moon Inn

BY PAUL FLEISCHMAN

Grades 2–6   88 pages   *Harper, 1980*

A chilling fantasy-adventure story about a mute boy separated from his mother by a blizzard and later kidnapped by the wicked proprietress of a village inn. Fast-moving, white-knuckle reading. Also by the author: *Bull Run*; *Seedfolks*; and *Weslandia*; for older readers: *The Borning Room*.

Help! I'm a Prisoner in the Library

BY ETH CLIFFORD

Grades 1–4　　106 pages　　　　　　　　　　　　　*Houghton, 1979*

When their father's car runs out of gas in a blizzard, Mary Rose and Jo-Beth are told to stay in the car while Dad goes for help. The two sisters, however, soon leave in search of a bathroom and end up mysteriously locked inside an empty old stone library. Before long, the lights go out, the phone goes dead, and a threatening voice cries out, "Off with their heads!" The tension is more dramatic than traumatic, and great fun. Sequels: *The Dastardly Murder of Dirty Pete*; *Just Tell Me When We're Dead!*; *Scared Silly*; and *Never Hit a Ghost with a Baseball Bat*. Also by the author: *Harvey's Horrible Snake Disaster* and *The Man Who Sang in the Dark*.

Herbie Jones

BY SUZY KLINE

Grades 1–4　　95 pages　　　　　　　　　　　　　*Putnam, 1985*

Third-grader Herbie and his irrepressible pal Raymond meet the challenges and trials of third grade—from escaping the bottom reading group to escaping the girls' bathroom. All of it is done with a blend of sensitivity and humor, topped off with some side-splitting "gross-outs." Also by the author: *Herbie Jones and the Birthday Showdown*; *Herbie Jones and the Class Gift*; *Herbie Jones and the Dark Attic*; *Herbie Jones and the Monster Ball*; *Herbie Jones and Hamburger Head*; and *What's the Matter with Herbie Jones?* For younger readers, see Kline's Horrible Harry series.

How to Be a Perfect Person in Just Three Days!

BY STEPHEN MANES

Grades 3–6　　76 pages　　　　　　　　　　　　　*BDD, 1982*

This laugh-out-loud book is not quite great literature but very close to the funny bone. A young boy, tired of bearing the brunt of everyone's taunts, begins a do-it-yourself course in becoming "perfect"—with hilarious and surprising results. Related books: *The Hoboken Chicken Emergency* by Daniel Pinkwater; *The Shrinking of Treehorn* (p); *Sideways Stories From Wayside School* (n); *The Secret Knowledge of Grown-ups* (p); and *Skinnybones* (s). See also John Scieszka's Time Warp series of zany short novels listed under *The True Story of the Three Little Pigs* (p).

The Hundred Dresses

BY ELEANOR ESTES

Grades 3–6   *78 pages*   *Harcourt, 1944*

Wanda Petronski comes from the wrong side of the tracks and is the object
of class jokes until her classmates sadly realize their awful mistake and cruelty. But by then it's too late. Though written more than a half century
ago, the book's message about peer pressure has lost none of its power or
relevancy. Related books: *The Bears' House* (s); *Crow Boy* by Taro Yashima;
Mandy by Julie Edwards; and *Queeny Peavy* by Robert Burch.

The Iron Giant: A Story in Five Nights

BY TED HUGHES

Grades 1–4   *58 pages*   *Harper, 1987*

The excellent children's movie of the same name was loosely based on this
science fiction–fantasy, a modern fairy tale, but the book is more nuanced.
It describes an invincible iron giant—a robot without a master—that stalks
the land, devouring anything made of metal. Suddenly the earth faces a
threat far greater than from the giant when an alien creature lands—forcing the iron man into a fight for his life. Sequel: *The Iron Woman*, with
handsome Barry Moser illustrations. On the Web: www.uni-leipzig.de/
~angl/hughes/huchild.htm.

Jacob Two-Two Meets the Hooded Fang

BY MORDECAI RICHLER

Grades 3–5   *84 pages*   *Knopf, 1975*

For the crime of insulting a grown-up, Jacob is sent to Children's Prison,
where he must confront the infamous Hooded Fang. A marvelous tongue-
in-cheek adventure story, sure to delight all. Sequel: *Jacob Two-Two's First
Spy Case.*

Junie B. Jones and the Stupid Smelly Bus

BY BARBARA PARK

K–1   *70 pages*   *Random House, 1992*

Don't be put off by the title of this book, part of a wonderfully funny series (more than fifteen books to date). Junie B. is Ramona, Little Lulu, and
Lucy all rolled into one determined kindergartner. No one in children's
publishing approaches Barbara Park when it comes to children's humor. For
a complete list of all the Junie B. books and activities, check out the author's
Web site: www.randomhouse.com/kids/junieb/. Park's other books, like

Mick Harte Was Here (s) and *Skinnybones* (s), are aimed at older students and demonstrate why she's consistently a state award–winner with children.

Lafcadio, the Lion Who Shot Back

BY SHEL SILVERSTEIN

Grades 2–6   90 pages   *Harper, 1963*

Lafcadio decides he isn't satisfied being a lion—he must become a marksman and man-about-town and painter and world traveler and. . . . He tries just about everything and anything in hope of finding happiness. If only he'd try being himself. A witty and thought-provoking book, Silverstein's first for children; for his other titles, see *Where the Sidewalk Ends* (po).

Leon's Story

BY LEON WALTER TILLAGE

Grades 2–6   105 pages   *FSG, 1997*

For years, the custodian spellbound the children at his Baltimore school with his story of growing up in segregated North Carolina, how families and community managed to survive, and then the tumultuous civil rights years when they unleashed the dogs. This is his amazingly simple but powerful true story. Related books: *From Miss Ida's Porch* by Sandra Belton; *Little Cliff and the Porch People* by Clifton Taulbert; *Uncle Jed's Barbershop* (p); and *A School for Pompey Walker* (p).

A Lion to Guard Us

BY CLYDE ROBERT BULLA

K–4   117 pages   *Crowell, 1981*

In a simple prose style that is rich in character and drama, one of America's best historical writers for children offers a poignant tale of the founding fathers of the Jamestown colony and the families they left behind in England. Here we meet a plucky heroine named Amanda who is determined to hold fast to her brother and sister despite the grim agonies of their mother's death, poverty and shipwreck. All the while she clings to the dream that someday she will find the father who left them all behind. In another historical novel, *Charlie's House*, the author portrays a dreamy English boy turned out by his family and eventually indentured to colonial farmers around 1750. Also by the author: *The Chalk Box Kid*; *Daniel's Duck*; *Ghost Town Treasure*; *Pirate's Promise*; *The Poppy Seeds* (p); *Shoeshine Girl* (s); and *The Sword in the Tree*.

The Littles

BY JOHN PETERSON

Grades 1–4   80 pages   *Scholastic, 1970*

Children have always been fascinated with the idea of "little people"—from leprechauns to Lilliputians, from Thumbelina to hobbits. Unfortunately, much of the famous fantasy literature is too sophisticated for reading aloud to young children. The Littles series is the exception—fast-paced short novels centering on a colony of six-inch people who live inside the walls of the Bigg family's home and have dramatic escapades with gigantic mice, cats, gliders, and telephones. Also in the series: *The Littles and the Lost Children*; *The Littles and the Terrible Tiny Kid*; *The Littles and the Trash Tinies*; *The Littles and Their Amazing New Friends*; *The Littles Give a Party*; *The Littles Go Exploring*; *The Littles Go to School*; *The Littles Have a Wedding*; *The Littles Take a Trip*; *The Littles to the Rescue*; and *Tom Little's Great Halloween Scare*. On the Web: www.geocities.com/Athens/Olympus/2597/. Related books: *The Minpins* (p); for older students: *The Borrowers* and *Poor Stainless*, both by Mary Norton; *The Indian in the Cupboard* (n); *The Smartest Man in Ireland* (s); and *Stuart Little* (n).

Mick Harte Was Here

BY BARBARA PARK

Grades 3–5   88 pages   *Knopf, 1995*

This is Barbara Park at her *serious* best. Told through the eyes of an angry, grieving, yet plucky and funny thirteen-year-old sister, it's the story of her younger brother's death from a bike accident, which would have ended otherwise had he been wearing a helmet. Park fills it with warm and often hysterically funny recollections of this terrific boy, who could unnerve anyone with his creative antics. Far from maudlin, it has won numerous children's-choice state awards. More than a decade ago, the author was able to pull off a similar feat with her poignant book on divorce, *Don't Make Me Smile*. See also *Skinnybones* (s). Web site: www.randomhouse.com/kids/junieb/.

The Monster's Ring

BY BRUCE COVILLE

Grades 2–4   87 pages   *Pantheon, 1982*

Just the thing for Halloween reading, this is the Jekyll-and-Hyde tale of timid Russell and the magic ring he buys that can turn him into a monster—not a *make-believe* monster but one with hairy hands, fangs and claws, one that roams the night, one that will make short order of Eddie the bully, and one that will bring out the worst in Russell. An exciting fantasy of magic gone awry. Sequel: *Jennifer Murdley's Toad*.

My Father's Dragon

BY RUTH S. GANNETT

K–2   78 pages   *Knopf, 1948*

This is the little fantasy novel that has stood the test of time—surviving in print for a half century. So it must be good! The three-volume series is bursting with hair-raising escapes and evil creatures. The tone is dramatic enough to be exciting for even mature preschoolers but not enough to frighten them. The narrator relates the tales as adventures that happened to his father when he was a boy. This is an excellent transition series for introducing children to longer stories with fewer pictures. The rest of the series, in order: *Elmer and the Dragon* and *The Dragons of Blueland*. All three tales are combined in a single volume for *My Father's Dragon: 50th Anniversary Edition*.

Old Yeller

BY FRED GIPSON

Grades 3–6   117 pages   *Harper, 1956*

While father is away on a cattle drive, the family must fend for itself in this nonstop novel set on a Texas farm in the 1860s. Together with their adopted stray dog, the mother and two sons battle skunks, wild boars, bulls, bears, stubborn mules, and rabies in a tale that tugs on both your attention and heartstrings. Sequel: *Savage Sam*. An interesting contrast can be made with the pioneer family in *Caddie Woodlawn* (n). See also listing of dog stories with *A Dog Called Kitty* (n).

On My Honor

BY MARION DANE BAUER

Grades 5–9   90 pages   *Clarion, 1986*

When his daredevil best friend drowns in a swimming accident, Joel tells no one and returns home to deny the reality and truth of the tragedy. This gripping drama of conscience and consequences is also a story of choices—the ones we make and those we refuse to make. Also by the author: *Rain of Fire*. Related book: *Liars* by P. J. Petersen; and *A Taste of Blackberries* (s).

Owls in the Family

BY FARLEY MOWAT

Grades 2–6   108 pages   *Little, 1961*

No child should miss the author's reliving of his rollicking boyhood on the Saskatchewan prairie, where he raised dogs, gophers, rats, snakes, pigeons, and owls. It is an era we will never see again. Mowat would grow up to become a world-famous writer and naturalist (author of *Never Cry Wolf*, book and film). Also by the author: *Lost in the Barrens*; and for older readers and adults, his irreverent, entertaining autobiography: *Born Naked*. Related books: *Capyboppy* by Bill Peet; *Gentle Ben* (n); and *My Side of the Mountain* (n).

Purple Death: The Mysterious Flu of 1918

BY DAVID GETZ

Grades 6 and up   76 pages   *Holt, 2000*

Secondary science teachers who say there's nothing to read aloud: Look no further than this slim volume. Here is the true story of the greatest epidemic to strike the world since the Black Plague, told in short chapters with a scientific slant. Since one variation of flu strikes the population every other year, and our difficulty in eradicating it rivals our woes with AIDS, this is a very relevant subject for the classroom. Also by the author: *Frozen Girl*; *Frozen Man*; and *Life on Mars*. Related titles: *Fever 1793* by Laurie Halse Anderson.

The Reluctant Dragon

BY KENNETH GRAHAME; ERNEST H. SHEPARD, ILLUS.

Grades 3–5   54 pages   *Holiday, 1938*

The author of the classic *Wind in the Willows* gives us here a simple boy-and-dragon story. The dragon is not a devouring dragon but a reluctant one who wants nothing to do with violence. The boy is something of a local scholar, well versed in dragon lore and torn mightily between his desire to view a battle between the dragon and St. George and his desire to protect his friend the dragon. For experienced listeners. Related books: *The Book of Dragons* by E. Nesbit; *My Father's Dragon* (s); *Saint George and the Dragon*, retold by Margaret Hodges; and *The Story of Ferdinand* (p).

The Rifle

BY GARY PAULSEN

Grades 6 and up   104 pages   *Harcourt, 1995*

This short biography of a weapon, from its artistic birth on the eve of the Revolutionary War to the present time, offers a moving portrait of the many people whose paths intersect with the rifle during its 230-year history. Although the weapon is always at the center of this tale, American history shares much of the stage as the rifle's role changes with the social structures of the times. Also by the author: see *Hatchet* (n). Related book: *Bull Run* by Paul Fleischman, a collection of narratives from sixteen characters involved in the first great battle of the Civil War.

Rip-Roaring Russell

BY JOHANNA HURWITZ

K–2   96 pages   *Morrow, 1983*

In this delightful introduction to chapter and series books, we follow little Russell, his younger sister, Elisa, and their family and friends through preschool, kindergarten, and primary grades. Hurwitz understands children and families. No one can resist loving the characters in her books. After this first book, the series reads in this order: *Russell Sprouts*; *Russell Rides Again*; *Russell and Elisa*; *E Is for Elisa*; *Make Room for Elisa*; *Ever Clever Elisa*; *Elisa in the Middle*; and *Elisa in the Summer*. Related titles: *Ramona the Pest* (n); and Janice Lee Smith's series about Adam Joshua and his primary-grade classmates, beginning with *The Monster in the Third Dresser Drawer*.

Sara Crewe

BY FRANCES HODGSON BURNETT

Grades 3–6   79 pages   *Scholastic, 1986*

This tale, as powerful today as it was more than one hundred years ago when it was written, is the story of the star boarder at Miss Minchin's exclusive London boarding school who is suddenly orphaned and becomes a ward of the cruel headmistress. Friendless, penniless, and banished to the attic as a servant, Sara holds fast to her courage and dreams—until at last she finds a friend and deliverance in a heartwarming surprise ending. Try comparing this story with that of the orphan child in *Peppermints in the Parlor* (n). *Sara Crewe* was expanded by the author into an equally successful longer novel, *A Little Princess*; both are for experienced listeners. Also by the author: *The Secret Garden* (n). Related books: *Little Kit* by Emily Arnold McCully; *Mandy* by Julie Edwards; and *Understood Betsy* (n).

Shoeshine Girl

BY CLYDE ROBERT BULLA

Grades 1–4   84 pages   *Harper, 1989*

A spoiled ten-year-old girl, having driven her parents to the edge, is sent to spend the summer with her aunt. Immediately she's in trouble for conning a neighbor child into a loan. Determined to have spending money, she lands a job at a local shoeshine stand and there she receives a maturing dose of reality and responsibility. For other books by the author, see *A Lion to Guard Us* (s). Related books: *Bud, Not Buddy* (n); *The Pinballs* (n); and *Queeny Peavy* by Robert Burch.

Skinnybones

BY BARBARA PARK

Grades 3–5   112 pages   *Knopf, 1982*

Park is one of the funniest voices writing for middle-grade children. Her characters may not always be lovable, but they are remarkably alive and interesting as they deal with losing ball games, moving, camp, or sibling rivalries. Best of all, they are funny—not cutesy or caustic, but genuinely and interestingly funny. Typical is Alex Frankovitch of *Skinnybones*, who is an uncoordinated smart aleck who throws tantrums; he's also a laugh a minute. Sequel: *Almost Starring Skinnybones*. Also by the author, *Junie B. Jones and the Stupid Smelly Bus* (s) and *Mick Harte Was Here* (s).

The Smartest Man in Ireland

BY MOLLIE HUNTER

Grades 1–5   110 pages   *Gulliver, 1996*

Because of the lilt of its language, the tightness of its plot, and its audacious protagonist, this is one of my all-time favorite short novels for read-aloud. It is now back in print in paperback and worth any price you pay for it. Patrick is full of himself and thinks he's the smartest man in Ireland. For certain, he's one of the laziest. While he just irritates his neighbors, his trickery has insulted the fairies who steal his only son in revenge. To win him back, Patrick will have to be not only the smartest but also the *bravest* man in Ireland. It is a great adventure-fantasy, one that Harry Potter fans will surely enjoy. Also by the author: *A Stranger Came Ashore* (n) and *The Walking Stones*. Related book about "wee folk": *The Lost Flower Children* by Janet Taylor Lisle.

Soup

BY ROBERT NEWTON PECK

Grades 4–6   96 pages   *Knopf, 1974*

Two Vermont pals share a genius for getting themselves into trouble. The stories are set in the rural 1930s when life was simpler and the days were longer. But the need for a best friend was just as great then as now. There are a dozen books in the series. For older readers: *A Day No Pigs Would Die* (n). Related books: *Homer Price* (n); *The Great Brain* (n); and *Owls in the Family* (n).

Stargone John

BY ELLEN KINDT MCKENZIE

Grades 1–5   67 pages   *Holt, 1990*

In a turn-of-the-century one-room schoolhouse, six-year-old John meets the new teacher on his first day at school. Her iron-willed and iron-handed approach to teaching sends the introverted child even deeper into his imaginary cave, where he is determined to stay until this teacher leaves. John eventually saves the day and learns to read—thanks to secret lessons from the town's retired but blind school mistress. Related books: *Caddie Woodlawn* (n); and *One-Room School* by Raymond Bial, a book of photographs of actual one-room schoolhouses.

Stone Fox
BY JOHN R. GARDINER
Grades 1–7   96 pages   *Crowell, 1980*
Here is a story that, like its ten-year-old orphan hero, never stands still. Since it has sold more than one million copies in twenty years with little or no corporate advertising, there must be great word-of-mouth out there for this book about the love of a child for his grandfather, and the loyalty of a great dog for his young master. Based on a Rocky Mountain legend, the story recounts the valiant efforts of young Willy to save his grandfather's farm by attempting to win the purse in a local bobsled race. Also by the author: *Top Secret.* Related dog books, see *A Dog Called Kitty* (n).

The Stories Julian Tells
BY ANN CAMERON
K–3   72 pages   *Pantheon, 1981*
The author takes six short stories involving Julian and his brother and weaves them into a fabric that glows with the mischief, magic, and imagination of childhood. Though centered on commonplace subjects like desserts, gardens, loose teeth, and new neighbors, these stories of family life are written in an uncommon way that will both amuse and touch young listeners. Sequels: *Julian's Glorious Summer; Julian Secret Agent; More Stories Julian Tells; The Stories Huey Tells; More Stories Huey Tells;* and *Gloria's Way.*

The Story of Holly and Ivy
BY RUMER GODDEN; BARBARA COONEY, ILLUS.
K–5   31 pages   *Viking, 1985*
This is the loving tale of a lonely, runaway orphan girl, an unsold Christmas doll, and a childless couple on Christmas Eve. But with Rumer Godden's talent combined with Barbara Cooney's lustrous illustrations, it is unforgettable. Though it is formatted like a picture book, the large amount of text makes it more of a short novel. The true story of *Polar, the Titanic Bear* by Daisy C. S. Spedden makes an excellent companion book. Related orphan books: *Aunt Minnie McGranahan* (p); *Mandy* by Julie Edwards; and *Raising Sweetness* (p).

A Taste of Blackberries

BY DORIS B. SMITH

Grades 4–7   52 pages   *Crowell, 1973*

In viewing death from a child's point of view, the author allows us to follow the narrator's emotions as he comes to terms with the death of his best friend, who died as a result of an allergic reaction to bee stings. The sensitivity with which the attendant sorrow and guilt are treated makes this an outstanding book. It blazed the way for the many other grief books that quickly followed, but few have approached the place of honor this one holds. Related books about death: *Bridge to Terabithia* (n); *A Day No Pigs Would Die* (n); and *On My Honor* (s); for younger children, see picture books listed with *A Gift for Tia Rosa* (p).

When the Soldiers Were Gone

BY VERA W. PROPP

Grades 2–5   101 pages   *Putnam, 1999*

World War II and the German occupation of the Netherlands are over, and life is returning to normal. That is when a young schoolboy is turned over to a man and woman who are his mother and father. But years ago he had been taken in by another Dutch couple to be sheltered during the occupation. Having lived with them for so long, he has forgotten they are not his real parents and that he is, in fact, Jewish, not a Christian. While the author has reduced the terrors of the war to the believable scale of an eight-year-old, she neither traumatizes the reader-listener nor trivializes the war because, as a classroom teacher for twenty-five years, she truly understands children. It is a heartwarming but powerful tale. Related titles: *The Butterfly* by Patricia Polacco; *Forging Freedom* by Hudson Talbott; *Hilde and Eli: Children of the Holocaust* by David A. Adler; *The Little Riders* by Margaretha Shemin; *Tell Them We Remember: The Story of the Holocaust* by Susan D. Bachrach; and *Twenty and Ten* by Claire H. Bishop.

The Whipping Boy

BY SID FLEISCHMAN

Grades 3–6   90 pages   *Greenwillow, 1986*

The brattish medieval prince is too spoiled ever to be spanked, so the king regularly vents his anger on Jeremy, a peasant "whipping boy." When circumstances lead the two boys to reverse roles, à la *The Prince and the Pauper*, each learns much about friendship and sacrifice. Painted with Fleischman's broad humor, this is a fast-paced Newbery-winning melodrama with short, cliff-hanger chapters. Also by the author: *Humbug Mountain* (n).

Wolf Story

BY WILLIAM MCCLEERY

K–3   82 pages   *Shoe String Press, 1988*

A great chapter-book read-aloud, this is a story on two tracks: (1) the affectionate contest of wills between a five-year-old and his father as the latter attempts to tell a bedtime story and the child insists on editing the tale; and (2) the bedtime story itself in which a crafty wolf tries to outwit an equally determined hen.

The Wonderful World of Henry Sugar and Six More

BY ROALD DAHL

Grades 4 and up   235 pages   *Puffin, 1988*

Here is a seven-story collection by Roald Dahl for experienced listeners. Two of the stories—"Lucky Break" and "A Piece of Cake"—are not good read-alouds, but the other five pieces are excellent (including one of his rare nonfiction pieces), and most especially the sixty-nine-page title story ("Henry Sugar"), which is really a novella, and one of his most imaginative.

Full-Length Novels

The Adventures of Pinocchio

BY CARLO COLLODI; ROBERTO INNOCENTI, ILLUS.

Grades 1–5   144 pages   *Knopf, 1988*

Unfortunately, most children's familiarity with this 1892 classic comes from the emasculated Disney or TV versions. Treat your children to the original story of the poor woodcarver's puppet who faces all the temptations of childhood, succumbs to many, learns from his follies, and gains his boyhood by selflessly giving of himself for his friends. The Knopf edition, the most lavishly illustrated ever, is the *real* Pinocchio.

The Animal Family

BY RANDALL JARRELL

Grades 3–7   180 pages   *Pantheon, 1965*

In a beautiful allegory on the social need for community and family, a lonely hunter brings a mermaid home to his island cabin. Over time he adopts a bear cub, lynx, and, finally, an orphaned child. Jarrell, an honored poet, wraps this unconventional family in the warm humor and love that permeate the best of family and community situations. Though no great plot unfolds, the reader/listener is drawn into the characters so deeply you begin to care for them as family. As one teacher described the book: "It's like a warm glove." For experienced listeners. Related books: *The Boy Who Lived With the Seals* by Rafe Martin and *Charlotte's Web* (n).

Bambi

BY FELIX SALTEN

Grades 2–5   191 pages   *Minstrel paper, 1988*

Don't be misled by the Disney version of this tale. Salten's original forest is far deeper than the film. Originally a protest against hunting, the story follows the young roe deer from birth to the arrival of danger—man. This is an accessible classic for children, but for experienced listeners. If you insist upon an abridged version, then use Janet Schulman's (Atheneum).

The Bad Beginning

BY LEMONY SNICKET

Grades 2–4   162 pages   *Harper, 1999*

The only thing wrong with this series of novels was its unfortunate timing— it debuted in the U.S. within a year of Harry Potter and thus was overshadowed. But once you read this first book, you won't want to miss its sequels. It's a splendid beginning to a series that follows the "riches-to-rags" tale of three resilient orphans who no sooner overcome one Dickensian misfortune and villain than even darker ones appear. The children must and do resist these threats with determined quick wits. Sending up the moralistic Victorian adventure tales of a century ago, as well as old-time Saturday movie serials, the author's asides to the reader/listener are humorous, helpful, and enlightening (especially with vocabulary). Sequels: *The Reptile Room*; *The Wide Window*; *The Miserable Mill*; *The Austere Academy*; and *The Vile Village*.

Because of Winn-Dixie

BY KATE DICAMILLO

Grades 2–5   182 pages   *Candlewick, 2000*

Ten-year-old Opal Buloni is not only the new kid in town, she's also a preacher's kid. And she is one of the most refreshing characters to come to children's literature in a dog's age. Speaking of dogs, she picked up a stray at the neighborhood Winn-Dixie grocery (that's how it got its name) and charms her daddy into letting her keep him. She also charms everyone she meets, collecting the weirdest assortment of cast-off grown-ups and kids you'll ever meet and grow fond of. Related books: *A Blue-Eyed Daisy* (s); *Foxy* by Helen Griffith; *Ida Early Comes over the Mountain* (n); and *The Wreck of the Zanzibar* by Michael Morpurgo.

Black Beauty

BY ANNA SEWELL; CHARLES KEEPING, ILLUS.

Grades 4–8   214 pages   *Farrar, 1990*

In this classic animal novel, and the first with the animal as narrator, the author vividly describes the cruelty to horses during the Victorian period, as well as giving a detailed picture of life at that time. Related books: *Bambi* (n); *The Black Stallion* (series), by Walter Farley; and *King of the Wind: The Story of the Godolphin Arabian* by Marguerite Henry.

Bridge to Terabithia

BY KATHERINE PATERSON

Grades 4–7   128 pages   *Crowell, 1997*

Few novels for children have dealt with so many emotions and issues so well: sports, school, peers, friendship, death, guilt, art, and family. This popular Newbery winner deserves to be read or heard by everyone. Also by the author: *The Great Gilly Hopkins* and *The Pinballs* (n). Related books: *A Taste of Blackberries* (s); *Tuck Everlasting* (n); and *A Gift for Tia Rosa* (p). For author studies: *Katherine Paterson* by Alice Cary (Learning Works, Santa Barbara, CA). On the Web: www.terabithia.com.

Bud, Not Buddy

BY CHRISTOPHER PAUL CURTIS

Grades 4–8   243 pages   *Delacorte, 1999*

After escaping a succession of bad foster homes, ten-year-old Buddy sets out to find the man he suspects to be his father—a popular jazz musician in Grand Rapids, Michigan. Told in the first person, this engaging Newbery winner brims with humor and compassion, while offering a keen insight into the workings of a child's mind during the Great Depression. Want the exact pulse of the book? Read page four! Related books: *A Family Apart* (n); *No Promises in the Wind* by Irene Hunt; and *Roll of Thunder, Hear My Cry* (n).

Caddie Woodlawn

BY CAROL RYRIE BRINK

Grades 4–6   286 pages   *Simon & Schuster, 1935*

You take *The Little House on the Prairie*; I'll take *Caddie Woodlawn*. Ten times over, I'll take this tomboy of the 1860s with her pranks, her daring visits to Indian camps, her one-room schoolhouse fights, and her wonderfully believable family. Try to pick up the 1973 edition with Trina Schart Hyman's illustrations. For experienced listeners. Sequel: *Magical Melons*. Related books: *Daily Life in a Plains Indian Village, 1868* by Michael Bad Hand Terry; and *One-Room School* by Raymond Bial provides a spectrum of American one-room schoolhouses, including classroom artifacts, along with rare photographs of classes attending school in the 1800s. Related book: *The Wreck of the Zanzibar,* by Michael Morpurgo.

The Call of the Wild

BY JACK LONDON

Grades 6 and up   126 pages   Viking (Whole Story edition), 1996
This 1903 dog story, set amidst the rush for gold in the Klondike, depicts the savagery and tenderness between man and his environment in unforgettable terms. The Whole Story edition includes extensive sidebars and illustrations that add greatly to the story's setting in time and place. For experienced listeners. Also by the author: *White Fang* (look for the edition illustrated by Ed Young). On the Web: http://sunsite.berkeley.edu/London/. Related books: *Jason's Gold* (n); *Yukon Gold: The Story of the Klondike Gold Rush* by Charlotte Foltz Jones; see *A Dog Called Kitty* (n) for related dog novels.

Captain Grey

BY AVI

Grades 4–7   141 pages   Morrow, 1993
A swashbuckling pirate story told in the classic adventure style, it deals with a young boy's determination to free himself from a band of pirates based on the New Jersey shoreline just after the Revolutionary War. For experienced listeners. See Author Index for a list of Avi titles. Related pirate books: *The Ghost in the Noonday Sun* by Sid Fleischman; *Stowaway* by Karen Hesse; and *Weasel* (n).

The Case of the Baker Street Irregular

BY ROBERT NEWMAN

Grades 4–8   216 pages   Atheneum, 1978
This finely crafted mystery novel is an excellent introduction for young readers to the world of Sherlock Holmes. A young orphan is suddenly pitted against the dark side of turn-of-the-century London when his tutor-guardian is kidnapped. Complete with screaming street urchins, sinister cab drivers, bombings, murder, back alleys, and a child's-eye view of the great sleuth himself—Sherlock Holmes. For experienced listeners. Sequels: *The Case of the Vanishing Corpse* and *The Case of the Watching Boy.* Related books: *Peppermints in the Parlor* (n).

The Cay

BY THEODORE TAYLOR

Grades 2–6   144 pages   *Doubleday, 1969*

An exciting adventure about a blind white boy and an old black man ship-wrecked on a tiny Caribbean island. The first chapters are slow but it builds with taut drama to a stunning ending. Sequel/prequel: *Timothy of the Cay*. Also by the author: *The Bomb* (atomic); *Sniper*, an outstanding suspense story set at a "big cat" preserve in Southern California; and *Rogue Wave and Other Red-Blooded Sea Stories*. See *Hatchet* (n) for other survival books.

Charlotte's Web

BY E. B. WHITE; GARTH WILLIAMS, ILLUS.

K–4   184 pages   *Harper, 1952*

One of the most acclaimed books in children's literature, it is loved by adults as well as children. The tale centers on the barnyard life of a young pig who is to be butchered in the fall. The animals of the yard (particularly a haughty gray spider named Charlotte) conspire with the farmer's daugh-ter to save the pig's life. While there is much humor in the novel, the au-thor uses wisdom and pathos in developing his theme of friendship within the cycle of life. Also by the author: *Stuart Little* (n). Beverly Gherman's *E. B. White: Some Writer!* is an excellent children's biography of the author; and *The Annotated Charlotte's Web*, which contains the complete text with annotations by Peter F. Neumeyer that span the eight different drafts of the book, is the most complete view of the book ever offered. Related books: *Inside and Outside Spiders* by Sandra Markle is an excellent picture book on the world of spiders; *The Animal Family* (n); *Cricket in Times Square* by George Selden; and *Poppy* (n).

The Chocolate Touch

BY PATRICK SKENE CATLING

Grades 1–4   122 pages   *Morrow, 1979*

Here is a new and delicious twist to the old King Midas story. Young John learns a dramatic lesson in self-control when everything he touches with his lips turns to chocolate—toothpaste, bacon and eggs, water, pencils, trumpet. What would happen, then, if he kissed his mother? Either before or after reading this story, read the original version, "The Golden Touch" (for fifth grade and up, the tale is included as one of the stories in Nathaniel Hawthorne's *A Wonder Book*). Related books: *Chocolate Fever* (s) and *The Search for Delicious* (n).

The Curse of the Blue Figurine

BY JOHN BELLAIRS

Grades 4–8   200 pages   *Dial, 1983*

If you are looking for intelligent alternatives to the Goosebumps series, look no further than the works of John Bellairs. In this book, Johnny Dixon removes a small figurine from the basement of his church, only to be haunted by the evil spirits attached to it. Johnny and his professor friend continue their spinetingling exploits down twisted tunnels in: *The Mummy, the Will and the Crypt*; *The Revenge of the Wizard's Ghost*; and *The Spell of the Sorcerer's Skull*. For a complete list of all Bellairs books, see: www.compleatbellairs.com.

Danny, Champion of the World

BY ROALD DAHL

Grades 3–6   196 pages   *Knopf, 1975*

In what might be Dahl's most tender book for children, a motherless boy and his father—"the most wonderful father who ever lived"—go on an adventure together. Teachers and parents should explain the custom and tradition of "poaching" in England before going too deeply into the story (Robin Hood was a poacher). See *James and the Giant Peach* for other books by the author. Related books: Try comparing the experiences of Danny with those of Leigh Botts, the boy in *Dear Mr. Henshaw* (n).

Dave at Night

BY GAIL CARSON LEVINE

Grades 4–8   281 pages   *Harper, 1999*

This engaging tale of childhood resilience and adventure is set in a Jewish orphan asylum in 1926. If you're familiar with Broadway musicals, you could say this is a Jewish *Annie*, without the music. Dave Caros is an eleven-year-old orphan whose noisy and rambunctious nature intimidates his relatives enough to keep them from adopting him. Thus he ends up at the HHB, the Hebrew Home for Boys in New York at the edge of Harlem. In a freezing dormitory with forty-one other boys, Dave finds the food is bad, school is awful, and the administrators are tyrants.

But he soon discovers a nighttime escape route, one that allows him to roam through what we now know as the Harlem Renaissance, vibrant with authors, artists, musicians, and wealthy dowagers. A benevolent old Jewish soothsayer takes Dave under his wing and ushers him on weekly visits into this unique society, where he becomes the darling friend of a wealthy young black girl. But like Cinderella, Dave must always return before dawn to the orphanage. But if the HHB is so dreadful, why does he go back? That is the heart of the tale. Also by the author: *Ella Enchanted* and *The Wish*. For related orphan books, see list with *A Family Apart* (n); and *Bud, Not Buddy* (n).

A Day No Pigs Would Die
BY ROBERT NEWTON PECK
Grades 6 and up   150 pages   *Knopf, 1972*
Set among Shaker farmers in Vermont during the 1920s, this is the poignant story of the author's coming of age at thirteen, his adventures, fears, and triumphs. As a novel of life and death, it should be read carefully by the teacher or parent before it is read aloud to children. A very moving story for experienced listeners. Sequel: *A Part of the Sky*. Also by the author: the Soup series (s).

Dear Mr. Henshaw
BY BEVERLY CLEARY
Grades 3–6   134 pages   *Morrow, 1983*
In this 1984 Newbery winner, Beverly Cleary departs from her Ramona format to write a very different but every bit as successful book—perhaps the finest in her long career. Using only the letters and diary of a young boy (Leigh Botts), the author traces his personal growth from first grade to sixth. We watch the changes in his relationship with his divorced parents, his schools (where he always ends up the friendless "new kid"), an author with whom he corresponds over the years, and finally the changes in himself. Along with the usual Cleary humor, there is also genuine sensitivity to the heartaches that confront the growing number of Leigh Bottses in our homes and classrooms. Sequel: *Strider*. For other books by the author, see *Ramona the Pest* (n). Related books: *Danny, Champion of the World* (n) and *Thank You, Jackie Robinson* (n). An author profile of Beverly Cleary can be found at www.trelease-on-reading.com/cleary.html.

A Dog Called Kitty
BY BILL WALLACE
Grades 1–5   137 pages   *Holiday, 1980*
In this first-person narrative, a young boy struggles to overcome the deep-seated fear of dogs caused by his traumatic experience with a vicious dog during early childhood. Don't be misled by the cutesy title of this book; it is a powerfully moving story of childhood and family. Also by the author: *Beauty*; *Blackwater Swamp*; *Red Dog*; *Shadow on the Snow*; and *Trapped in Death Cave*.

Other great dog stories: *Big Red* by Jim Kjelgaard; *Call of the Wild* (n); *Foxy* by Helen Griffith; *Hero, Kavik the Wolf Dog*, and *Scrub Dog of Alaska*—all three by Walt Morey; *Hurry Home, Candy* (n); *Lassie Come Home* (n); *Sable* by Karen Hesse; *Old Yeller* (s); Phyllis Naylor's excellent series—*Shiloh*; *Shiloh Season*; and *Saving Shiloh*; *Stone Fox* (s); *Where the Red Fern Grows* (n); and (nonfiction) *Woodsong* (n).

A Family Apart

BY JOAN LOWERY NIXON

Grades 3–7   *162 pages*   *Bantam, 1987*

The popular Orphan Train series is based on the years between the Civil War and the Great Depression when 150,000 homeless children were shipped west to families willing to give them shelter. Some were looking to adopt a first child, some were reaching out to enlarge their present family, and some were looking for unpaid laborers—under the guise of family. This opening book in the series follows the six Kelly children from New York City to Missouri after their widowed mother turns them over to the Children's Aid Society, which sends them to Missouri and parcels them out to farm families. Much of the book focuses on thirteen-year-old Frances and her attempts to masquerade as a boy in order to be "adopted" by the same family that takes her youngest brother. Also in the series: *Caught in the Act*; *In the Face of Danger*; *A Place to Belong*; *A Dangerous Promise* (Civil War); *Keeping Secrets*; and *Circle of Love*.

Other historical books about children in orphaned circumstances: *Street Child* (n) and *Gratefully Yours* (n). Among the last of the orphan train children was Lee Nailling in 1926, whose true but happy life is told movingly in *Orphan Train Rider: One Boy's True Story* by Andrea Warren, a fifty-four-page book that includes excellent photographs documenting the history of the orphan trains. Also Eve Bunting's picture book *Train to Nowhere*, which follows fourteen orphans through the "train" experience.

After the orphan trains came the orphanage movement, or children living on the streets. Outstanding books on these circumstances include: Avi's *Beyond the Western Sea I—The Escape From Home* and *Beyond the Western Sea II—Lord Kirkle's Money*; *Dave at Night* (n); *Nowhere to Call Home* by Cynthia DeFelice, about two orphans living as hobos during the Great Depression; and *Slake's Limbo* (n), which follows a modern orphan living in the construction cracks of the New York subway system. For a less serious treatment of the orphan melodrama, see *The Bad Beginning* (n).

Finding Buck McHenry

BY ALFRED SLOTE

Grades 3–6   250 pages   *Harper, 1991*

Eleven-year-old Jason, baseball card collector extraordinaire, is convinced that school custodian Mr. Mack Henry is really the legendary Buck McHenry of Negro Leagues fame. Before either of them can stop it, the idea steamrolls out of control. The author creates a rich blend of baseball history, peer relationships (male and female), family, and race relations while never losing sight of a good story. Also by the author: *Hang Tough, Paul Mather* and *The Trading Game*. See also the excellent paperback series of Dan Gutman about a boy who time travels using his baseball cards: *Jackie and Me* (Jackie Robinson); *Babe and Me* (Babe Ruth); and *Honus and Me* (Honus Wagner); see also *Thank You, Jackie Robinson* (n); *Bud, Not Buddy* (n); older readers, see books listed with *The Rebounder* (n). Also, "Inning Six" from Ken Burns's baseball video for PBS (*The National Pastime*) offers an excellent portrayal of the color line being broken in baseball.

Francie

BY KAREN ENGLISH

Grades 3 and up   199 pages   *FSG, 1999*

Thirteen-year-old Francie Weaver is strong-willed, determined, impetuous, honest to a fault, generous, intelligent, and doesn't suffer fools gladly. This last quality made life complicated in Alabama when segregation ruled, and Francie's troubles multiply even more when she befriends an illiterate sixteen-year-old boy and begins to teach him to read. When he is accused of attempted murder, she launches a personal campaign to save him. This is a heartwarming, compelling first novel. For related books, see *Roll of Thunder, Hear My Cry* (n).

Freak, the Mighty

BY RODMAN PHILBRICK

Grades 6–9   165 pages   *Scholastic, 1993*

Many popular entertainment tales have involved teams—Batman and Robin, the Lone Ranger and Tonto, Skywalker and Solo. Each member is usually of vastly different stature. In that tradition comes the team of Max and Kevin, two unlikely teenage heroes. Middle-schooler Max is gigantic, powerful, and a remedial student. The wise-cracking Kevin suffers from a birth defect that limits his growth and keeps him on crutches; his body cannot grow to more than a few feet in height, but his mind has expanded to brilliant proportions. The two become fast friends and give themselves the nickname "Freak (Kevin) the Mighty (Max)." Their adventures run the gamut from escaping street bullies and outwitting school authorities, to educating Max and surviving his homicidal father. While some parts are implausible, the friendship between the two is a thing of beauty, and Max's first-person voice rings true as he painfully explores the anxieties of adolescence. Sequel: *Max, the Mighty*.

From the Mixed-up Files of Mrs. Basil E. Frankweiler

BY E. L. KONIGSBURG

Grades 4–7   162 pages   *Macmillan, 1967*

A bored and brainy twelve-year-old girl talks her nine-year-old brother into running away with her. To throw everyone off their trail, Claudia chooses the Metropolitan Museum of Art in New York City as a refuge, and amid centuries-old art they sleep, dine, bathe, and pray in regal secret splendor. An exciting story of hide-and-seek and a wonderful art lesson to boot. For experienced listeners. Related runaway books: a city boy hides in the wilderness in *My Side of the Mountain* (n); a city boy hides n the subway system in *Slake's Limbo* (n); see also *The Wreck of the Zanzibar* by Michael Morpurgo.

Gentle Ben

BY WALT MOREY

Grades 3–6   192 pages   *Dutton, 1965*

A young boy adopts a huge bear and brings to his family in Alaska all the joys and tears such a combination might invite. Though the struggle to save animals from ignorant but well-intentioned human predators is one that has been written many times over, Morey's handling of characters, plot, and setting makes an original and exciting tale. He supports the pace of his story with many lessons in environmental science, from salmon runs to hibernation. Also by the author: *Canyon Winter*; *Hero*; *Kavik the Wolf Dog*; and *Scrub Dog of Alaska*. Related book: *The Grizzly* by Annabel and Edgar Johnson.

The Gift of the Pirate Queen

BY PATRICIA REILLY GIFF

Grades 2–4   164 pages   *Delacorte, 1982*

By the time their father's cousin arrives from Ireland, the O'Malley girls and their father have pretty well unraveled without a mother in the house. But within a week, the newcomer helps each of them to "do the hard thing" that will heal their melodramas. Also by the author: *Lily's Crossing* (n). Related books: *Ida Early Comes Over the Mountain* (n) and *Understood Betsy* (n).

Good Night, Mr. Tom

BY MICHELLE MAGORIAN

Grades 6 and up   318 pages   *Harper, 1981*

This is one of the longest novels listed in this Treasury; it might also be the most powerful. Adults should preview it carefully before reading it aloud. It's the story of an eight-year-old London boy evacuated during the blitz to a small English village, where he is reluctantly taken in by a grumpy old man. The boy proves to be an abused child, terrified of everything around him. With painstaking care, the old man begins the healing process, unveiling to the child a world he never knew existed—a world of kindness, friendship, laughter, and hope. For experienced listeners. Related books: *The Lion and the Unicorn* (p); *North to Freedom* (n); *The Kingdom by the Sea* (n); and *So Far from the Bamboo Grove* by Yoko Watkins.

Good Old Boy

BY WILLIE MORRIS

Grades 5–8   128 pages   *Yoknapatawpha, 1981*

If Mark Twain had been writing *Tom Sawyer* in the 1940s, this is the book he'd have written. One of the South's most distinguished authors gives us the heartwarming tale of growing up in a town on the banks of the Mississippi. For experienced listeners. Sequel: *My Dog Skip*, upon which the wonderful movie was *loosely* based, but read the book first. Related books: *The Adventures of Tom Sawyer* by Mark Twain; *The Great Brain* (n); *Homer Price* (n); and *Soup* (s).

Gratefully Yours

BY JANE BUCHANAN

Grades 2–5   117 pages   *FSG, 1997*

Between 1854 and 1929, more than 150,000 orphaned or homeless children were shipped West to families intent on adopting them. Some of those families were motivated by goodness; others were seeking a free laborer in the family fields. Thus we find nine-year-old Hattie adopted by a Nebraska farmer who hopes that her presence will bring his wife out of the deep depression that has plagued her since the death of their two children. The moody Hattie has her work cut out for her. Not only has she never farmed before; she is also tired of people telling her how grateful she should be. Gradually, amidst the pain and struggle of farm life, she and her new family discover the warmth of each other. An excellent historical novel with characters we come to care for deeply. Related books: the

Orphan Train Riders series—see *A Family Apart* (n); *Good Night, Mr. Tom* (n); and *The Pinballs*.

The Great Brain
BY JOHN D. FITZGERALD
Grades 5 and up   175 pages   *Dial, 1967*

This is the first book in a series dealing with the hilarious—and often touching—adventures of an Irish-Catholic family surrounded by Utah Mormons in 1896, told through the eyes of a younger brother. Tom Fitzgerald is part boy-genius and part con man, but in command of every situation. The series reads well on many levels, including a perspective of daily life at the turn of the century. For experienced listeners. Sequels (in order): *More Adventures of the Great Brain*; *Me and My Little Brain*; *The Return of the Great Brain*; and *The Great Brain Is Back*.

Harry Potter and the Sorcerer's Stone
BY J. K. ROWLING
Grades 2–6   309 pages   *Scholastic, 1998*

Harry is the best thing to happen to children's books since the invention of the paperback! No book (adult or children's) in publishing history ever sold as quickly and as often as the fourth book in the series (*Goblet of Fire*). While the series' plot is surely original, it follows in the path of C. S. Lewis's dual "Narnia" world, George Lucas's *Star Wars* struggles with the "dark side," and Dorothy's search for the Wizard of Oz. It is also blessed with an abundance of Roald Dahl's cheeky childhood humor.

Harry is the orphan child of two famous wizards who died mysteriously when he was very young. Rescued at age eleven from abusive relatives, he is sent to Hogwarts School (sorcery's equivalent of an elite boarding school), where he experiences high adventure when he and his friends (boy and girl) struggle with classes in potions, charms, and broom-flying, all the while battling a furtive faculty member working for the dark side.

This is not an *easy* read-aloud and the reader-aloud should be aware the first two chapters of the first book are a bit complicated as they set the scene for Harry's dual world. Definitely for experienced listeners. Actor Jim Dale has done a masterful job of recording (unabridged) all of the Potter books for Listening Library. Other books to date in the projected seven-volume series (in order): *Harry Potter and the Chamber of Secrets*; *Harry Potter and the Prisoner of Azkaban*; and *Harry Potter and the Goblet of Fire*.

For author studies: Marc Shapiro's unauthorized paperback biography, *J. K. Rowling: The Wizard Behind Harry Potter* (St. Martin's); Rowling's interview with NPR's Diane Rehm, October 20, 1999, is available as both an audiocassette and a RealAudio archived file (found at www.wamu.org/ram/1999/r1991020.ram); cassette: $10, WAMU Cassette Services, Harry Potter 10/20/99 Interview, 4400 Massachusetts Avenue N.E., Washington, D.C. 20016; or call (202) 885-1200. The tape will be available through the year 2002, and possibly longer.

Younger fans of Harry will also enjoy: *The Lion, the Witch, and the Wardrobe* (n); the Redwall series, beginning with *Martin the Warrior* (n); *A Stranger Came Ashore* (n); and *Which Witch?* by Eva Ibbotson; older fans may be ready for *The Hobbit* by J.R.R. Tolkien.

Hatchet

BY GARY PAULSEN

Grades 6 and up   195 pages   *Bradbury, 1987*

The lone survivor of a plane crash in the Canadian wilderness, this thirteen-year-old boy carries three things away from the crash: a fierce spirit, the hatchet his mother gave him as a gift, and the secret knowledge that his mother was unfaithful to his father. All play an integral part in this Newbery Honor survival story for experienced listeners. Sequels: *The River*; *Brian's Winter*; and *Brian's Return*.

Other books by Paulsen include: *The Foxman* (a precursor to his later *Harris and Me*); the frontier series—*Mr. Tucket*; *Call Me Francis Tucket*; *Tucket's Gold*; *Tucket's Home*; also: *Nightjohn* and its sequel, *Sarny: A Life Remembered*; *The Rifle* (s); *Soldier's Heart*; *The Tent*; and a survival-at-sea novel, *The Voyage of the Frog*.

Paulsen has written an adult autobiography, *Eastern Sun, Winter Moon*, that details his painful childhood years, as well as a memoir for children of his relationships with dogs, *My Life in Dog Years*. For author studies: *Presenting Gary Paulsen* by Professor Gary M. Salvner, (Twayne Publishers/Simon & Schuster); less scholarly and written as a children's biography is *Gary Paulsen* by Stephanie True Peters (Learning Works: Santa Barbara, CA). A Paulsen profile is also available at www.trelease-on-reading.com/paulsen.html.

Holes

BY LOUIS SACHAR

Grades 4–8   233 pages   *FSG, 1998*

Too often, when a children's book captures a large number of prizes from adult committees (this book won the 1999 Newbery Medal, National Book Award, and *The Horn Book* Award), it turns out to be inaccessible to most children. Not so here! *Holes* is an adventure tale, a mystery, fantasy, and quest book. An important ingredient is Sachar's wit. Set in a juvenile detention station on the Texas desert, it traces the sad life of fourteen-year-old Stanley Yelnats, who has just been sentenced (mistakenly) for stealing a pair of sneakers. Not only has the friendless, hopeless Stanley been haunted all his life by a dark cloud of events, so has his family. Indeed, there is a family legend that his grandfather's long-ago selfishness in Latvia has rusted every golden opportunity for the family since then. Forced by the abusive camp police to dig holes all day long in the baking desert, he experiences an epiphany, makes his first friend, and gradually discovers courage he never knew he had. In so doing, he slowly and painfully unwinds the century-old family curse.

Sachar's acceptance speech for the Newbery (July–August 1999 issue, *The Horn Book*) offers an excellent view of how the book was created, and is reprinted with a personal profile of the author by his wife and daughter. Also by the author: *Sideways Stories From Wayside School* (n). Related books: *Maniac Magee* (n) and *Queeny Peavy* by Robert Burch.

Homer Price
BY ROBERT MCCLOSKEY
Grades 2–5   160 pages   *Viking, 1943*
A modern children's classic, this is a collection of humorous tales about a small-town boy's neighborhood dilemmas. Whether telling how Homer foiled the bank robbers with his pet skunk or of his uncle's out-of-control doughnut maker, these six tales will long be remembered. Sequel: *Centerburg Tales*. For a biographical profile of the author, see *Hey! Listen to This* (a). Related books: *Humbug Mountain* (n); *Good Old Boy* (n); *The Great Brain* (n); *Pinch* by Larry Callen; and *Soup* (s).

Humbug Mountain
BY SID FLEISCHMAN
Grades 4–6   172 pages   *Little, 1978*
Reminiscent of Mark Twain humor, suspense, and originality, here are the captivating adventures of the Flint family as they battle outlaws, crooked riverboat pilots, ghosts, and their creditors on the banks of the Missouri River in the late 1800s. Also by the author: *By the Great Horn Spoon*; *Chancy and the Grand Rascal*; *The Ghost in the Noonday Sun*; *Mr. Mysterious & Company*; *The Midnight Horse*; and *The Whipping Boy* (s).

Hurry Home, Candy

BY MEINDERT DEJONG

Grades 2–6   244 pages   *Harper, 1953*

With a childlike sense of wonder and pity, this book details the first year in the life of a dog—from the moment she is lifted from her mother's side, through the children, adults, punishments, losses, fears, friendships, and love that follow. See *A Dog Called Kitty* (n) for related dog stories.

Ida Early Comes Over the Mountain

BY ROBERT BURCH

Grades 2–6   145 pages   *Viking, 1980*

During the Depression, an ungainly young woman shows up to take over the household chores for Mr. Sutton and his four motherless children. The love that grows between the children and the unconventional Ida is, like her tall tales, a joyous experience. She has been rightly described as a "Mary Poppins in the Blue Ridge Mountains." Sequel: *Christmas With Ida Early*. Also by the author: *Queenie Peavy*; three of the author's best and earliest works are back in print through the University of Georgia Press: *Skinny*; *Tyler, Wilkin, and Skee*; *D.J.'s Worst Enemy*. Related book: *Gift of the Pirate Queen* (n).

In the Year of the Boar and Jackie Robinson

BY BETTE BAO LORD

Grades 1–5   169 pages   *Harper, 1984*

Over the course of the year 1947, we watch a nine-year-old Chinese immigrant girl as she and her family begin a new life in Brooklyn. Told with warmth and humor and based on the author's own childhood, Shirley Temple Wong's cultural assimilation will ring true with any child who has had to begin again—culturally or socially. To know this little girl is to fall in love with her—and her neighbors and classmates. (One of the students in Bette Bao Lord's childhood classroom was the future children's novelist Avi.) Compare this book with a reading of Frances Hodgson Burnett's classic *Little Lord Fauntleroy*, in which a poor American boy must move into his grandfather's English estate.

Incident at Hawk's Hill

BY ALLAN W. ECKERT

Grades 6 and up   174 pages   *Little, 1971*

An extremely timid six-year-old who wandered away from his family's farm in 1870 is adopted by a ferocious female badger, à la Mowgli in *The*

Jungle Books. The boy is fed, protected, and instructed by the badger through the summer until the family manages to recapture the now-wild child. Definitely for experienced listeners. Reading this aloud, paraphrase a large portion of the slow-moving prologue. In the sequel: *Return to Hawk's Hill*, young Ben is again missing, this time adrift in a canoe in Indian territory among the feared Cree. Related books: *Hatchet* (n); *My Side of the Mountain* (n); *Weasel* (n); and *The Wild Child* by Mordicai Gerstein.

The Indian in the Cupboard
BY LYNNE REID BANKS
Grades 2–6   *182 pages*   *Doubleday, 1981*
A witty, exciting, and poignant fantasy tale of a nine-year-old English boy who accidentally brings to life his three-inch plastic American Indian. Once the shock of the trick wears off, the boy begins to realize the immense responsibility involved in feeding, protecting, and hiding a three-inch human being from another time (1870s) and culture. Anyone concerned about the political correctness of the series will feel relieved by reading the review by Native American author Michael Dorris in *The New York Times Book Review* (May 16, 1993). Sequels: *Return of the Indian*; *The Secret of the Indian*; *The Mystery of the Cupboard*; and *The Key to the Indian*. Related books: *The Borrowers* by Mary Norton.

James and the Giant Peach
BY ROALD DAHL
K–6   *120 pages*   *Knopf, 1961*
Four-year-old James, newly orphaned, is sent to live with his abusive aunts and appears resigned to spending his life as their humble servant. Then a giant peach begins growing in the backyard. Waiting inside that peach is a collection of characters that will captivate your audience as they did James. Few books hold up over six grade levels as well as this one does, and few authors for children understand their world as well as Dahl did. Also by the author: *The BFG*; *Danny, Champion of the World* (n); *Fantastic Mr. Fox*; *Matilda*; *The Minpins* (p); *The Wonderful Story of Henry Sugar* (s); and *The Roald Dahl Treasury*, which contains the best collection of his work. Two recent collections of his adult short stories, marketed for adolescents: *Skin and Other Stories* and *The Umbrella Man and Other Stories*. If you have any Roald Dahl fans in your midst, see how they do with the 300 questions based on seven of his most popular books in *The Roald Dahl Quiz Book* by Richard Maher and Sylvia Bond. On the Web: www.nd.edu/~khoward1/dahl/.

Jason's Gold

BY WILL HOBBS

Grades 4 and up   *240 pages*   *Harper, 1999*

One of the most promising young authors of adventure tales for young adults, Will Hobbs appears to be the heir-apparent to Gary Paulsen. In this book, Hobbs's most decorated novel to date, we follow a fifteen-year-old boy as he joins the rush for gold in the Klondike. The vivid historical and social details of the period are all there, along with an excellent blend of fictional adventure. Sequel: *Down the Yukon*. Related books: *The Call of the Wild* (n) and *White Fang* by Jack London; and *Yukon Gold: The Story of the Klondike Gold Rush* by Charlotte Foltz Jones, which includes nearly a hundred historic photos. Also by the author: *Beardance*; *Bearstone*; *Downriver*; *Far North*; *Kokopeli's Flute*; *The Maze*, and *River Thunder*. On the Web www.willhobbsauthor.com. Hobbs fans will enjoy all of Gary Paulsen's books, see *Hatchet* (n).

Killing Mr. Griffin

BY LOIS DUNCAN

Grades 7 and up   *224 pages*   *Little, 1978*

This young-adult novel offers a chilling dissection of peer pressure and group guilt. Because of the subject matter and occasional four-letter words, care should be used in its presentation. The story deals with five high school students who attempt to scare their unpopular English teacher by kidnapping him. When their carefully laid plans unravel toward a tragic catastrophe, they find themselves unable to handle the situation. For experienced listeners. Also by the author: *Ransom*; and *I Know What You Did Last Summer*. Duncan on the Web: www.iag.net/~barq/lois.html. Related books: *Deathwatch* by Robb White; *Holding Me Here* by Pam Conrad; *On My Honor* (s); *Plague Year* (n); and *Wolf Rider* (n).

The Kingdom by the Sea

BY ROBERT WESTALL

Grades 6 and up   *176 pages*   *FSG, 1990*

Lest today's child think the wartime terrors in the Balkans, the Middle East, and Africa are new to human experience, this award-winning author takes us on the quest of a twelve-year-old boy in 1942 London. His family has been lost in the bombing, and rather than risk being sent to an orphanage, he takes his chances on the run. It's an orphan's odyssey, filled with dangers, surprises, risks, villains, and heartwarming friendships. Also by the author: *Children of the Blitz* and *Blitzcat*. Related books: *Dave at Night* (n); *Slake's Limbo* (n); and *Street Child* (n).

The Land I Lost
BY HUYNH QUANG NHUONG
Grades 2–6   126 pages   *Harper, 1982*
Most American children today know Vietnam only as a word associated
with a bitter war that divided the nation. The author of this remembrance
grew up there, one of eight children in a farming family along a river, not
far from the jungle. This is the dramatic and affectionate tale of how his
tiny hamlet worked together to survive the constant assaults from wild animals and a climate that would destroy lesser souls. Each of the fifteen
chapters is an adventure into a long-lost world. Sequel: *Water Buffalo Days*.

Lassie Come Home
BY ERIC KNIGHT
Grades 4 and up   200 pages   *Holt, 1940*
This classic dog story reads so easily, the words ringing with such feeling,
that you'll find yourself coming back to it year after year. As with many
dog stories, there are the usual themes of loss, grief, courage, and struggle—but here they are taken to splendid heights. Set between the Scottish
Highlands and Yorkshire, England, in the early 1900s, the novel describes
the triumphant struggle of a collie dog to return the one hundred miles to
her young master. Unfortunately, Hollywood and television have badly
damaged the image of this story with their tinny, affected characterization.
This is the *original* Lassie story. See listing with *A Dog Called Kitty* (n) for related books.

Lily's Crossing
BY PATRICIA REILLY GIFF
Grades 3–6   180 pages   *Delacorte/Dell, 1997*
This coming-of-age novel focuses on the summer of 1944 and one feisty
yet frightened young girl in a Long Island beach community. With her
beloved father shipped overseas and her best friend moved away, Lily befriends a Hungarian refugee (Albert). They experience together the great
fears and small triumphs that keep children afloat during war years. Lily,
reader and future writer, learns the hard way that tall tales, spun out of
control, can become dangerous lies. And Albert finds in Lily a friend who
will change his life forever. This is a multiple award-winner, including
Newbery Honor. Also by the author: *The Gift of the Pirate Queen* (n). Related books: *Alan and Naomi* by Myron Levoy; *Because of Winn-Dixie* (n); *A
Blue-Eyed Daisy* (s); and *The Wreck of the Zanzibar* by Michael Morpurgo.

The Lion, the Witch, and the Wardrobe

BY C. S. LEWIS

Grades 3–6   186 pages   *HarperCollins, 1950*

Four children discover that the old wardrobe closet in an empty room leads to the magical kingdom of Narnia—a kingdom filled with heroes, witches, princes, and intrigue. This is the most famous (but second) of seven enchanting books called the Chronicles of Narnia, which can be read as adventures or as Christian allegory. The series in order: *The Magician's Nephew; The Lion, the Witch, and the Wardrobe; The Horse and His Boy; Prince Caspian; The Voyage of the "Dawn Treader"; The Silver Chair;* and *The Last Battle. The Land of Narnia* by Brian Sibley is an excellent guide to Narnia. Also try HarperCollins' *The Narnia Trivia Book.* On the Web: http://cslewis.cache.net/. Many reasonable comparisons have been made between the dual world of Narnia and the *Harry Potter* (n) books; also *Martin the Warrior* (n).

Lupita Mañana

BY PATRICIA BEATTY

Grades 4–8   192 pages   *Harper paper, 2000*

After the death of her father, thirteen-year-old Lupita emigrates illegally to the United States. In slums, under cover of night, in damp freight cars, across the desert, plucky Lupita—posing as a boy—learns the meaning of fear as immigration police haunt her thoughts night and day. Here is the hope and heartbreak of poor families everywhere.

Maniac Magee

BY JERRY SPINELLI

Grades 5–9   184 pages   *Little, Brown, 1990*

One of the most popular Newbery winners ever, this is the tale of a legendary twelve-year-old runaway orphan, athlete extraordinaire, who touches countless families and peers with his kindness and wisdom. Could he be a modern Huck Finn? The book deals with racism, homelessness, and community violence in a most effective, almost allegorical manner. Also by the author: *The Library Card; Space Station Seventh Grade;* and *Wringer.* Author studies: Spinelli's autobiography is one of the best of its kind: *Knots in My Yo-Yo String: The Autobiography of a Kid.* On the Web: www.carr.lib.md.us/authco/spinelli-j.htm. Related books: *Bud, not Buddy* (n); *No Promises in the Wind* by Irene Hunt; *The Pinballs* (n); and *Street Child* (n).

Martin the Warrior

BY BRIAN JACQUES

Grades 4–7   376 pages   *Philomel, 1994*

In the tradition of *The Hobbit*, but for younger readers, is the Redwall series. Built around an endearing band of courageous animals inhabiting
an old English abbey, the books describe their fierce battles against evil
creatures. There is high adventure galore, cliff-hanger chapter endings,
gruesome behavior by evil outsiders, and rollicking fun. For experienced
listeners. *Martin the Warrior* is a prequel, going back to the founding of the
abbey, and should be read first, followed by *Redwall*; *Mossflower*; *Mattimeo*;
Mariel of Redwall; *Outcast of Redwall*; *Pearls of Lutra*; *Marlfox*; *The Long Patrol*;
The Legend of Luke; and *Lord Brocktree*. Related books: *Harry Potter and the
Sorcerer's Stone* (n); *The Lion, the Witch, and the Wardrobe* (n); *Which Witch?*
by Eva Ibbotson; for grade 6 and up: *The Hobbit* by J.R.R. Tolkien. On the
Web: www.redwall.org/dave/jacques.html.

The Mennyms

BY SYLVIA WAUGH

Grades 3–6   230 pages   *Morrow, 1994*

In the distinguished tradition of British fantasies, including *Peter Pan*; *The
Wind in the Willows*; *The Borrowers*; and *Harry Potter* (n), comes *The Mennyms* series.

    In a small English village live the Mennyms, a quiet, nondescript fam-
ily—at least, that's the way their neighbors would describe them. "They
keep to themselves." And they have—for forty years. Out of necessity, for
they possess a dark secret. This family of ten turns out to be a family of
life-size, living-and-breathing *rag dolls*—as in Raggedy Ann and Andy, but
without their sugar-coated innocence. The Mennym family has all the travails of a normal family (including three stubborn teenagers and two dom-
ineering grandparents), except their crises can't always be solved routinely:
after all, no one must know they are dolls. So they travel by night, work by
mail, and keep up the least of appearances. For experienced listeners. Sequels (in order): *The Mennyms in the Wilderness*; *The Mennyms Under Seige*;
The Mennyms Alone; and *The Mennyms Alive*.

The Midnight Fox

BY BETSY BYARS

Grades 4–6   160 pages   *Viking, 1968*

From the very beginning, young Tommy is determined he'll hate his aunt
and uncle's farm where he must spend the summer. His determination suf-

fers a setback when he discovers a renegade black fox. His desire to keep the fox running free, however, collides with his uncle's wish to kill it, and the novel builds to a stunning moment of confrontation and courage. For an excellent profile of the author, see her children's autobiography, *The Moon and I.* Also by the author: *Cracker Jackson; The Pinballs* (n); *Summer of the Swans; Trouble River;* and *The Winged Colt of Casa Mia.* On the Web: www.betsybyars.com.

The Monster Garden
BY VIVIEN ALCOCK
Grades 3–6   164 pages   *Houghton, 1988*
Young Frances has come into possession of a tiny glob of jelly, part of a chunk stolen by her brother from their father's laboratory. While the brother's jelly is useless, his sister's is sitting on a windowsill during an electrical storm—and something untoward happens. Dad's laboratory is involved in genetic engineering and electrical shock from the storm is enough to bring the jelly to *life,* though not in a form humans can recognize. To complicate matters, the girl can't bring herself to tell anyone but some friends—in secret. But secrets are almost as hard to keep as a mysterious glob of life that keeps growing and growing. This is an excellent exploration of social and familial relationships, as well as the very topical subject of genetic engineering. Related book: *Mrs. Frisby and the Rats of NIMH* (n).

The Mouse and the Motorcycle
BY BEVERLY CLEARY
K–2   158 pages   *Morrow, 1965*
When young Keith and his family check into a run-down motel one day, the mice in the walls are disappointed. They'd hoped for young children, messy ones who leave lots of crumbs behind. What Ralph S. Mouse gets instead is a mouse-size motorcycle. He and the boy guest become fast friends and embark on a series of hallway-to-highway escapades that make this tale a long-time favorite. Sequels: *Runaway Ralph* and *Ralph S. Mouse.* For other books by the author, see *Ramona the Pest* (n); for a list of mice books, see *Stuart Little* (n).

Mr. Popper's Penguins
BY RICHARD AND FLORENCE ATWATER; ROBERT LAWSON, ILLUS.
Grades 2–4   140 pages   *Little, 1938*
When you add twelve penguins to the family of Mr. Popper, the house painter, you've got immense food bills, impossible situations, and a freezer full of laughs. The short chapters will keep your audience hungry for

more. Related books: *Capyboppy* by Bill Peet; *Owls in the Family* (s); *Rabbit Hill* by Robert Lawson; and *The Story of Doctor Doolittle* by Hugh Lofting.

Mrs. Frisby and the Rats of NIMH
BY ROBERT C. O'BRIEN

Grades 4–6   232 pages   *Atheneum, 1971*

In this unforgettable fantasy–science fiction tale, we meet a group of rats that has become super-intelligent through a series of laboratory injections. Though it opens with an almost fairy-tale softness, it grows into a taut and frighteningly realistic tale. Two decades after its publication, the fiction grows closer to fact with genetic engineering; see December 27, 1982, issue of *Newsweek,* "The Making of a Mighty Mouse," p. 67. Sequels: *Racso and the Rats of NIMH* and *R-T, Margaret, and the Rats of NIMH*, both by Jane L. Conly (Robert C. O'Brien's daughter). Also by the author: *The Silver Crown.* On the Web: www.binary.net/camoon/rcob. Related book: *The Monster Garden* (n).

My Brother Sam Is Dead
BY JAMES LINCOLN COLLIER AND CHRISTOPHER COLLIER

Grades 5 and up   251 pages   *Simon & Schuster, 1974*

In this Newbery-winning historical novel, the inhumanity of war is examined through the experiences of one divided Connecticut family during the American Revolution. Told in the words of a younger brother, the heartache and passions hold true for all wars in all times, and the authors' balanced accounts of British and American tactics allow readers to come to their own conclusions. This book makes a good comparative study with *Rain of Fire* by Marion Dane Bauer, in which a young brother is shocked by the effect World War II had upon his brother.

Related book on the Revolutionary period: *American Revolution* by Joy Masoff, part of Scholastic's Chronicle of America series that uses photographs from America's living history museums to illustrate this excellent forty-eight-page reference volume. Other related books: *The Fighting Ground* by Avi; *Sarah Bishop* (n); *Toliver's Secret* (s); related war books: *Otto of the Silver Hand* (n); *The Rifle* and *Soldier's Heart*, both by Gary Paulsen; and *So Far from the Bamboo Grove* by Yoko Watkins.

My Daniel
BY PAM CONRAD

Grades 4–7   137 pages   *Harper, 1989*

As an eighty-year-old grandmother leads her grandchildren through the natural history museum toward the dinosaur room, she recounts the one great adventure of her life: when, at age twelve, she and her sixteen-year-old brother Daniel discovered the bones of a giant brontosaurus on their Nebraska farm. It is these same dinosaur bones she is going to view now in the museum—for the first time since the death of her beloved brother sixty-eight years ago. Each room of the museum serves as another chapter in a poignant tale that goes back to a time when dirt-poor farmers and greedy bone hunters and paleontologists scoured the west for buried fortune. For related dinosaur books, see *Dinosaurs! The biggest, baddest, strangest, fastest* (p). Also by the author: *Call Me Ahnighito* (p); *Holding Me Here*; *Willow*; and *Our House: The Stories of Levittown*, which contains six short stories, one for each decade from 1950 through 2000, set in the first preplanned community in America. Each story involves a different family and child who lived, laughed, loved, and cried there.

My Side of the Mountain
BY JEAN CRAIGHEAD GEORGE
Grades 3–8   178 pages   *Dutton, 1959*
A modern teenage Robinson Crusoe, city-bred Sam Gribley describes his year surviving as a runaway in a remote area of the Catskill Mountains. His diary of living off the land is marked by moving accounts of the animals, insects, plants, people, and books that helped him survive. For experienced listeners. Sequel: *On the Far Side of the Mountain* and *Frightful's Mountain*. Related survival books: *Hatchet* (n). For author studies: *Jean Craighead George* by Alice Cary (Learning Works, Santa Barbara, CA). On the web: www.jeancraigheadgeorge.com.

North to Freedom
BY ANNIE HOLM
Grades 4 and up   190 pages   *Harcourt, 1974*
This is a magnificent and unforgettable book. Picture a twelve-year-old boy, raised in an East European prison camp, who remembers no other life. Suddenly the opportunity to escape presents itself, and he begins not only a terrifying odyssey across Europe but also a journey into human experience. David must now deal with the normal experiences and knowledge denied him in prison. There are wondrous but confusing moments when he meets for the first time: a crying baby, flowers, fruit, a church bell peeling, children playing, and a toothbrush. Meanwhile, he learns how to smile, the meaning of conscience, and the need to trust. For experienced listeners.

Nothing but the Truth: A Documentary Novel

BY AVI

Grades 7 and up   177 pages   *Orchard, 1991*

In this Newbery Honor winner, a ninth-grader decides to irritate his teacher until she transfers him to another class. But what begins benignly soon escalates into a slanderous attack on the teacher when parents, faculty, media, and school-board members join the conflict. In the end, everyone loses. Told exclusively through documents like memos, letters and diary entries, this is a dramatic example of how freedom of speech can be abused. For other Avi books, and Web site, see *The True Confessions of Charlotte Doyle* (n). Related books: *Plague Year* (n) and *Tangerine* (n).

Nothing to Fear

BY JACKIE FRENCH KOLLER

Grades 4 and up   279 pages   *Harcourt, 1991*

This is a good old-fashioned historical novel that grabs you right by the heart and throat for 279 pages. Set in the Depression, it follows the travails and triumphs of a poor Irish family—especially young Danny and his mother—as they try to hold on against all odds. This is a vivid depiction of life in the 1930s, but the acts of love and courage displayed by the Garvey family are repeated daily in many families wherever poverty abides. Related books: *Bud, Not Buddy* (n); *No Promises in the Wind* by Irene Hunt; and a look at the Irish immigrant experience in Avi's *Lord Kirkle's Money*.

Number the Stars

BY LOIS LOWRY

Grades 4–7   137 pages   *Houghton, 1989*

In 1943, as the occupying Nazi army attempted to extricate and then exterminate the 7,000 Jews residing in Norway, the Danish people rose up as one in a determined and remarkably successful resistance. Against that backdrop, this Newbery winner describes a ten-year-old Danish girl joining forces with her relatives to save the lives of her best friend and her family. *Darkness Over Denmark* by Ellen Levine is an excellent nonfiction companion to this book, with photos of Denmark and the resistance fighters; the popular novel *Snow Treasure* by Marie McSwigan is about Danish children smuggling gold past the Nazis. Also by Lois Lowry: *Autumn Street*; and for older readers, *The Giver*. For author studies: *Looking Back: A Photographic Memoir* by Lois Lowry; and *Lois Lowry* by Lois Markham (Learning Works, Santa Barbara, CA).

Related books on the Holocaust, for younger children: *The Butterfly* by Patricia Polacco; *Hilde and Eli: Children of the Holocaust* by David A. Adler; *The Little Riders* by Margaretha Shemin; *Rose Blanche* by Roberto Innocenti and Christophe Gallaz; *Terrible Things: An Allegory of the Holocaust* by Eve Bunting; and *Twenty and Ten* by Claire Bishop. For older students: *Alan and Naomi* by Myron Levoy; and *Forging Freedom* by Hudson Talbott.

Otto of the Silver Hand

BY HOWARD PYLE

Grades 5–8   132 pages   *Dover, 1967*

First published in 1888 and written by one of the leading figures of early American children's literature, this is an ideal introduction to the classics. Intended as a cautionary tale about warfare (and inspired by the wounded Union soldiers he saw on railroads during the Civil War), Pyle describes a young boy's joy and suffering as he rises above the cruelty of the world, while caught between warring medieval German tribes. Though the language may be somewhat foreign to the listener at the start, it soon adds to the flavor of the narrative. For experienced listeners. Related books: *Castle Diary* by Richard Platt, the year-long diary of a young page serving in the castle of his uncle in 1285, a large picture book with rich text and illustrations describing everyday life; *Matilda Bone* by Karen Cushman, about a female apprentice bonesetter in a medieval village; and *The Fox Man* and *The Rifle* (s), both by Gary Paulsen.

Peppermints in the Parlor

BY BARBARA BROOKS WALLACE

Grades 3–7   198 pages   *Atheneum, 1980*

When the newly orphaned Emily arrives in San Francisco, she expects to be adopted by her wealthy aunt and uncle. What she finds instead is a poverty-stricken aunt held captive as a servant in a shadowy, decaying home for the aged. Filled with Dickensian flavor, this novel has secret passageways, tyrannical matrons, eerie whispers in the night, and a pair of fearful but plucky kids. Following the success of this book, the author has produced four more in the same genre: *Cousins in the Castle*; *Ghosts in the Gallery*; *The Twin in the Tavern*; and *Sparrows in the Scullery*, the latter two winning the Edgar Allan Poe Award from the Mystery Writers of America. Other gothic mysteries: *The Case of the Baker Street Irregular* (n); *The Curse of the Blue Figurine* (n); and *The Wolves of Willoughby Chase* (n).

The Pinballs

BY BETSY BYARS

Grades 5–7 136 pages Harper, *1977*

Brought together under the same roof, three foster children prove to each other and the world that they are not pinballs to be knocked around from one place to the next; they have a choice in life—to try or not to try. The author has taken what could have been a maudlin story and turned it into a hopeful, loving, and very witty book. Short chapters with easy-to-read dialogue. See *The Midnight Fox* for Byars's other books. Related books: *A Family Apart* (n); *The Loner* by Ester Wier; and *No Promises in the Wind* by Irene Hunt.

Plague Year

BY STEPHANIE S. TOLAN

Grades 7 and up 198 pages Fawcett, *1991*

When Bran arrives in his aunt's neatly manicured middle-class town, his clothes, hair style, and manner make him the immediate target of the high school's "jock" crowd. That he can handle, but a month later a tabloid newspaper announces his secret—that his father is about to go on trial in New Jersey as an accused serial killer. Suddenly, the town is consumed by Bran's presence and the danger this "bad seed" poses for its children, and mob mentality takes over for common sense and justice. Reading like today's headlines, it is fast-paced, thought-provoking, and offers powerful examples of all that is good and bad in school and community. Related books: *Nothing But the Truth* (n) and *Tangerine* (n).

Poppy

BY AVI

K–4 160 pages Orchard, *1995*

A great horned owl keeps the growing deer mice population in Dimwood Forest under his fierce control like an evil dictator, eating those who dare to disobey his orders. When he kills her boyfriend, little Poppy dares to go where no mouse has gone before—to the world beyond Dimwood. Indeed, she uncovers the hoax the evil owl has perpetrated through the years and leads her frightened family to the promised land. Told with wit and high drama, this is an excellent start to the "Tales from Dimwood Forest" that have followed: *Poppy and Rye*; *Ragweed*; and *Ereth's Birthday*. Older fans of this series will enjoy: *Martin the Warrior* (n); younger fans: *Charlotte's Web* (n). See *The True Confessions of Charlotte Doyle* (n) for more Avi information.

Ramona the Pest
BY BEVERLY CLEARY

K–4   144 pages   Morrow, 1968

Not all of Beverly Cleary's books make good read-alouds, though children love to read her silently. Some of her books move too slowly to hold read-aloud interest, but that's not the case with the Ramona series, which begins with *Ramona the Pest*. The book follows this outspoken young lady through her early months in kindergarten. Children will smile in recognition of Ramona's encounters with the first day of school, show-and-tell, seat work, a substitute teacher, Halloween, young love—and dropping out of kindergarten. Long chapters can easily be divided. Early grades should have some experience with short novels before trying Ramona. The sequels follow Ramona as she grows older and, with her family, experiences the challenges of modern life: *Ramona and Her Father; Ramona and Her Mother; Ramona Quimby, Age 8; Ramona Forever;* and *Ramona's World*. Also by the author: *Dear Mr. Henshaw* (n) and *The Mouse and the Motorcycle* (n). On the web: www.teleport.com/~krp/cleary.html. Beverly Cleary fans will enjoy her two-volume adult autobiography: *A Girl from Yamhill* and *My Own Two Feet* (Morrow).

The Rebounder
BY THOMAS J. DYGARD

Grades 5–10   180 pages   Puffin, 1996

Sixty years ago there was a Harvard grad named John R. Tunis who wrote boys' sports novels, mixing sports and social commentary, that were unrivaled for almost four decades. His most worthy successor is Thomas Dygard. In this book on high school basketball, Dygard sees the game through the players' and coach's eyes, reads the athlete's psyche, and puts the game into the social framework of community and school. Also by the author: *Backfield Package; Forward Pass; Game Plan; Halfback Tough; Infield Hit; Outside Shooter; The Rookie Arrives; Running Wild; Second Stringer;* and *Tournament Upstart*. Early primary sports fans will want to check out the books of Matt Christopher; middle graders, see *Finding Buck McHenry* (n); for middle school and high school, John H. Ritter's two baseball books, *Choosing Up Sides* and *Over the Wall*.

Roll of Thunder, Hear My Cry
BY MILDRED TAYLOR

Grades 5 and up   276 pages   Dial, 1976

Filled with the life blood of a black Mississippi family during the Depression, this Newbery winner depicts the pride of people who refuse to give in to threats and harassments from white neighbors. The story is told through daughter Cassie, age nine, who experiences her first taste of social injustice and refuses to swallow it. She, along with her family, her classmates and neighbors, will stir listeners' hearts and awaken many children to the tragedy of prejudice and discrimination. For experienced listeners. Caution: There are several racial epithets used in the dialogue. Other books in the series: *Let the Circle Be Unbroken*; *The Road to Memphis*; and four short novels, *The Friendship* (s); *Mississippi Bridge*; *Song of the Trees*; and *The Well*. Also by the author: *The Gold Cadillac*.

Related novels: *The Borning Room* by Paul Fleischman; *Francie* (n); *Nightjohn* by Gary Paulsen; *Sour Land* (n)—the sequel to *Sounder*; and *Words by Heart* (n).

Related nonfiction titles: *Christmas in the Big House, Christmas in the Quarters* by Patricia and Fredrick McKissack; *Mary Banneky* (n); *More Than Anything Else* (Booker T. Washington learns to read), by Marie Bradby; *Now Is Your Time! The African-American Struggle for Freedom* by Walter Dean Myers; and *Rosa Parks: My Story* by Rosa Parks.

A classroom *must:* The March 31, 1999, issue of *Education Week* carries the story of a Colorado fourth-grade class studying slavery, and how their highly publicized subsequent investigation revealed frightening modern-day slavery in "Sudan: Liberating Lesson" by Linda Jacobson, pp. 22–24 (www.edweek.com/ew/1999/29sudan.h18).

Video recommendations: "Once Upon a Time . . . When We Were Colored," an affectionate look back at life in a black Mississippi neighborhood from the mid-1940s to the dawn of the civil rights movement, based on the autobiographical novel by Clifton Taubert; and "4 Little Girls," Spike Lee's acclaimed 1997 documentary of the turning point in the civil rights movement, the bombing of the 16th Street Baptist Church.

Rules of the Road

BY JOAN BAUER

Grades 6 and up   201 pages   *Putnam/Puffin, 1998*

Jenna Boller is a savvy sixteen-year-old salesgirl at a Chicago shoe store when she is spotted by the crusty matriarch of the shoe chain and given an unusual summer job; driving her from Chicago to Dallas. Considering Jenna just got her driver's license, this is no small challenge. Along the way, they visit various stores in the chain, assess the strengths and weaknesses of each, and discover the shoe company is the object of a takeover bid by a cheapskate rival chain. In Dallas, the bid comes to a head and Jenna's courage—something she honed while coping all her life with an alcoholic father—comes to the rescue. The "rules of the road," as applied here, are the rules of life, family, and business that keep us balanced when un-expected curves appear. This is a wise, witty, and moving novel that has deservedly won awards and praise. Also by the author: *Hope Was Here; Back-water*, and *Squashed*.

Sarah Bishop
BY SCOTT O'DELL
Grades 5 and up   184 pages   *Houghton, 1980*
Based on a historic incident, this is the story of a determined young girl who flees war-torn Long Island after her father and brother are killed at the outbreak of the Revolutionary War. In the Connecticut wilderness, she takes refuge in a cave, where she begins her new life. Sarah Bishop makes an interesting comparative study with two other read-aloud novels dealing with children running away: *Slakes's Limbo* (n) and *My Side of the Mountain* (n). Each depicts the subject of the "runaway" at a different point in history. For experienced listeners. O'Dell's stories often focus on indepen-dent, strong-willed young women. Also by the author: *Sing Down the Moon* (s). For related Revolutionary War titles, see *My Brother Sam Is Dead* (n).

Scorpions
BY WALTER DEAN MYERS
Grades 7 and up   216 pages   *Harper, 1988*
This award-winning novelist has drawn upon his childhood in Harlem to give us a revealing and poignant look at an African-American family fac-ing the daily pressures of urban poverty. While seventh-grader Jamal Hicks struggles to resist the pressures to join a neighborhood gang, he is watch-ing his family being torn apart by the crimes of an older brother and a wayward father. Moreover, his relationship with school is disintegrating under a combination of his own irresponsibility and an antagonistic prin-cipal. Unable to resist the peer pressure, Jamal makes a tragic decision in-volving a handgun. Readers-aloud should be aware that some of the book's dialogue is written in black dialect. Author study: *Bad Boy, a Memoir*. Re-lated books: *Killing Mr. Griffin* (n); *Make Lemonade* by Virginia Euwer Wolff; *The Outsiders* by S. E. Hinton; and *Twelve Shots: Outstanding Short Stories about Guns*, collected by Harry Mazer.

The Search for Delicious
BY NATALIE BABBITT
Grades 3–7   160 pages   *Farrar, 1969*
After a nasty argument among the King, Queen, and their court over the correct meaning of the word "delicious," the Prime Minister's adopted son

is dispatched to poll the kingdom to determine the choice of the people. The poll brings out people's foolishness, pettiness, and quarrelsome natures: Everyone has his own personal definition of "delicious" and civil war looms. Also by the author: *Tuck Everlasting* (n). Related books: *The Butter Battle Book* by Dr. Seuss, and *The War with Grandpa* by Robert K. Smith.

The Secret Garden
BY FRANCES HODGSON BURNETT

Grades 2–5   240 pages   *numerous publishers*

Few books spin such a web of magic about their audiences as does this 1911 children's classic about the sulky orphan who comes to live with her cold, unfeeling uncle on the windswept English moors. Wandering the grounds of his immense manor house one day, she discovers a secret garden, locked and abandoned. This leads her to discover her uncle's invalid child hidden within the mansion, her first friendship, and her own true self. While this is definitely for experienced listeners, try to avoid the abridged versions, since too much of the flavor is lost in those. Also by the author: *Sara Crewe* (s); *Little Lord Fauntleroy*; *A Little Princess*; and *The Lost Prince*. Related books: *Good Night, Mr. Tom* (n); *Mandy* by Julie Edwards; and *Understood Betsy* (n).

Sideways Stories from Wayside School
BY LOUIS SACHAR

Grades 2–5   124 pages   *Random House, 1990*

Thirty chapters about the wacky students who inhabit the thirtieth floor of Wayside School, the school that was supposed to be built one story high and thirty classes wide, until the contractor made a mistake and made it thirty stories high! If you think the building is bizarre, wait until you meet the kids who inhabit it. Sequels: *Wayside School Is Falling Down*; and *Wayside School Gets a Little Stranger*. Also by the author: *Holes* (n); *Johnny's in the Basement*; *Sixth Grade Secrets*; *Someday Angeline*; and *There's a Boy in the Girls' Bathroom*. Other humorous books: *Skinnybones* (s); *The Best Christmas Pageant Ever* (s); and *Tales of a Fourth-Grade Nothing* (n).

The Sign of the Beaver
BY ELIZABETH GEORGE SPEARE

Grades 3 and up   135 pages   *Houghton, 1983*

This is the story of two boys—one white, the other American Indian— and their coming of age in the Maine wilderness during the Colonial period. It is also a study of the awkward relationship that develops when the starving white boy is forced to teach the reluctant Indian to read in order for both of them to survive. Also by the author: *The Witch of Blackbird Pond*. Related books on the relationship between white settlers and Indian neighbors: *Clearing in the Forest: A Story About a Real Settler Boy* by Joanne Landers Henry; *Encounter* (p); *Return to Hawk's Hill* by Allan W. Eckert; *Sing Down the Moon* (n); and *Weasel* (n).

Sing Down the Moon

BY SCOTT O'DELL

Grades 3–6   138 pages   *Houghton, 1970*

Through the first-person narrative of a fourteen-year-old Navaho girl, we follow the plight of the American Indian in 1864 when the U.S. government ordered the Navahos out of their Arizona homeland and marched them 300 miles to Fort Sumner, New Mexico, where they were imprisoned for four years. Known as "The Long Walk," it is a journey that has since become a part of every Navaho child's heritage. The injustices and the subsequent courage displayed by the Indians should be known by all Americans. The novel also provides a detailed account of daily Indian life during the period. Short chapters are told with the vocabulary and in the style appropriate to a young Indian child. Also by the author: *Sarah Bishop* (n). See listing with *Sign of the Beaver* (n) for related titles.

Slake's Limbo

BY FELICE HOLMAN

Grades 5–8   117 pages   *Atheneum, 1984*

A fifteen-year-old takes his fears and misfortunes into the New York City subway one day, finds a hidden construction mistake in the shape of a cave near the tracks, and doesn't come out of the system for 121 days. The story deals simply but powerfully with the question: Can anyone be an island unto himself? It is also a story of survival, personal discovery and the plight of today's homeless. This book makes interesting comparative study with three other books that discuss running away, hiding, and personal discovery: *My Side of the Mountain* (n); *North to Freedom* (n); and *Sarah Bishop* (n).

Snow Bound

BY HARRY MAZER

Grades 5–8   146 pages   *Dell, 1975*

Two teenagers, a boy and a girl, marooned by a car wreck during a severe snowstorm, fight off starvation, frostbite, wild dogs, broken limbs, and personal bickering in order to survive. An excellent example of people's lives being changed for the better in dealing with adversity. Occasional four-letter words in the dialogue. Also by the author: *When the Phone Rang.* Related survival stories: See *Hatchet* (n).

Sour Land
BY WILLIAM H. ARMSTRONG
Grades 4–8   116 pages   *Harper, 1971*
This is the little-known sequel to the Newbery-winning *Sounder*, and a better read-aloud. Here we meet the nameless boy from *Sounder*, now grown, teaching in a small black school, maintaining his decency and dignity while the lethal shadow of racism lurks in the corner. Related books: see *Roll of Thunder, Hear My Cry* (n).

Street Child
BY BERLIE DOHERTY
Grades 3–8   154 pages   *Puffin, 1996*
It is London in the 1860s, and Jim Jarvis is a lovable street orphan living by his wits and fast feet but teetering on the edge of starvation and despair. This tale follows him from the time his mother dies in the workhouse until he finally is rescued by a man who could be classified as an early social worker. The author gives the reader a powerful dose of the resilience and courage that enabled people to survive those times. Though fictionalized, it is carefully researched and based on actual characters and events that offer striking contrasts with both the plight of today's homeless and present-day child welfare agencies and laws.

The Academy Award–winning film *Oliver!* would be an ideal video to share with this reading. See *A Family Apart* (n) for related "orphan" books; also an excellent abridgment of Dickens's *Oliver Twist* by Lesley Baxter (Dial). For a similar tale, set in the wartime of the 1940s, see *The Kingdom by the Sea* (n).

Stuart Little
BY E. B. WHITE
K–3   130 pages   *Harper, 1945*
Stuart is a very, very small boy (two inches) who unfortunately looks exactly like a *mouse.* This leaves him at a decided disadvantage living in a house where everyone else is normal size, including the family cat. White's first book for children, it is filled with beautiful language and lots of adventures as Stuart struggles to find his way in the world—an important job for all children, even if they don't look like a mouse. (*Stuart Little* is such a good book that (even though the most influential librarian in the U.S. tried

to block its publication,) it's still around fifty-five years later.) Also by the author: *Charlotte's Web* (n) and *Trumpet of the Swans*. Related books: *The Mouse and the Motorcycle* (n); the "Dimwood Forest" tales by Avi, beginning with *Poppy* (n); for older listeners: the *Redwall* series by Brian Jacques (see *Martin the Warrior* [n]).

A Stranger Came Ashore

BY MOLLIE HUNTER

Grades 4–7   163 pages   *Harper, 1975*

The handsome stranger who claims to be the sole survivor of a shipwreck off the Scottish coast is really the Great Selkie, come to lure the Henderson family's beautiful daughter to her death at the bottom of the sea. Also by the author: *The Smartest Man in Ireland* (s). Related books: *The Animal Family* (n); *The Crane Wife*, retold by Katherine Paterson; *The Sea Man* by Jane Yolen; and *The Selkie Girl* by Susan Cooper.

Tales of a Fourth-Grade Nothing

BY JUDY BLUME

Grades 3–5   120 pages   *Dutton, 1972*

A perennial favorite among schoolchildren, this novel deals with the irksome problem of a kid brother whose hilarious antics complicate the life of his fourth-grade brother, Peter. Sequels: *Superfudge*; *Fudge-a-Mania* (readers-aloud should be cautioned that the latter book deals with the question: Is there a Santa Claus?). Also by the author: *Freckle Juice*. Related books: see *Rip-Roaring Russell* (s); *Junie B. Jones and the Smelly Bus* (s). On the Web: www.judyblume.com.

Tangerine

BY EDWARD BLOOR

Grades 6 and up   294 pages   *Harcourt, 1997*

To call this a sports novel (though it certainly is that) is to narrow its wide range of topics: prejudice, evil, repressed memories, corruption, ecology, botany, and good old academic bureaucracy. Add those topics to the friendships developed on the athletic field and you've got a remarkable first novel by Mr. Bloor, who has spent years in the classroom with adolescents—and it shows. The book does start a bit slowly for a read-aloud, so you'll need to give it thirty pages or so. By then, the pattern of seventh-grader Paul Fisher's life and family are in bold relief: a commandeering mother, a father who lives exclusively through the high school football exploits of his oldest son (Erik), and Erik—a dark figure who moves through the corners of Paul's life like a hand grenade with a loose pin. Side note:

the Florida tourism office will *not* be recommending this book. Related book: *Plague Year* (n).

Thank You, Jackie Robinson

BY BARBARA COHEN

Grades 5–7   126 pages   *Lothrop, 1988*

In the late 1940s, we meet young Sam Green, a rare breed known as the True Baseball Fanatic and a Brooklyn Dodger fan. His widowed mother runs an inn, and when she hires a sixty-year-old black cook, Sam's life takes a turn for the better. The two form a fast friendship and begin to explore the joys of baseball in a way the fatherless boy has never known. A tender book that touches on friendship, race, sports, personal sacrifice, and death. Related books: *Finding Buck McHenry* (n); *In the Year of the Boar and Jackie Robinson* (n); *Teammates* by Peter Golenbock; and an excellent paperback series by Dan Gutman about a boy who time travels using his baseball cards: *Jackie and Me* (Jackie Robinson); *Babe and Me* (Babe Ruth); and *Honus and Me* (Honus Wagner). Also, "Inning Six" from Ken Burns's Baseball video for PBS (*The National Pastime*) offers an excellent portrayal of the color-line being broken in baseball.

Thunder Cave

BY ROLAND SMITH

Grades 4–8   250 pages   *Hyperion, 1997*

For "buckle-your-seatbelts" adventure, this one ranks with the best. After the sudden death of his mother, fourteen-year-old Jacob (half Hopi Indian) makes his way to Kenya, Africa, in search of his father, a biologist studying elephant behavior in a remote area. Along the way, he masters the fine art of international politics (with Kenyan immigration officials); survives a trio of local thugs who beat him unconscious, strip him to his underwear, and steal his mountain bike; and encounters a Kenyan brush fire, a marauding lion, and a life-threatening bout of diarrhea.

Thanks to the author's background knowledge of African and exotic animals, the twists are done quite plausibly. He also connects the wandering boy to a Masai witch doctor (college graduate with a degree in philosophy) who offers an excellent study in similarities between American Indian and Masai cultures. (Caution: Jacob occasionally utters an expletive, nothing integral to the story, but be prepared.) The book received national social studies citations. Sequel: In *Jaguar*, Jacob joins his father in the Amazon. Related books: *Bud, Not Buddy* (n); *Nightwalkers* by Judy K. Morris; and *A Perfect Friend* by Reynolds Price. Fans of *Thunder Cave* will enjoy books by Gary Paulsen and Will Hobbs.

Toliver's Secret

BY ESTHER WOOD BRADY

Grades 3–5   166 pages   *Crown, 1988*

During the Revolutionary War, ten-year-old Ellen Toliver is asked by her ailing grandfather to take his place and carry a secret message through British lines. What he estimates to be a simple plan is complicated by Ellen's exceptional timidity and an unforeseen shift by the British. The book becomes a portrait of Ellen's personal growth—complete with a heart-stopping crisis in each chapter. Related books: *The Courage of Sarah Noble* (s); *The Little Ships* by Louise Borden, in which a young girl poses as a boy to sail with her father in the dramatic rescue of British soldiers at Dunkirk in WWII; *The Secret Soldier: The Story of Deborah Sampson* by Ann McGovern; and *American Revolution* by Joy Masoff, part of Scholastic's Chronicle of America series that uses photographs from America's living history museums to illustrate this excellent forty-eight-page reference volume.

The Trolls

BY POLLY HORVATH

Grades 3–6   135 pages   *FSG, 1999*

Only out of sheer desperation would the Andersons ever invite eccentric Aunt Sally to babysit the children. Not only is Sally an artist, she's also got a very vivid imagination for family history, which she spins each night as a bedtime story. As the children discover these ancient family tales (including the day the trolls carried their father off when he was a child), they find it harder and harder to separate fact from fancy. But they also find it impossible not to love Aunt Sally. Related title: *Ida Early Comes Over the Mountain* (n); *The Lost Flower Children* by Janet Taylor Lisle; and *The Smartest Man in Ireland* (n).

The True Confessions of Charlotte Doyle

BY AVI

Grades 4 and up   215 pages   *Orchard, 1990*

Winner of a Newbery Honor medal, this is the exciting tale of an obstinate thirteen-year-old girl who is the lone passenger aboard a merchant ship sailing from England to the U.S. in 1832. The crew is bent on mutiny, the captain is a murderer, and within weeks the girl is accused of murder, tried by captain and crew, and sentenced to hang at sea. Avi is at his finest with this "first-person" adventure, exploring history, racism, feminism, and mob psychology.

Other books by Avi: *The Barn*; Beyond the Western Sea series: I—*The*

Escape from Home; II—*Lord Kirkle's Money*; *Captain Grey* (n); *Don't You Know There's a War On?*; *The Fighting Ground*; *Nothing But the Truth* (n); *Poppy* (n); *What Do Fish Have to Do with Anything and Other Stories*; and *Wolf Rider* (n). Avi's Web site: www.avi-writer.com. For author studies: *Avi* by Lois Markham (Learning Works, Santa Barbara, CA).

Tuck Everlasting

BY NATALIE BABBITT

Grades 4–7   124 pages   *Farrar, 1975*

A young girl stumbles upon a family that has found the "Fountain of Youth," and in the aftermath there is a kidnapping, a murder, and a jailbreak. This touching story suggests a sobering question: What would it be like to live forever? For experienced listeners. Also by the author: *Search for Delicious* (n). Related book: *The Lost Flower Children* by Janet Taylor Lisle.

The Twenty-One Balloons

BY WILLIAM PÈNE DU BOIS

Grades 4–6   180 pages   *Viking, 1947*

This long-ago Newbery winner is a literary smorgasbord; there are so many different and delicious parts one hardly knows which to mention first. The story deals with a retired teacher's attempts to sail by balloon across the Pacific in 1883, his crash landing and pseudo-imprisonment on the island of Krakatoa, and, finally, his escape. The book is crammed with nuggets of science, history, humor, invention, superior language, and marvelous artwork. For experienced listeners. Be sure to have available *Why Do Volcanoes Blow Their Tops?* by Melvin and Gilda Berger (Scholastic) and its instructions for building a volcano.

Understood Betsy

BY DOROTHY CANFIELD FISHER

Grades 2–5   229 pages   *Holt, 1999*

Written in 1917 by one of America's most celebrated writers, this is the classic story of a timid, almost neurotic orphan child (Betsy) being raised by her overprotective city-dwelling aunts. Then a family illness requires the child be sent to live with "stiff-necked" rural relatives in Vermont and she must stand on her own two feet, do chores, and speak for herself—all of which causes a heartwarming metamorphosis. As a novel, even as a psychological or historical profile, the book is enormously successful. One of its original intentions was to promote the Montessori method of education at the beginning of the twentieth century. Related books: *Gift of the Pirate Queen* (n); *Good Night, Mr. Tom* (n); *Mandy* by Julie Edwards; and *The Secret Garden* (n).

Under the Bridge
BY ELLEN KINDT MCKENZIE
Grades 3–6   *140 pages*   *Harper, 1996*
Fifth-grader Ritchie and his four-year-old sister are desperate: Their
mother has been hospitalized with a breakdown and their father answers
none of their questions. Each child is sinking into despair when a letter arrives from an unusual source—the tiny troll who lives under the bridge
next door. His succession of letters provide the distracting and coping device the children desperately need. At the same time, Ritchie is befriended
by the mysterious man who lives in the shack next door (source of the troll
letters). Far from depressing, this is a realistic and uplifting tale of siblings
caring deeply for each other, a story that is resolved happily with the
mother's return. Also by the author: *Stargone John* (s). Related book: *The
Lost Flower Children* by Janet Taylor Lisle.

The War of Jenkins' Ear
BY MICHAEL MORPURGO
Grades 6 and up   *171 pages*   *Putnam, 1995*
This is *not* a book for public school read-aloud. As you'll see, the subject
matter makes it safest in private and parochial schools, as well as at home—
if you are comfortable with the subject matter. Set in a private English prep
school, it deals with the mysterious new student, Christopher, and his reluctance to do any of the cruel or deceitful things most of the boys do. He
is fearless, as though nothing could harm him—even the school bully.
Then he confides in a friend that he is the "next Christ," that he's been sent
by Christ to finish the work begun 2000 years earlier. It's too difficult a secret for the classmate to keep to himself and it soon spreads through the
disbelieving student body and faculty. In the end, the question of his identity is not determined, for they have driven him away from the school with
their cruelty—an emotional crucifixion. The layers of the story, the power
of the relationships, and the trueness of the characters' behavior make this
a powerful young-adult novel. One could say it's *The Chocolate War* meets
The Lion, the Witch, and the Wardrobe. Also by the author: *Waiting for Anya*
and *The Wreck of the Zanzibar.*

Weasel
BY CYNTHIA DEFELICE
Grades 2–6   *119 pages*   *Atheneum, 1990*
Set in Ohio in 1839, this realistic look at the American frontier focuses on
a widower and his two children as they confront racism, violence, and the

elements. Most of the challenge comes in the person of Weasel, a former government "Indian fighter" who captures both father and son. A fast-paced, first-person adventure story, it also describes the plight of the American Indian and America's own "ethnic cleansing." Also by the author: *The Apprenticeship of Lucas Whittaker* and *Nothing to Fear* (n). Related books: *Buffalo Knife*; *Flaming Arrows*; *Perilous Road*; and *Winter Danger*, all by William Q. Steele; *The Sign of the Beaver* (n); and *Sing Down the Moon* (n).

When the Tripods Came

BY JOHN CHRISTOPHER

Grades 5 and up   151 pages   *Dutton, 1988*

An updating of H. G. Wells's *War of the Worlds*, this is the prequel to one of modern science fiction's most popular juvenile series: *The Tripods*. When invaders from space take over Earth and begin implanting brain-control devices among the humans, a group of rebellious teens lay the groundwork for the invaders' destruction. The series includes (in order): *The White Mountains*; *The City of Gold and Lead*; and *The Pool of Fire*. Related books: *Fallout* by Robert Swindells; and *War of the Worlds* by H. G. Wells.

Where the Red Fern Grows

BY WILSON RAWLS

Grades 3–7   212 pages   *Doubleday, 1961*

A ten-year-old boy growing up in the Ozark mountains, praying and saving for a pair of hounds, finally achieves his wish. He then begins the task of turning the hounds into first-class hunting dogs. It would be difficult to find a book that speaks more definitively about perseverance, courage, family, sacrifice, work, life, and death. Long chapters are easily divided, but bring a box of tissues for the final chapters. Also by the author: *Summer of the Monkeys*. The author's recitation of his life story ("Dreams Can Come True"), is available on audiocassette; for details: www.trelease-on-reading. com/rawls.html. See *A Dog Called Kitty* for related dog titles.

The Wish Giver: Three Tales of Coven Tree

BY BILL BRITTAIN

Grades 4–8   181 pages   *Harper, 1983*

Into the town of Coven Tree comes a mysterious stranger who sets up a tent at the church social, promising wishes-come-true for fifty cents. Three young people in this tiny New England town find out the hard way that sometimes we'd be better off if our wishes didn't come true. There is plenty of homespun merriment and fast-moving suspense here. Also by the author: *Wings*. Related book: *The Pied Piper* (p).

Wolf Rider: A Tale of Terror

BY AVI

Grades 7 and up   224 pages   *Aladdin, 2000*

This is breathtaking, plausible, and nonstop reading and my first recommendation for "reluctant-reader" teens. When fifteen-year-old Andy accidentally receives a random phone call from a man claiming he's killed a college coed, nobody believes him. And when everyone writes it off as a prank, Andy sets out to find the anonymous caller in a race against death and the clock. Read any version of "The Boy Who Cried Wolf" before reading aloud this book. Caution: There is a small number of expletives in the text. For other books about and by Avi, see *The True Confessions of Charlotte Doyle* (n). Related books: *Killing Mr. Griffin* (n) and *Plague Year* (n).

The Wolves of Willoughby Chase

BY JOAN AIKEN

Grades 3–6   168 pages   *Dell, 1987*

Here is Victorian melodrama in high gear by a master storyteller: a great English estate surrounded by hungry wolves, two young girls mistakenly left in the care of a wicked, scheming governess, secret passageways and tortured flights through the snow in the dark of night. For experienced listeners. Sequels: *Black Hearts in Battersea*; *Nightbirds on Nantucket*; and *The Stolen Lake*. Related books: *Peppermints in the Parlor* (n); *The Secret Garden* (n); and *Street Child*, (n).

The Wonderful Wizard of Oz

BY L. FRANK BAUM

Grades 1 and up   260 pages   *Numerous publishers*

Before your children are exposed to the movie version, treat them to the magic of this 1900 book, which many regard as the first American fairy tale, as well as our earliest science fiction. (Incidentally, the book is far less terrifying for children than the film version.) The magical story of Dorothy and her friends' harrowing journey to the Emerald City is but the first of many books about the Land of Oz. Sequels: *Dorothy and the Wizard of Oz*; *The Emerald City of Oz*; *The Marvelous Land of Oz*; *Ozma of Oz* (the best of the sequels); *The Patchwork Girl of Oz*; and *The Road to Oz*. Author study: Nothing compares with Michael Patrick Hearn's *The Annotated Wizard of Oz: The Centennial Edition* (Norton, 2000). On the Web: www.eskimo.com/~tiktok/index.htm.

Woodsong

BY GARY PAULSEN

Grades 5 and up   *132 pages*   *Simon & Schuster, 1990*

Using the same tension he infuses into his novels, the author gives us a nonfiction journal about living off the land while training a dog team for the Iditarod. Powerful and breathtaking nonfiction—but not for the faint of heart or weak-stomached. Also by the author: *My Life in Dog Years*, reminiscences of his favorite dogs. For other Paulsen titles, see *Hatchet* (n); for more dog stories, *A Dog Called Kitty* (n).

Words by Heart

BY OUIDA SEBESTYEN

Grades 5 and up   *162 pages*   *Little, 1979*

A young girl and her family must summon all their courage and spirit in order to survive as the only black family in this 1910 Texas community. The child's spunk, her father's tireless patience, and the great faith in God he leaves with her make this an unforgettable book. For experienced listeners. The slow-moving first chapter can be edited with prereading. Sequel: *On Fire*. Related books: *Bud, Not Buddy* (n); *Francie* (n); and *Roll of Thunder, Hear My Cry* (n).

Poetry

And the Green Grass Grew All Around: Folk Poetry from Everyone

BY ALVIN SCHWARTZ; SUE TRUESDELL, ILLUS.

K–4   *148 pages*   *Harper, 1992*

From a top folklorist comes this delightful collection of more than 250 poems, limericks, chants, jump-rope rhymes, taunts, riddles, and much more—all part of the great American folklore tradition. Truesdell's riotous illustrations add the perfect touch to a book that you'll find your children trying to memorize just for the fun of it.

Casey at the Bat

BY ERNEST L. THAYER; BARRY MOSER, ILLUS.

Grades 4 and up   *32 pages*   *Godine, 1988*

This description of a small-town baseball game and a local hero is one of the most famous pieces in America's literary quilt, and this centennial edition from Godine includes Barry Moser's illustrations depicting the original period. "Casey" is as topical today as it was in 1888. For a biographical profile of Thayer and the history of the poem, as well as a copy of the lesser known "Casey's Revenge" by Grantland Rice, see *Read All About It!* (a). Also: *Casey at the Bat*, Christopher Bing, illus.

The Cremation of Sam McGee
BY ROBERT W. SERVICE; TED HARRISON, ILLUS.

Grades 4 and up   *30 pages*   *Greenwillow, 1987*

Once one of the most memorized poems in North America, this remains the best description of the sun's strange spell over the men who toil in the North. After seeing this edition, you will find it difficult to hear the words without picturing Harrison's artwork. Also by the author and illustrator: *The Shooting of Dan McGrew*. Two excellent collections of Service poetry: *Best Tales of the Yukon* (Running Press) and *Collected Poems of Robert Service* (Dodd). For a biographical profile of the poet, see *Read All About It!* (a). See *Call of the Wild* (n) for related Yukon books.

Honey, I Love
BY ELOISE GREENFIELD; DIANE AND LEO DILLON, ILLUS.

PreS.–3rd   *42 pages*   *Harper, 1976*

Sixteen short poems about the things and people children love: friends, cousins, older brothers, keepsakes, mother's clothes, music, and jump ropes. Set against an urban background, the poems elicit both joyous and bittersweet feelings.

If I Were in Charge of the World and Other Worries
BY JUDITH VIORST

Grades 3 and up   *56 pages*   *Atheneum, 1981*

If the meter or rhyme in these forty-one poems is occasionally imperfect, it is easily overlooked in light of their pulse and timing. In prescribing these short verses "for children and their parents," this contemporary American humorist offers a two-point perspective: Children reading these poems will giggle, then recognize themselves, their friends and enemies, and think, "That's really the way it is!" Parents will recognize in the poems the child they used to be. Also by the author: *Alexander and the Terrible, Horrible, No Good, Very Bad Day* (p).

If You're Not Here, Please Raise Your Hand: Poems About School

BY KALLI DAKOS; G. BRIAN KARAS, ILLUS.

Grades 1–8   64 pages   *Simon, 1990*

As a classroom teacher, Kalli Dakos has been down in the trenches with all the silliness, sadness, and happiness of elementary school. Can't you tell just from the title? Also by the author: *Don't Read This Book What Ever You Do! More Poems About School.* Related books: *I Thought I'd Take My Rat to School: Poems for September to June,* selected by Dorothy M. Kennedy; *Lunch Money and Other Poems About School* by Carol D. Shields; *Somebody Catch My Homework* and *A Thousand Cousins,* both by David L. Harrison.

Kids Pick the Funniest Poems

COMPILED BY BRUCE LANSKY; STEPHEN CARPENTER, ILLUS.

K–8   105 pages   *Meadowbrook, 1991*

Here are the seventy-five funniest poems as chosen by 300 schoolchildren, from a broad cross section of poets.

Mother Goose (see *The Lucy Cousins Book of Nursery Rhymes,* page 244)

Never Take a Pig to Lunch and Other Poems about the Fun of Food

SELECTED AND ILLUSTRATED BY NADINE BERNARD WESTCOT

K–4   62 pages   *Orchard, 1994*

In this collection of silly or hilarious poems about food, the compiler has divided the sixty selections into four fun categories: (1) eating silly things; (2) eating foods we like; (3) eating too much; and (4) manners at the table. Included are most of the best children's poets of today and yesterday.

The New Kid on the Block

BY JACK PRELUTSKY; JAMES STEVENSON, ILLUS.

K–4   160 pages   *Greenwillow, 1984*

One of our most prolific poets for children, Prelutsky has collected more than a hundred of his most outrageous and comical characters, attempting simply to amuse and please children—which he does, for example, with a poem about the taken-for-granted blessings of having your nose on your face instead of in your ear, and the one about Sneaky Sue who started playing hide-and-seek a month ago and still can't be found. Also by the author: *The Dragons Are Singing Tonight; It's Raining Pigs and Noodles; Nightmares: Po-*

ems to Trouble Your Sleep; A Pizza the Size of the Sun; also his *Random House Book of Poetry* (see below) and *Read-Aloud Rhymes for the Very Young* (po).

The Random House Book of Poetry for Children
SELECTED BY JACK PRELUTSKY; ARNOLD LOBEL, ILLUS.
K–5   248 pages   Random House, 1983
One of the best children's poetry anthologies ever, showing that poet Jack Prelutsky recognizes the common language of children. The 572 selected poems (from both traditional and contemporary poets) are short—but long on laughter, imagery, and rhyme. They are grouped into fourteen categories that include food, goblins, nonsense, home, children, animals, and seasons. This is an excellent companion to *Read-Aloud Rhymes for the Very Young* (see below).

Read-Aloud Rhymes for the Very Young
COLLECTED BY JACK PRELUTSKY; MARC BROWN, ILLUS.
Tod–K   88 pages   Knopf, 1986
Here are more than 200 little poems (with full-color illustrations) for little people with little attention spans, to help both to grow. Related books: *The Lucy Cousins Book of Nursery Rhymes* (p); and *Whiskers and Rhymes* by Arnold Lobel.

Side by Side: Poems to Read Together
COLLECTED BY LEE BENNETT HOPKINS; HILARY KNIGHT, ILLUS.
PreS.–2nd   80 pages   Simon & Schuster, 1998
Teacher, poet, and anthologist Lee Bennett Hopkins assembles the work of traditional and contemporary poets to be read aloud to young children. Covering the seasons, holidays, animals, and lullabies, the fifty-seven poems also include several of the classic narrative poems for young children, like "Poor Old Lady," "The House That Jack Built," and "A Visit from St. Nicholas."

Sing a Song of Popcorn: Every Child's Book of Poems
SELECTED BY DEREGNIERS, MOORE, WHITE, AND CARR
K–5   160 pages   Scholastic, 1988
What distinguishes this volume from other excellent poetry collections is that each of the nine sections has been assigned to a different Caldecott Award–winning illustrator, including Maurice Sendak, Trina Schart Hyman, and Arnold Lobel. Thus both the sounds and sights of this book make it outstanding.

Where the Sidewalk Ends

BY SHEL SILVERSTEIN

K–8   166 pages   *Harper, 1974*

Without question, this is the best-loved collection of poetry for children, selling more than two million hardcover copies in twenty years. When it comes to knowing children's appetites, Silverstein was pure genius. The titles alone are enough to bring children to rapt attention: "Bandaids"; "Boa Constrictor"; "Crocodile's Toothache"; "The Dirtiest Man in the World"; and "Recipe for a Hippopotamus Sandwich." Here are 130 poems that will either touch childen's hearts or tickle their funny bones. Silverstein's second collection of poems, *A Light in the Attic*, was the second children's book to make *The New York Times* best-seller list, where it remained for 186 weeks. His last collection was *Falling Up*. Also by the author: *The Giving Tree* and *Lafcadio, the Lion Who Shot Back* (s).

Anthologies

Does God Have a Big Toe?

BY MARC GELLMAN

Grades 1–7   88 pages   *Harper, 1989*

Along with being a mother lode of wisdom and inspiration, the Bible has been a rich source of literature and inspiration for those who look for the common thread of story in all life. Because the Bible lends itself to diverse interpretations, scholars often create stories of their own to explain it. In this case, Rabbi Marc Gellman has taken twenty Biblical episodes and given us twenty midrosh—"new stories about old stories." Its success is largely due to Gellman's wit and the reverence he maintains throughout. Sequel: *God's Mailbox: More Stories about Stories in the Bible*. Also *How Do You Spell God? Answers to the Really Big Questions from Around the World* by Rabbi Marc Gellman and Monsignor Thomas Hartman.

Great Lives: Human Rights

BY WILLIAM JAY JACOBS

Grades 6 and up   266 pages   *Atheneum, 1990*

This is one in a series of excellent biographical anthologies covering the entire curriculum. (So no matter what subject you teach, you'll easily find something to choose from here.) Written by respected historians, each volume contains more than twenty-five biographies (approximately fifteen pages each) from a particular area, such as Human Rights. Others in the series: American Frontier; American Government; American Journalism; American Literature; Exploration; Human Culture; Invention and Technology; Medicine; Nature and the Environment; Painting; Sports; Theater; World Government; and World Religions.

Her Stories: African American Folktales, Fairy Tales, and True Tales

BY VIRGINIA HAMILTON; LEO AND DIANE DILLON, ILLUS.
Grades 3 and up   *193 pages*   *Scholastic, 1995*
This is a collection of nineteen short tales that have been retold through the ages by African-American women, including stories of magic and mischief, fairy folk and vampires, tricksters and slaves.

Hey! Listen to This: Stories to Read Aloud

BY JIM TRELEASE
K–4   410 pages   *Penguin, 1992*
Here are forty-eight read-aloud stories from the top authors of yesterday and today. Arranged in categories like school days, food, families, folk and fairy tales, and animals, the selections include entire chapter excerpts as well as complete stories. There are also full-page biographical profiles of the authors. Also by the author: *Read All About It!*, an anthology for grades five and older; and *The Read-Aloud Handbook*. On the web: www.trelease-on-reading.com/hey.html.

Never Cry "Arp!"

BY PATRICK MCMANUS
Grades 4 and up   *133 pages*   *Holt, 1996*
Patrick McManus has long been breaking up readers of *Outdoor Life*, and this collection of essays on his wilderness and camping adventures expertly displays his funny-bone talents. You could say he's the Dave Barry of the outdoors. If you can read the first two pages of this book with a straight face, you'll *hate* this book. Related book: *The Secret Knowledge of Grown-ups* (p).

Paul Harvey's "The Rest of the Story"

BY PAUL HARVEY, JR.
Grades 6 and up   *234 pages*   *Bantam, 1978*
This collection of essays from broadcaster Paul Harvey's five-minute radio show, "The Rest of the Story," is perfect for teachers and parents trying to

win older students to the art of listening. Nearly all of these pieces deal with famous people, past and present. The person's name is saved for the last few lines of the tale and serves as an O. Henry–type punch line. The eighty-one stories average four minutes in length. Sequel: *More of Paul Harvey's "The Rest of the Story."*

The Random House Book of Humor for Children

SELECTED BY PAMELA POLLACK; PAUL O. ZELINSKY, ILLUS.

Grades 3–7   309 pages   *Random, 1988*

Here are thirty-four short stories and novel excerpts centered upon children and humor, featuring many famous authors in children's fiction—from Mark Twain and Rudyard Kipling to Robert McCloskey and Beverly Cleary. Though each stands on its own, they are an excellent way to lure children into the author's complete works. This is part of an excellent series by Random House that includes: *The Random House Book of Fairy Tales*; *The Random House Book of Ghost Stories*; *The Random House Book of Science Fiction Stories*; and *The Random House Book of Sports Stories*.

Read All About It!

BY JIM TRELEASE

Grades 5 and up   487 pages   *Penguin, 1993*

For parents and teachers at a loss for what to read to preteens and teens, here are fifty selections—from classics to newspaper columns, fiction and nonfiction, humor and tragedy. Each story is introduced by a biographical profile of the author—like "Whatever happened to Harper Lee?" (*To Kill a Mockingbird*). Also by the author: *Hey! Listen to This*, an anthology for grades K–4; and *The Read-Aloud Handbook*. On the Web: www.trelease-on-reading.com/aai.html.

Scary Stories to Tell in the Dark

COLLECTED BY ALVIN SCHWARTZ; STEPHEN GAMMELL, ILLUS.

Grades 5 and up   112 pages   *Lippincott, 1981*

Dipping into the past and the present, the author presents twenty-nine American "horror" stories and songs guaranteed to make your listeners cringe. The text includes suggestions for the reader-aloud on when to pause, when to scream, even when to turn off the lights. The selections run the gamut from giggles to gore and average two pages in length. In addition, a source section briefly traces each tale's origin in the U.S. (Discretion is advised because of the subject matter.) Sequels: *More Scary Stories to Tell in the Dark*; *Scary Stories 3: More Tales to Chill Your Bones*. Other scary story collections: *Ask the Bones: Scary Stories from Around the World*, retold by

Arielle North Olson and Howard Schwartz; *Chills in the Night* by Jackie Vivelo; *Haunts* by Angela Shelf Medearis, and *In a Creepy, Creepy Place and Other Scary Stories* by Judith Gorog.

Uncle John's Great Big Bathroom Reader

FROM THE BATHROOM READERS' INSTITUTE

Grades 5 and up　　450 pages　Bathroom Readers' Press (Ashland, OR), 1998
Crude as the title may sound, the book's contents make up for it. You'll need a pretty strong immune system to resist the short but true anecdotes included here. The thousands of articles cover history, politics, family, death, movies, science, law and order, and myths. My bookstore had numerous editions, but not in the children's section; look for it in Humor/Reference. On the Web: www.bathroomreader.com.

Uncle Remus: The Complete Tales

RETOLD BY JULIUS LESTER; JERRY PINKNEY, ILLUS.

Grades 1–6　　600 pages　　　　　　　　　　　　　Fogelman, 1999
Just as captured slaves in America adapted their African folktales to a Southern locale, Prof. Julius Lester has moved them off the plantation and into the twentieth century without losing any of their wit, wisdom, or flavor. This celebrated black author has replaced Joel Chandler Harris's heavy dialect with a more contemporary and accessible Southern tongue in the mouth of an Uncle Remus who might be sitting on the front porch telling these forty-eight tales to his grandchild. This volume contains the text of four separate Uncle Remus retellings: *The Tales of Uncle Remus*; *More Tales of Uncle Remus*; *Further Tales of Uncle Remus*; and *The Last of the Uncle Remus Tales*.

Fairy and Folk Tales

The Arabian Nights

RETOLD BY BRIAN ALDERSON; MICHAEL FOREMAN, ILLUS.

Grades 4 and up　　191 pages　　　　　　　　　　　　Morrow, 1995
No collection of fairy or folk tales ever surpassed these tales from the Middle East, which inspired no less than Dickens and Andersen as children. Magnificently illustrated, the tales are retold here by the chief children's book reviewer for *The London Times*, and include "Sinbad," "Ali Baba," and "Aladdin."

Eric Carle's Treasury of Classic Stories for Children

BY ERIC CARLE

K–3   154 pages   *Orchard, 1988*

Here are twenty-two of the world's classic tales, from Aesop, Andersen, and the Brothers Grimm, retold and handsomely illustrated by one of today's great children's author-illustrators. On the Web: www.eric-carle.com.

From Sea to Shining Sea: A Treasury of American Folklore and Folk Songs

COMPILED BY AMY COHN

Grades 1–6   273 pages   *Scholastic, 1993*

More than 300 years' worth of songs, poems, stories, tall tales, celebrations, legends, tricksters, riddles, sports, animals, wars and struggles are packed in here. To give you an idea of the sweep of this volume (illustrated by eleven Caldecott Medal winners), "Yankee Doodle" is here, and so is Martin Luther King, Jr.'s, "I Have a Dream," and Abbott and Costello's "Who's on First?" routine.

Hans Andersen's Fairy Tales

TRANSLATED BY L. W. KINGSLAND; RACHEL BIRKETT, ILLUS.

Grades 3 and up   268 pages   *Oxford University Press, 1985*

This includes twenty-six of Andersen's best known tales in a single volume, complete with color and black-and-white illustrations. A Puffin paperback edition by the same name, edited by Naomi Lewis, is also excellent. Be sure to introduce children to Andersen's marvelous but largely unknown art work in *The Amazing Paper Cuttings of Hans Christian Andersen* by Beth Wagner Brust.

Individual Andersen volumes: *The Emperor's New Clothes*, translated by Naomi Lewis, illustrated by Angela Barrett; *The Match Girl*, retold and illustrated by Jerry Pinkney; *The Nightingale*, retold by Anthea Bell; *The Princess and the Pea*, illustrated by Dorothee Duntze; *The Snow Queen*, adapted by Naomi Lewis; *The Steadfast Tin Soldier*, illustrated by Fred Marcellino; *Thumbeline*, translated by Anthea Bell; *Seven Tales*, by Eva Le Gallienne; *The Snow Queen*, retold by Naomi Lewis; and *The Swan's Stories*, translated by Brian Alderson, illustrated by Chris Riddell (twelve lesser-known tales by Andersen, none dealing with people, but with household items that serve as small fables).

Household Stories of the Brothers Grimm

TRANSLATED BY LUCY CRANE; WALTER CRANE, ILLUS.

Grades 2 and up   269 pages   *Dover paperback, 1963*

This collection of fifty-three tales contains the Grimms' most popular works in a translation that is easily read aloud and includes more than one hundred illustrations. The maturity and listening experience of your audience should determine their readiness to handle the subject matter, complexity of plot, and language of these unexpurgated versions.

Individual Grimm volumes: *The Elves and the Shoemaker*, retold by Freya Littledale; *The Four Gallant Sisters*, retold by Eric A. Kimmel; *Hansel and Gretel*, retold by Rika Lesser; *Iron Hans*, illustrated by Marilee Heyer; *Rapunzel*, retold by Barbara Rogasky; *Rose Red and the Bear Prince*, retold by Dan Andreasen; *Rumpelstiltskin*, retold by Paul O. Zelinski; *Seven in One Blow*, retold by Eric A. Kimmell, illustrated by Megan Lloyd; *Sleeping Beauty*, retold by Trina Schart Hyman; and *Snow White & Rose Red*, illustrated by Gennady Spirin.

The Maid of the North: Feminist Folk Tales from Around the World

by Ethel Johnston Phelps

Grades 2 and up   174 pages   *Holt, 1981*

A collection of twenty-one fast-moving tales with witty, resourceful and confident heroines (not heroes) from seventeen different cultures. Also by the author: *Tatterhood and Other Tales*.

The People Could Fly: American Black Folktales

by Virginia Hamilton; Leo and Diane Dillon, illus.

Grades 3–6   174 pages   *Knopf, 1985*

Rich with rhythm, energy, and humor, these twenty-four stories were kept alive by slave tellers and include Bruh Rabbit, Gullah, and freedom-trail adventures. Related books: *Tales of Uncle Remus* (a).

The Serpent Slayer and Other Stories of Strong Women

BY KATRIN TCHANA; TRINA SCHART HYMAN, ILLUS.

Grades 3–6   105 pages   *Little, Brown, 2000.*

This handsome collection of eighteen fairy tales from around the world focuses on heroines and is handsomely illustrated by one of the most talented Caldecott winners ever.

Appendix A:

A Note for Doomsayers
Who Think Things Have
Never Been Worse

If you are among the many who think today's schools and students are appreciatively inferior to those of, let's say, 1941—think again. The last decade has not only seen an increase in the volume of calls to reform America's decaying schools, there also has been an increase in the amount of research that proves such indictments are hollow, self-serving rants.

Every time a national education report is issued, there's a feeding frenzy among pessimists and hearse followers. There was, for example, the national survey of adult literacy that led the news in September 1993—the one that showed almost one-half of the adult U.S. population cannot function adequately in reading or math.[1] The critics couldn't wait to declare, "I told you today's kids were dumb as posts compared to the ones in the good old days."

Were they right? Not quite. In their rush to judgment, they neglected to examine the report carefully—something Daniel Tanner did five years later.[2] He found the study had included a disproportionate number of immigrants who had never attended American schools; of the 25 percent who finished in the lowest levels of literacy, one-fifth were legally blind, and 25 percent had serious health problems; and prison inmates were over-represented in the study by 1200 percent. In other words, the adults in the sampling were *not* a representative sample of American adults.

Why this rush to indict the schools? The first thing to understand is the strong inclination of some people to burn their neighbor's house down in order to make their own house look better. When this is transferred to generations, we end up with insecure older citizens imagining their childhoods as better, smarter, and more civilized than the present one.

Those anchored to the dream of the "good old days" might consider these headlines, which read like today's newspaper:

*Don't ring in the "good old days"
until you know exactly
how bad they were.*

- *Yale Review* laments the admission of poorly prepared students.
- Of 331 students at the University of Wisconsin, only forty-one attend regular classes.
- Over one-half of students enrolled at Harvard, Princeton, Yale, and Columbia do not meet entrance requirements; developmental (remedial) courses are established.

Each of those headlines occurred *before* 1908.[3] The great institution of American education didn't turn sour in the last twenty-five years. If the truth be known, it has never been as great as the previous generation thought it was.

If you think the rhetoric and writing of our founding fathers was reflected in their citizenry, guess again. Prior to 1845, nearly all school examinations were done orally. When Boston tried written exams, a review of their results showed "beyond a doubt, that a large proportion of the scholars in our first classes, boys and girls of 14 or 15 years of age, when called upon to write simple sentences, to express their thoughts on common subjects, without the aid of a dictionary . . . , cannot write, without such errors in grammar, in spelling, and in punctuation."[4]

On a higher academic level, a dismayed and reform-minded university president indicted his own school with these words: "The school admitted students without any evidence of academic requirements; the classes were not graded; students entered any time and attended lectures then in progress; the school never examined the students, who left after eighteen months of lectures—with a degree." The school? The most prestigious law school in America—Harvard Law—in 1869.[5]

Those who bemoan today's video culture in favor of the days of yore when families sat around the open hearth reading should consider the lament of Dartmouth Professor of English C. F. Richardson in 1906: "A house without books has been well called a literary Sahara; and how many of them there are! We are a 'reading people'; but nothing is easier to find than homes in which the furniture, the pictures, the ornaments—everything, is an object of greater care and expense than the library. Is it any wonder that their inmates, whatever their so-called wealth or comfort, are intellectual starvlings?"[6]

Until 1890, most rural areas of America had no high schools and the urban centers had no standard curriculum. In Massachusetts, which boasted the most developed public school system, only one in ten high schools had college preparatory courses in 1890. By 1920, the situation had improved to where the average student completed *just one year* of high school and only 20 percent graduated that year. The graduation rate did jump dramatically during the 1930s—thanks to the Great Depression, which eliminated millions of jobs that adolescents would have left school to fill.[7] By 1940, we could boast the following:

♦ The school dropout rate was 76 percent[8] (compared to 10 percent in 1999[9]).
♦ Only 5 percent of the population had a college diploma (26 percent today).
♦ Only 8 percent of the black population had a high school diploma (75 percent in 1993).[10]

What About the SAT decline?

The story behind the mirage of the SAT decline begins in 1941—the golden year selected by the College Board as the "average" year's score for the SAT—500 points for either math or verbal. Each succeeding year's test takers would be measured against that score. And when the scores began to decline in the 1960s and continued to do so until the 1980s, many of us associated the drop with a lowered interest in reading and more time in front of the television. Those factors may have contributed, but they were minor next to a greater cause, largely ignored until the 1990s. It was a reason so obvious and powerful, it forced a dramatic revamping of the SAT scoring system in 1994.

Who exactly were the SAT class of 1941, the "whiz kids" who allegedly made today's students look so paltry? When "education archeologists" began digging, they came up with surprising answers. For one thing, they were 10,654 in number. Moreover, they were 98 percent white, 40 percent from private schools, and 60 percent male.[11] We also know the Depression was still affecting the nation, so the only people who could afford college in 1941 were the wealthy. The SAT class of 1941 was 10,654 rich white guys who became the national average for a half century.

The *real* change in school scores can be traced not to 1963, as is most commonly done, but to 1950 when the original G.I. Bill opened the doors of previously sacrosanct colleges and universities to thousands of World War II veterans, men who never would have qualified for college admission otherwise. To everyone's surprise, those non–college prep veterans survived college and graduated. With that, the halls of Ivy were wedged open, and it was impossible to close them again. Quietly, without fanfare, the barrier of elitism had been broken at American colleges and universities.

So with G.I. vets opening the collegiate dams, the wave of students that soon flooded campuses was not made up of the elite sons and daughters of college-educated parents, but *average* kids, the first generation to go beyond high school. Once average students began to take the SAT or college classes, the scores dropped. It was not because the top students were dumber or the teachers were worse. We had moved from a hand-picked class of all-stars to an assembly of average students.

The more select and elite the group taking the test, the higher the scores. For example, on the 2000 SAT, Mississippi's students scored 562 in the verbal, while Connecticut's averaged 508. Why the low score for Connecticut and the high score for Mississippi? Because only 4 percent of graduates took the test in Mississippi (elite, achieving seniors) while 81 percent took it in Connecticut—more of the average students. The truest test of each state's reading abilities is not the SAT but the NAEP assessments. In 1998, Connecticut had 42 percent of its eighth-graders reading at proficient or advanced levels and 18 percent below basic level; Mississippi had only 19 percent reading at the highest levels and 39 percent below basic.[12] The NAEP assessments, unlike the SAT, are not selective but represent a cross section of all children in the state and country.

By the turn of the millennium, the 10,654 who took the SAT in 1941 had grown to 1.2 million, with 83 percent from public schools, 54 percent women, 30 percent minorities (many from the lower socioeconomic levels), and 34 percent coming from families whose income was $40,000 or lower.[13] The class of 2000 was a national average.

Another advantage for that class of 1941 was they were a product of a peculiar decade in which the U.S. had its lowest immigration rate in one hundred years. Students of the 1990s come from a decade (1991–1999) in which immigration figures were the highest in a century.[14] By 1994, Massachusetts suburban school districts like Brookline could count 27 different languages being spoken by its students, while Miami, Florida, averaged 44, and Anaheim, California, included 67 different languages.[15]

The cynics who were scandalized by the poor showing by U.S. seventeen-year-olds and college seniors in the general history exam sponsored by the National Endowment for the Humanities in the late 1980s can take some solace in this headline from *The New York Times* front page on April 4, 1943: "Ignorance of U.S. History Shown by College Freshmen." The study included 7,000 college freshmen (then a very elite group), and when a follow-up exam was given to college seniors and military college freshmen, they also failed it.[16]

As one writer noted, the high school of 1940 might have been a superficially pleasanter, quieter place than the high school of today, but we need to remember that 49 percent of the students were excluded in 1940—the "pregnant, handicapped, learning disabled, emotionally disturbed, poor, and minority."[17] How much of a democratic experience could schooling have been if 49 percent of the students were excluded? Those who thought of schools as the great equalizers never checked the attendance records.

Those who think schools did such a better job in the good old days might want to consider how many actually finished school with any kind of a degree.[18]

Ages 25–34	High School Degree	
	1940	*1998*
Both Sexes	35%	87%

Ages 25–34	College Degree	
	1940	*1998*
Males	7%	26%
Females	5%	28.6%

A common failing of older generations is to set higher standards for today's children than existed for themselves. This was evident the day Gilbert Grosvenor, president of the National Geographic Society, held a press conference to announce U.S. students' failing grade in a geography survey. He announced that "We have found another lost generation." But when a reporter in the audience asked him if he himself could name the states that border Texas, he could not.[19]

If the Good Old Days Were Bad,
Where's the Good News Today?

For all the doomsaying we've heard in the last twenty years, you're about to read a most amazing accomplishment. *Fact:* There has been no significant drop in student reading or math scores since 1970. With that in mind, consider the rate of *household* changes since 1970: increases in the percentage of teen moms; of children living in single-parent households; of working moms; of fatherless homes; and of children living in poverty. Then factor in the number of TVs in the home (doubled) and the time they're watched per day (an hour more), and add all the video stores and cell phones (nonexistent in 1970). With those distractions working against the classroom, the miracle is there's been no *decline* in school scores in three decades. And it's another miracle we've managed the following:

+ A record percentage of African-American children now attend preschool, higher than even whites.[20]
+ There has been no decline in student IQ, and the number of students with 130 IQ (gifted) has doubled in the last two decades.[21]
+ Current NAEP math assessment showed 60 percent of seventeen-year-olds achieving advanced proficiency (up from 49 percent).[22]
+ Since 1982, the average high school student has increased to 25 the number of courses taken (from 22).[23]
+ The number of students taking highest-level math is up to 27 percent (from 11 percent in 1982) and chemistry and physics rests at 19 percent (up from only 7 percent).[24]
+ The number of bachelor's degrees in engineering, computer science, physical science, and mathematics has increased by more than 75 percent in the last twenty years, despite a decline in the college-age population.[25]
+ Today's faculties are the best educated in U.S. history. In 1961, only 23 percent of teachers had master's or doctoral degrees; by 1999, that figure had climbed to 52 percent.[26]
+ In a measurement of prose, document, and mathematical literacy, half of all teachers exceed 80 percent of all U.S. adults, and the average teacher is the equal of her college classmates, including physicians and lawyers, on the same tests.[27]
+ Women now make up 57 percent of college enrollments, up from 41 percent in 1970.[28]

♦ For the first time in U.S. history, women now outpace men in college and high school diplomas, greatly expanding the income base for women.[29]

How Do We Account for Lower U.S. Scores in International Competition?

Comparing U.S. students with other nations isn't logical unless the other country's demographics are similar to ours, and it almost never is. Do we compare the mileage of brand-new cars with ones that are twenty years old? So it doesn't make sense to compare America (owning a child poverty rate of 22 percent) with Germany (7 percent) or Finland (3 percent). U.S. teenagers' scores are not comparable to Japan's unless you separate teen moms from the study; in the U.S. the rate is sixty per thousand births, in Japan it's four.[30] Quite simply, the higher the poverty rate, the lower the school scores—everywhere in the world.

On the other hand, when international comparisons are made between the best in the U.S. and the best in other nations, we do very well, thank you. In the study, *How in the World Do Students Read?*[31], comparing more than two hundred thousand students (ages nine and fourteen) from thirty-two countries, the U.S. finished second among the nine-year-olds and eighth among the fourteen-year-olds. But when our *best* readers were singled out for comparisons, they were the best in the thirty-two countries.

Anyone wishing to dig deeper into these issues could do no better than to read *Setting the Record Straight: Responses to Misconceptions About Public Education in the United States* by Gerald W. Bracey.[32]

Nothing is more responsible for the good old days than a bad memory.

—FRANKLIN PIERCE ADAMS

Internet Sites for Children's Literature and Education

The Internet, like the U.S. interstate highway system, is a great time-saver—*if* you know where you're going! Without signposts, both systems can bog you down in traffic for hours. So here are Internet signposts (links) to my favorite children's literature, publishing, and education sites. (If you're looking for my site, it's included on the bio page at the front of this book.)

One word of caution: Because the Internet changes so rapidly, it's always risky to provide Internet addresses. This book will be unchanged for the next five years, but a Web address may change tomorrow. So if you encounter difficulty in reaching one of the sites below—let's say www.nces.gov/nationsreportcard/—you have two options: You can truncate the address, entering just www.nces.gov/ in the URL window of your browser, or you can go to a search engine like Metacrawler and enter the name of the site or organization—*National Assessment of Educational Progress*—as a phrase to find its new address.

Children's Book Publishers' Internet Home Pages

Publicity, news, author appearances, freebies, and publishers' catalogs:

Atheneum www.simonsays.com
Bantam Doubleday Dell www.bdd.com
Crown Publishers, Inc. www.randomhouse.com/kids
DK INK (DK, Dorling Kindersley) www.dk.com
Dial Books www.penguinputnam.com
Dutton Children's Books www.penguinputnam.com
Gulliver Books (Harcourt Trade Publishers) www.harcourtbooks.com

Harcourt Brace www.harcourtbooks.com

HarperCollins Children's Books www.harperchildrens.com

Houghton Mifflin www.hmco.com

Alfred A. Knopf, Inc. www.randomhouse.com/kids

Little, Brown Co. www.littlebrown.com

Margaret K. McElderry Books www.simonsayskids.com

Orchard Books www.grolier.com

Philomel Books www.penguinputnam.com

Puffin Books www.penguinputnam.com

G.P. Putnam's Sons www.penguinputnam.com

Random House Children's www.randomhouse.com/kids

Scholastic Inc. www.scholastic.com

Simon & Schuster www.simonsayskids.com

Viking Children's Books www.penguinputnam.com

Children's Book Council (The CBC) www.cbcbooks.org

> Dating back to its origins in 1944, this nonprofit trade association of children's book publishers has had one great purpose: to promote the reading of children's books. The site includes a wealth of material for teachers, librarians, parents, and students of children's literature.

Booksellers

♦ **The World Wide Web Virtual Library Publishers–Bookstores**
www.comlab.ox.ac.uk/archive/publishers/bookstores.html
The largest list of on-line bookstores anywhere in the world; you can't buy books here but you sure can find out where they're sold.

♦ **Amazon** www.amazon.com
The first and largest of on-line booksellers.

♦ **Barnes & Noble** www.bn.com
Runner-up to Amazon on the Web.

♦ **The BookWire Index** www.bookwire.com/index/booksellers.html
A comprehensive list of U.S. booksellers, on-line and off. BookWire is also the publishing industry's "insider's view"—an on-line source for news, reviews, author interviews and appearances, literary events, and links to hundreds of book and author sites.

♦ **BookFinder** www.bookfinder.com

Looking for that favorite childhood book (or any book) that's out of print? Find a free search here that will locate it in a database of inventories from used bookstores in North America. For example, when I searched for Mel Ellis's adolescent novel *This Mysterious River* (out of print for fifteen years), BookFinder provided me with twenty sale sites, physical descriptions of each copy, prices ranging from $4.75 to $27, and e-mail connections to many of these stores if I wished to make a purchase.

♦ **Bibliofind** www.bibliofind.com

An excellent used/out-of-print book search vehicle.

♦ **ALibris** www.alibris.com

This used/out-of-print book search has become one of the largest and most popular.

♦ **Advanced Book Exchange** www.abebooks.com

One of the largest vehicles for searching used, OP, or rare books, including a database of twelve million titles.

♦ **The Big Link** www.booksearch.com

This site operates in a fashion similar to BookFinder (above).

♦ **Language Education Associates** input.languagebooks/com/
   education/

If you're shopping for the published works of Stephen Krashen, Frank Smith, and Jeff McQuillan, here's your one-stop shopping spot. It is the most complete resource for the hundreds of articles published by Krashen.

Children's Literature and Reading

♦ **The Children's Literature Web Guide** www.acs.ucalgary.ca/
   ~dkbrown/

This is the ultimate Web site for Children's Lit, constructed by Professor David K. Brown of the Doucette Library of Teaching at the University of Calgary. Consider the list of subjects addressed at the site: Essential Kid Lit Web sites; Discussion Boards; Children's Book Awards; The Year's Best Books; Children's Bestsellers; Teaching Ideas for Children's Books; Authors on the Web; Readers' Theatre; Journals and Book Reviews; Resources for Teachers; Resources for Parents; Resources for Storytellers; Resources for Writers and Illustrators; Children's Literature Organizations on the Internet; Children's Publishers and Booksellers on the Internet.

♦ **"Choices" Awards** www.reading.org/choices/
Each year, 10,000 students and teachers across America vote on the best
books published in a given year. Under the auspices of the International
Reading Association and the Children's Book Council, each year's tally is
divided into three categories (Children; Young Adults; and Teachers) and
can be found here at the IRA home site. (Adobe Acrobat files)

♦ **Carol Hurst's Children's Literature Site** www.carolhurst.com/index.
html
Long-time children's book critic for K–8/*Learning Years* magazine, children's librarian, author, and nationally acclaimed storyteller, Carol Otis
Hurst offers up a wealth of collected children's literature ideas, reviews,
and curriculum ideas.

♦ **Center for the Study of Books in Spanish for Children &**
Adolescents coyote.csusm.edu/campus_center/csb/english/
This is the most comprehensive site for children's literature in Spanish.
Under the direction of Dr. Isabel Schon (California State University, San
Marcos, CA), the site includes reviews, conferences, and extensive lists of
outstanding children's titles that are available in both English and Spanish.

♦ **Book Links** www.ala.org/BookLinks/
Here's the best new children's literature print journal to appear in the last
twenty-five years. Published by the American Library Association, it is an
outstanding resource for teachers and librarians, as well as parents interested
in extending their knowledge of children's lit.

♦ **School Library Journal's "Best Books of the Year"** www.slj.com/
articles/articles/articlesindex.asp
School Library Journal's reviewers (school librarians from across America)
comb through the 4,000 books they review annually and select the best
sixty-plus of the year (grades K–12, fiction and nonfiction). They're listed
at the SLJ Web site, along with brief reviews.

♦ **International Reading Association** www.reading.org and www.
readingonline.org
The home site of the largest organization of reading professionals in the
world, the International Reading Association (IRA), it includes featured
articles from the most recent issue of *The Reading Teacher*.

History

♦ **American Studies WEB** www.georgetown.edu/crossroads/asw
For older students, here is a guide to American studies on the Internet—
the whole academic ball game is here.

♦ **Smithsonian Exhibitions on the Web** www.sil.si.edu/SILPublications/
Online-Exhibitions/online-exhibitions-title.htm
When a special exhibit is mounted at a major museum almost anywhere in
the world, it now is accompanied by a digital version on-line. In addition,
many museums create special on-line exhibition halls to promote their libraries and archives. This single site, based on the Smithsonian Institution's
Web page, provides a master list of hundreds of digital exhibitions.

♦ **American Memory** lcweb2.loc.gov/ammem/
The historical collection for the National Digital Library (within the Library of Congress) is a collection of digital photos, images, documents,
films, maps, and sound recordings. It contains ongoing exhibits of important American documents and is the on-line equivalent of an American
history museum.

Internet Skills

♦ **Miss Rumphius Awards** web.syr.edu/~djleu/RTEACHER/
rumphius.html
Every day, tens of thousands of new Web pages are added to the Internet,
including those created by teachers and their classes. The best of those are
cited here, honored by the teachers' board at the RTEACHER listserv.
Named after Barbara Cooney's award-winning character, who spreads
lupine seeds wherever she goes, these sites spread literacy and creativity
across the World Wide Web.

♦ **Surf For** www.slj.com/articles/surffor/surfforarchive.asp
Reading Gail Junion-Metz's columns on surfing the Internet is like having
a full-time guide at your side. If it's any good, Metz has been there. Her
column runs monthly in *School Library Journal* and back columns are listed
by subject, from holidays and chat room safety to biography and science
sites. The site listed here will take you to her column archives.

- **American Library Association Guide to Cyberspace**
  www.ala.org/parentspage/greatsites/guide.html
  ALA offers a straightforward introduction to the Internet for Web-amateur parents and children. The same skills needed to negotiate your neighborhood library's shelves and catalogs must be used to surf the net in a meaningful way.

Libraries and Research

- **Britannica** www.ebig.com/
  Britannica editors have searched the Web and offer here more than 75,000 sites—rated, reviewed, and classified for your research convenience. (See also AskERIC below.)

- **The Library of Congress** www.loc.gov/
  The nation's most comprehensive library offers a catalog of its holdings, as well as exhibitions of its treasures (American Memory), pending legislation before Congress, and catalogs of its holdings.

- **America's Story** www.americastory.gov
  This is a more user-friendly site for the Library of Congress (see previous listing), extremely story- and entertainment-oriented, and sure to be a favorite of families.

- **StudyWeb** www.studyweb.com
  Here are 68,000 links to education research, sorted according to grade levels, and includes downloadable images for reports and projects, and an excellent subject index.

- **Metacrawler** www.metacrawler.com
  Here's my favorite *comprehensive* search engine, finding even the most obscure items on the Web. It queries almost a dozen other search engines (including many of the famous ones), organizes and ranks the results by relevance. You're able to use not just one engine, but all of them at once! An added incentive: Almost no advertising! *Caution:* This is not a search engine for children, so they should not use it unattended. For adults, it's excellent. Also: www.google.com.

- **Kid-Safe Search Sites**
  Here are three excellent search sites geared for children, with filters built in to protect them from adult Web sites. Searches with Yahooligans and

Searchopolis produce numerous high-quality sites, under category headers. Yahooligans and Ask Jeeves For Kids are geared for children 7–12, while Searchopolis aims at the 10–18 audience, with the results for the latter producing more mature but not offensive material. You might also consider the two excellent "homework" search sites listed in the Parenting section.

♦ **Ask Jeeves For Kids** www.ajkids.com
Unlike traditional search engines, the seeker types in a complete sentence or question and Jeeves provides sites that will answer the query.

♦ **Yahooligans** www.yahooligans.com

♦ **Searchopolis** www.searchopolis.com

Parents

♦ **Infoplease Homework Center** www.infoplease.com/homework/index.html
Here's a site *The New York Times* called a "strong, reliable solution to homework troubles." It offers a comprehensive list of search categories. Also receiving equally high accolades in the *Times'* homework article was HomeworkCentral.com, with an even larger list of categories for "kid-friendly" searches.

♦ **ALFY** www.alfy.com/ALFY
Here's a Web portal or entry that is extremely "kid-friendly," providing access and entry to thousands of safe, child-oriented Web sites—an excellent family portal to the World Wide Web. The subjects and contents of the sites in its portal have been carefully scrutinized and deemed both safe and user-friendly for children. ALFY is geared for children ages 3–10, and includes a graphical index that can be used by young children who are preliterate or nonreaders. The site also includes educational and entertaining games.

♦ **Book Adventure** www.bookadventure.org
Call this a "poor man's" *Accelerated Reader*. Sponsored by Sylvan Learning Center Foundation, Barnes&Noble.com, Houghton Mifflin, and R. R. Bowker, it amounts to a reading club that a child joins, chooses one of the 3,000 titles from among dozens of categories and reading levels (K–8 range), obtains the book from the library, reads it, and then returns to take a brief quiz on the story. Successful scores are rewarded with very simple

prizes or points. While its simplicity offers no threat to the major reading incentive programs, that same simplicity will do no harm to young readers who might enjoy competing against the computer for answers.

♦ **LD Online: Learning Disabilities Information & Resources**
www.ldonline.org

Much of what a parent or teacher needs to know about learning disabilities, including the latest research findings on a wide variety of disabilities, can be found here. There are lists of resources—national and state organizations and agencies—as well as on-line resources, along with LD chat, and an "ask the expert" area connecting you via bulletin boards.

♦ **National Geographic XPEDITIONS** www.nationalgeographic.
com/xpeditions

Families and teachers looking for a Web site that offers activities that reinforce geography (as well as the new U.S. classroom standards) need look no further than this site. Every other week you'll find a new activity, along with teacher-tested ideas and family activities.

Teaching

♦ **Education Week** www.edweek.com

No one covers education the way this weekly newspaper does. From politics and curriculum issues to the latest in research, they've got it all, and the weekly opinion essays draw some of the nation's best education thinkers. The on-line site contains a well-loaded archive with search.

♦ **AskERIC** www.askeric.org/about

ERIC is an acronym for Educational Resources Information Center, a federally funded national information system providing information on education-related issues. Primarily used in research by librarians, teachers, and administrators, it also is available for parents. The site enables the visitor to either ask an education-related question ("What are the effects of year-round schooling on elementary students?"), search for and obtain accredited lesson plans for given subjects, or search ERIC's database for research articles and books on a given subject (a search for "reading aloud" returned the titles and authors of 921 documents on the subject). With such titles in hand, your local college or university usually can give you a printout of the actual microfiched documents or directions for purchasing same from an ERIC Support Component. The AskERIC net site will not give you the actual research but it sure points you in the right direction.

♦ **National Assessment of Educational Progress** www.nces.gov/
nationsreportcard/
By far the most reliable assessment of student scores for the last thirty years, this site provides the latest scoring patterns in reading, math, science, and writing—state by state, regionally or nationally. This is truly the Nation's Report Card.

♦ **NPR Transcripts** www.npr.org/inside/transcripts/
Remember that program you heard three months ago on National Public Radio, the one about advertising's influence on children? It would be perfect for the unit you're writing, if only you had a copy of the show. "If only . . ." is no longer wishful thinking. Here you can wend your way through the index of past and present programs, find your show, and then: (1) listen to it as a Webcast; or (2) order it on either audiocassette or as a printed transcript.

♦ **The English Companion** www.englishcompanion.com
Jim Burke, a California high school English teacher and author, has created a comprehensive and practical Web site for English teachers. It features NCTE news, censorship alerts and resources, English newsletters, news on TV shows connected to language arts, recommended readings, a collection of Burke's articles, and test-taking and college essay tips. Burke is the author of *I Hear America Reading* (Heinemann) and *The English Teacher's Companion* (Boynton/Cook).

♦ **Teachnet.Com** www.teachnet.com/
A *must* stop on the internet for professional educators, this site covers the profession of teaching from A to Z. Syntheses on new research in all curricula, information on academic competitions from math to music and art, information on new school products, listings of teacher resources in various geographic regions of the U.S., and guides to Web sites like the one devoted to classrooms with one or two Macs.

♦ **Teacher's Online Notebook** www.technology4u.com/ton/
This site offers a collection of continually updated, excellent links to education-oriented sites, including the Arts, Language Arts, Science, Current Events, Educational Technology, Math, Social Studies, Exceptional Needs, Multicultural, and a Research Toolkit.

Notes

Introduction

1. Jay R. Campbell, Catherine M. Hombo, and John Mazzeo, *NAEP 1999 Trends in Academic Progress: Three Decades of Student Performance*, U.S. Department of Education (Washington, DC: National Center for Education Statistics, 2000). Also available at http://nces.ed.gov/nationsreportcard.
2. Kenneth Gray, "The Baccalaureate Game: Is it Right for all Teens?" *Phi Delta Kappan*, April 1996, pp. 528–34.
3. Ibid.
4. Ibid.
5. Gerald W. Bracey, "Time Outside School," *Phi Delta Kappan*, September 1991, p. 88: "Starting at birth, a child spends only 9 percent of his or her life in school, 91 percent of it elsewhere."
6. Jerry West, Kristin Denton, Elvira Germino-Hausken, *America's Kindergartners: Findings from the Early Childhood Longitudinal Study, Kindergarten Class of 1998–99, Fall 1998,* Office of Educational Research and Improvement, NCES 2000-070 (Washington, DC: U.S. Department of Education, 2000).
7. Ibid. See also: *The Condition of Education 2000,* Rebecca Pratt, managing editor, U.S. Department of Education, Office of Educational Research and Improvement, NCES 2000-062 (Washington, DC: U.S. Government Printing Office, 2000), p. 147. Also available at http://nces.ed.gov/pubsearch/index/asp.
8. Lawrence E. Gladieux and Watson Scott Swail, "Beyond Access: Improving the Odds of College Success," *Phi Delta Kappan*, May 2000, pp. 688–92.
9. Ruben G. Rumbaut, "The New Californians: Assessing the Educational Progress of Children of Immigrants," ERIC document: ED398 294, based upon chapter 2, *California's Immigrant Children: Theory, Research, and Implications for Education Policy,* Ruben G. Rumbaut and Wayne A. Cornelius, eds. (San Diego, CA: April 1996, Center for U.S.–Mexican Studies, University of California).
10. Ronald Steel, "America Remains No. 1," *The New York Times Magazine,* September 29, 1996, pp. 111.
11. Paul E. Barton and Richard J. Coley, "Captive Students: Education and Training in America's Prisons" (Princeton, NJ: ETS Policy Information Center, 1996).
12. Tim Simmons, "A Crisis out of Hiding," from Special Section: "Worlds Apart: The Racial Education Gap," *Charlotte* (NC) *News & Observer,* December 27, 1999, pp. 1, 3.
13. Hilary T. Holbrook, "Sex Differences in Reading: Nature or Nurture," *Journal of Reading,* 31, March 1988, pp. 574–77.

14. A. D. Gross, "Sex Role Standards and Reading Achievement: A Study of an Israeli Kibbutz System," *The Reading Teacher,* 1978, 32, pp. 149–56.

15. Hilary T. Holbrook, "Sex Differences in Reading: Nature or Nurture?"; also J. Downing and C. K. Leong, *Psychology of Reading* (New York: Macmillan, 1982).

16. Cornelius Riordan, "The Silent Gender Gap: Reading, Writing, and Other Problems for Boys," *Education Week,* November 17, 1999, pp. 46, 49. See also Christina Hoff Sommers, "Where the Boys Are," *Education Week,* June 22, 1996, pp. 52, 42; Christina Hoff Sommers, "The War Against Boys," *The Atlantic Monthly,* May 2000, pp. 59–74; and *Trends in Educational Equity of Girls and Women,* U.S. Department of Education (Washington, DC: National Center for Education Statistics, March 2000).

17. Henry Wechsler, Ph.D., and others, "Binge Drinking, Tobacco, and Illicit Drug Use and Involvement in College Athletics: A Survey of Students at 140 American Colleges," *Journal of American College Health,* March 1997, pp. 195–200. In a study of 28,000 students at 140 American colleges, researchers found the single worst group of binge drinkers on campus were student athletes.

18. *Trends in Educational Equity of Girls and Women,* U.S. Department of Education (Washington, DC: National Center for Education Statistics, March 2000).

19. You could start with H. G. Bissenger's book about the year he spent in the high school football capital of America, Odessa, Texas: *Friday Night Lights* (DaCapo); next, travel to an affluent New Jersey suburb in *Our Guys* by Bernard Lefkowitz (University of California Press), describing the infamous Glen Ridge, New Jersey, gang-rape case involving the community's star athletes and a retarded girl; and finally, the book *Sports Illustrated* suggested "might be the greatest sports biography ever written," David Maraniss's *When Pride Still Mattered: A Life of Vince Lombardi* (Simon & Schuster), about the glory and emotional havoc that come with an unchecked obsession with sports.

20. Clyde C. Robinson, Jean M. Larsen, and Julia H. Haupt, "Picture Book Reading at Home: A Comparison of Head Start and Middle-Class Preschoolers," *Early Education & Development,* July 1995, vol. 6, no. 3, pp. 241–52.

21. Photo by Jean Shifrin, *The Atlanta Journal-Constitution,* September 25, 1996; used by permission.

22. Janelle M. Gray, "Reading Achievement and Autonomy as a Function of Father-to-Son Reading" (master's thesis 1991, California State University, Stanislaus, CA, 1991).

23. Mary A. Foertsch, *Reading In and Out of School,* Educational Testing Service/Education Information Office (Washington, DC: U.S. Department of Education, May 1992).

24. Richard C. Anderson, Elfrieda H. Hiebert, Judith A. Scott, Ian A.G. Wilkinson, *Becoming a Nation of Readers: The Report of the Commission on Reading* (Champaign-Urbana, IL: Center for the Study of Reading, 1985). See also Diane Ravitch and Chester Finn, *What Do Our 17-Year-Olds Know?* (New York: Harper & Row, 1987).

25. "Students Cite Pregnancies as a Reason to Drop Out," Associated Press, in *The New York Times,* September 14, 1994, p. B7.
26. Melissa Lee, "When It Comes to Salary, It's Academic," *The Washington Post,* July 22, 1994, p. D1. The Census Bureau reports the following lifetime earnings:

No high school diploma	$609,000
High school diploma	$821,000
Some college	$993,000
Associate's degree	$1,062,000
Bachelor's degree	$1,421,000
Master's degree	$1,619,000
Doctorate	$2,142,000
Profession—doctor, lawyer	$3,013,000

See also Gerald W. Bracey, "The Fourth Bracey Report on the Condition of Public Education," *Phi Delta Kappan,* October 1994, p. 123; Robert B. Reich, "The Fracturing of the Middle Class," *The New York Times,* August 31, 1994, p. A19. Reich notes that a male with a college degree will earn 83 percent more than his counterpart with only a high school diploma.
27. Every time a student's family income increases by $5,000, the student's SAT score (either math or verbal) rises; for each $5,000 decrease, the score drops. This holds true every year and for every ethnic group. See Christopher de Vinck, "An Open Book," The *College Board Review,* Spring 1991, pp. 9–12, vol. 159; also *USA Today* chart, August 19, 1993, p. 3D.
28. Eugene Rogot, Paul D. Sorlie, and Norman J. Johnson, "Life Expectancy by Employment Status, Income, and Education in the National Longitudinal Mortality Study," *Public Health Reports,* July–August 1992, vol. 107, pp. 457–61; see also Jack M. Guralnik and others, "Educational Status and Active Life Expectancy Among Older Blacks and Whites," *The New England Journal of Medicine,* July 8, 1993, pp. 110–16; E. Pamuk and others, *Health, United States, 1998: Socioeconomic Status and Health Chartbook* (Hyattsville, MD: National Center for Health Statistics, 1998).
29. Paul E. Barton and Richard J. Coley, "Captive Students: Education and Training in America's Prisons," Educational Testing Service (Princeton, NJ: ETS Policy Information Center, 1996). More education lowers the chance of going to prison, and twenty years of research (J. Gerber) shows a positive connection to a lower recidivism rate with more education while in prison. Nonetheless, some states spend less than $300 a year per inmate on education, with Wisconsin, California, Mississippi, and Alaska being the lowest.
30. Harold L. Hodgkinson, *The Same Client: The Demographics of Education and Service Delivery Systems* (Washington, DC: Institute of Educational Leadership/Center for Demographic Policy, 1989), p. 15.
31. Paul E. Barton and Richard J. Coley, "Captive Students: Education and Training in America's Prisons."
32. Edward B. Fiske, "Can Money Spent on Schools Save Money That Would Be Spent on Prisons?," *The New York Times,* September 27, 1989, p. B10.
33. Hodgkinson, *The Same Client,* p. 16.

34. The listing below indicates the bottom ten states for high school graduation rates (1998) and their ranking in prison population (1999): "Prison and Jail Inmates at Midyear 1999," U.S. Department of Justice (Washington, DC: Bureau of Justice Statistics, April 2000), p. 3; and "Dropout Rates in the United States: 1998," National Center for Education Statistics, NCES 2000-022 (Washington, DC: U.S. Department of Education, November 1999), p. 57. The listing here shows each of the ten states' national ranking in high school graduation rates and rank in per capita prison population.

Oregon	50	13
Arizona	49	41
Nevada	48	42
New Mexico	47	12
Texas	45	48
California	44	40
Louisiana	43	49
Mississippi	42	46
Florida	41	37
Alabama	40	44

35. Kate Zernike, "Gap Widens Again on Tests Given to Blacks and Whites," *The New York Times,* August 25, 2000, p. A14. The article plots the racial gap in NAEP scores that has widened since the 1980s between white and black students in math, science, and reading, including a decline among students coming from the best-educated black families.

Chapter 1: Why Read Aloud?

1. Mary A. Foertsch, *Reading In and Out of School,* Educational Testing Service/Education Information Office (Washington, DC: U.S. Department of Education, May 1992), pp. 6–7, 35–36.
2. Richard C. Anderson, Elfrieda H. Hiebert, Judith A. Scott, Ian A.G. Wilkinson, *Becoming a Nation of Readers: The Report of the Commission on Reading* (Champaign-Urbana, IL: Center for the Study of Reading, 1985), p. 23.
3. Ibid., p. 51.
4. *Literacy: Profiles of America's Young Adults,* National Assessment of Educational Progress (Princeton, NJ: Educational Testing Service, 1987).
5. "Illiteracy Seen as Threat to U.S. Economic Edge," *The New York Times,* September 7, 1988, p. B8.
6. "Foreign-Aid Agency Shifts to Problems Back Home," *The New York Times* June 26, 1994, pp. A1, A18.
7. Edward A. Gargan, "India Among the Leaders in Software for Computers," *The New York Times,* December 29, 1993, pp. A1, A7.
8. Anne D. Neal and Jerry L. Martin, "Losing America's Memory: Historical Illiteracy in the 21st Century" (Washington, DC: American Council of Trustees and Alumni, 2000). See also "History 101: Snoop Doggy Roosevelt," *The New York Times,* July 2, 2000, p. WK7. The *Times* article contains all thirty-four questions and answers from the exam.
9. Kenneth Gray, "The Baccalaureate Game: Is It Right for All Teens?" *Phi Delta Kappan,* April 1996, pp. 528–34.

10. Ibid.

11. Ibid.

12. Ina V.S. Mullis and others, *NAEP 1992 Trends in Academic Progress,* Office of Educational Research and Improvement (Washington, DC: U.S. Department of Education, June 1994). See also *America's Smallest School,* Policy Information Center (Princeton, NJ: Educational Testing Service, 1992). Also Patricia L. Donahue and others, *NAEP 1998 Reading Report Card for the Nation and the States,* U.S. Department of Education, NCES 1999-500 (Washington, DC: National Center for Education Statistics, 1999). Also at http://nces.ed.gov/.

13. Ibid.

14. Jay R. Campbell, Catherine M. Hombo, and John Mazzeo, *NAEP 1999 Trends in Academic Progress: Three Decades of Student Performance,* U.S. Department of Education (Washington, DC: National Center for Education Statistics, 2000), pp. 31–40.

15. Jacques Barzun, *Begin Here* (Chicago, IL: University of Chicago Press, 1991), pp. 114–16.

16. Thomas Jefferson in letter to Colonel Charles Yancey, January 6, 1816.

17. Gordon Rattray Taylor, *The Natural History of the Brain* (New York: E. P. Dutton, 1979), pp. 59–60.

18. Keith E. Stanovich, "Matthew Effects in Reading: Some Consequences of Individual Differences in the Acquisition of Literacy," *Reading Research Quarterly,* Fall 1986, pp. 360–407; Richard L. Allington, "Oral Reading," in *Handbook of Reading Research,* P. David Pearson, ed. (New York: Longman, 1984), pp. 829–64; Warwick B. Elley and Francis Mangubhai, "The impact of reading on second language learning," *Reading Research Quarterly,* Fall 1983, pp. 53–67; Mary A. Foertsch, *Reading In and Out of School.*

19. Mary A. Foertsch, *Reading In and Out of School.*

20. Warwick B. Elley, *How in the World Do Students Read?* (Hamburg: International Association for the Evaluation of Educational Achievement, July 1992). Available from the International Reading Association, Newark, DE, $16/$12.

21. "How to Make a Better Student," *Time,* October 19, 1998, pp. 78–96.

22. Jacques Steinberg, "Experts Call for Mix of 2 Methods to Teach Reading: Phonics and Meaning," *The New York Times,* March 19, 1998, pp. A1, A15.

23. Kathleen Kennedy Manzo, "Reading Scores Fall in Some Schools Awarded Grants to Emphasize Phonics," *Education Week,* January 12, 2000, p. 12.

24. Elton G. Stetson and Richard P. Williams, "Learning from Social Studies Textbooks: Why Some Students Succeed and Others Fail," *Journal of Reading,* September 1992, pp. 22–30.

25. Christopher Hitchens, "Why We Don't Know What We Don't Know," *The New York Times Magazine,* May 13, 1990, p. 32.

26. Jerry West, Kristin Denton, Elvira Germino-Hausken, *America's Kindergartners: Findings from the Early Childhood Longitudinal Study, Kindergarten Class of 1998–99, Fall 1998,* Office of Educational Research and Improvement, NCES 2000-070 (Washington, DC: U.S. Department of Education, 2000).

27. Courtney B. Cazden, *Child Language and Education* (New York: Holt, Rinehart and Winston, 1972).

28. Psychologist Burton L. White interviewed in "Training Parents Helps Toddlers," *The New York Times*, October 2, 1985, p. C1.
29. George A. Miller and Patricia M. Gildea, "How Children Learn Words," *Scientific American*, September 1987, pp. 94–99.
30. *Starting Points: The report of the Carnegie Task Force on Meeting the Needs of Young Children*, Carnegie Corporation of New York (New York: Carnegie Corporation, 1994), p. 5.
31. "How Frequently Do You . . . ?" *Education Week*, PTA/Dodge national parent survey/*Newsweek*, April 4, 1990, p. 22.
32. Betty Hart and Todd Risley, *Meaningful Differences in the Everyday Experience of Young American Children* (Baltimore, MD: Brookes Publishing, 1996). See also Paul Chance, "Speaking of Differences," *Phi Delta Kappan*, March 1997, pp. 506–7.
33. M. J. Adams and A. W. F. Huggins, "The Growth of Children's Sight Vocabulary: A Quick Test with Educational and Theoretical Implications," *Reading Research Quarterly*, vol. 20, 1985, pp. 262–81.
34. M. F. Graves and others, "Word Frequency as a Predictor of Students' Reading vocabularies," *Journal of Reading Behavior*, vol. 12, 1980, pp. 117–27.
35. M. F. Graves, G. J. Brunetti, and W. H. Slater, "The Reading Vocabularies of Primary Grade Children of Varying Geographic and Social Backgrounds," in J. A. Niles and L. A. Harris, eds. *New inquiries in reading research and instruction* (Rochester, NY: National Reading Conference, 1982), pp. 99–104. Also T. G. White, M. F. Graves, and W. H. Slater, "Growth of Reading Vocabulary in Diverse Elementary Schools: Decoding and Word Meaning," *Journal of Educational Psychology*, vol. 82, no. 2, 1990, pp. 281–90.
36. Linda Jacobson, "Study: Program Started in Infancy Has Positive Effect in Adult Years," *Education Week*, October 27, 1999, p. 6. Also at www.fpg.unc.edu/overview/abc/abcov.htm.
37. Georges Vernez, Richard Krop, and C. Peter Ryde, "Closing the Education Gap: Benefits and Costs," RAND Corporation (Santa Monica, CA: RAND Corporation, 1999), p. 143. The figures I used here were an *average* for all ethnic groups, though each projects slightly different incomes, according to their social and ethnic demographics.
38. Donald P. Hayes and Margaret G. Ahrens, "Vocabulary Simplification for Children: A Special Case for 'Motherse,'" *Journal of Child Language*, vol. 15, 1988, pp. 395–410.
39. Ibid., pp. 401, 403.
40. Caroline Hendrie, "Chicago Data Show Mixed Summer Gain," *Education Week*, September 10, 1999, pp. 1, 14. See also Diane Ravitch, "Summer School Isn't a Solution," *The New York Times*, March 3, 2000, p. A25.
41. Mary A. Foertsch, *Reading In and Out of School*.
42. "In School: A Photocopier Salesman Does His Job Too Well, and the Taxpayers Foot the Bill," *The New York Times*, June 29, 1994, p. A12.
43. Patricia L. Donahue and others, *NAEP 1998 Reading Report Card for the Nation and the States*, U.S. Department of Education, NCES 1999-500 (Washington, DC: National Center for Education Statistics, 1999), p. 20. Also at http://nces.ed.gov/.

44. *1992 NAEP Reading Assessment, National Assessment of Educational Progress* (Princeton, NJ: Educational Testing Service, 1993). The worksheet category was not included in the 1998 assessment data, but there is nothing to indicate any change in classroom strategies between the 1992 assessment and 1998 (scores remained the same); if anything, with the increased emphasis on systematic intensive phonics instruction in California and Texas, there may be even more emphasis on worksheets.

45. Patricia L. Donahue and others, *NAEP 1998 Reading Report Card for the Nation and the States,* p. 99.

46. George Vecsey, "Mystique Returns to Yankees," *The New York Times*, sports column, July 12, 1985.

47. K. Jackym, Richard L. Allington, and Kathleen A. Broikou, "Estimating the Cost," *The Reading Teacher,* October 1989, pp. 30–35.

48. Olga Emery and Mihaly Csikszentmihalyi, "The Socialization Effects of Cultural Role Models in Ontogenetic Development and Upward Mobility," *Child Psychiatry and Development and Human Development,* Fall 1981, pp. 3–18.

49. Bruno Bettelheim, *The Uses of Enchantment: The Meaning and Importance of Fairy Tales* (New York: Knopf, 1976), pp. 3–6.

50. Robert Penn Warren, "Why Do We Read Fiction," *The Saturday Evening Post,* October 20, 1962, pp. 82–84.

51. *Time,* February 1, 1988, pp. 52–58; also Mark D. O'Donnell, "Boston's Lewenberg Middle School Delivers Success," *Phi Delta Kappan,* March 1997, pp. 508–12. The *Kappan* article describes how Tom O'Neill didn't just affect the language arts curriculum. He also spearheaded a physical rebirth in the school, and a remarkable six-week physical education program built around Project Adventure, an intense climbing regimen. There is also a detailed description of O'Neill's adventures with an often inept school department and an obstructionist custodial union, and the resulting triumph of the school. For his work at Lewenberg, O'Neill was named one of the inaugural recipients of the "Heroes in Education" award, presented by *Reader's Digest* to educators with original and effective methods. The award included $10,000 to the school. He is now retired from education.

52. Howard W. French, "Tokyo Dropouts' Vocation: Painting the Town," *The New York Times,* March 12, 2000, pp. A1, A18: "In the place of the nose-to-the-grindstone ethic of long study hours and single-minded focus on exams and careers that helped build postwar Japan, the motto of the current 15- to 18-year-olds seems to be that girls and boys just want to have fun." Since 1997, Japan has seen its school dropout rate increase by 20 percent.

53. Kazue Suzuki, " 'Reading Hour' Transports Children to a World of Imagination," *Asahi Evening News* (daily Japanese English-language newspaper), May 17, 1998, LIFE Section, p. 9. According to the Japanese publisher Tohan, the number of schools using SSR in the morning had grown to 3,500 by March 2000.

54. Geoffrey C. Godbey and John P. Robinson, *Time for Life* (University Park, PA: Pennsylvania State University Press, 1997).

55. Jodi Wilgoren, "After Success with Poor, Schools Try Cloning," *The New York Times,* August 16, 2000, pp. A1, A26.

56. Chris Erskine, "Book Habit Puts Dad, Son on the Same Page," *The Los Angeles Times,* April 22, 1998, pp. 1E, 3E: Used by permission of the author.

Chapter 2: When to Begin Read-Aloud

1. These remarks were made during a half-hour interview (September 3, 1979) with Dr. Brazelton conducted by John Merrow for *Options in Education,* a co-production of National Public Radio and the Institute for Educational Leadership of the George Washington University.
2. Anthony J. DeCasper and Melanie J. Spence, "Prenatal Maternal Speech Influences Newborns' Perception of Speech Sounds," *Infant Behavior and Development,* 1986, 9 (2), pp. 133–50.
3. Marjory Roberts, "Class Before Birth," *Psychology Today,* May 1987, p. 41; Sharon Begley and John Carey, "The Wisdom of Babies," *Newsweek,* January 12, 1981, pp. 71–72.
4. Dorothy Butler, *Cushla and Her Books* (Boston: The Horn Book, 1980).
5. One year after my first meeting with Mrs. Kunishima, *Reader's Digest* made her family's story its lead article: "The Family That Wouldn't Be Broken," by John Pekkanen, *Reader's Digest,* December 1993, pp. 45–50.
6. Vera Propp, "All Babies Are Born Equal."
7. Gerald W. Bracey, "American Students Near the Top in Reading," *Phi Delta Kappan,* February 1993, pp. 496–97. You'll find everything you need to know about the Finnish reading philosophy in the following: Leonard B. Finkelstein, "Finland's Lessons: Learning Thrives in a Land Where It Is Respected," Commentary, *Education Week,* October 18, 1995, p. 31; Viking Brunell, and Pirjo Linnakylä, "Swedish speakers' literacy in the Finnish society," *Journal of Reading,* February 1994, pp. 368–75; Pirjo Linnakylä, "Subtitles prompt Finnish children to read," *Reading TODAY* (Newark, DE: International Reading Association, October/November 1993), p. 31.
8. Warwick B. Elley, *How in the World Do Students Read?* (Hamburg: International Association for the Evaluation of Educational Achievement, July 1992). Available from the International Reading Association, Newark, DE, $16/$12.
9. Mark B. Thogmartin, *Teaching a Child to Read with Children's Books,* ERIC Clearinghouse (Bloomington, IN: EDINFO Press, 1996).
10. Laura A. Petitto and Paula F. Marentette, "Babbling in the Manual Mode: Evidence for the Ontogeny of Language," *Science,* March 1991, pp. 1493–96. See also Natalie Angier, "Deaf Babies Use Their Hands to Babble, Researcher Finds," *The New York Times,* March 22, 1991, pp. A1, B6.
11. Jerome Kagan, "The Child: His Struggle for Identity," *Saturday Review,* December 1968, p. 82. See also Steven R. Tulkin and Jerome Kagan, "Mother-Child Interaction in the First Year of Life," *Child Development,* March 1972, pp. 31–41.
12. Further examples of "concept-attention span" can be found in Kagan, "The Child: His Struggle for Identity," p. 82.
13. These two became the seminal studies for read-aloud research: Dolores Durkin, *Children Who Read Early* (New York: Teachers College, 1966), and Margaret M. Clark, *Young Fluent Readers* (London: Heinemann, 1976). See

also Anne D. Forester, "What Teachers Can Learn from 'Natural Readers,'" *The Reading Teacher,* November 1977, pp. 160–66.

14. Ina V. S. Mullis and others, *NAEP 1992 Trends in Academic Progress,* Office of Educational Research and Improvement (Washington, DC: U.S. Department of Education, June 1994). See also Paul E. Barton and Richard J. Coley, *America's Smallest School* (Princeton, NJ: Educational Testing Service, Policy Information Center, 1992), pp. 12–19.

15. Dina Feitelson and Zahava Goldstein, "Patterns of Book Ownership and Reading to Young Children in Israeli School-Oriented and Nonschool-Oriented Families," *The Reading Teacher,* May 1986, pp. 924–30. See also here chapter 6: Libraries.

16. Donald Roberts, Ph.D., and others, *Kids & Media @ The New Millennium* (Menlo Park, CA: The Henry J. Kaiser Family Foundation, November 1999). Also at www.kff.org/content/1999/1535/ChartPack.pdf.

17. Richard C. Anderson, Elfrieda H. Hiebert, Judith A. Scott, Ian A. G. Wilkinson, *Becoming a Nation of Readers: The Report of the Commission on Reading,* U.S. Department of Education (Champaign-Urbana, IL: Center for the Study of Reading, 1985), p. 51.

18. The survey's results were shared privately with me and therefore the community name cannot be used.

19. G. Robert Carlsen and Anne Sherrill, *Voices of Readers: How We Come to Love Books,* National Council of Teachers of English (Urbana, IL: NCTE, 1988).

20. In the interests of fairness, four different factors were taken into account by reading specialist Kathy Nozzolillo in determining the Harris–Jacobson reading level for the script: semantic difficulty; syntactic difficulty; vocabulary; and sentence length.

21. Personal correspondence with Thomas G. Devine. See also: Thomas G. Devine, "Listening: What Do We Know After Fifty Years of Research and Theorizing?" *Journal of Reading,* January 1978, pp. 296–304.

22. Judith and Neil Morgan, *Dr. Seuss and Mr. Geisel* (New York, NY: Random House, 1995), p. 155. This is the definitive biography of Dr. Seuss.

23. "David Ogilvy, 88, Creator of Advertising Empire and Images Known Worldwide, Dies," *The New York Times,* July 22, 1999, pp. A1, C25.

24. Miriam Martinez and William H. Teale, "Reading in a Kindergarten Classroom Library," *The Reading Teacher,* February 1988, pp. 568–72.

25. "High School Seniors Discuss Future Plans," "Morning Edition," National Public Radio, Record ID: 9606030104, June 13, 1996.

26. Robert McCrum, William Cran, and Robert MacNeil, *The Story of English* (New York, NY: Viking, 1986), pp. 19, 20, 32.

27. John Ritter, "Why English is Language of Aviation," *USA Today,* January 18, 1996, p. 2A.

28. "In Sweden, Proof of the Power of Words," *The New York Times,* December 8, 1993, p. C17.

29. Carl B. Smith and Gary M. Ingersoll, "Written Vocabulary of Elementary School Pupils," ERIC document ED323564, pp. 3–4.

30. John Holt treated this concept at length in "How Teachers Make Children Hate Reading," *Redbook,* November 1967.

31. Krashen, *The Power of Reading;* also William Powers, John Cook, and Russell Meyer, "The Effect of Compulsory Writing on Writing Apprehension," *Research in the Teaching of English,* 13, 1979, pp. 225–30; and Harry Gradman and Edith Hanania, "Language Learning Background Factors and ESL Proficiency," *Modern Language Journal,* 75, 1991, pp. 39–51.

32. Arthur Applebee and others, *NAEP 1992 Writing Report Card,* Educational Testing Service (Washington, DC: U.S. Department of Education, 1994).

33. Jacques Barzun, *Begin Here* (Chicago, IL: University of Chicago Press, 1991) pp. 114–16.

34. Tom Parker, quoted in "How to Make a Better Student," *Time,* pp. 78–96; Parker was then admissions director at Williams College, but is now at Amherst.

35. Adam Woog, "How Tony Hillerman Won the West," *USAir Magazine,* September 1993, pp. 61–63, 113.

36. Roger C. Schank, *Tell Me a Story: A New Look at Real and Artificial Memory* (New York: Scribners, 1990).

37. Lawrie Mifflin, "The Stopwatch Ticks On: As Television Changes, '60 Minutes' Holds Its Own," *The New York Times,* May 19, 1997, pp. B1, B4.

38. Robert Coles, "Gatsby at the Business School," *The New York Times Book Review,* October 25, 1987, p. 1; "There's a Lot to be Learned from Literature, Owners Find," *The Wall Street Journal,* May 20, 1985, p. 29; also Robert Coles, *The Call of Stories: Teaching and the Moral Imagination* (Boston: Houghton Mifflin, 1989).

Chapter 3: The Stages of Read-Aloud

1. Peter W. Jusczyk and Elizabeth A. Hohne, "Infants' Memory for Spoken Words," *Science,* September 26, 1997, pp. 1984–85.

2. "Rapid Changes Seen in Young Brain," *The New York Times,* June 24, 1986, p. A17.

3. Anthony J. DeCasper and Melanie J. Spence, "Prenatal Maternal Speech Influences Newborns' Perception of Speech Sounds," *Infant Behavior and Development,* 1986, vol. 9(2), pp. 133–50. See also "Rhyme's Reason: Linking Thinking to Train the Brain?" by Gina Kolata, *The New York Times,* February 19, 1995, p. E3.

4. "The Experience of Touch: Research Points to a Critical Role," *The New York Times,* February 2, 1988, Science Times, p. 17.

5. Linda Lamme and Athol Packer, "Bookreading Behaviors of Infants," *The Reading Teacher,* February 1986, pp. 504–9; Michael Resnick and others, "Mothers Reading to Infants: A New Observational Tool," *The Reading Teacher,* May 1987, pp. 888–94.

6. "Talking to Baby: Some Experts' Advice," *The New York Times,* May 1987, p. C20.

7. Bess Altwerger, Judith Diehl-Faxon, and Karen Dockstader-Anderson, "Read Aloud Events as Meaning Construction," *Language Arts,* September 1985, pp. 476–84.

8. Dorothy White, *Books Before Five* (Portsmouth, NH: Heinemann, 1984), p. 2.

9. Bruno Bettelheim, *The Uses of Enchantment: The Meaning and Importance of Fairy Tales* (New York: Knopf, 1976), pp. 17–18.

10. David Yaden, "Understanding Stories Through Repeated Read-Alouds: How Many Times Does It Take?" *The Reading Teacher,* February 1988, pp. 556–60.

11. David B. Yaden, Jr., Laura B. Smolkin, and Alice Conlon, "Preschoolers' Questions About Pictures, Print Conventions, and Story Text During Reading Aloud at Home," *Reading Research Quarterly,* Spring 1989, pp. 188–214.

12. David K. Dickinson and Miriam W. Smith, "Long-term Effects of Preschool Teachers' Book Readings on Low-Income Children's Vocabulary and Story Comprehension," *Reading Research Quarterly,* April/May/June 1994, pp. 104–22.

13. Joannis K. Flatley and Adele D. Rutland, "Using Wordless Picture Books to Teach Linguistically/Culturally Different Students," *The Reading Teacher,* December 1986, pp. 276–81; Donna Read and Henrietta M. Smith, "Teaching Visual Literacy Through Wordless Picture Books," *The Reading Teacher,* May 1982, pp. 928–52; J. Stewig, *Children and Literature* (Chicago: Rand McNally, 1980), pp. 131–58.

14. Miriam Martinez and William H. Teale, "Reading in a Kindergarten Classroom Library," *The Reading Teacher,* February 1988, pp. 568–72. See also Gail Heald-Taylor, "Predictable Literature Selections and Activities for Language Arts Instruction," *The Reading Teacher,* October 1987, pp. 6–12; Lynn K. Rhodes, "I Can Read! Predictable Books as Resources for Reading and Writing Instruction," *The Reading Teacher,* February 1981, pp. 511–18.

15. G. K. Chesterton, *Orthodoxy: The Romance of Faith* (New York: Doubleday-Image, 1990), pp. 46–65.

16. "Seeing Rise in Child Abuse, Hospitals Step In to Try to Stop the Battering," *The New York Times,* April 5, 1994, p. A18.

17. Ibid.

18. Ann Jones, "Crimes Against Women," *USA Today*, March 10, 1994, p. 9A.

19. Carol Jago, "An Interview with Alfie Kohn," *California English,* Winter 1995.

20. Mary A. Foertsch, *Reading In and Out of School,* National Center for Statistics/U.S. Department of Education (Princeton, NJ: Educational Testing Service, 1992), pp. 10–11.

21. Mary Budd Rowe, "Wait Time: Slowing Down May Be a Way of Speeding Up!" *Journal of Teacher Education,* 37: 1 (1986).

22. James V. Hoffman, Nancy L. Roser, and Jennifer Battle, "Reading Aloud in the Classroom: From the Modal Toward a 'Model,'" *The Reading Teacher,* March 1993, pp. 496–503.

23. Judy Pearson and Richard West, "College Kids Compliant in Class," *Communication Education,* January 1991.

24. They have their own burdens to carry, so I don't want to burden them any more by naming the town; suffice it to say it's in the Northeast and the average per capita income is $100,000.

25. Patricia Greenfield and Jessica Beagles-Roos, "Radio vs. Television: Their Cognitive Impact on Children of Different Socioeconomic and Ethnic Groups," *Journal of Communications,* Spring 1988, pp. 71–92.

26. Robertson Davies, *One Half of Robertson Davies* (New York: Viking, 1977), p. 1.

27. Kurt Vonnegut, Jr., "Despite Tough Guys, Life Is Not the Only School for Real Novelists," *The New York Times,* May 24, 1999, pp. B1, B2.

28. Dr. Marie Carbo today is a nationally recognized figure in reading circles, heading the National Learning Styles Institute. For more information, see www.nrsi.com/homepage.html.

29. Marie Carbo, "Teaching Reading With Talking Books," *The Reading Teacher,* December 1978, pp. 267–73.

30. Personal e-mail correspondence.

31. Keith Baker, " 'Have you been dead?' Questions and letters from children," *The Reading Teacher,* February 1993, pp. 372–75.

32. Linda Carlton, Lisa Mistretta, Vickie Morris, Crystal Thompson, and Allan Thomson, "Reading Aloud in the Midde Grades," (master's paper, Institute of Educational Transformation, George Mason University, Fairfax, VA, May 1999).

33. Personal interviews; also: "A Soothing 'Late Show' for Troubled Teen-Agers," *The Los Angeles Times,* January 28, 1993, pp. 1, 12A.

34. Read Aloud Virginia, Project Manager, Library of Virginia, (800) 336-5266; also Gary Anderson, c/o RAV Inc., 4506 Riverside Drive, Richmond, VA 23225.

35. Jim Burke, *I Hear America Reading: Why We Read, What We Read* (Portsmouth, NH: Heinemann, 1999). Burke also wrote *The English Teacher's Companion* (Boynton/Cook). His Web site is www.englishcompanion.com.

Chapter 5: Sustained Silent Reading: Reading-Aloud's Natural Partner

1. Keith E. Stanovich, "Matthew Effects in Reading: Some Consequences of Individual Differences in the Acquisition of Literacy," *Reading Research Quarterly,* Fall 1986, pp. 360–407; Richard L. Allington, "Oral Reading," in *Handbook of Reading Research,* P. David Pearson, editor (New York: Longman, 1984), pp. 829–64; Warwick B. Elley and Francis Mangubhai, "The impact of reading on second language learning," *Reading Research Quarterly,* Fall 1983, pp. 53–67; Mary A. Foertsch, *Reading In and Out of School.*

2. Warwick B. Elley, *How in the World Do Students Read?* (Hamburg: International Association for the Evaluation of Educational Achievement, July 1992). Available from the International Reading Association, Newark, DE, $16/$12 (U.S.).

3. Ina V. S. Mullis et al., *NAEP 1992 Trends in Academic Progress,* ETS/Office of Educational Research and Improvement (Washington, DC: U.S. Department of Education, June 1994). Also found in *America's Smallest School: The Family*, Educational Testing Service, at www.ets.org/research.

4. Richard Anderson, Linda Fielding, and Paul Wilson, "Growth in Reading and How Children Spend Their Time Outside of School," *Reading Research Quarterly,* Summer 1988, pp. 285–303.

5. John I. Goodlad, *A Place Called School: Prospects for the Future* (New York: McGraw-Hill, 1984), p. 107.
6. Jodi Wilgoren, "After Success with Poor, Schools Try Cloning," *The New York Times,* August 16, 2000, pp. A1, A26.
7. Robert A. McCracken, "Instituting Sustained Silent Reading," *Journal of Reading,* May 1971, pp. 521–24, 582–83.
8. Stephen Krashen, *The Power of Reading* (Englewood, CO: Libraries Unlimited, 1993).
9. S. Jay Samuels, "Decoding and Automaticity: Helping Poor Readers Become Automatic at Word Recognition," *The Reading Teacher,* April 1988, pp. 756–60; Richard Anderson et al.
10. Richard C. Anderson, Elfrieda H. Hiebert, Judith A. Scott, Ian A. G. Wilkinson, *Becoming a Nation of Readers: The Report of the Commission on Reading* (Champaign-Urbana, IL: Center for the Study of Reading, 1985), p. 119.
11. Mark Sadoski, "An Attitude Survey for Sustained Silent Reading Programs," *Journal of Reading,* May 1980, pp. 721–26.
12. Kenneth Gray, "The Baccalaureate Game: Is it Right for All Teens?" *Phi Delta Kappan,* April 1996, pp. 528–34.
13. Richard Allington, "If They Don't Read Much, How They Gonna Get Good," *Journal of Reading,* October 1977, pp. 57–61.
14. Anderson et al., "Growth in Reading," p. 152.
15. Edward Fry and Elizabeth Sakiey, "Common Words Not Taught in Basal Reading Series," *The Reading Teacher,* January 1986, pp. 395–98.
16. Patricia L. Donahue, Kristen E. Voelki, Jay R. Campbell, and John Mazzeo, *NAEP 1998 Reading Report Card for the Nation and States,* Office of Educational Research and Improvement, NCES 1999-500 (Washington, DC: U.S. Department of Education, March 1999), pp. 98–100.
17. Robert A. McCracken and Marlene J. McCracken, "Modeling Is the Key to Sustained Silent Reading," *Reading Teacher,* January 1978, pp. 406–8. See also Linda B. Gambrell, "Getting Started with Sustained Silent Reading and Keeping It Going," *The Reading Teacher,* December 1978, pp. 328–31.
18. Richard L. Allington, "The Reading Instruction Provided Readers of Differing Reading Abilities," *The Elementary School Journal,* May 1983, vol. 83, no. 15, pp. 548–59.
19. Reni Herda and Francisco Ramos, "How Consistently Do Students Read During Sustained Silent Reading? A Look Across the Grades," unpublished paper, Rossier School of Education, University of California.
20. Martha Efta, "Reading in Silence," *Teaching Exceptional Children,* Fall 1978, pp. 12–24.
21. Rosalie P. Fink, "Successful Dyslexics: A Constructivist Study of Passionate Interest Reading," *Journal of Adolescent & Adult Literacy,* December 1995/January 1996, pp. 268–79.
22. Barbara Heyns, *Summer Learning and the Effects of Schooling* (New York: Academic Press, 1978). See also Doris R. Entwistle and Karl L. Alexander, "Summer Setback: Race, Poverty, School Composition, and Mathematical Achievement in the First Two Years of School," *American Sociological Review,* 57, 1992, pp. 72–84; Barbara Heynes, "Schooling and Cognitive Develop-

ment: Is There a Season for Learning," *Child Development,* vol. 58, 1987, pp. 1151–60; Larry J. Mikulecky, "Stopping Summer Learning Loss Among At-Risk Youth," *Journal of Reading,* April 1990, pp. 516–21.

23. Catherine Gewertz, "More Districts Add Summer Coursework," *Education Week,* June 7, 2000, pp. 1, 12.

24. See chart on page 14.

25. Barbara Heyns, *Summer Learning and the Effects of Schooling.*

26. Hank Whittemore, "The Most Precious Gift," *Parade Magazine,* December 22, 1991, p. 4; and personal interview.

27. Jay R. Campbell, Catherene M. Hombo, and John Mazzeo, *NAEP 1999 Trends in Academic Progress: Three Decades of Student Performance,* U.S. Department of Education (Washington, DC: National Center for Education Statistics, 2000). Also available at http://nces.ed.gov/nationsreportcard.

28. Steve Sternberg, "Michael DeBakey's living legacy," *USA Today,* November 2, 1998, pp. 1D–2D.

29. Benjamin Fine, "Ignorance of U.S. History Shown by College Freshmen," *The New York Times,* April 4, 1943, pp. 1, 32, 33.

30. "America's Students Know Little About U.S. History, Survey Says," Associated Press in *The New York Times,* November 2, 1995.

31. Jason Burke and Stuart Wavell, "Winston Who? Pupils Cannot Name War Heroes," (London) *Sunday Times,* April 30, 1995, pp. 1, 6.

32. Gerald W. Bracey, "Research: Many Visions, Many Aims, One Test," *Phi Delta Kappan,* January 1997, p. 411; Paul Gagnon, "What Should Children Learn?" *Atlantic Monthly,* December 1995, pp. 65–77; Julie Johnson, "Teacher union faults history books," *The New York Times,* September 14, 1989, p. A20; Debra Viadero, "A textbook case: U.S. history in the making," *Education Week,* January 26, 1994, pp. 30, 31.

33. "History 101: Snoop Doggy Roosevelt," *The New York Times,* July 2, 2000, p. WK7. The American Council of Trustees and Alumni is a Washington, DC, nonprofit organization for the promotion of liberal arts study.

34. Ibid. All thirty-four questions and answers were reprinted with the *Times* article.

35. Esther B. Fein, "Immersed in Facts, the Better to Imagine Harry Truman's Life," *The New York Times,* August 12, 1992, pp. C1, C10.

36. Accelerated Reader, from Advantage Learning Systems, Inc., 2610 Industrial Street, PO Box 36, Wisconsin Rapids, WI 54495-0036 (tel: 800 338-4204).

37. Reading Counts, from Scholastic Reading Counts!, P. O. Box 7502, Jefferson City, MO 65102-7502 (tel: 877-268-6871).

38. Jean M. Stevenson and Jenny Webb Camarata, "Imposters in Whole Language Clothing: Undressing the Accelerated Reader Program," *Talking Points,* Whole Language Umbrella/National Council of Teachers of English, April/May 2000, vol. 11, no. 2, pp. 8–11. Although I agree with only small parts of their arguments, it is another point of view to consider.

39. Alfie Kohn, *Punished by Rewards* (Boston: Houghton Mifflin, 1993).

40. Paul Chance, "The Rewards of Learning," *Phi Delta Kappan,* November, 1992, pp. 200–207.

41. Anne P. Sweet and John T. Guthrie, "How Children's Motivations Relate to Literacy Development and Instruction," *The Reading Teacher,* May 1996, pp. 660–61.

42. Harold Bloom, "Can 35 Million Book Buyers Be Wrong? Yes," *The Wall Street Journal,* July 11, 2000, op-ed page. In this curmudgeonly essay, the noted Yale professor proclaimed the Potter series to be a waste of valuable reading time because its pedestrian prose style failed to elevate the mind sufficiently. I am assuming, because Dr. Bloom finished reading the book, he read it for another purpose than mental or spiritual enrichment—perhaps for the fame or fortune that would accompany his *Journal* essay—which could be equated with "points."

43. Mel Gussow, "Orville Prescott, *Times* Book Critic for 24 Years, Dies at 89," *The New York Times,* April 30, 1996, p. B14.

44. Rochelle Sharpe, "Book Case Study: Cassandra Mozley Is an Inspired Reader," *The Wall Street Journal,* July 17, 1995, pp. A1, A4.

45. Jodi Wilgoren, "After Success With Poor, Schools Try Cloning," *The New York Times,* August 16, 2000, pp. A1, A26.

46. Stephen D. Krashen and Kyung-Sook Cho, "Acquisition of Vocabulary from the Sweet Valley Kids Series: Adult ESL Acquisition," *Journal of Reading,* May 1994, pp. 662–67; similar results were accomplished in the Sponce English Language Program at the University of Southern California–Los Angeles using Harlequin romances. See also: Rebecca Constantino, "Pleasure Reading Helps, Even If Readers Don't Believe It," *Journal of Reading,* March 1994, pp. 504–5.

47. G. Robert Carlson and Anne Sherrill, *Voices of Readers: How We Come to Love Books* (Urbanna, IL: National Council of Teachers of English, 1998).

48. Viking Brunell and Pirjo Linnakylä, "Swedish Speakers' Literacy in the Finnish Society," *Journal of Reading,* February 1994, pp. 368–75.

49. Stephen Krashen, "Comic Book Reading and Language Development," a monograph from Abel Press, P.O. Box 6162, Station C, Victoria Station, BC, Canada V8P 5L5; Emma Halstead Swain, "Using Comic Books in Teaching Reading and Language Arts," *Journal of Reading,* December 1978, pp. 253–58. See also Larry Dorrell and Ed Carroll, "Spider-Man at the Library," *School Library Journal,* August 1981, pp. 17–19.

50. Joanne Ujiie and Stephen D. Krashen, "Comic Book Reading, Reading Enjoyment, and Pleasure Reading Among Middle Class and Chapter I Middle School Students," *Reading Improvement,* vol. 33, no. 1, pp. 51–54; also Joanne Ujiie and Stephen D. Krashen, "Is Comic Book Reading Harmful?" *California State Library Association Journal,* vol. 19, no. 2, Spring 1996, pp. 27–28.

51. *Archie*—1.8 grade level; *Spiderman*—4.4; and *Batman*—6.4; from Krashen, *The Power of Reading,* p. 53.

52. Leslie Campbell and Kathleen Hayes, "Desmond Tutu," interview from *The Other Side's Faces of Faith,* pp. 23–26. For a free copy of this booklet, write to 300 Apsley St., Philadelphia, PA 19144.

53. Arthur Schlesinger, Jr., "Advice from a Reader-Aloud-to-Children," *The New York Times Book Review,* November 25, 1979.

54. Sid T. Womack and B. J. Chandler, "Encouraging Reading for Professional Development," *Journal of Reading,* February 1992, pp. 390–94.
55. Stanley I. Mour, "Do Teachers Read?" *The Reading Teacher,* January 1977, pp. 397–401. This study was somewhat skewed in favor of teachers because the subjects were more motivated professionally as graduate students. If anything, the results would be worse with teachers not as professionally involved. Included in the numbers were 202 females and 22 males; 6 counselors; 6 principals; 5 supervisors; most of the teachers (145) were elementary level; see also Kathleen Stumpf Jongsma, "Just Say Know!" *The Reading Teacher,* March 1992, pp. 546–48.
56. Nicholas Zill and Marianne Winglee, *Who Reads Literature?* (Cabin John, MD: Seven Locks Press, 1990).
57. Cheryl B. Littman and Susan S. Stodolsky, "The Professional Reading of High School Academic Teachers," *The Journal of Educational Research,* vol. 92, (2), November 1998, p. 75.
58. Clifton Fadiman, *Party of One: The Selected Writings of Clifton Fadiman* (New York: The World Publishing Company, 1955), p. 369.
59. Von Sprecken, Kim, and Stephen Krashen, "The Home Run Book: Can One Positive Reading Experience Create a Reader?," *California School Library Journal,* vol. 23(2), pp. 8–9; Jiyoung Kim and Stephen Krashen, "Another Home Run," *California English,* in press, 2000.
60. Dr. Beers is currently in the education department, University of Houston.
61. G. Kylene Beers, "No Time, No Interest, No Way!" *School Library Journal,* two parts: February 1996, pp. 30–33, March 1996, pp. 110–13.
62. Krashen, *The Power of Reading,* pp. 76–78. This offers an overview of research on writing as a boost for intelligence.
63. W. E. Nagy, P. Herman, R. Anderson, "Learning Words from Context."
64. Stephen Krashen, *Writing: Research, Theory and Applications* (Torrence, CA: Laredo Publishing Company, 1984); Krashen, *The Power of Reading.*
65. Susan Ohanian, "A Not-So-Tearful Farewell to William Bennett," *Phi Delta Kappan,* September 1988, pp. 11–17.
66. Nicholas Zill and Marianne Winglee, *Who Reads Literature?* pp. 20–33.
67. Connie C. Epstein, "The Well-Read College-Bound Student," *School Library Journal,* February 1984, pp. 32–35.

Chapter 6: Libraries: Home, School, and Public

1. Tom Weir, "City's Refrain: 'Sammy Lived Here,'" *USA Today,* August 20, 1998, pp. 1A, 2A.
2. Stephen S. Krashen, *The Power of Reading* (Englewood, CO: Libraries Unlimited, 1993).
3. Jeff McQuillan, *The Literary Crisis: False Claims, Real Solutions* (Portsmouth, NH: Heinemann, 1998).
4. Richard Allington, Sherry Guice, Kim Baker, Nancy Michaelson, and Shouming Li, "Access to Books: Variations in Schools and Classrooms," *The Language and Literacy Spectrum,* Spring 1995, pp. 23–25. Also "Something to Read: Putting Books in Their Desks, Backpacks, and Bedrooms," Richard

L. Allington and Sherry Guice, in Phillip Dreyer, ed., *Vision and realities in literacy: Sixtieth Yearbook of the Claremont Reading Conference* (Claremont, CA: Claremont Reading Conference, 1996), p. 5.

5. Keith Curry Lance, Marcia J. Rodney, and Christine Hamilton-Pennell, *How School Librarians Help Kids Achieve Standards: The Second Colorado Study,* Colorado State Library, Colorado Department of Education; Keith Curry Lance, Lynda Welborn, and Christine Hamilton-Pennell, *The Impact of School Media Centers on Academic Achievement,* Colorado Department of Education. Copies may be ordered through Libraries Unlimited, PO Box 6633, Englewood, CO 80155 (tel: 800 237-6124). Also "Dick and Jane Go to the Head of the Class" by Christine Hamilton-Pennell, Keith Curry Lance, Marcia J. Rodney, and Eugene Hainer, *School Library Journal,* April 2000, pp. 44–47.

6. Jeff McQuillan, *The Literacy Crisis.*

7. Warwick B. Elley, *How in the World Do Students Read?* (Hamburg: International Association for the Evaluation of Educational Achievement, July 1992). Available from the International Reading Association, Newark, DE, $16/$12 (U.S.).

8. Keith Curry Lance and others, *How School Librarians Help Kids Achieve Standards.*

9. C. Snyder and C. Hoffman, *Digest of Education Statistics* (Washington, DC: U.S. Department of Education, 1995).

10. Richard Moore, "California Dreamin'," *California Librarian* (1993), vol. 21, 1 and 2, p. 17.

11. Richard Allington, Sherry Guice, Kim Baker, Nancy Michaelson, and Shouming Li, "Access to Books: Variations in Schools and Classrooms," *The Language and Literacy Spectrum,* Spring 1995, pp. 23–25.

12. C. Contantino and Stephen Krashen, "Differences in Print Environment for Children in Beverly Hills, Compton, and Watts," *Emergency Librarian,* 24, 1997, 4, pp. 8–9. See also Stephen Krashen, "Bridging Inequity with Books," *Educational Leadership,* January 1998, pp. 19–22.

13. Many of Krashen's findings and recommendations can be found in the document *Every Person a Reader: An Alternative to the California Task Force Report on Reading* by Stephen D. Krashen, from Language Education Associates, PO Box 7416, Culver City, CA 90233, FAX: (310) 568-9040.

14. Jean Merl, "Funding Effort Is One for the Books," *The Los Angeles Times,* January 11, 1999, p. 3A. Also Kritina Sauerwein, "State Weeds Out Old, Inaccurate Books at Schools," *The Los Angeles Times,* May 30, 1999, pp. 1A, 32A.

15. Kathleen Kennedy Manzo, "California Continues Phaseout of Whole Language Era," *Education Week,* July 9, 1997, p. 15.

16. Susan Edelman, "Our Worst Schools Have Fewest Books," *The New York Post,* June 1, 1999, pp. 4–5.

17. Jerry West, Kristen Denton, Elvira Germino-Hausken, *America's Kindergartners: Early Childhood Longitudinal Study—Kindergarten Class of 1998–99, Fall 1998,* National Center for Education Statistics (Washington, DC: U.S. Department of Education, 1999), p. 51.

18. Dina Feitelson and Zahava Goldstein, "Patterns of Book Ownership and Reading to Young Children in Israeli School-Oriented and Nonschool Oriented Families," *The Reading Teacher,* May 1986, pp. 924–30.

19. Hayes, Palmer and Zaslow, *Who cares for America's children: Child care policy for the 1990's* (Washington, DC: National Academy Press, 1990). In an extensive evaluation of the Defense Department's day-care system, Nancy Duff Campbell, Judith C. Applebaum, Karin Martinson, and Emily Martin (*Be All That You Can Be,* National Women's Law Center, Washington, DC), noted the reform of the system between 1990 and 2000 corrected the previous situations in which there was often an annual turnover of 300 percent in the government-run child-care system.

20. Susan B. Neuman, "Books Make a Difference: A Study of Access to Literacy," *Reading Research Quarterly,* July/August/September 1999, pp. 286–311.

21. Doreen Carvajal, "Reading the Bottom Line," *The New York Times Magazine,* April 6, 1997, pp. 76–77.

22. Deirdre Donahue, "A Haven for the Intellect: In an Isolated World, Bookstores Appeal as a Sanctuary of Civility," *USA Today,* July 10, 1997, pp. 1D–2D.

23. Charli O'Dell, "What Works: Thanks-a-Latte; Coffee in the School Library?" *School Library Journal,* December 1999, p. 35.

24. Helen Werner Cox, Lindbergh Middle School, 1022 E. Market Street, Long Beach, CA 90805.

25. Jack Hitt, "The Theory of Supermarkets," *The New York Times Magazine,* March 10, 1996, pp. 56–61, 94, 98.

26. Robin Fields, and Melinda Fulmer, "Markets' Shelf Fees Put Squeeze on Small Firms," *The Los Angeles Times,* Jan. 29, 2000, pp. 1A, 26A.

27. Jann Sorrell Fractor and others, "Let's Not Miss Opportunities to Promote Voluntary Reading: Classroom Libraries in the Elementary School," *The Reading Teacher,* March 1993, pp. 476–84.

28. Mary B. W. Tabor, "In Bookstore Chains, Display Space Is for Sale," *The New York Times,* January 15, 1996, pp. A1, D8.

29. Mike Oliver is now principal at Barbara Bush Elementary in Mesa, Arizona.

30. Dr. Kylene Beers, "The 'Good Books' Solution," *School Library Journal,* March 1996, p. 113. This is a sidebar to a two-part series entitled "No Time, No Interest, No Way!" by Dr. Kylene Beers, *School Library Journal,* February and March 1996.

31. Fox Butterfield, "Crime Keeps Falling, but Prisons Keep on Filling," *The New York Times,* September 28, 1997, Section 4, pp. 1, 4.

32. Paul E. Barton and Richard J. Coley, "Captive Students: Education and Training in America's Prisons," Educational Testing Service (Princeton, NJ: ETS Policy Information Center, 1996).

33. Frank Deford, "A Gentleman and a Scholar," *Sports Illustrated,* April 17, 1989, pp. 87–99.

34. Pamela Harper, "After a Long Search, He Finds a Real Treasure," *Santa Barbara News Press,* December 7, 1988, p. B5.

35. Anthony Brandt, "Literacy in America," *The New York Times,* August 25, 1980, p. 25.

36. To date, only Scholastic Books has been a fully cooperating partner in the book section of the program.

Chapter 7: Lessons from Oprah, Harry, and the Internet

1. *A Nation at Risk*, U.S. Department of Education, Washington, DC: 1995.
2. W. S. Hinchman, "Reading Clubs Instead of Literature Classes," *English Journal,* vol. 6 (2), 1917, pp. 88–95. Also G. Kylene Beers, "No Time, No Interest, No Way!" *School Library Journal,* March 1996, p. 111.
3. Adele A. Greenlee, Dianne L. Monson, and Barbara M. Taylor, "The Lure of Series Books: Does It Affect Appreciation for Recommended Literature?" *The Reading Teacher,* vol. 50, no. 3, November 1996, pp. 216–25.
4. D. T. Max, "The Oprah Effect," *The New York Times Magazine,* December 26, 1999, pp. 36–41.
5. Laurel Graeber, "New Book Clubs: Mothers, Daughters and Discussion," *The New York Times,* April 24, 1997, p. B4.
6. Steven J. Zipperstein, "If It's Goodbye Books, Then Hello . . . What?" *The New York Times,* September 23, 2000, p. A21.
7. Robert Giroux, "Thomas Merton's Durable Mountain," *The New York Times Book Review,* October 11, 1998, p. 35. Giroux recalled taking a class with Van Doren and hearing him offer that definition.
8. Dorren Carvajal, "Revolution Aside, Paperbacks Losing Battle for Readers," *The New York Times,* March 15, 1999, pp. A1, A13.
9. Elizabeth Weise, "Net Use Doubling Every 100 Days," *USA Today,* April 16, 1998, p. 1.
10. *Caddie Woodlawn* by Carol Ryrie Brink; *Bridge to Terabithia* by Katherine Paterson; *Roll of Thunder, Hear My Cry* by Mildred Taylor; *Maniac Magee* by Jerry Spinelli; and *Holes* by Louis Sachar, to name a few.
11. Warren E. Leary, "Violent Crime Continues to Decline, Survey Finds," *The New York Times,* August 28, 2000, p. A10.
12. Catherine Sheldrick Ross, "If They Read Nancy Drew, So What?: Series Book Readers Talk Back," *Library and Information Science Research* (LISR) vol. 17, 1995, pp. 201–36. This research won the American Library Association's research award in 1995. A shortened version appeared in *School Library Media Quarterly,* Spring 1996, pp. 165–71.
13. Franklin K. Mathiews, "Blowing Out the Boy's Brains," *Outlook,* November 18, 1914, p. 653.
14. Harvey Graff, *The Literacy Myth* (San Diego, CA: Academic, 1979), p. 39. Quoting an editorial from the *Christian Guardian,* July 31, 1850.
15. Ronald B. Schwartz, *For the Love of Books* (New York: Grosset/Putnam, 1999), p. 107. Recalled by Pete Hammill during an interview with Schwartz.
16. Anna Quindlen, "Aha! Caught You Reading," *Newsweek,* July 17, 2000, p. 64.
17. Adele A. Greenlee, Dianne L. Monson, and Barbara M. Taylor, "The Lure of Series Books: Does It Affect Appreciation for Recommended Literature?" *The Reading Teacher,* November 1996, pp. 216–25.
18. Catherine Sheldrick Ross, "If They Read Nancy Drew, So What?"
19. " 'For it was indeed he,' " *Fortune Magazine,* April 1934; also found in *Only Connect,* Sheila Egoff, G. T. Stubbs, and L. F. Ashley, eds. (New York: Oxford University Press, 1969), pp. 41–61.

20. Barbara A. Bruschi and Richard J. Coley, "How Teachers Compare: The Prose, Document, and Quantitative Skills of America's Teachers," ETS Policy Information Center (Princeton, NJ: Educational Testing Service, March 1999). Available on the Web at www.ets.org/research/pic/compare.html.

21. G. Robert Carlsen and Anne Sherrill, *Voices of Readers: How We Come to Love Books* (Urbana, IL: National Council of Teachers of English, 1988).

22. Elizabeth Weise, "One Click Starts the Avalanche," *USA Today,* August 8, 2000, p. 3D.

23. Elizabeth Weise, "Net Use Doubling Every 100 Days," *USA Today,* April 16, 1998, p. 1.

24. Ian Austen, "Study Reveals Web as Loosely Woven," *The New York Times,* May 18, 2000, p. D8. The study was funded by IBM, Compaq, and the search engine Alta Vista.

25. Ian Austen, "The Case of the Flickering Pixels," *The New York Times,* February 3, 2000, pp. D1, D9.

26. Catherine Greenman, "Printed Page Beats PC Screen for Reading, Study Finds," *The New York Times,* August 10, 2000, p. E11.

27. Quoted in Robert Darnton, "The New Age of the Book," *New York Review,* March 18, 1999, p. 5.

28. Mark F. Goldberg, "Joltin' Joe and the Pursuit of Excellence," *Phi Delta Kappan,* January 1997, pp. 395–97.

29. Nate Stulman, "The Great Campus Goof-Off Machine," *The New York Times,* May 15, 1999, Op-ed page.

30. Greg Miller and P. J. Huffstutter, "File-Sharing PC Software Shakes Up Music World," *The Los Angeles Times,* February 24, 2000, p. 1A, 12A; Jefferson Graham, "Caught between rock and a hard drive," *USA Today,* May 15, 2000, pp. 1D, 2D.

31. Patrick Welsh, "Hooking Up Kids to Computers Won't Make Them Smart," *USA Today,* June 4, 1999, Op-ed commentary, p. 13A.

32. *NAEP 1994 U.S. History Report,* National Library of Education, U.S. Department of Education (Washington, DC: Office of Educational Research and Improvement, 1994).

33. Daniel J. Rocha, "The Emperor's New Laptop: Are the Outcomes in Line with the Hype? One School's Story," *Education Week,* September 27, 2000, pp. 42, 46–47. Rocha was the academy's head of middle school.

34. Colleen Cordes and Edward Miller, *Fool's Gold: A Critical Look at Computers in Childhood,* Alliance for Childhood (College Park, MD: Alliance for Childhood, 2000). Available for $8.00 at Alliance for Childhood, PO Box 444, College Park, MD, 20741; also available for free as a downloadable PDF file at www.allianceforchildhood.net/projects/computers/computers_reports/htm.

35. M-L Chu, "Reader Response to Interactive Computer Books: Examining Literary Responses in a Non-traditional Reading Setting," *Reading Research and Instruction,* vol. 34, pp. 352–66.

36. Marco R. della Cava, "Are Heavy Users Hooked or Just On-line Fanatics?" *USA Today,* January 16, 1996, pp. 1A, 2A.

37. Alison Armstrong and Charles Casement, *The Child and the Machine: How Computers Put Our Children's Education at Risk* (Beltsville, MD: Robins Lane Press, 2000).

38. Jane M. Healey, *Failure to Connect: How Computers Affect Our Children's Minds—for Better and Worse* (New York: Simon & Schuster, 1998).

Chapter 8: Television

1. Lawrie Mifflin, "Pediatricians Urge Limiting TV Viewing," *The New York Times,* August 4, 1999, p. A1, A11.
2. Patricia A. Williams, Edward H. Haertel, Geneva D. Haertel, and Herbert J. Walberg, "The Impact of Leisure-Time Television on School Learning: A Research Synthesis," *American Educational Research Journal,* Spring 1982, vol. 19, no. 1, pp. 19–50.
3. Daniel R. Anderson and Patricia A. Collins, "The Impact on Children's Education: Television's Influence on Cognitive Development," U.S. Department of Education (Washington, DC: Office of Educational Research and Improvement, April 1988).
4. Jay R. Campbell, Catheriene M. Hombo, and John Mazzeo, *NAEP 1999 Trends in Academic Progress: Three Decades of Student Performance,* U.S. Department of Education (Washington, DC: National Center for Education Statistics, 2000); also available at http://nces.ed.gov/nationsreportcard.
5. Ibid.
6. Ruben G. Rumbaut, "The New Californians: Assessing the Educational Progress of Children of Immigrants," ERIC document: ED398 294, based upon chapter 2, *California's Immigrant Children: Theory, Research, and Implications for Education Policy,* Ruben G. Rumbaut and Wayne A. Cornleius, eds., San Diego, CA: Center for U.S.–Mexican Studies, University of California, April 1996.
7. "2000 Report on Television: The First 50 Years," New York, NY: Nielsen Media Research, 2000, p. 14.
8. Ibid., p. 16.
9. Donald Roberts, Ph.D., Ulla G. Foehr, Victoria Rideout, and Mollyann Brodie, Ph.D., Kids & Media @ The New Millennium, The Henry J. Kaiser Family Foundation, November 1999.
10. Judith Owens et al., "Television-Viewing Habits and Sleep Disturbance in School Children," *Pediatrics,* September 8, 1999, p. 552.
11. The single best exploration of the gap appeared in an award-winning newspaper series by Tim Simmons of the *Charlotte News & Observer,* reprinted in a special section, "Worlds Apart: The Racial Education Gap," December 27, 1999; see also Kate Zernike, "Gap Widens Again on Tests Given to Blacks and Whites," *The New York Times,* August 25, 2000, p. A14: The article plots the racial gap in NAEP scores that has widened since the 1980s between white and black students in math, science, and reading, includin a decline among students coming from the best-educated black families; Pam Belluck, "Reason Is Sought for Lag by Blacks in School Effort," *The New York Times,* July 4, 1999, pp. A2, A12; and Kate Zernike, "Racial Gap in Student Test Scores Polarizes Town," *The New York Times,* August 4, 2000, pp. A1, A25; Debra Viadero, "Lags in Minority Achievement Defy Traditional Explanations," *Education Week,* March 22, 2000, pp. 1, 18–22.

12. Pam Belluck, "Reason Is Sought for Lag by Blacks in School Effort," *The New York Times,* July 4, 1999, pp. A1, A12.

13. Donald Roberts, Ph.D., Ulla G. Foehr, Victoria Rideout, and Mollyann Brodie, Ph.D., Kids & Media @ The New Millennium, The Henry J. Kaiser Family Foundation, November 1999.

14. Paul Copperman, *The Literacy Hoax: The Decline of Reading, Writing, and Learning in the Public Schools and What We Can Do About It* (New York: Morrow, 1980), p. 166.

15. "Zapping of TV Ads Appears Pervasive," *The Wall Street Journal,* April 25, 1988. p. 29.

16. Neil Postman, *Teaching as a Conserving Activity* (New York: Delacorte, 1980), pp. 77–78.

17. Michael Liberman, "The Verbal Language of Television," *The Journal of Reading,* April 1983, pp. 602–9.

18. "Gadgets That Help Parents Wean Kids from TV-itis," *U.S. News and World Report,* September 20, 1993, p. 79.

19. Susan B. Neuman and Patricia Koskinen, "Captioned Television as 'Comprehensible Input': Effects of Incidental Word Learning from Context for Language Minority Students," *Reading Research Quarterly,* 27, 1992, pp. 95–106; Koskinen, P. S., Wilson, R. S., Gambrell, L. and Jensema, C. J., *ERS Spectrum: Journal of School Research and Information* 4(2), pp. 9–13; Patricia S. Koskinen, Robert M. Wilson, Linda B. Gambrell, Susan B. Neuman, "Captioned Video and Vocabulary Learning: An Innovative Practice in Literacy Instruction," *The Reading Teacher,* September 1993, pp. 36–43; Robert J. Rickelman, William A. Henk, Kent Layton, "Closed-Captioned Television: A Viable Technology for the Reading Teacher," *The Reading Teacher,* April 1996, pp. 598–99.

20. Pirjo Linnakylä, "Subtitles Prompt Finnish Children to Read," *Reading TODAY* (IRA bimonthly), October/November 1993, p. 31.

21. Rosemarie Truglio, Aletha Huston, John Wright, "The Relation Between Children's Print and Television Use to Early Reading Skills," Center for Research on the Influences of Television on Children, Department of Human Development, University of Kansas, 1988.

22. John C. Wright and Aletha C. Huston, "Effects of Educational TV Viewing of Lower Income Preschoolers on Academic Skills, School Readiness, and School Adjustment One to Three Years Later," Center for Research on the Influences of Television on Children, June 1995; the report can be obtained from Children's Television Workshop, 1 Lincoln Plaza, NY, NY, 10023, (212) 595-3456; also at www.critc.he.utexas.edu/CRITC/Manuscripts/effects_of_education_tv_viewin.htm or www.cyfc.umn.edu/television/html; see also Mark Walsh, "Study Links Television Viewing, School Readiness," *Education Week*, June 7, 1995, p. 5.

23. Barbara Fowles Mates and Linda Strommen, "Why Ernie Can't Read: Sesame Street and Literacy," *The Reading Teacher,* January 1996.

24. Sven Birkerts, "Close Listening," *Harper's,* January 1993, pp. 86–91.

25. Helen Aron, "Bookworms Become Tapeworms: A Profile of Listeners to Books on Audiocassette," *Journal of Reading,* November 1992, pp. 208–12.

26. Kylene Beers, "Listen While You Read: Struggling Readers and Audio-books," *School Library Journal,* April 1998, pp. 30–35.

Appendix A

1. "Half of Adults Lack Skills to Function Fully in Society, Literacy Study Finds," *The New York Times,* September 15, 1993. See also Irwin Kirsch and others, *Adult Literacy in America,* Educational Testing Service/National Center for Educational Statistics (Princeton, NJ: 1993); and *1992 National Adult Literacy Survey* (Princeton, NJ: Educational Testing Service, 1993).
2. Daniel Tanner, "The Social Consequences of Bad Research," *Phi Delta Kappan,* Janauary 1998, pp. 345–49.
3. Monica Wyatt, "The Past, Present, and Future Need for College Reading Courses in the U.S.," *The Journal of Reading,* September 1992, pp. 10–20. The article contains a page-long list of remedial headlines from 1828 to the present.
4. David J. Hoff, "Made to Measure," *Education Week,* June 16, 1999, p. 21. Quoting from Robert M. W. Travers's book, *How Research Changed American Schools.*
5. Henry J. Perkinson, *Two Hundred Years of American Educational Thought* (New York: David McKay, 1976), p. 141.
6. C. F. Richardson, "The Home Library," *Self Culture for Young People,* Andrew Sloan Draper, editor in chief, St. Louis: 1906, p. 35.
7. Daniel P. Resnick, "Historical Perspectives on Literacy and Schooling," *Daedulus,* Spring 1990, pp. 15–32.
8. "Educational Attainment in the US," *Education Week,* November 22, 1989, p. 3.
9. Phillip Kaufman, Jin Y. Kwon, Steve Klein, Christopher D. Chapman, "Dropout Rates in the United States: 1998," National Center for Education Statistics, NCES 2000-022 (Washington, DC: U.S. Department of Education, November 1999), p. 57.
10. "Educational Attainment in the US," *Education Week,* November 22, 1989, p. 3; "Gains for Blacks in Education," *USA Today,* November 21, 1994, p. 1D, based upon U.S. Census Bureau reports.
11. "SAT Increases the Average Score, by Fiat," *The New York Times,* June 11, 1994, pp. 1, 10.
12. Patricia Donahue, Kristin E. Voelkl, Jay R. Campbell, and John Mazzeo, *NAEP 1998 Reading Report Card for the Nation,* Office of Educational Research and Improvement, National Center for Education Statistics (Washington, DC: U.S. Department of Education, March 1999), p. 121.
13. "2000 Profile of College-Bound Seniors," The College Board (New York, NY: August 2000) Table 1, Table 4–2, Table 8.
14. Dina Temple-Raston, "Immigrants Filled Critical Gap in Wide-Open Job Market," *USA Today,* June 23, 2000, pp. 1B–2B.
15. William Celis 3d, "Schools Pay for Diversity in Languages of Students," *The New York Times,* September 11, 1994, pp. 37, 53.
16. This and other performance studies are compared in "The Condition of Education: Why School Reformers Are on the Right Tracks," by Lawrence

C. Stedman, *Phi Delta Kappan,* November 1993, pp. 215–25; see also "Correction," *Phi Delta Kappan,* February 1994, p. 504.

17. "Backtalk/Remembering 1940—The Author (Mike Males) Responds," *Phi Delta Kappan,* December 1992, pp. 351–52.

18. U.S. Census Bureau, Education and Social Stratification Branch, 1998.

19. Gerald W. Bracey, "Research: The New Lost Generation?" *Phi Delta Kappan,* March 1997, pp. 578–79.

20. "The Condition of Education 2000," Office of Educational Research and Improvement, NCES 2000-062 (Washington, DC: U.S. Department of Education, June 2000).

21. David C. Berliner and Bruce J. Biddle, *The Manufactured Crisis* (New York: Addison-Wesley, 1996).

22. "The Condition of Education 2000."

23. Ibid.

24. Ibid.

25. Daniel Tanner, "A Nation 'Truly' at Risk," *Phi Delta Kappan,* December 1993, pp. 288–97. The article highlights, among other things, the government-suppressed report "Perspectives on Education in America," Final Draft, Sandia National Laboratories, Albuquerque, NM, April 1992, which reports the state of American education is not as bad as the government claims.

26. *The Condition of Education 2000,* p. 164 (Appendix 1). Also http://nces. ed.gov/pubsearch/index.asp. See also Cornelius Riordan, "The Silent Gender Gap: Reading, Writing, and Other Problems for Boys," *Education Week,* November 17, 1999, pp. 46, 49; see also Christina Hoff Sommers, "Where the Boys Are," *Education Week,* June 22, 1996, pp. 52, 42; Christina Hoff Sommers, "The War Against Boys," *The Atlantic Monthly,* May 2000, pp. 59–74.

27. Barbara A. Bruschi and Richard J. Coley, "How Teachers Compare: The Prose, Document, and Quantitative Skills of America's Teachers," ETS Policy Information Center, Educational Testing Service, Princeton, NJ, March 1999. Available on the Web at http://www.ets.org/research/pic/compare. html.

28. "The Condition of Education 2000."

29. Anita Manning, "Women Outpacing Men in Degrees," *USA Today,* June 29, 1998, p. 1A.

30. "The Kids Count Data Book 2000," Baltimore, MD: The Annie E. Casey Foundation, 2000. pp. 28, 32; on-line at www.aecf.org.

31. Warwick B. Elley, *How in the World Do Students Read?* (Hamburg: International Associaton for the Evaluation of Educational Achievement, July 1992). Available from the International Reading Association, Newark, DE, $16/$12.

32. Gerald W. Bracey, *Setting the Record Straight: Responses to Misconceptions About Public Education in the United States* (Alexandria, VA: Association for Supervision and Curriculum Development, 1997).

Bibliography

Adams, Marilyn Jager. *Beginning to Read: Thinking and Learning about Print—A Summary.* Champaign-Urbana: University of Illinois, Center for the Study of Reading, 1990.

Anderson, Daniel R. and Patricia A. Collins. *The Impact on Children's Education: Television's Influence on Cognitive Development.* Washington, DC: U.S. Department of Education, Office of Educational Research and Improvement, 1988.

Anderson, Richard C., Elfrieda H. Hiebert, Judith A. Scott, and Ian A. G. Wilkinson. *Becoming a Nation of Readers: The Report of the Commission on Reading.* Champaign-Urbana, IL: Center for the Study of Reading, 1985.

Applebee, Arthur N., Judith A. Langer, and Ina V. S. Mullis. *Who Reads Best?* Princeton, NJ: National Assessment of Educational Progress, 1988.

Applebee, Arthur N., Judith A. Langer, Ina V. S. Mullis, Andrew S. Latham, and Claudia A. Gentile. *NAEP 1992 Writing Report Card,* Educational Testing Service. Washington, DC: U.S. Department of Education, 1994.

Armstrong, Alison and Charles Casement. *The Child and the Machine: How Computers Put Our Children's Education at Risk.* Beltsville, MD: Robins Lane Press, 2000.

Bae, Yupin, Susan Choy, Claire Geddes, Jennifer Sable, and Thomas Snyder. *Trends in Educational Equity of Girls and Women.* Washington, DC: U.S. Government Printing Office, 2000.

Barton, Paul E. and Richard J. Coley. *America's Smallest School: The Family.* Princeton, NJ: Educational Testing Service, 1992.

———. *Captive Students: Education and Training in America's Prisons.* Princeton, NJ: Educational Testing Service, 1996.

Barzun, Jacques. *Begin Here.* Chicago, IL: University of Chicago Press, 1991.

Beatty, Alexandra S., Clyde M. Reese, Hilary R. Persky, and Peggy Carr. *NAEP 1994 U.S. History Report Card.* Washington, DC: U.S. Department of Education, Office of Educational Research and Improvement, 1994.

Berliner, David C. and Bruce J. Biddle. *The Manufactured Crisis.* Reading, MA: Addison-Wesley, 1996.

Bettelheim, Bruno. *The Uses of Enchantment: The Meaning and Importance of Fairy Tales.* New York: Knopf, 1976.

Bissenger, H. G. *Friday Night Lights.* New York: Da Capo Press, 2000.

Bracey, Gerald W. *Setting the Record Straight: Responses to Misconceptions About Public Education in the United States.* Alexandria, VA: Association of Supervision and Curriculum Development, 1997.

Bruer, John T. *The Myth of the First Three Years.* New York: The Free Press/ Simon & Schuster, 1999.

Bruner, Jerome S. and Sylva, K. editors. *Play—Its Role in Development and Evolution.* New York: Penguin 1976

Burke, Jim. *I Hear America Reading: Why We Read, What We Read.* Portsmouth, NH: Heinemann, 1999.

Butler, Dorothy. *Cushla and Her Books.* Boston: The Horn Book, 1980.

Campbell, Jay R., Catherine M. Hombo, and John Mazzeo. *NAEP 1999 Trends in Academic Progress: Three Decades of Student Performance.* Washington, DC: National Center for Education Statistics, NCES, 2000. Also available at: http://nces.ed.gov/nationsreportcard.

Carlsen, G. Robert and Anne Sherrill. *Voices of Readers: How We Come to Love Books.* Urbana, IL: National Council of Teachers of English, 1988.

Carson, Ben. *Gifted Hands: The Ben Carson Story.* Grand Rapids: Zondervan, 1990.

Cazden, Courtney B. *Child Language and Education.* New York: Holt, Rinehart and Winston, 1972.

Chesterton, G. K. *Orthodoxy: The Romance of Faith.* New York: Doubleday-Image, 1990.

Clark, Margaret M. *Young Fluent Readers.* London: Heinemann, 1976.

Coles, Robert. *The Call of Stories: Teaching and the Moral Imagination.* Boston: Houghton Mifflin, 1989.

Copperman, Paul. *The Literacy Hoax: The Decline of Reading, Writing, and Learning in the Public Schools and What We Can Do About It.* New York: Morrow, 1980.

Cordes, Colleen and Edward Miller. *FOOL'S GOLD: A Critical Look at Computers in Childhood.* College Park, MD: Alliance for Childhood, 2000. Also available at www.allianceforchildhood.net/projects/computers/computers_reports.htm.

Csikszentmihalyi, M., K. Rathnude, K., and S. Whalen. *Talented Teenagers: The Roots of Success and Failure.* New York: Cambridge University Press, 1993.

Davies, Robertson. *One Half of Robertson Davies.* New York: Viking, 1977.

Donahue, Patricia L., Kristen E. Voelki, Jay R. Campbell, and John Mazzeo. *NAEP 1998 Reading Report Card for the Nation and States.* Washington, DC: U.S. Department of Education, NCES, 1999.

Donahue, Patricia L., Voelkl, Kristin E., Campbell, Jay R., and John Mazzeo. *NAEP 1998 Reading Report Card for the Nation and the States.* Washington, DC: US Department of Education, NCES, 1999. Also at: http://nces.ed.gov/.

Downing, J., and C. K. Leong. *Psychology of Reading.* New York: Macmillan, 1982.

Dreyer, Phillip. *Vision and Realities in Literacy: Sixtieth Yearbook of the Claremont Reading Conference.* Claremont, CA: Claremont Reading Conference, 1996.

Duff, Nancy, Judith Campbell, C. Applebaum, Karin Martinson, and Emily Martin. *Be All That You Can Be.* Washington, DC: National Women's Law Center, 2000.

Durkin, Dolores. *Children Who Read Early.* New York: Teachers College, 1966.

Egoff, Sheila, G. T. Stubbs, and L. F. Ashley. *Only Connect.* New York: Oxford University Press, 1969.

Elkind, David. *The Hurried Child: Growing Up Too Soon Too Fast.* Reading, MA: Addison Wesley, 1981.

————. *Miseducation: Preschoolers at Risk.* New York: Knopf, 1987.

Elley, Warwick B. *How in the World Do Students Read?* Hamburg: International Association for the Evaluation of Educational Achievement, 1992.

Fadiman, Clifton. *Party of One: The Selected Writings of Clifton Fadiman.* New York: World Publishing Company, 1955.

Foertsch, Mary A. *Reading In and Out of School.* Princeton, NJ: National Assessment of Educational Progress, 1992.

Goleman, Daniel. *Emotional Intelligence: Why it can matter more than IQ.* New York: Bantam, 1995.

Goodlad, John I. *A Place Called School: Prospects for the Future.* New York: McGraw-Hill, 1984.

Goodman, Kenneth, Patrick Shannon, Yvonne Freeman, and S. Murphy. *Report Card on Basal Readers.* New York: Richard Owen, 1988.

Gopnik, Alison, Andrew N. Meltzoff, and Patricia K. Kuhl. *The Scientist in the Crib.* New York: Morrow, 1999.

Hart, Betty and Todd Risley. *Meaningful Differences in the Everyday Experience of Young American Children.* Baltimore, MD: Brookes Publishing, 1996.

Healy, Jane M. *Failure to Connect: How Computers Affect Our Children's Minds—for Better and Worse.* New York: Simon & Schuster, 1998.

Heyns, Barbara. *Summer Learning and the Effects of Schooling.* New York: Academic Press, 1978.

Hodgkinson, Harold L. *The Same Client: The Demographics of Education and Service Delivery Systems.* Washington, DC: Institute of Educational Leadership, 1989.

Kohn, Alfie. *Punished by Rewards: The Trouble with Gold Stars, Incentive Plans, A's, Praise, and Other Bribes.* Boston: Houghton Mifflin, 1993.

Krashen, Stephen. *The Power of Reading.* Englewood, CO: Libraries Unlimited, 1993.

————. *Writing: Research: Theory and Applications.* Torrance, CA: Laredo Publishing Company, 1984.

Kubey, Robert and Mihaly Csikszentmihalyi. *Television and the Quality of Life,* Hillsdale, NJ: Erlbaum, 1990.

Lance, Keith Curry, Lynda Welborn, and Christine Hamilton-Pennell. *The Impact of School Media Centers on Academic Achievement.* Englewood, CO: Libraries Unlimited, 1993.

Lance, Keith Curry, Marcia J. Rodney, and Christine Hamilton-Pennell. *How School Librarians Help Kids Achieve Standards: The Second Colorado Study.* Denver, CO: Colorado State Library, 2000.

Lefkowitz, Bernard. *Our Guys: The Glen Ridge Rape and the Secret Life of the Perfect Suburb.* Berkeley, CA: University of California Press, 1997

Leonhardt, Mary. *Parents Who Love Reading, Kids Who Don't: How It Happens and What You Can Do About It.* New York: Crown, 1993.

Maraniss, David *When Pride Still Mattered: A Life of Vince Lombardi.* New York: Simon & Schuster, 1999.

McCrum, Robert, William Cran, and Robert MacNeil. *The Story of English.* New York: Viking, 1986.

McQuillan, Jeff. *The Literacy Crisis: False Claims, Real Solutions.* Portsmouth, NH: Heinemann, 1998.

Morgan, Judith and Neil. *Dr. Seuss and Mr. Geisel.* New York: Random House, 1995.

Mullis, Ina V. S., J. R. Campbell, and A. E. Farstrup. *1992 NAEP Reading Report Card for the Nation and States.* Washington, DC: National Center for Education Statistics, U.S. Government Printing Office, 1993.

Mullis, Ina V. S., John A. Dossey, Jay R. Campbell, Claudia A. Gentile, Christine O'Sullivan, and Andrew Latham. *NAEP 1992 Trends in Academic Progress.* Washington, DC: Office of Educational Research and Improvement, U.S. Department of Education, 1994.

Neal, Anne D. and Jerry L. Martin. *Losing America's Memory: Historical Illiteracy in the 21st Century.* Washington, DC: American Council of Trustees and Alumni, 2000.

Newell, G. and R. K. Durst. *Exploring Texts: The Role of Discussion and Writing in the Teaching and Learning of literature.* Norwood, MA: Christopher-Gordon, 1993.

Nielsen Media Research. *2000 Report on Television: The First 50 Years.* New York, NY: Nielsen Media Research, 2000.

Niles, J. A. and L. A. Harris. *New inquiries in reading research and instruction,* Rochester, NY: National Reading Conference, 1982.

Ohanian, Susan. *One Size Fits Few: The Folly of Educational Standards.* Portsmouth, NH: Heinemann, 1999.

Pamuk, E., D. Makuc, K. Heck, C. Reuben, and K. Lockner. *Health, United States, 1998: Socioeconomic Status and Health Chartbook.* Washington, DC: U.S. Government Printing Office, 1998.

Pearson, P. David. *Handbook of Reading Research.* New York: Longman, 1984.

Pennac, Daniel. *Better than Life.* York, ME: Stenhouse Publishers, 1999.

Perkinson, Henry J. *Two Hundred Years of American Educational Thought.* New York: David McKay, 1976.

Postman, Neil. *Teaching as a Conserving Activity.* New York: Delacorte, 1980.

Pratt, Rebecca, and others. *The Condition of Education 2000.* Washington, DC: U.S. Department of Education, NCES, 2000. Also available at: http:// nces.ed.gov/pubsearch/index/asp.

Ravitch, Diane and Chester Finn. *What Do Our 17-Year-Olds Know?* New York: Harper & Row, 1987

Roberts, Donald, Ulla G. Foehr, Victoria Rideout, and Mollyann Brodie. *Kids & Media @ The New Millennium.* Menlo Park, CA: The Henry J. Kaiser Family Foundation, 1999. Also at www.kff.org/content/1999/1535/ ChartPack.pdf.

Rumbaut, Ruben G. and Wayne A. Cornleiu. *California's Immigrant Children: Theory, Research, and Implications for Education Policy.* San Diego, CA: Center for U.S.-Mexican Studies, University of California, 1996.

Schank, Roger C. *Tell Me a Story: A New Look at Real and Artificial Memory.* New York: Scribners, 1990.

Schwartz, Ronald B. *For the Love of Books.* New York: Grosset/Putnam, 1999.

Snow, Catherine E., M. Susan Burns, and Peg Griffin, editors. *Preventing Reading Difficulties in Young Children.* Washington, DC: National Academy Press, 1998.

Starting Points: The Report of the Carnegie Task Force on Meeting the Needs of Young Children. New York: Carnegie Corporation, 1994.

Taylor, Gordon Rattray. *The Natural History of the Brain.* New York: E. P. Dutton, 1979.

The 2000 Kids Count Data Book. Baltimore, MD: Annie E. Casey Foundation, 2000. Also available online at: www.aecf.org/kidscount/kc2000/.

Thogmartin, Mark B. *Teaching a Child to Read With Children's Books.* Bloomington, IN: EDINFO Press, 1996.

Vernez, Georges, Richard Krop, and C. Peter Ryde. *Closing the Education Gap: Benefits and Costs.* Santa Monica, CA: RAND Corporation, 1999.

West, Jerry, Kristin Denton, and Elvira Germino-Hausken. *America's Kindergartners: Findings from the Early Childhood Longitudinal Study, Kindergarten Class of 1998–99, Fall 1998.* Washington, DC: US Department of Education, NCES, 2000.

White, Dorothy. *Books Before Five.* Portsmouth, NH: Heinemann, 1984.

Zill, Nicholas and Marianne Winglee. *Who Reads Literature?* Cabin John, MD: Seven Locks Press, 1990.

Subject Index for the Text

(*See* Author-Illustrator Index for books listed in the Treasury; **bold** indicates section devoted to subject.)

Abecedarian Project, 16, 62

Accelerated Reader, 122–123

Adams, Franklin Pierce, 339

Advanced Book Exchange, 164

Advanced Placement exams, xxii

Advantage Learning System, 122

Adventures of Tintin, The, 135

affirmations of child, 15–16, 42

African-American students, 200–201, 335, 336, 337, 338

Alaska, 144

Albom, Mitch, 172

Alexander and the Terrible, Horrible, No Good Very Bad Day, 81

ALibris.com, 164

Alice Ramsey's Grand Adventure, 85

aliterates, 135–138

All About Alfie, 78

Allen, Dr. Robert, 116–117

Allen, Steve, 175

Alliance for Childhood, 191

Allington, Richard, 111, 144

Alma Elementary, 157–158

American Academy of Pediatrics, 197

American Library Association, 162, 183

Amherst College, 9

Ammon, Bette D., 81

Anderson, Gary, 96–97

anthologies, 90, 326

Antinoff, Melissa Olans, 78–79

Appomattox, VA, 11

Archie comic, 134

Armstrong, Alison, 193

Aron, Helen, 210

Asch, Frank, 34

AT&T Labs, 61

at-risk, *see* poverty

athletics, *see* sports

Atkins, Jeannine, 85

Atlanta, GA, 115

attention span, 40–42, 64, 76–80, 83–84

Atwater, Richard and Florence, 80

Auchincloss, Louis, 182

audio book, 12, 18, 71–72, 87–89, 209–213

  abridged vs. unabridged, 210–211

  in middle school, 212–213

  profile of users, 210–211

author, writing to, 101–102

Author Autobiography series, 90

Author Day, 91

author information, 89–92

Avi, 90

Babbitt, Natalie, 74

Baby-Sitters' Club series, 176

background knowledge, 10–11

Baker, Keith, 91

Baltimore, MD, 3

Bart's Books, 165

Barzun, Jacques, 5, 53, 182

basal reader, *see:* textbook,

baseball text, 10

Basic Lexicon (vocabulary), 17

Batman comic, 134

Battery Park City Day Nursery, 79–80

Bauer, Caroline Feller, 102

Bauermeister, Erica, 75, 173

Bears' House, The, xv

Beavis and Butthead, 14

Beck, Ellen, 88–89

Becoming a Nation of Readers, 2–3, 110, 111

bed lamp, 44

Beers, Dr. G. Kylene, 137–138, 158–159, 171, 212

Behrens, Walter and Nancy, 129–130

Belmore, Rev. Kent, xxiii–xxiv

Belmore, Thomas, xxiii–xxiv

Bennett, William, 140

Berners-Lee, Tim, 185

Berman, Matt, 163

Bernstein, Richard, 73–74

Bethel College, 117

Bethlehem Steel, 3

Bettelheim, Bruno, 21, 68, 73

Better Than Life, 169

Between the Lions, 208–209

Beverly Hills, CA, 145

Bible, 116

Bibliofind.com, 164

bicycle effect on reading, 116

Big Alfie and Annie Rose Storybook, 78

Big Alfie Out-of-Doors Storybook, 78

Big Book of Urban Legends, The, 56

Big Link, The, 164

Biggest Bear, The, 77

biographies, 54–55

Birkerts, Sven, 141

Black Books Galore!, 163–164

black-white test score gap, 200–201

Blessing Way, The, 54

blind date, and reading, 83–84

Bloom, Harold, 128

Blos, Joan, 81

Bobbin Girl, The, 85

Bobbsey Twins, The, 181

Boltz Junior High, 151–152

Bomba, the Jungle Boy, 182

book basket, 43

Book Links, 90, 162

book(s),

access to, *see* print climate

anthologies, 55–56, 90, **326**

audio, 12, 71–72, 87–89, 209–213

and babies, 29–36, 62–69

banning, *see* censorship

basket, 43–44

Best of Year, 163

board, 33, 66, 67

childhood favorite, 86–87, 164–165

Children's Choices, 162

children's publishers, 341

classics, 140–142, 172, 176–177

club(s), 169–175

comic, 116, 133–135

computerized, 187–188, 192–193

controlled vocabulary, 45–46, 70

cover(s), 156–158

discussion, 47, 64–66, 70–71,.75–76, 169–176

encyclopedia, 119, 148

face-out shelving of, 155–158

fairy/folk tales, 73–75, 330

fiction, 21–22, 57–59, 74, 181

in "good books" box, 158–159

in the home, 42–44, 67, 117–118, 335

"home run," 115, 136–137

and infant behavior, 32–34, 63–65

interactive, 67

and Internet, 185–193

"junk," 132–134

lifetime readers of, 97–98

lists of recommended, 162–164

nonfiction, 114–115, 138, 181, **222**

novels, **284**

ownership of, 42, 43–44, 66, 117–118, 146, 164–165, *see also:* print climate

personalized, 66

picture, 64–65, **223**

plot-driven, 84, 178

poetry, **323**

predictable, 70, 71–72, 220

protests, *see* censorship

Reading Rainbow choices, 163

reference, **222**

repeat readings of, 33, 62–63

reports, 92–93, 171–172

reviews, 162–163

search, 164–165, 341–342

series, 47, 86–87, 114, 129, 176–185
sexism in, 74–75
short novels, **269**
in Spanish, 163, 343
sports, 161
talks, 47, 95, 124, 135–136, 166, 170–176
teacher favorites, 86–87, 162
teen favorites, 162
"too many," 159, 165–166
trade, 111
used, 149, 164
visual-puzzle, 72–73
vs. computer, 148
vs. video, 69
vs. worksheets, 19–20, 35–36, 116–117
wordless, 71–72, **219**
see also: library; novels; textbooks
Book-of-the-Month Club, 136
BookFinder.com, 164
Booklist, 162
Books Aloud project, 147
Books Before Five, 66
Books in Print, 164
bookseller Web sites, 341–342
bookstore(s), 149–150, 157
Boston City Hospital, 167–168
Boy Scouts of America, 181
boys and reading, *see:* gender differences
Bracey, Gerald, 339
Bradbury, Ray, 134
brain research, 60–63
Brave Companions, 56
Brazelton, Dr. T. Berry, 28–29, 36
Brenner, Barbara, 78, 85
bribery and reading, 128–132
Brigham Young University, 165
Britton-Macon Area School District (MI), 172–173
Brown, Don, 85
Bruer, John T., 61
Brunvand, Jan, 56
Burgess, Thornton W., 129
Burke, Jim, 97–98
Burlingame High School (CA), 97–98
Bush, Pres. George, 206
Butler, Dorothy, 29–30
Butter Battle Book, The, 81
Byars, Betsy, 126

California, print climate, 144, 153, 160
Cal. State University-San Marcos, 163
captioned TV, *see:* close captioning
Carbo, Marie, 88–89
Carle, Eric, 34, 35, 69
Carlson, G. Robert, 184
Carnegie Foundation, 12
Carson, Dr. Ben, 194–196
Carson, Sonya, 119, 194–196
Carter, Noelle & David, 67
Casemont, Charles, 193
cassette player, *see:* audio book
Cat in the Hat, The, 46, 62–63, 72
Cate School, The, 165
censorship, 179, 181
Center for the Study of Books in Spanish, 163
Cerf, Bennet, 170
chapter books,
in kindergarten, 78–79
in preschool, 79–80
see also: novels
Charlotte's Web, xi, xxiv, 79–80, 88, 89, 149
Chesterton, G. K., 73
Chibi: A True Story from Japan, 85
Chicago Public Schools, 115
Child and the Machine, The, 193
Children's Books and Their Creators, 90
Children's Choices, 162
children's literature Web sites, 342–343
Cho, Kyung-Sook, 132–133
Choking Doberman, The, 56
Chocolate War, The, 217
Christmas Tree in the White House, 85
Christopher, Matt, 161
Chronicles of Narnia, 176
Churchill, Winston, 121–122
Cinderella, 73
Clark, Joe, 23
classic(s), 140–142, 176–177, 178
definition of, 177
classroom library, *see:* library
Cleary, Beverly, 102, 176
clergy, 166–167
Cliffs Notes, 177
Cline-Ransome, Lesa, 85
Clinton, President Bill, 115
closed-captioning, 206–207
Coerr, Eleanor, 78
Coles, Robert, 58, 85
Collier, James and Christopher, 54

Colorado, 144
Colorado State Library, 144
Comer, Dr. James, xx–xxi
Comer, Maggie, xx–xxi
comic book, 116, 133–135, 176
   vocabulary, 132–135
Commission on Reading, 2, 110, 111
compliments to child, 15–16
comprehension, 8, 38–39, 45–46
Compton (CA) schools, 145
computer(s), 148, 185–186
   as addiction, 193
   and developmental threats, 190–192
   and e-books, 187–188, 192–193
   jobs, 4
   and learning, 187–189, 190
   in preschool and elementary, 186, 190–192
   reading on, 187–188
   and teachers, 189–190
   as "time-waster", 188–190
   and writing skills, 190
   see also: Internet
Conger, Lesley, 143
Connecticut, 336
Connecticut Farms Elementary (NJ), 1
Conrad, Pam, 56, 82
Contra Costa Juvenile Hall, 95–96
controlled-vocabulary books, 45–46, 70, 72
conversation vocabulary, 13–15, 16, 17–18,
   49–50
Cook, Alistair, 175
Cooney, Barbara, 85
Copperman, Paul, 201
Corduroy, 69
Cormier, Robert, 217
Cosby, Bill, 45, 50–51
Cosby Show, The, 45
Courage of Sarah Noble, The, 78
Cox, Helen, 152–154
cricket (sport) text, 10
Cricket in Times Square, 80
Cronkite, Walter, 175
Crosby, Texas, 88, 175
Cuomo, Mario, 50
Curses! Broiled Again, 56
Cushla and Her Books, 29–30

Dahl, Roald, 89, 91, 178
Dale, Jim, 212
Dalgliesh, Alice, 78

Dallas, Texas, 19
Dartmouth College, 334
Davies, Robertson, 83
day care, 16, 41–42
Day No Pigs Would Die, A, 49
deaf children, 38
Dear Mr. Henshaw, 102
DEAR time, *see:* SSR
DeBakey, Dr. Michael, 119
DeCasper, Dr. Anthony, 29, 62
Deep in the Forest, 71
Deford, Frank, 161
Dertouzos, Dr. Michael L., 185–186
Detroit, MI, 194
Deuker, Carl, 161
Dickens, Charles, 83, 84
DiMaggio, Joe, 19
discussion clubs,
   book, 169–175
   mother-daughter, 173
   mother-son, 174–175
dish washing, while listening, 93
Distant Trumpet, A, 137
DODDS, program, 165–166
Dodson, Shireen, 173
Dominican Republic, 143–144
Don't Go Near That Rabbit, Frank!, 56, 82
Donahue, Phil, 175
dosage device for TV, 206
do's and don'ts of read-aloud, **99–105**
Down Syndrome, 30
dropout rates, 335
Duncan, Lois, 212
Durkin, Doloris, 42–43
Duxbury (MA) Free Public Library, 150
Dygard, Thomas J., 161
dyslexia and SSR, 114–115
Dyson, Marianne J., 189

E. B. White: Some Writer!, 89
early fluent readers, 37–38, 42–43
education,
   emotional, 57–59
   and income, xxiv–xxv, 16, 20–21
   Web sites, 340–209
educational TV (PBS), 207–209
Efta, Martha, 113–114
Eisner, Michael, 205
Eleanor, 85
Ella Enchanted, 75

email and writing skills, 192
Emotional Intelligence, 58
Encounter, 81
encyclopedia, 119, 148
Encyclopedia Britannica, 119
England, 121
English language, 49–51, 186
  advantage of, 4
  in Pacific Rim nations, 4
  as second language (ESL), 49–50, 71–72,
    133–134, 186
Erskine, Chris, 25–27
Everything Book, The, 65–66, 84
extrinsic vs. intrinsic rewards, 122–132

face-out shelving, 155–158
faculty education level, 338
Fadiman, Clifton, 58, 99, 136
Failure to Connect, 193
fairy tales, 73–74, **330**
  heroines in, 74
  purpose of, 73–74
fathers, xxi–xxiv
  see also: parents
Faulkner, William, 161
favorite books of teachers, 86–87
Ferguson, Prof. Ronald F., 201
Fernands, Ellie, 40–41
fiction, 74
  as "danger," 181
  purpose of, 21–22, 57–59
Fifth Book of Junior Authors and Illustrators, 90
Fink, Rosalie, 114
Finland, 7–8, 36, 37, 133, 207
Fitzgerald, F. Scott, 171
Fleming, Denise, 65, 84
food and reading, 33–34, 43–44, 150–152
*FOOL'S GOLD: A Critical Look at Computers
  in Childhood,* 191–192
Fort Collins, CO, 151
Foster, Sheila, 163–164
Fox, Mem, 81
Foxman, The, 49
France, 7
Frandsen, Betty, 95–96
Frank Merriwell, 182
Franklin, John Hope, xxi
Freeman, Don, 69
French language, 51
French, Vivian, 85

Gacon, Paul, 81
Gannett, Ruth Stiles, 78, 114
Gates, Bill, 187–188
gender differences, xxi–xxiii, 75
George, Jean, 54
German language, 51
Germany, 59
Gettysburg Address, 4, 93, 121
Getz, David, 85
Gherman, Beverly, 89
Ghost Girl, 56
Giamatti, Bart, 161
G.I. Bill, 336
Gifted Hands: The Ben Carson Story, 196
Gillilan, Strickland, xi
Gingrich, Newt, 129–130
girls (females), *see:* gender differences
Giver, The, 174
Godden, Rumer, 78
Gold, Prof. Arthur, 141–142
Goleman, Daniel, 58
Gone With the Wind, 81, 125–126
Good Old Boy, 49
"good old days" myth, 333–339
Good-Bye House, 34
"good books" box, 158–159
Goodlad, John, 107
Goodwill thrift shops, 149
Goosebumps books, 176–177, 181
Gould, Stephen Jay, 188
graduation rates, 334, 352
grammar, 49–50, 52
Grandaddy's Place, 78
Graveyards of the Dinosaurs, 85
Great Gatsby, The, 140, 172
Great Lives, 54–55
Green Eggs and Ham, 46
Green, Gerald, 137
Greene, Bob, 56, 93
Greene, Graham, 1
Greenwich, CT, 174
Griffith, Helen, 78
grocery lessons for libraries, 155–158
Grosvenor, Gilbert, 337
Groton School, The, 171
Guatemala, xxi

Haley, Alex, 90
Hamill, Pete, 182
Hamilton, Virginia, 74–75

Handford, Martin, 72–73
Happily Ever After, 75
Hard, Andrew and Jacob, 201–202
Hard, Mike and Sally, 201–202
Hardy Boys, The, 181
Harris-Jacobson Wide Range Readability
    formula, 45
Harry Potter, xxiii, 36, 75, 124, 176–183, 212
    as fairy tale, 73–74
Harry Potter and the Goblet of Fire, xxiii, 36,
    177, 212
Hart, Dr. Betty, 13–15
Harvard Business School, 58
Harvard Law School, 334
Harvard University, 141, 188, 334
Harvey, Paul, 92
Hasbro Children's Hospital, 200
Hassett, Erin, 32–36
Hassett, Jim and Linda, 32–36
Hatchet, 89
Hayashi, Hiroshi, 23–24
Hayden, Torey, 56
Head Start, 11
Healy, Jane M., 193
heart quotient (HQ), 57–59
Heidi, 176–177
Hemingway, Ernest, 161
Henkes, Kevin, 77
Her Stories, 74
Herda, Reni, 113
Here Come the Aliens!, 77
Hergé, 134–135
heroine books, 74–75
Hewitt, Don, 57
Hey! Listen to This, 90
Hill, Eric, 64–65, 67
Hill, Lee Sullivan, 107
Hillerman, Tony, 53–54
Hinchman, W. S., 171
Hines, Gary, 85
Hiroshima No Pika, 81
history,
    tests, 120–122
    Web sites, 344
Hitler, Adolf, 121, 166
Hobbit, The, 177
Hoffman, Dustin, 135
Holden, Robert, 81
Holm, Anne, 49
Holman, Felice, 49

Holmes, Beverly, 113
Holmes, Mark, 188
Holt, Dr. Charles Allen, 148
home,
    hours at, 117, 146
    language, 49–50
    reading materials, 42–43
    schooling, 34, 37
    see also: print climate
"home run" book, 115, 136–137
homework, 198–199
Homework Help on the Internet, 188–189
Hop on Pop, 46
Horgan, Paul, 137
Horn Book, The, 162, 178
hours in school vs. home, 117, 146
House on East 88th Street, The, 78
How in the World Do Students Read?, 339
Howe, John, 75
HQ (heart quotient), 57–59
Huff, Sam, 127
Hughes, Shirley, 78
    see also: author index
Hunchback of Notre Dame, The, 177
Hunt, Jr., Lyman C., 109
Hunt, Marie, 202
Hurwitz, Johanna, 78
Hyman, Trina Schart, 75, 77

I'm a Little Mouse, 67
I Hear America Reading, 97–98
I SPY books, 72–73
I.B.M., 4
Idaho Falls Public Library, 91–92
illiteracy, 3–4
    see also: aliteracy
illiterates and reading to children, 12, 18,
    71–72, 209–210
illustrations, *see:* picture book
imitation, 11, 38
immigrant, 18, 71–72
    children, xix, 198–199
in utero learning, 29
incentives to read, 122–132
income and education, xxiv–xxv, 325
India, 4
Indian in the Cupboard, The, 176
information highway, *see:* Internet; computer
International Assoc. for the Evaluation of
    Educational Achievement, 107

International Reading Association (IRA), 162, 163

Internet, 122, 164, **185–193,** 340–348
 reliability, 187
 research links, 345–346
 vs. the library, 185, 187

intrinsic vs. extrinsic rewards, 122–132

IQ vs. HQ, 57–59

Island of the Skog, The, 77

Israel, 4, 43, 143, 146, 186

Israeli hockey syndrome, 143

Jack and the Beanstalk, 75

Jacobs, Dr. Jim, 165–166

Japan, student reading in, 23–24

Jefferson, Thomas, 5

Johnny on the Spot, 82

Johns Hopkins Medical Center, 196

Johns Hopkins University, 4, 61

Johnson, Samuel, 176

Jones, Rebecca C., 85

Josefina Story Quilt, The, 78

Joyce, William, 84

Just Another Kid, 56

juvenile offenders and reading, 96–97

Kagan, Jerome, 40

Kahn, Merry, 91

Kaiser Family Foundation, 199, 200

Katcavich, Jim, 127

Kate and the Beanstalk, 75

Kate Shelley: Bound for Legend, 75, 81

Kellogg, Steven, 77

Kilborne, Allerton, 67–68

Killing Mr. Griffin, 212

kindergarten students, xix, 12, 13, 43, 146

King, Larry, 175

King, Stephen, 141

Kipling, Rudyard, 142

KIPP Academies, 109, 131

Kirkus Reviews, 162

Kline, Derek and Kelly, xi–xii

Kohn, Alfie, 75–76, 127

Koppel, Ted, 175

Kosciusko, MS, 175

Kotlowitz, Alex, 56

Krashen, Stephen, 52, 106, 132–134, 144, 145, 342

Kunhardt, Dorothy, 67

Kunishima, Geri and Lindy, 31–32

Kunishima, Steven, 31–32

Lafcadio, the Lion Who Shot Back, 78

Lance, Keith Curry, 144

language development, 41–42, 68, 167

Last Angry Man, The, 137

Last Princess, The, 85

learning disabilities, 113–114, 347

Lebowitz, Fran, 138

Lee, Harper, 37

Leon's Story, 85

Leslie College, 114

Let's Hear It for the Girls, 75, 173

Levine, Ellen, 85

Levine, Gail Carson, 75

library, 43, **143–168**
 access to print in, 130–132, 137–138, 144–154, 156,
 card, 137
 circulation and reading scores, 2, 130–132, 144–146, 147
 in classroom, 47, 144–145
 collection, 114–115, 123, 144–146
 compared to bookstores, 149–158
 cost, 145, 160
 cost vs. inmate expense, 160
 exemplary school, 151–154
 and face-out shelving, 155–158
 and grocery stores, 155–158
 in home, 42, 147–149
 and immigrants, 18
 and incentive programs, 123
 marketing, 151–159
 in 1906 home, 334–335
 and poverty children, 130–133, 144–146, 147, 152–154, 160
 in preschools, 147
 in Tatum (TX) Primary, 130–133
 with "too many" books, 159, 165–166
 usage by grade, 2
 vs. book stores, 149–158
 vs. the Internet, 149
 Web sites, 345
 see also: print climate

Lieberman, Jan, 124, 163, 210

Lilly's Purple Plastic Purse, 77

Lincoln County, OR, 129–130

Lindbergh Middle School (CA), 152–154

Lindsay, Vachel, 142

Linnakylä, Pirjo, 207
listening, 82, 83
    comprehension, 8–9, 10, 39–40
    vocabulary, 8–9, 12, 34, 45–46
Listening Library, 212
literature, purpose of, 20–22, 57–59, 97–98
Little House on the Prairie, 34
Little Red Riding Hood, 77
Littles, The, 78
Lodi, CA, xviii
(London) *Sunday Times,* 121
London Times, 124
London, Jack, 142
Long Beach, CA, 152
Longmont, CO, 36
Louisiana, 145
Love You Forever, 33
Lowry, Lois, 174
Lucy Cousins Book of Nursery Rhymes, The, 63
Lyle the Crocodile series, 78

MacLachlin, Patricia, 183
magazine reading, 138, 160–161
Magazines for Children, 163
Magic School Bus, The, 85
Magic Treehouse series, 184
Maid of the North, The, 75
Maine, 143–144
Make Way for Ducklings, xv, 203
Maniac Magee, 89–90
Mann, Horace, 5
Maquoketa, Iowa, 91
Marquand, J. P., 161
Maruki, Toshi, 81
Mary Anning and the Sea Dragon, 85
Marzollo, Jean, 72–73
math scores and television, 198
M.I.T., 185
Mathiews, Franklin K., 181
McCleery, William, 78
McCloskey, Robert, xv, 203
McCracken, Robert and Marlene, 109, 112
McCullough, David, 56, 122
McCully, Emily Arnold, 75, 85
McDonald's, 44
McNaughton, Colin, 77
McPartland, Margie, 174–175
McQuillan, Jeff, 144, 342
Meaningful Differences, 13–15, 62

Meek, Margaret, 183
Merrow, John, 36
Metropolis, IL, 202
Mexican Pet, The, 56
Mick Hart Was Here, 85
Mirette and Bellini Cross Niagara Falls, 75
Mirette on the Highwire, 75
Mississippi, 336
Modesto, CA, xxiv
Moerbeek, Kees, 33
Montclair Kimberly Academy, 190
Moore, Clement, 67–68
Morris, Mary McGarry, 51
Morris, Willie, 49
Morrison, Toni, 51
Mosel, Arlene, 77
Mother Goose, 60, 62–63
Mother-Daughter Book Club, 173
mothers, xix, 173–175, 194–196
Motor Boys, The, 181
Motorola, 4
Mr. Coffee, *see:* Joe DiMaggio
Mr. Popper's Penguins, 80
Munsch, Robert, 33
Murphy's Boy, 56
Murrow, Edward R., 175
My Brother Sam Is Dead, 54
My Father's Dragon, 78, 114
My First Word Book, 65–66
My Side of the Mountain, 54
Myth of the First Three Years, The, 61

Nancy Drew, 176, 181
Natl. Assessment of Educational Progress
    (NAEP), 1, 4–5, 19, 52–53, 107,
    111–112, 117–118, 190, 198, 336, 338
Natl. Education Association (NEA), 46,
    183
National Geographic, 153
National Geographic Society, 188, 337
National Public Radio (NPR), 49
Natl. Reading Research Center, 127
national standards, 57–59
Needlman, Dr. Robert, 167–168
Nepal, 186
Netanyahu, Benjamin, 186
Neuman, Dr. Susan, 147
New York City schools, 145–146
New York Giants, 127

New York Times, 3, 5, 9, 73, 120–121, 124, 129, 155, 189
Newport Elementary, 88
newspaper vocabulary, 17
Night Before Christmas, The, 67–68
Nintendo, 206
Nixon, Joan Lowery, 212
North Carolina, 16
North to Freedom, 49
Not One Damsel in Distress, 75
novel(s), 82–84,
   list of short, **269–283**
   list of full, **284–322**
   transition from picture books to, 76–80, 82–85

OCLC, 163
O'Dell, Charli, 151–152
O'Donnell, Rosie, 179
O'Farrell, Jill, 131–132
Ogilvy, David, 47
Ohanian, Susan, 140
Old Henry, 81
Oliver, Mike, 157–158
On Cassette, 211
One Child, 56
O'Neill Jr., Thomas P., 22–24
one-on-one time, 40, 47–48
100 Books for Girls to Grow On, 173
Oprah's Book Club, 76, 90, 112, 120
oral reading liabilities, 112–113
Osborne, Mary Pope, 75
Other Side of the River, The, 56
Outdoor Girls, The, 181
Overall Boys, The, 136
Oxenbury, Helen, 71

Paar, Jack, 175
parent(s),
   and brain development, 60–63
   conversation, 17–18
   education level, xix, 13
   mothers, xix, 173–175
   fathers, xxi–xxiv, 175
   parenting Web sites, 346–347
   as role model, 9, 11, 12, 20–21, 38, 42–43, 66, 117, 208
   see also: poverty families
Park, Barbara, 85

Parker, Tom, 9
Parker, Toni T., 163–164
Pat the Bunny, 67
Patten, William Gilbert, 182
Paul Harvey's The Rest of the Story, 92
Paulsen, Gary, 49, 54, 89
Peck, Robert Newton, 49
pediatricians, 167–168
Peet, Bill, 77
Pennac, Daniel, 169
Pennsylvania, 144
personalized book, 66
Peterson, John, 78
Phelps, David, 129–130
Phelps, Ethel Johnston, 75
Phi Delta Kappan, 173,188
Philippines, 4
Phoenicians, 10
phonies, 9–10, 37
picture book(s), 64–65, 69
   in upper grades, 80–82
   list of, **223–269**
   predictable, 70, 71–72, **220–221**
   recommended, **223–269**
   transition to novels, 76–80
   visual-puzzle, 72–73
   wordless, **219**
Pied Piper of Hamelin, The, 81
Pink and Say, 81
Pinkwater, Daniel, 91
Place Called School, A, 107
Plato, 28, 37
pleasure role in reading, *see:* reading for pleasure
poetry, 62–63, 323; *see also:* Mother Goose
points for reading, *see:* incentives
Polacco, Patricia, 81
Porto Bello Gold, 164–165
Postman, Neil, 203
Potter, Beatrix, 74, 204
Potter-Burns School, 113
poverty families, xviii, xix–xxi, xxiii, 3–4, 10, 13–15, 16–17, 22–24, 71–72
   and book ownership, xix, 144–145, 146, 147, 167–168
   and libraries, 18, 144–145, 147, 152–154

Power of Reading, The, 52, 106, 109–110, 133
Powers, Jack, 188

predictable books, 70, 71–72, **220–221**
Prelutsky, Jack, xi, 33
preschoolers and chapter books, 79–80
Prescott, Orville, 60, 129
President Has Been Shot!, The, 85
Princeton University, 334
print climate, 20–21, 42, 43–44, 117–118,
    130–133, 144–148, 165–166, 167–168,
    208
prison,
    costs, 16, 160
    population, xxi, xxv, 160, 352
Proctor, Dr. Samuel DeWitt, 210
prohibitions uttered to child, 15
Public Broadcasting System (PBS), 207–209
publisher Web sites, 340–341
publishers and face-out shelving, 157
Punished by Rewards, 127
Purple Death: The Mysterious Flu of 1918, 85

questions
    in classroom, 70–71
    kinds asked by children, 68, 69
Quindlen, Anna, 75, 179

rain gutters for books, 157–158
Ramona Quimby series, 127–128
RAND Corp., 16
Rand, Donna, 163–164
rare words, 17
Ravich, Diane, 189
Rawls, Sophie, 91–92
Rawls, Wilson, 84, 91–92
Reach Out and Read (ROR), 167–168
Read Across America, 46, 183
Read All About It!, 55–56, 90
Read-Aloud Handbook, history of, xv–xviii
Read Aloud Virginia, 96–97
Read-Aloud Rhymes for the Very Young, xi, 33
Reader's Guide to Periodic Literature, 90
reading
    and access to print, *see:* print access
    as accrued skill, 3, 6–7, 107, 109, 111,
        112, 130–133, 176–177, 183–184
    by adolescents, 94–95, 97–98, 141, 195
    by adults, 182
    by advanced placement students, 9, 140
    affect on spelling, 52–54
    age for instruction, 8

and aliterates, 137–138
amount in school, 108
and audio books, 12, 18, 71–72, 87–89,
    209–213
as "blind date" experience, 83–84
by boys (males), xxi–xxiv
and bribery (rewards), 128–130
and childhood diseases, 25–27
class vs. club, 171
by college students, xiii, 4, 111
comic books, 116, 132–135
compared to TV, 17, 194–205
comprehension, 8, 38–39, 45–46
on computer screen, 187–188, 191
early fluent, 37–38, 42–43
and eating, 33–34, 43–44, 150–152
in elementary school day, 107
"facts," 6
fiction, 21–22, 57–59, 74, 181
formula, xxiv–xxv
gender differences, xxi–xxiii
and grammar, 49–50
in high school, 2, 4, 46–47, 107
and illness, 25–27
incentives/rewards, 122–132
and income, xix–xx, 20–21, 146, 351
in India, 4
instruction, 8, 9, 10–11, 18–20, 34–36,
    42–43, 116–117
international scores, 7–8, 107
in Israel, 146
as job skill, 3
"junk," 132–134
level in workplace, 3
level vs. listening level, 45–46
and life span, xxiv–xxv
lifetime readers, 2, 127
magazines, 138, 160–161
in middle school day, 107, 137–138
among minorities, 5
and mothers, 173–175
motivation, 9, 46–47, 137–138
and pain (unpleasure), 7, 46–47, 137–138
per day by 5th graders, 108
for pleasure, 1–2, 6–7, 22–24, 72–73, 94,
    110, 114, 131, 132–135, 137–138, 140,
    176–177, 178, 183
for points, *see:* incentives
and poverty, *see:* poverty families

purposes of, xxiv–xxv, 20–21, 74, 97–98, 128–129

recreational, 1–2, 7, 44, 137–138; *see also* reading for pleasure; SSR

related to time and scores, 109, 130–132

remedial, 112–115, 133

required, 118–119, 195–196

schooltime readers, 46–47

school time devoted to, 107

scores, xiii, 3, 4, 5, 7–8, 10, 108, 145–146, 200–201

silent vs. oral, 112–113

skills, 72

as social factor, 20–21, 45, 57–59

and special needs child, 29–36, 113–114

and spelling, 52–53

sports, xxii–xxiii, 161

student age for, 8

during summer vacation, 35, 115–116, 120

by teachers, 86–87, 135–136

and travel affect, 11

and vocabulary, 17–18, 49–50, 68, 72, 146

who reads best? 107

without tests, 116–117

"work" mentality, 138–140

and worksheets, 18–20

and writing skills, 42, 52–54, 138–140, 171–172

see also: SSR

reading aloud

and activities, 69, 70–71, 102

to adolescent, 2, 22–24, 46–47, 48–49, 55–56, 80–85, 92–95

as advertisement for pleasure, 7, 12, 44–46, 47

and attention span, 40–42, 76–80

on audio, *see:* audio book(s)

award books, 86–87

as blind date experience, 83–84

classics, 83, 84

in classroom, 55, 56, 57, 70–71, 80–85, 93–95

and clergy, 166–167

decline in upper grades, 44, 46–47

to discipline problems, 95–96

and discussion, 70–71, 75–76

do's and don'ts, 94–95, **99–105**

editing what is read, 82–83

and emotional bond, xxiv, 48–49, 63

with expression, 101

as grammar lesson, 17–18, 49–50

in high school, 93–95

and imagination, 82

by income level, 146

to infants, 12, 28–36, 60–67, 167

interruptions during, 68, 70–71

Israeli study on, 146

in juvenile detention centers, 95–96

to kindergartners, 45–46, 47, 76, 78–79, 146

magazine articles, 54, 92–93

in math class, 54–55, 93–95

and McDonald's, 44

in middle school, 44, 46–47, 54–59, 80–85, 92–95

as motivation to read, 47, 94, 137–138, 212–213

newspaper articles, 54, 92–93

one-on-one, 47–48

by parents, xi–xii, xix, xxiii–xxiv, 11, 12–13, 20–21, 25–27, 29–36, 40–42, 44–48, 62–63, 67–69, 103, 137–138, 146, 173–175

and pediatricians, 167–168

position, 104

to preschoolers, 9, 41–42, 45–46, 69, 70–71, 76–80

purposes for, xxiv, 6, 9, 11, 39, 44–47, 49–51, 62–63, 65–66, 106

questions by child, 42, 68, 69, 70–71

repeat readings, 67–69

research support for, xxiv, 2, 8, 17–18, 29, 42–43, 44, 47, 61–63, 93–95, 107, 137–138, 146, 167

in science class, 54–55

in social studies, 54–55, 93–95

in special ed./family studies, 93–95

to special needs child, 29–36, 113, 114

and speech development, 41–42

stages of, 33–36, **60–98**

styles, 70–71

to teach standard English, 49–50

by teachers, 11, 22–24, 46–47, 54–55, 70–71, 93–95

time of day for, xxiii–xxiv, 33–34, 92, 95

in utero, 29

and vocabulary development, 17–18, 41–42, 45, 61, 62–63

reading aloud (*cont.*)
what makes a good read-aloud, 84–85
when to begin, **28–59**
when to stop, 44–47, 54–59
while student follows in text, 87–89,
212–213
vs. television, 82
see also: picture book(s); novel(s)
Reading Counts, 122–123
reading lamp, 44
Reading Mother, The, xi
Reading Rainbow, 163, 208
reading scores and book ownership, 117–118
reading scores and TV, 197, 200–201,
206–209
Reading Teacher, The, 173
Recorded Books, Inc., 211–212
reference books, **222**
remedial student, 87–89, 333–334
repeat readings, purpose of, 67–69
rewards, *see:* incentives
rhymes, 62–63
Richardson, Prof. C. F., 334–335
Riordan, Prof. Cornelius, xxi
Rip-Roaring Russell, 78
Risley, Dr. Todd, 13–15
Ritter, John H., 161
ROAR, *see* ROR
Robustelli, Andy, 127
Rolie Polie Olie, 84
Roll of Thunder, Hear My Cry, 49
Roots, 90
ROR (Reach Out and Read), 167–168
Rosen, Michael, 71
Roseville (MN) Public Library, 150
Ross, Dr. Catherine Sheldrick, 180–181, 183
Rover Boys, The, 181
Rowling, J. K., 176, 212
Royko, Mike, 56, 89
Rumpelstiltskin, 77
Run with the Horseman, 55
Rylant, Cynthia, 134

Sachs, Marilyn, xv
SAT, 335–336
preparation, 9
St. Louis, MO, 11
Salvation Army thrift shop, 149
Sams, Ferrol, 55

Samurai's Daughter, The, 75
San Diego, CA, 198–199
San Francisco Chronicle, 97
San Pedro de Macoris, 143–144
San Souci, Robert D., 75, 81
Santa Clara (CA) Public Library, 209–210
Sarah Plain and Tall, 183
Satchel Paige, 85
Saturday Evening Post, The, 54
Sawyer, Diane, 175
Schank, Roger C., 57
Schjeldahl, Dave, 92
Schlesinger, Jr., Arthur, 135
Scholastic, Inc. 122
Schon, Dr. Isabel, 163
School Library Journal, 141, 162
school reform, 333–339
Scientist in the Crib, The, 61
Scieszka, Jon, 81
Seance, The, 212
Secret Knowledge of Grown Ups, The, 82
Selden, George, 80
Sendak, Maurice, 84
series books, 47, 86–87, 114, 129, 176–185
advantages of, 132–133, 183
and ESL students, 132–133
by top students, 183, 184
history of, 180–184
kinds of, 176, 184
Serpent Slayer, The, 75
Service, Robert W., 142
Sesame Street, 208
Setting the Record Straight, 339
Seulling, Barbara, 71
Seuss, Dr., 45–46, 62–63, 72, 81
sexism in literature, 74–75
Shaker Heights, OH, 201
Shaywitz, Dr. Sally, 62
Sherman, Gale W., 81
short novels
in preschool, 79–80
recommended, **269–283**
Silver Pony, The, 71
Silverstein, Shel, 77, 78
Silvey, Anita, 90
Simmons, Ruth J., xxi
Simon, Seymour, 85
Simpson, Sir James Young, 179
60 Minutes, 57

skill sheets, *see:* worksheets,
Slake's Limbo, 49
sleep disorders and TV, 200
Sleeping Beauty, 75, 81
Sleeping Ugly, 75
Slote, Alfred, 161
slotting fees, 155
Smith, Arthur D. Howden, 164–165
Smith, Frank, 342
Smith, Holly, 75, 173
Smoky Mountain Rose, 73
Snoop Doggy Dog, 121
Solomon Lewenberg Middle School, 22–24
Somebody Else's Kid, 56
Somebody Loves You, Mr. Hatch, 81
Something About the Author, 90
Sorel, Edward, 82
Sosa, Sammy, 144
South Ozone Park, NY, 145–146
Spanish children's books, 163
special needs children, 29–32, 113–114
speech development, 41–42
speech patterns, 49–50
spelling, 52–53
Spider Watching, 85
Spiderman comic, 134
Spinelli, Eileen, 81
Spinelli, Jerry, 89–90
sports, xxi–xxiv, 143–144
Sports Illustrated, 161
Spot's First Walk, 64–65
Spot's Touch and Feel Day, 67
SSR (sustained silent reading), 22–24,
    106–142
    champion (Robt. Allen), 116–117
    and Commission on Reading, 110, 111
    and dyslexia, 114–115
    and educable retarded, 113–114
    as free voluntary reading, (FVR) 110
    by grade level, 111
    guidelines for, 109, 113, 119, 120
    at home, 117–118
    in Japan, 23–24
    mistakes, 112, 113
    and reading scores, 8, 19, 130–132
    recommended amount, 110
    and remedial classes, 112–115, 137
    research, 8, 19, 23–24, 107, 109, 111–112,
        137

required, 94, 118–119, 195,
schools without, 19, 53, 107, 111
at secondary level, 110–111
and special needs students, 113–115,
    137
at Tatum Primary, 130–132
teacher's role in, 112
as vocabulary builder, 111
standard English, 49–51
standards, national, 57–59
Standish, Burt L., 182
Stanley, Diane, 85
Stanley, Fay, 85
Starring Mirette & Bellini, 75
State University of New York-Albany, 20,
    111
story (narrative), 56–57
Story of English, The, 51
Story of Ferdinand, The, 81
Story of Holly and Ivy, The, 78
Story of Ruby Bridges, The, 85,
Strange Mysteries from Around the World, 85
Stratemeyer, Edward, 181
Stuart Little, 79–80
Stulman, Nate, 189
Styron, William, 140
Substance of Things Hoped For, The, 210
Summer of the Monkeys, 91–92
summer reading, 115
    list, 120, 173
summer school, 115–116, 146
Sun Microsystems, 187
Susanna of the Alamo, 81
sustained silent reading, *see: SSR*
Swarthmore College, 189
Sweden, 7
Sweet Valley High series, 176
Sweet Valley Kids series, 132–133

Taft Elementary, 129–130
Takaya, J., 85
Tale of Peter Rabbit, The, 74, 204
Tanaka, Shelley, 85
Tanner, Daniel, 333
tape recorder, *see:* audio book
Tatterhood and Other Tales, 332
Tatum Primary School, 130–132
Taylor, Mildred, 49
Tchana, Katrin, 75

teacher Web sites, 347–348
teachers as readers/nonreaders, 22–24, 54,
    123–124, 135–136, 154, 169–193
teachers' favorite books, 86–87
*Teaching a Child to Read With Children's Picture
    Books,* 37
Teaching as a Conserving Activity, 203
Tebo, Bob, 172–173
Teeny Tiny Woman, The, 71
television, **194–209**
    and American Academy of Pediatrics, 197
    as antisocial experience, 202–203
    and child sleep disorders, 200
    in child's bedroom, 197, 199–200, 201
    and closed-captioning, 206–207
    compared to reading, 17, 69, 202–204
    dosage device, 206
    educational (PBS), 207–209
    in Finland, 207
    and imagination, 82
    and immigrant children, xix
    impact on brain, 197
    impact on math score, 198
    impact on reading score, 197
    in kitchen, 44, 203
    over-viewing of, 197–201
    and parents, 42, 201–202
    PBS, 207–209
    racial differences in viewing, 200–201
    as time consumer, 197–200, 201–202
    Trelease family viewing, 204–205
    vs. picture book, 69
    viewing by gender, 197
    viewing statistics, 197–201
    vocabulary, 17, 44, 203, 204
Tell Me a Story, 57
testing, 57–59
Texas Assessment of Academic Skills, 89
Texas Instruments, 4
textbooks' vocabulary deficits, 19, 111
"the", meaning and usage of word, 38–39
There Are No Children Here, 56
Theroux, Phyllis, xviii
Thogmartin, Mark B., 37
Thomas, Marcia and Jennifer, 30–31
three B's, 43–44
Tikki Tikki Tembo, 77
Tillage, Leon Walter, 85
time, 24–25
Tintin in Tibet, 134–135

Tips and Titles of Books, 163
To Kill a Mockingbird, 37
Tolkien, J. R. R., 74
Tom Sawyer, 217
Tom Swift, 81
Too Good to Be True, 56
travel, impact on reading, 11
Tree That Would Not Die, The, 85
Trelease, Brian, 136–137
True Adventure of Daniel Hall, The, 85
True Confessions of Charlotte Doyle, The, 90
True Story of the Three Little Pigs, The, 81
Tuck Everlasting, 103
Tuesday, 71
Tuesdays With Morrie, 172–173
Tunis, John R., 161
Turkle; Brinton, 71
Tutu, Bishop Desmond, 134
TV Allowance, 206
Twain, Mark, 217

Uncle John's Great Big Bathroom Reader, 93
Union, NJ, 1
Union College (NJ), 210
University of North Carolina, 29
University of Southern California, 109, 144
University of Tennessee-Martin, 117
University of Vermont, 109
University of Virginia, 11
University of Western Ontario, 180
University of Wisconsin, 334
unpleasure, 7
Updike, John, 134, 140
Upfield, Arthur, 54
urban schools, xviii–xix
USA Today, 189–190

Van Buren, Abigail ("Dear Abby"), xvii
Van Doren, Mark, 177
Van Hoegarden, Ann, 38
Van Hoegarden, Frank and Linda, 38
Vanderbilt University, 117
Vanishing Hitchhiker, The, 56
Velveteen Rabbit, The, 81
Very Hungry Caterpillar, The, 34, 35, 69
videos vs. books, 69
Viorst, Judith, 81
Virginia, 11, 93–94, 96–97
Virginia, Read Aloud, 96–97
vocabulary 17–18, 34, 39, 61, 146

and income, 15–16, 146
listening, 9, 12, 13, 34, 39
print vs. oral, 17–18, 146
ireading, 9, 17, 52–54, 139–140, 177
of TV scripts, 17
speaking, 8–9, 17–18, 49–51, 146
Voices of Readers, 184
Vonnegut Jr., Kurt, 83, 142

Waber, Bernard, 78
Wagon Wheels, 78
Waldman, Karleen, 79–80
Walker, Alice, 140
Wallace, Mike, 175
Walters, Barbara, 175
Ward, Lynd, 71, 77
Warren, Robert Penn, 21–22
Watts (CA) schools, 145
We're Going on a Bear Hunt, 71
Wellesley College, 141
Welsh, Patrick, 189
What Else Should I Read?, 163
Where the Red Fern Grows, 84, 91–92
Where the Sidewalk Ends, 77
Where the Wild Things Are, 84
Where's Spot?, 67
Where's Waldo?, 72–73
Whingdingdilly, The, 77
White, Dorothy, 66
White, E. B., 79–80, 89, 194
Who's Peeking at Me?, 33
Who Reads Literature?, 140
Wiesner, David, 71
Wilfred Gordon McDonald Partridge, 81
Wilkes, Angela, 65–66
Williams College, 9

Williams, Margery, 81
Williams, William Carlos, 58
Wilson Company, H. W., 181
Winfrey, Oprah, 169–176
  see also: Oprah's Book Club,
Winglee, Marianne, 140
Wisniewski, David, 82
Wolf Rider, 93
Wolf Story, 78
Wolfe, Thomas, 142
Woodsong, 54
Wood, Joan and Marty, 204
Woodworth, Stanley, 164–165
wordless books, 71–72, **219**
worksheet, 7, 18–19, 20, 35–36, 39, 47, 110,
  111, 117
World Book Encyclopedia, 148
World Wide Web, see Internet
Worth a Thousand Words, 81
writing
  and computer usage, 190
  as "copy-cat" experience, 52–54
  curriculum, 138–140
  and email, 192
  purpose, 139
  reading connection, 42, 138–140
  skills, 52–54
  utensils, 42, 190

Yale, 161, 334
Yeoman, Cushla, 29–30
Yolen, Jane, 75, 81

Zelinsky, Paul, 77
Zill, Nicholas, 140
Zuckerman, Dr. Barry, 167–168

Author-Illustrator Index
for the Treasury

Italics are for illustrator only; * after page number gives location of a group of books by an author or illustrator.

Abolafia, Yossi, 236
Ackerman, Karen, 265
Adler, David, 233, 237, 271–272, 283, 307
Aesop, 223
Ahlberg, Allan, 264
Ahlberg, Janet, 264
Aiken, Joan, 322
Alborough, Jez, 220, 243, 267*
Alcock, Vivien, 304
Alderson, Brian, 330, 331
Allard, Harry, 224, 249
Allen, Debbie, 225
Alley, R. W., 250
Andersen, Hans Christian, 253, 330*
Anderson, Laurie Halse, 277
Andreasen, Dan, 226, 331
Andrews, Jan, 249
Anno, Mitsumasa, 223
Archambault, John, 220, 226, 236, 244
Ardizzone, Edward, 225, 243*
Armstrong, William H., 315
Arnold, Marsha Diane, 226, 242, 272
Arnold, Tedd, 221, 251*
Ash, Russell, 222
Atkins, Jeannine, 231
Atwater, Florence, 304
Atwater, Richard, 304
Avi, 287, 291, 305, 307, 309, 315, 318–319*, 322
Aylesworth, Jim, 221

Babbitt, Natalie, 312–313, 319
Bachrach, Susan D., 283
Bader, Barbara, 223
Baker, Olaf, 244
Bang, Molly, 219, 245, 252
Banks, Lynne Reid, 299
Bannerman, Helen, 260
Barrett, Angela, 253, 331
Barrett, Judi, 228
Barrett, Ron, 228
Bauer, Joan, 311–312
Bauer, Marion Dane, 278
Baum, L. Frank, 322
Baxter, Lesley, 314
Beatty, Patricia, 302
Bell, Anthea, 331
Bellairs, John, 289*
Belton, Sandra, 264, 265, 275
Bemelmans, Ludwig, 245
Beneduce, Ann Keay, 236
Benson, Patrick, 248, 252
Berger, Gilda, 231, 318–319
Berger, Melvin, 231, 318–319
Best, Cari, 254
Bial, Raymond, 249, 281, 286
Bing, Christopher, 323
Birdseye, Debbie, 221
Birdseye, Tom, 221
Birkett, Rachel, 331
Bishop, Claire H., 283, 307

Blake, Quentin, 219, 220, 221
Bloor, Edward, 316
Blos, Joan, 226, 252
Blume, Judy, 316
Blundell, Tony, 263
Bolognese, Don, 265
Bond, Felicia, 238
Bond, Sylvia, 299
Bonson, Richard, 231
Borden, Louise, 241–242, 317
Bradby, Marie, 261, 310
Brady, Esther Wood, 318
Brenner, Barbara, 246, 265, 269
Brett, Jan, 253
Bridges, Ruby, 260
Briggs, Raymond, 219, 240, 263–264
Brink, Carol Ryrie, 286–287
Brittain, Bill, 321
Brooke, William J., 264
Brown, Marc, 224, 326
Brown, Margaret Wise, 220, 221, 235
Brown, Ruth, 220
Browning, Robert, 252
Bruchac, Joseph, 244
Brunvand, Jan Harold, 232
Brust, Beth Wagner, 331
Buchan, Elizabeth, 229
Buchanan, Jane, 294
Bulla, Clyde Robert, 253, 265, 276*, 280
Bunting, Eve, 226, 230, 235, 255, 291, 307
Burch, Robert, 270, 274, 280, 296, 298*
Burnett, Frances Hodgson, 280, 298, 313*
Burton, Virginia Lee, 242, 248*
Butterfield, Moira, 222
Byars, Betsy, 303–304, 309

Callen, Larry, 297
Calmenson, Stephanie, 253
Cameron, Alice, 220
Cameron, Ann, 282
Cannon, Janell, 259
Carle, Eric, 220, 221, 226, 265*, 331
Carpenter, Stephen, 325
Carr, Jan, 326
Carrick, Carol, 235, 258*
Carrick, Donald, 258
Carter, David, 259
Carter, Noelle, 259
Cary, Alice, 286, 305–306

Casanova, Mary, 233, 241, 262
Catling, Patrick Skene, 288
Catrow, David, 255
Chambers, Veronica, 249
Chesworth, Michael, 219
Child, Lydia, 255
Christopher, John, 321
Christopher, Matt, 310
Cleary, Beverly, 290, 304, 310*
Clements, Andrew, 273
Clifford, Eth, 274
Clifton, Lucille, 235, 265
Climo, Shirley, 258
Coerr, Eleanor, 225, 265
Cohen, Barbara, 249, 317
Cohn, Amy, 331
Cole, Bruce, 237
Coles, Robert, 260
Collier, Christopher, 305
Collier, James Lincoln, 305
Collington, Peter, 219
Collodi, Carlo, 284
Conrad, Pam, 227, 231, 250, 262, 300,
    305–306*
Conly, Jane L., 304
Cooney, Barbara, 282
Cooper, Helen, 226
Cooper, Susan, 247, 252, 315
Cousins, Lucy, 244, 246*, 259
Coville, Bruce, 277
Crane, Lucy, 332
Crane, Walter, 332
Cruz, Ray, 223
Curtis, Christopher Paul, 286
Cushman, Karen, 307
Cuyler, Margery, 221, 238

Dabcovich, Lydia, 225
Dahl, Roald, 248, 284, 289, 299*
Dakos, Kalli, 325
Dalgliesh, Alice, 249, 272
Day, Alexandra, 219
DeFelice, Cynthia, 291, 320–321
DeJong, Meindert, 298
Delaney, A., 220, 243
Delf, Brian, 222
Deming, A. G., 221
dePaola, Tomie, 219, 233, 235, 236, 238,
    240, 240–241*, 244, 245, 259, 261

deRegniers, Beatrice S., 326
deRosa, Dee, 235
DiCamillo, Kate, 285
Dillon, Diane, 324, 328, 332
Dillon, Leo, 324, 328, 332
Doherty, Berlie, 315
Dougherty, James, 247, 260
Downey, Lynn, 220, 250
Dragonwagon, Crescent, 221
Du Bois, William Pène, 268–269, 319
Duncan, Lois, 300
Duntze, Dorothee, 331
Dupasquier, Philippe, 227
Dygard, Thomas J., 310

Eastman, P. D., 220, 252, 259
Eckert, Allan W., 244, 298–299, 313
Eckstein, Joan, 237
Edwards, Julie, 274, 282, 312, 319
Egielski, Richard, 235
Eisenberg, Lisa, 237
Elleman, Barbara, 241
Emberly, Barbara, 220
Emberly, Michael, 243, 264
English, Karen, 292
English, Mark, 231
Ernst, Lisa Campbell, 230, 243, 264
Estes, Eleanor, 261, 275

Fancher, Lou, 244
Farley, Walter, 285
Feiffer, Jules, 239
Fisher, Dorothy Canfield, 320
Fisher, Leonard Everett, 240
Fitzgerald, John D., 295
Flack, Marjorie, 220, 224*
Fleischman, Paul, 232, 273–274*, 279, 283, 310
Fleischman, Sid, 287, 297*
Fleming, Denise, 233
Floca, Brian, 255
Ford, George, 260
Forman, Michael, 330
Fox, Mem, 220
Frazee, Marla, 257
Freeman, Don, 229

Gag, Wanda, 221
Galdone, Paul, 220, 230
Gallaz, Christophe, 307

Gammell, Stephen, 250
Gannett, Ruth S., 278
Gardiner, John R., 282
Gauch, Patricia Lee, 252, 262
Gellman, Marc, 327
George, Jean Craighead, 306
Geraghty, Paul, 238
Gerstein, Mordicai, 298
Getz, David, 279
Gherman, Beverly, 288
Gibbie, Mike, 221
Giff, Patricia Reilly, 293, 301
Ginsburg, Mirra, 235, 240, 266
Gipson, Fred, 278
Gleit, Joyce, 237
Goble, Paul, 244
Godden, Rumer, 282
Golenbock, Peter, 258, 316
Goode, Diane, 240
Gorey, Edward, 257
Gorog, Judith, 329
Graham, Bob, 247
Grahame, Kenneth, 279
Grambling, Lois G, 238
Gray, Libba Moore, 221, 242, 248
Greenfield, Eloise, 324
Griffith, Helen, 236*, 285, 290
Grimm, Brothers, 331
Grossman, Bill, 221
Guevara, Susan, 228
Gutman, Dan, 291, 316
Gwynne, Fred, 224, 264

Hall, Katy, 237
Hamilton, Virginia, 328, 332
Handford, Martin, 267–268
Harris, Jim, 240
Harris, Joel Chandler, 329
Harrison, David L., 323, 324
Harrison, Ted, 324
Harshman, Marc, 242
Hartman, Thomas Msgr., 327
Harvey, Jr., Paul, 328–329
Hawkes, Kevin, 232, 246
Hawthorne, Nathaniel, 288
Hayes, Sarah, 221
Hearn, Lafcadio, 262
Hearn, Michael Patrick, 322
Heide, Florence Party, 223, 243, 257

Hendry, Diana, 226
Henkes, Kevin, 241*, 258
Henry, Joanne Landers, 313
Henry, Marguerite, 285
Hergé, 263
Hesse, Karen, 287, 290
Hest, Amy, 236, 253, 264, 266
Heyer, Marilee, 331
Hickam, Jr., Homer, 270
Hickox, Rebecca, 258
Hill, Eric, 221, 259
Himler, Ronald, 230
Hinton, S.E., 312
Hoban, Lillian, 260–261
Hoban, Russell, 226
Hobbs, Will, 300*, 317
Hoberman, Mary Ann, 257
Hodges, Margaret, 252, 278
Holden, Robert, 252
Holm, Anne, 306
Holman, Felice, 314
Hooks, William H., 258
Hopkins, Lee Bennett, 326
Horvath, Polly, 318
Houston, Gloria, 264
Howard, Arthur, 238
Howard, Ellen, 235, 236, 265
Howe, John, 240
Huck, Charlotte, 258
Hughes, Shirley, 223*, 241, 244
Hughes, Ted, 275
Hunt, Irene, 302, 306, 308
Hunter, Mollie, 281, 316
Hurd, Clement, 235
Hurmence, Belinda, 249
Hurwitz, Johanna, 280
Hutchins, Pat, 219, 261
Hyman, Trina Schart, 243, 331, 332

Ibbotson, Eva, 295, 302
Innocenti, Roberto, 284, 307
Ivimey, John, 221

Jackson, Alison, 220
Jacobs, William Jay, 327–328
Jacques, Brian, 303
Jaffe, Nina, 258
Janovitz, Marilyn, 220, 221
Jarrell, Randall, 284–285

Jesse, Harley, 236
Johnson, Annabel, 294
Johnson, Edgar, 294
Johnson, Stephen T., 255
Johnson, Steve, 244
Johnston, Tony, 236, 249, 263, 265
Jones, Charlotte Foltz, 286, 299
Jordan, Deloris, 225
Jordan, Roslyn, 225
Joyce, William, 221, 230*, 255

Karas, G. Brian, 256, 264–265, 325
Keats, Ezra Jack, 227, 254
Keeping, Charles, 286
Kellogg, Steven, 239*, 250
Kennedy, Dorothy M., 324
Ketteman, Helen, 233
Khalsa, Dayal Kaur, 236
Kimmel, Eric A., 258, 331
Kingsland, L. W., 331
Kinsey, Helen, 272
Kinsey-Warnock, Natalie, 225, 272
Kipling, Rudyard, 254
Kjelgaard, Jim, 290
Kline, Suzy, 274
Knight, Eric, 301
Knight, Hilary, 326
Koide, Tan, 247
Koide, Yasuko, 247
Koller, Jackie French, 307
Konigsburg, E. L., 293
Koopmans, Loek, 258
Kovalski, Maryann, 221
Kramer, Ann, 222
Kraus, Robert, 247
Kroll, Steven, 226

Lansky, Bruce, 325
Lasky, Kathryn, 246, 255
Latimer, Jim, 252
Lawson, Robert, 260, 304
Leaf, Munro, 260
Lee, Spike, 310–311
Le Gallienne, Eva, 331
Lent, Blair, 262–263
Lesser, Rika, 331
Lester, Julius, 330
Levine, Arthur A., 245, 262
Levine, Ellen, 263

Levine, Evan, 252, 307
Levine, Gail Carson, 258, 289–290
Levinson, Riki, 265
Levitin, Sonia, 244, 251
Levoy, Myron, 301, 307
Lewin, Betsy, 224, 238
Lewin, Ted, 238
Lewis, C. S., 302
Lewis, Naomi, 253, 330, 331
Lia, Simone, 253–254
Lichtenheld, Tom, 227
Lillegard, Dee, 221
Lindsay, William, 231
Lionni, Leo, 234
Lisle, Janet Taylor, 264, 280, 318, 319
Littledale, Freya, 331
Lloyd, Megan, 331
Lobel, Arnold, 223, 234*, 244, 326
Lofting, Hugh, 304
London, Jack, 287, 299
London, Jonathan, 220, 234*
Lord, Bette Bao, 298
Louie, Ai-Ling, 258
Lowell, Susan, 243, 258
Lowry, Lois, 307–308
Lynch, P. J., 266

Madrigal, Antonio H., 233
Maestro, Betsy, 266
Maestro, Giulio, 237
Magorian, Michelle, 294
Maher, Richard, 299
Mahy, Margaret, 250, 262
Manes, Stephen, 274
Manson, Christopher, 221
Marcellino, Fred, 260, 331
Markham, Lois, 307, 318
Markle, Sandra, 288
Marshall, James, 229*, 236–237, 249
Martchenko, Michael, 262
Martin Jr., Bill, 220, 221, 226*, 236, 244, 258
Martin, Rafe, 244, 284
Marzollo, Jean, 267
Masoff, Joy, 272, 305, 317
Mayer, Mercer, 219, 243
Maynard, Bill, 232
Mazer, Anne, 250
Mazer, Harry, 312, 314
McCleery, William, 284

McCloskey, Robert, 246*, 266, 297
McCully, Emily Arnold, 248*, 249, 255, 262, 269
McGill, Alice, 249
McGovern, Ann, 317
McKenzie, Ellen Kindt, 251, 281–282, 319
McKissack, Fredrick, 252, 310
McKissack, Patricia, 243, 252, 310
McLerran, Alice, 242
McManus, Patrick, 328
McMullan, Jim, 221, 251
McMullan, Kate, 221, 251
McNaughton, Colin, 227*, 237
McPhail, David, 232, 261
McSwigan, Mary, 307
Medearis, Angela Shelf, 329
Miles, Miska, 244
Miller, Virginia, 235
Miller, William, 254
Minarik, Else Holmelund, 242
Minters, Frances, 258, 263
Mitchell, Margaree K., 265
Monjo, F. N., 265
Moore, Elaine, 236
Moore, Eva, 326
Mora, Pat, 254
Morey, Walt, 290, 293
Morgan, Judith, 234
Morgan, Neil, 234
Morpurgo, Michael, 271, 285, 286, 292, 301, 320*
Morris, Judy K., 317
Morris, Willie, 294
Mosel, Arlene, 221, 262–263
Moser, Barry, 274, 323–324
Mowat, Farley, 278–279
Muller, Robin, 245
Munsch, Robert, 240, 249, 262*
Murphy, Jim, 269
Myers, Walter Dean, 310, 312

Naylor, Phyllis, 290
Nelson, Kadir, 225
Nesbit, E., 278
Neumeyer, Peter F., 288
Newman, Robert, 287
Nhuong, Huynh Quang, 301
Nixon, Joan Lowery, 291
Nolen, Jerdine, 225

Norton, Mary, 276, 298
Numeroff, Laura, 220, 238

O'Brien, Robert C., 305
O'Dell, Scott, 312, 314
Olson, Arielle North, 329
Orr, Richard, 222
Osborne, Mary Pope, 238, 273
Oxenbury, Helen, 266

Palatini, Margie, 257
Parish, Peggy, 224
Park, Barbara, 275–276, 277, 281*
Parks, Rosa, 310
Paterson, Katherine, 270, 286, 315
Pattison, Darcy, 262
Paulsen, Gary, 252, 279, 296*, 299, 305,
    307, 310, 317, 323
Peck, Robert Newton, 281, 290
Peet, Bill, 225, 228, 238, 248, 268*, 277,
    304
Perrault, Charles, 258
Peters, Stephanie True, 296
Petersen, P. J., 277
Peterson, John, 277
Phelps, Ethel Johnston, 332
Philbrick, Rodman, 292–293
Phillips, Louis, 236–237
Pilkey, Dav, 237, 266
Pinkney, Andrea D., 249
Pinkney, Jerry, 223, 254, 330
Pinkwater, Daniel, 228, 237, 255, 261, 274
Platt, Richard, 222, 231, 307
Polacco, Patricia, 226, 232, 235, 252–253,
    261–262, 272, 283, 307
Pollack, Pamela, 329
Porte, Barbara Ann, 225, 228, 236*, 250
Potter, Beatrix, 228
Prelutsky, Jack, 326
Price, Reynolds, 317
Prigger, Mary Skillings, 224
Propp, Vera W., 283
Pulver, Robin, 250, 253
Pyle, Howard, 308

Quindlen, Anna, 263

Rand, Gloria, 225, 272
Rand, Ted, 225, 242, 245, 263

Ransome, James, 265
Rappaport, Doreen, 262
Rathmann, Peggy, 220, 235
Rattigan, Jama Kim, 264–265
Rawls, Wilson, 321
Ray, David, 245
Remkiewicz, Frank, 234
Rey, H. A, 229
Richler, Mordecai, 275
Riddell, Chris, 331
Ritter, John H., 310
Robart, Rose, 220
Robins, Arthur, 243, 266
Robinson, Aminah B., 256
Robinson, Barbara, 271
Rogasky, Barbara, 331
Rohmann, Eric, 219
Root, Phyllis, 221
Rosen, Michael J., 256
Rosen, Michael, 221, 266
Rosenberg, Liz, 250
Ross, Gayle, 244
Rowling, J. K., 295–296
Rylant, Cynthia, 271

Sachar, Louis, 296–297, 313*
Sachs, Marilyn, 270
Salten, Felix, 285
Salvner, Gary M., 296
San Souci, Robert D., 226, 249, 251, 255,
    269, 272
Santore, Scott, 248
Schindler, S. D., 252
Schneider, Howie, 228
Schotter, Roni, 232
Schroeder, Alan, 258
Schulman, Janet, 284
Schwartz, Alvin, 323, 329*
Schwartz, David M., 238
Schwartz, Howard, 329
Scieszka, John, 223, 264*, 274
Sebestyen, Ouida, 323
Seibel, Fritz, 224
Selden, George, 288
Sendak, Maurice, 220, 221, 226, 242, 267*
Service, Robert W., 324
Seuling, Barbara, 221
Seuss, Dr., 233, 239, 253, 312
Sewell, Anna, 286

Shannon, David, 232, 251, 257
Shaw, Charles, 221
Shapiro, Marc, 295
Shemin, Margaretha, 283, 307
Shepard, Aaron, 245
Shepard, Ernest H., 245, 279
Shields, Carol D., 255, 324
Shroeder, Alan, 258, 265
Sibley, Brian, 301
Silver, Norman, 232, 256
Silverstein, Shel, 276, 327*
Simms, Laura, 255
Skurzynski, Gloria, 252
Slavin, Bill, 220
Slote, Alfred, 292
Small, David, 234, 261
Small, Terry, 252
Smith, Cat B., 251
Smith, Doris B., 283
Smith, Janice Lee, 279
Smith, Joseph A., 247
Smith, Lane, 264
Smith, Robert K., 236, 272*, 312
Smith, Roland, 317
Sneed, Brad, 258
Snicket, Lemony, 285
Soentpiet, Chris K., 249
Sorel, Edward, 240
Soto, Gary, 228, 270*
Speare, Elizabeth George, 313–314
Spedden, Daisy C. S., 282
Sperry, Armstrong, 271
Spier, Peter, 219
Spinelli, Eileen, 249, 259
Spinelli, Jerry, 254, 261, 302*
Spirin, Gennady, 236, 331
Spurr, Elizabeth, 255
Stanley, Diane, 240, 256, 263–264*
Stanley, Fay, 240
Steele, William O., 252, 320*
Steig, William, 226, 240, 261*, 269
Steptoe, John, 258
Stevens, Carla, 270
Stevenson, James, 236, 266*, 325
Stewart, Sarah, 234, 254, 261
Strete, Craig Kee, 244
Stroud, Virginia A., 244
Swift, Jonathan, 236
Swindells, Robert, 320

Taha, Karen T., 235
Takaya, Julia, 246, 269
Talbott, Hudson, 283, 307
Tanaka, Shelley, 231
Taulbert, Clifton, 236, 275, 310
Taylor, Mildred, 273, 310–311*
Taylor, Theodore, 288
Tchana, Katrin, 332
Teague, Mark, 238, 251, 255, 257*, 264
Terry, Michael Bad Hand, 244, 286
Thayer, Ernest L., 323–324
Tillage, Leon Walter, 276
Tolan, Stephanie S., 309
Tolhurst, Marilyn, 230, 264
Tolkien, J.R.R., 295, 302
Tomes, Margot, 262
Trelease, Jim, 328
Truesdell, Site, 323
Tsuchiya, Yukio, 225
Tunnell, Michael O., 245
Turkle, Brinton, 219, 230
Turner, Ann, 272
Twain, Mark, 294

Ungerer, Tomi, 245, 262

Van Allsburg, Chris, 219, 237, 242, 252, 269*
Viorst, Judith, 223*, 235, 324
Vivelo, Jackie, 329
Vogel, Carole G., 231

Waber, Bernard, 220, 237*, 239
Waddell, Martin, 221, 235, 252
Wadsworth, Olive, 221
Wallace, Barbara Brooks, 308
Wallace, Bill, 290–291
Walsh, Jill Paton, 236
Ward, Lynd, 219, 225, 258
Warren, Andrea, 291
Watkins, Yoko, 293, 305
Waugh, Sylvia, 303
Weeks, Sarah, 221
Weisgard, Leonard, 272
Wells, H. G., 320
Wells, Rosemary, 235, 247*, 266
Welsch, Roger, 244
Westall, Robert, 300
Westcot, Nadine Bernard, 325
White, E. B., 288, 315–316*

White, Mary Michaels, 326
White, Robb, 300
Whybrow, Ian, 238
Wick, Walter, 267
Wier, Esther, 308
Widman, Christine, 264
Wiesner, David, 219
Wilkes, Angela, 231, 233
Williams, Garth, 288
Williams, Linda, 221, 243
Williams, Vera B., 227*, 236
Winter, Jeanette, 220
Wisniewski, David, 256
Wolff, Virginia Euwer, 312
Wood, Audrey, 221, 232, 235, 237, 250, 256
Wood, Don, 237, 250

Yalowitz, Paul, 259
Yashima, Taro, 249, 259, 262, 274
Yep, Laurence, 262
Yolen, Jane, 226, 232, 238, 250, 262, 264, 272, 315
Yorinks, Arthur, 237
Young, Ed, 243, 286
Younger, Barbara, 226

Zak, Drahos, 252
Zarin, Cynthia, 257
Zelinsky, Paul O., 329, 331
Zimmerman, Howard, 230
Zipes, Jack, 223
Zolotow, Charlotte, 235, 268–269*